What People Are Saying About...

Kids' Adventures Around San Francisco Bay

"This is definitely a great resource! *Kids' Adventures Around San Francisco Bay* will certainly be an indispensable guide for our family."
— **Kristi Yamaguchi**
Olympic Gold Medalist, Figure Skating

"**Following and Leading Kids!**
Children's minds are sponges that soak up what they experience.... Importantly, kids, being kids, absorb and retain material better when it is presented in a fun way. Look on it as planting seeds that have the potential to grow and develop a brain to its best capacity. You too may find these many and diverse gems of interest. By educating our kids we educate ourselves. ...Whether you are a local resident or a tourist, you will find this work stimulating and fun, just as it is for your kids."
— **Dr. Glenn Austin, M.D., F.A.A.P.**
Past President, The American Academy of Pediatrics

"Feel like you and your kids have done everything there is to do in Northern California? Think again. Elina Wong's *Kids' Adventures Around San Francisco Bay* is likely to become any parent's new favorite resource, offering countless suggestions for fun and educational activities for children of every age."
— *Diablo Magazine*

"**Los Gatos Author Cultivates a Love of Art and Science**
...This lively new book can help parents and educators introduce children to new things and support their learning through the area's vast array of exhibits, events, performances, outings, and classes."
— *Bay Area Parent*

"**Get out:** Pick pluots in Brentwood, rent rowboats at Lafayette Reservoir, cruise Oakland Harbor in FDR's yacht, tour Fairfield's Jelly Bellies factory. Elina Wong's *Kids' Adventures Around San Francisco Bay* ... is more fun for the postpubescent set than its title suggests."
— *East Bay Express*

"Children learn through play" says longtime Bay Area resident and author Elina Wong, and her new book is a testament to this....[It] is well organized and bursting with fun ideas and friendly advice."

— ANG Newspapers

(*Oakland Tribune, Tri-Valley Herald, San Mateo County Times, Argus, Daily Review, Marin Independent, Alameda Times Star, Vallejo Times Herald*)

"...there's a real point to its back cover blurb, 'Follow your child's passion ... all around the Bay.' ...it's her choice of adventures that makes the book. And she covers a lot of bases in between: fauna, flora, insects, astronomy, and other scientific matters; transportation of all sorts; fine, applied, and performing arts; historical outings; and sports and conditioning; plus almost 100 pages of related classes and workshops."

— *Parents' Press*

"Your expertise regarding the wealth of learning opportunities around the Bay Area—for all income levels and age ranges—made the show a real hit with the listeners. Your thoughtful and well-researched book is a treasure for families. We were delighted to have you on the show."

— **"Childhood Matters" radio show**

"One of the most valuable things about the book, not emphasized at all in the book itself, is its companion Web site, at www.kidsedventures.com....The book and Web site are complementary. The Web site allows you to search listings and easily link to the Web site of any listed venue. But the book provides descriptive information and other details."

— Jennifer Dees
San Francisco Homeschoolers

Greater San Francisco Bay Area City Locator Map

Greater San Francisco Bay Area City Locator Map

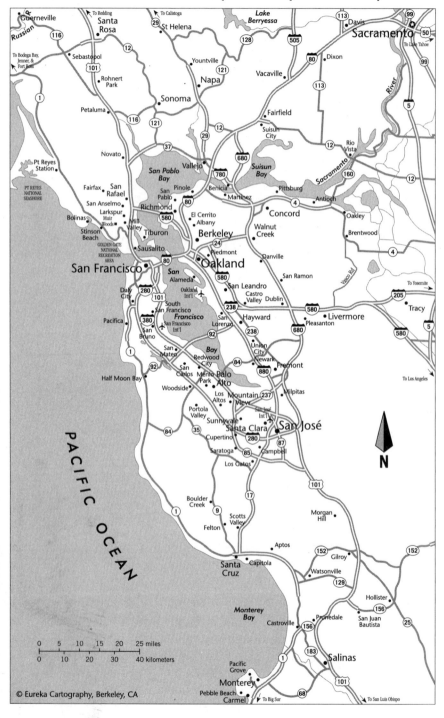

© Eureka Cartography, Berkeley, CA

Kids' Adventures
Around San Francisco Bay

Second Edition

Educational Places to Go, Things to Do, & Classes to Take
in the North Bay, Peninsula, East Bay, Silicon Valley, & Santa Cruz

Elina Wong
Copyright ©2007

Kids' Adventures Around San Francisco Bay: Educational Places to Go, Things to Do, and Classes to Take in the North Bay, Peninsula, East Bay, Silicon Valley, & Santa Cruz

Kids EdVentures
Post Office Box 1090
Los Gatos, CA 95031-1090, USA
Tel: (408) 356-2450; Fax: (408) 356-2714
www.KidsEdVentures.com

Printed in the United States of America
Cover Design: Robert Howard Graphic Design
Editors: Diane Feldman, Despina Gulides; Book Interior Design: Folio Bookworks
Back Cover Writing: Susan Kendrick Writing

Publisher's Cataloging-in-Publication
(Provided by Quality Books, Inc.)

Wong, Elina.
   Kids' adventures around San Francisco Bay :
   educational places to go, things to do, & classes to
   take in the North Bay, Peninsula, East Bay, Silicon
   Valley & Santa Cruz / Elina Wong. -- 2nd ed.
      p. cm.
   Includes index.
      CONTENTS: Animal kingdom -- Plant kingdom -- Bees,
   butterflies, & bugs -- Science & technology museums -- Planetariums &
   observatories -- Transportation favorites -- How things
   work -- Art & performing arts -- Historical outings --
   Seasonal events -- Local resources -- Science & arts
   education -- Physical activities.
      LCCN 2007900418
      ISBN-13: 978-0974361727
      ISBN-10: 0974361720

      1. San Francisco Bay Area (Calif.)--Guidebooks.
   2. Children--Travel--California--San Francisco Bay Area--
   Guidebooks.   I. Title.

F868.S156W6395 2007   917.94'60454
                        QBI07-600035

Distributed to the trade by Independent Publishers Group.
10 9 8 7 6 5 4 3 2

Contents

Section I
Places to Go & Things to Do

Section I
Places to Go & Things to Do Cont'd

Section II
Classes to Take

Section II
Classes to Take (Cont'd)

Appendices

Acknowledgments

The companies, product brands, organizations, and services mentioned in *Kids' Adventures Around San Francisco Bay: Educational Places to Go, Things to Do, and Classes to Take in the North Bay, Peninsula, East Bay, Silicon Valley, and Santa Cruz* retain all rights, trademarks, and service marks that belong to them.

Neither the author nor the publisher has any ownership nor received any compensation from any of the companies, products, organizations, or services included in this book.

I would like to thank the people who have helped make this book a reality. Ruby Wong: Thanks for your moral support and for reviewing the book. Ellen Gee: Thanks for reading and rereading the manuscript, for providing suggestions, and for catching the little details I missed. Alison Ahmed: Thanks for our many memorable outings that helped form the foundation and inspiration for this book. Thanks for sharing your knowledge of art education and the art world and for reviewing the art sections. Maria Mancini: Thanks for listening and your encouragement. Marcie Cayton: Thanks for evaluating the Web site on how airplanes fly. Thanks for your feedback and moral support. Anna Rozovsky: Thanks for reviewing the music sections and encouragement. Stanford and Margaret Gee: Thanks for your friendship and support, without which this book would not have been introduced to the marketplace. My husband: Thanks for taking over the nighttime chores, for giving me the time to write the book, and for providing moral and technical computer support.

Finally, I'd like to thank my team: my editors, cover designer, distributor, printers, publicists, Web site developers, back cover writer, and Publishers Marketing Association for making this such a wonderful journey. Thank you all!

Disclaimer

This book is designed to provide information on the educational and community resources available in the greater San Francisco Bay Area. It is sold with the understanding that the publisher and author are not providing any professional services. If expert professional assistance is required, the services of a competent professional should be sought.

Efforts have been made to make this guide as complete and as accurate as possible. However, there may be mistakes, both typographical and in content. Information can change. This text should be used as a general reference guide. To avoid disappointment, check the information with the organization prior to embarking on your trip.

Inclusion in this book should not be considered to be a recommendation, endorsement, or referral, nor a guarantee of the quality of the products, organizations, and services presented. Each individual must use his best judgment before purchasing products or engaging in any activities.

The author and Kids EdVentures are not liable nor responsible to any person, organization, or entity with respect to any loss or damage caused, or alleged to have been caused, directly or indirectly, whether or not negligent, by the information contained in this book.

By purchasing this book, the reader agrees to exempt the author and the publisher from any responsibility.

Introduction

Children learn through play. From play, they explore their world, test their theories about how things work, and learn through *all* of their five senses. Experiences that allow all their senses to be engaged help them to remember and understand. That's why it's so valuable to provide fun adventures to engage our children. When they play and experience, they are studying and learning about their world.

In 1997, milestone articles came out of the scientific community regarding the brain development of children. They answered the age-old question of nature versus nurture. Both play a role and interact with each throughout our lives. There are windows of opportunity when exposure to certain types of learning is the most optimal. The infant brain is born with billions of neurons and connections, but when the child's brain is not exposed to the necessary stimuli, the corresponding neurons are shut down since the brain deems them unnecessary. Besides being lots of fun, engaging experiences stimulate a child's natural curiosity about the world and help to develop his brain.

Earlier research has shown that the first few years of a child's life are critical. Most of the child's brain development happens prior to his entering kindergarten. The infant, toddler, and preschool years are critical to the child's overall development.

While parents must decide which activities should be undertaken, and when, it is important to remember that children need time to just day-dream or play, so that they are *not* overscheduled and overburdened. It is important to keep a balance between downtime and all the fun and educational adventures just outside our doorsteps.

Outings and field trips allow children to experience and learn from all of their senses. Being out in nature helps children understand how things are related. Exposure to the fine arts helps encourage and develop their creativity and imagination. Sports and physical play are important to their physical development and well-being. In today's world, where schools provide just the basics, it's more important than ever for parents to find resources in the community to provide the enrichment in science, art, music, drama, and sports that our schools are hard-pressed to offer due to the lack of funds. The saving grace is that our community is rich in resources, and we can get much of this enrichment without tremendous expense from our local parks, parks and recreation departments, and community groups that provide theater and concerts at affordable rates, and sometimes for free.

Finally, because motor skills are one of the first skills babies develop and continue to do so during their toddler, preschool, and elementary school years, I've included physical activities and parks that your child might enjoy.

I've lived in the Bay Area for more than thirty years, and I'm still finding new experiences and resources, especially after I have become a parent and as my children grow. Some of these I learned from other moms I've met who provided insider's tips to the abundant resources in our community. I've also seen travelers' guides to the Bay Area with an overwhelming list of things to see and do and Web sites with an equally overwhelming number of destinations. But I was frustrated trying to find the appropriate outings for an educational goal I had in mind. As a result, I've organized this book with an educational focus to help you find resources, outings, and classes based on an educational goal.

The outings and classes in this book cover a wide range of topics to help your child learn about the ocean, land, air, and space as well as art, music, dance, drama, and history.

This book is divided into two major parts. The first part focuses on places to go and things to do. The second part is dedicated to classes for kids.

"Places to Go & Things to Do" includes both destinations and outings:
- Destinations are museums, zoos, aquariums, nature centers, gardens, farms, planetariums and observatories, parks, etc.
- Outings include boating, air shows, factory tours, whale watching, tide pooling, fruit picking, living history demonstrations, shows and concerts, and annual seasonal events such as the Chinese New Year's Parade, Cinco de Mayo, July 4th celebrations, the Renaissance Faire, Holiday Tea Parties, etc.

"Classes to Take" provides information on the resources available for kids' classes covering a wide range of topics from art, music, drama, and science to dance, swimming, gymnastics, ice skating, and bowling. Many of these can be done also as one-time outings.

I've provided:
- a regional index to help you find resources in your locale.
- a calendar to help you plan outings year-round.
- a free activities index to help you find fun things to do without over-stretching your budget (and these are plentiful!).
- an alphabetical index to make your search for things to do easier.
- a rainy day ideas list.
- a check list of items to bring along.

I've developed a companion Web site <**www.KidsEdVentures.com**> to this book, so please visit!

I hope this book is helpful and useful. Let me know what you think as you go out to explore and enjoy!

Elina Wong

How to Use This Book

This book should be used as a general reference and for information purposes only. While I've researched the information and collated it to make your search easier, and I've tried to be as accurate as possible, please double check and confirm dates, hours, times, locations, etc. prior to your outing to avoid any disappointments.

Age appropriateness: When the entry is listed with a minimum age requirement, the age requirement is established by the facility. Some facilities are just not designed for younger children, so please pay attention to the minimum age requirement. Some facilities have an age recommendation. These are shown as "Recommended Age." When the entry says (Ages #+), it is my suggestion as a general guideline and not a requirement nor a recommendation of the facility. Use your best judgment based on the interest, attention span, maturity, physical development, etc. of your child to help you determine if it is an appropriate activity for your child. The recommendation is just a general guideline, and each child has his own interests and characteristics.

Most facilities will host birthday parties. It is a rare facility that does not host birthday parties these days. Nature Centers or Visitor Centers at Nature Preserves often provide a less expensive alternative for birthday parties, and the kids love them!

The classes section is an additional outing resource because many facilities will allow one-time visits such as ice skating, bowling, etc. Gymnastics, ice skating, bowling, art, and music are great activities for birthday parties, too.

Some facilities will not provide tours to individuals or small groups but will provide programs and tours for larger groups such as Mom's groups, Scouts, or school groups. If you have some friends who are also interested in a specific activity or you belong to a parent's group, consider setting up a group to do these outings so you can take advantage of the programs that are offered only to groups. Note that some facilities with programs for school groups or Scout groups may require reservations up to a year in advance.

Remember that many museums have specific days when admission is free to the public. So, plan ahead to take advantage of these days.

Tips for a Great Trip

1) Print out the visitor maps provided by the local Convention and Visitor Bureaus. Here are their Web sites:
   - Sonoma County Map: <www.sonomavalley.com/SonomaValleyMap. htm>; <www.sonomacounty.com/map.aspx>.
   - San Francisco has Bay Area wide, San Francisco citywide, and detailed area maps: <www.sfvisitor.org/maps/index.html>.
   - Oakland has East Bay and Oakland downtown maps: <www.oaklandcvb.com/visiting_getting_around.cfm>.
   - San Jose has Bay Area wide, San Jose downtown, uptown, and central San Jose area maps: <www.sanjose.org/visitors/maps/maps.php>.
   - Santa Cruz has the Santa Cruz County map: <www.santacruz.org/places/county.shtml>.
   - Monterey has a Monterey County map: <http://montereyinfo.org/?p=4382>.
   - Carmel has a city map: <www.carmelcalifornia.org/images/map.jpg>.
   - *Bay City Guide's* Web site has great maps on transportation including BART, Bay Area ferries, and MUNI (with cable car routes) as well as Bay Area wide, downtown San Francisco, Fisherman's Wharf, and Golden Gate Park maps: <www.baycityguide.com/maps.html>. The site also has a huge collection of online coupons to attractions, shops, restaurants, tours, etc.
   - Tri-Valley area (Pleasanton, Livermore, San Ramon area) map: <www.trivalleycvb.com> then select "Area Maps" on the right side below the "search" box.

2) Before you start your trip, call to confirm dates, times, and costs and to get specific directions. Look on Web sites for maps and directions. Sometimes the maps from the internet mapping software are wrong. Confirm directions prior to your trip. While every effort has been made to provide accurate information, things change frequently and without notice.

3) Prepare your younger child by explaining a bit about your destination and/or reading about the topic prior to your outing, to ensure an enriching experience. I've suggested some materials where appropriate to help prepare your child.

4) Bring some cash, in various denominations from quarters and dollar bills to larger bills. This will come in handy for parking (both metered and parking lots), food, and other necessities. Most facilities require cash for food, even if they will accept credit cards at the entrance for admission.

5) Have extra changes of clothing and shoes in the car (at least for the kids, but it's a good idea for the adults, too) for unexpected messes.

6) Bring lots of bottled water or drinks because fun can be a thirsty business. It's always a great idea to have some fruit, yogurt, cheese sticks, or other snacks handy for the trip home.

7) Have binoculars, camera, jackets, sunscreen, sunglasses, and umbrellas stocked in your car so they'll be handy at a moment's notice.

8) As a general rule of thumb, many museums are closed on Mondays and are open during some federal holidays like Memorial Day, July 4th, Labor Day, etc.

Web Site

www.KidsEdventures.com

The official Web site for *Kids Adventures Around San Francisco Bay* is www.KidsEdVentures.com or www.KidsEducationalAdventures. com. The book and Web site are complementary. The Web site is designed to provide:

* Information on current family educational events in the Greater San Francisco Bay Area.

* Links to Web sites that appear in this book to registered readers for one-stop convenience of locating up-to-date information. Register online.

* A community forum for readers to share their experiences and to seek others' reviews of the facilities and services that appear in this book. When sending in a review or when reading a review, please keep in mind that different people have different standards and expectations.

* Be a vehicle for readers to give feedback. Your feedback is greatly appreciated!

Section I
Places to Go & Things to Do

Chapter 1
Animal Kingdom

The animal kingdom is extremely diverse. From the smallest shrew to the giant blue whale, size is only one feature among many that differentiates us. We can expose our children to barnyard animals in local farms; to more exotic and colorful animals at zoos and aquariums; but, best of all, to animals in their natural habitats. This section covers farms, zoos and wildlife museums, aquariums, nature preserves, beaches for tidepool animals, and whale-watching cruises for marine life.

Farms

Help your child learn that eggs come from chickens, milk from cows, and sweaters from sheep's wool. Some farm tours allow visitors to gather the eggs that the hen has laid, feed the sheep, and learn about wool shearing. Recreational farms such as Ardenwood, Hidden Villa, Little Farm at Tilden Park, and Slide Ranch are wonderful places to learn that eggs, milk, and butter come from chickens and cows and not from the shelves of the local grocery store. Consider visiting Ardenwood first, because the animal feedings are scheduled during convenient times and there are a variety of fun experiences.

Ardenwood Historic Farm (Ages 2+)

(510) 796-0663; 34600 Ardenwood Boulevard, Fremont, CA 94555
<www.ebparks.org/parks/arden.htm> or City of Fremont's site for Ardenwood:
<www.fremont.gov/recreation/ardenwoodpark/default.htm>

Description: This farm has an historic house, the Patterson House; gardens; farm animals; a horse-drawn train; and a blacksmith shop. Plan your trip to coincide with the animal feeding and blacksmith demonstrations. Best days to visit are Thursday, Friday, and Sunday when most activities are open. Learn from the staff which part of the hay the animals love to eat. Follow the staff around to harvest the eggs the chickens have laid, feed the animals, and get them settled for the evening. Better yet, time your visit with the many special events that are offered.

Hours: *Tues–Sun*: 10am–4pm. Closed Monday.

Animal Feeding: Thur–Sun 3pm.

Summer Season (April to mid-November):

• Patterson House tours: Thur–Sun.

• Horse-drawn train: Thur, Fri, & Sun 10:15am–3:30pm.

• Blacksmith demonstrations: Thur, Fri, Sun, & every other Sat.

• Farmyard Café: Thurs–Sun.

• Family programs and naturalist programs: Sat & Sun.

Winter Season (mid-November–March 31): The horse-drawn train and blacksmith shop are closed during the winter season.

Cost: Tues, Wed, Sat: $2/adult or senior, $1/child, free/child under 4 years old. Thur, Fri, & Sun: $5/adult, $4/senior, $3.50/child, and free/child under 4 years old. Special event fees are higher.

Bathrooms: Yes.

Facilities: Dirt trails. Strollers are OK.

Food: Café open Thur–Sun only. Picnic tables available.

What to Bring: Sunscreen, sunglasses, hat, picnic lunch and drinks, or cash for food.

Follow-Up Activities: For the calendar of special events, check the Web site: <www.fremont.gov/Recreation/ArdenwoodPark/Events.htm> or <www.ebparks.org/spevents.htm>. Special events include: spring activities at the farm such as baby animals, butterflies, farm chores for kids, puppets of the world, old-fashioned games, corn planting, learning to knit, gardening and farming, candle making, sheep and wool, rope making, and more. There are many historic events, including Johnny Appleseed Day, Celtic Festival, Highland Scottish Games, Civil War Reenactment, an

Old-Fashioned Independence Day Celebration on July 4th, Historic Rail Fair over Labor Day weekend, Cajun-Zydeco Festival in late September, Harvest Festival in mid-October, Halloween trains on weekend evenings during the second half of October, and "An Ardenwood Christmas" in early to mid-December.

Deer Hollow Farm (Ages 2+)

(650) 903-6430, (650) 965-FARM for Farm Tour
Rancho San Antonio County Park: Cristo Rey Drive, Cupertino, CA 95014
<www.fodhf.org>; <www.openspace.org/activities/deer_hollow_farm.asp>; <www.ci.mtnview.ca.us/city_hall/comm_services/recreation_programs_and_services/deer_hollow_farm.asp>

Description: Deer Hollow Farm is located inside the Rancho San Antonio Preserve. It is a small farm with chickens, goats, pigs, and sheep. It requires about a mile walk from the parking lot to the farm.

Hours: *Tues, Thur–Sun:* 8am–4pm; *Wed:* 8am–1pm. Animals visible 9am-3pm. See the chicks and ducklings in the spring by taking the farm tours on select Saturdays of April, May, & June. Tours are at 10am–1pm and last 45 minutes. Call for reservations. For detailed information, visit the Friends of Deer Hollow Farm Web site: <www.fodhf.org>.

Cost: Free. Tours: $5/adult, $2/child, free/child under 2.

Bathrooms: At the main entrance to the park.

Facilities: Stroller accessible, but during a farm tour, consider putting younger ones in a baby carrier.

Food: Food kiosk serving hot dogs, icees, etc. during the summer only.

What to Bring: Sunscreen, hat, sunglasses, water, and cash for food.

Follow-Up Activities: 1)Mountain View Recreation Dept. offers after school classes and summer camps. <www.ci.mtnview.ca.us/citydepts/cs/recreation.htm>. 2)Schools can arrange for field trips focused on the "Farm and Garden, Sheep and Goats, Wilderness Adventure, Birds, Ohlone Habitat and Ohlone Village" through the farm. Register in August through the farm. 3) Ohlone Day in late October.

Elkus Youth Ranch (Ages 2+)

(650) 712-3151; 1500 Purisima Creek Road, Half Moon Bay, CA 94019
<http://cesanmateo.ucdavis.edu/Custom_Program>;
e-mail: elkusranch@ucdavis.edu

Description: Located a few miles off Highway One in Half Moon Bay, this operational ranch is an educational environmental center dedicated to teaching kids. Run by the University of California Extension, there are chickens, rabbits, goats, pigs, sheep, llamas, a burro, and a horse. There's also a garden, greenhouse, and a ranch house.

Hours: The time to visit is during the special events and camps. There's a "Sheep to Shawl" day on a Saturday in early June and a "Winter Family Day" in mid-December when the ranch is open to the public. The ranch also has a week-long summer camp and a 2-day winter camp (during the holiday break) for kids ages 6-11. All of the above events and program require pre-registration. Watch Web site for details and to register. Schools and other groups have access to field trips and overnight camps.

Cost: "Sheep to Shawl": $3/person. "Winter Family Day": free, but donation appreciated. 2-day Winter Discovery Day Camp: $40/child per day.

Bathrooms: At the main entrance to the park.

Facilities: Stroller accessible, but during a farm tour, consider putting younger ones in a baby carrier.

Food: No.

What to Bring: Sunscreen, hat, sunglasses, and water bottles. Bring lunch and snacks during camps.

Follow-Up Activities: The ranch is home to a weavers guild and a yarn spinners guild meeting on the second weekend of each month. Visit Web site for details.

Emma Prusch Farm Park (Ages 3+)

(408) 926-5555; 647 South King Road, San Jose, CA 95116
<www.pruschfarmpark.org>;
<www.sjparks.org/Parks/RegionalParks/emmaPRUSCH.asp>

Description: This farm has a small birds area that includes free range chickens, some rather territorial (and aggressive) geese, peafowl, and some rabbits. The barn houses a few animals such as pigs, cows, goats, and sheep. Unfortunately, this farm doesn't have tours for families on a regular basis, so choose a special event day to visit. Visit this farm for the community gardens and orchards, but visit Hidden Villa or Ardenwood Farm for animals and animal feedings. This farm has two demonstration orchards: a rare fruit orchard and a deciduous fruit orchard featuring some of the fruit grown here in Santa Clara Valley, previously known as "Valley of Heart's Delight." School groups can reserve farm tours. These tours include animal visits, butter making by the students and butter tasting, and a brief presentation of the history of the farm. There is a newly built kids' playground.

Hours: Daily: 8:30 am–sunset. Visitor Center: 8:30am–4pm. Closed Thanksgiving, Christmas, & New Year's days.

Cost: Free admission and parking.

Bathrooms: Indoor bathrooms available at the Meeting Hall building. Portable toilets available in the park and community gardens.

Facilities: Stroller friendly.

Food: No food sales. Picnic tables available, some with barbecues, and one vending machine that sells drinks located on the side of the Meeting Hall building.

What to Bring: Sunscreen, sunglasses, and picnic lunch.

Follow-Up Activities: 1) Summer camps and classes offered through the San Jose Parks, Recreation, & Neighborhood Services <www.sanjoseca. gov/prns/cagindex.asp>. 2) Annual Harvest Festival in early October. 3) Hollow Park & Zoo (part of History Park San Jose), the Children's Discovery Museum, and the Tech Museum are close by.

Hidden Villa (All Ages)

(650) 949-8650; 26870 Moody Road, Los Altos Hills, CA 94022
<www.hiddenvilla.org>

Description: This is one of my favorites; it is truly an oasis. Nestled in the Los Altos Foothills, just beyond Foothill College, Hidden Villa is the former estate of the Duvenecks. There's an organic garden, a small farm, a hostel, an environmental education center, and hiking trails. Don't miss the farm tour and the beautiful organic garden, which has a grapevine cave and a gourd vine tunnel that kids love. Learn about different plants and composting. Past the garden, there is a big barn where the cows and sheep are housed. Continue walking up the dirt road and you'll come to a T-intersection. Make a left at the T-intersection, just past the little bridge, and you'll see a small white barn on your left. Some of the horses and goats are housed here. On your right, across the way from the small white barn, there's a white house. Walk behind the white house into the yard to see the chicken coop. If you're lucky, you may be able to see the freshly laid eggs inside the henhouse. The roosters and the hens are left to roam in the yard on alternate days. There's a very small barn in the back of the yard that houses the pigs. Placards on the outside wire fence identify the pigs by name.

Hours: Tues–Sun during daylight hours. Closed to the public in the summer for summer camps except for certain weekends. Check the schedule on the Web site for summer weekend hours. Visitor Center: Tues–Sun: 10am–4pm. Guided farm and garden tours on most weekends at 11am and 1pm, rain or shine. Reservations required.

Cost: $5 parking fee per car—"honor box." Guided farm tours are $5/person, free/child under 2. Reservations are required. Other costs vary by program.

Bathrooms: Yes, at the Visitor Center, the Education Building, and the office in the Duveneck House. Pick up a trail map at the Visitor Center (the first building next to the first parking lot once you pass the farm stand at the entrance).

Facilities: Dirt and gravel paths. Strollers are fine here.

Food: No food available. Picnic tables available if you want to bring your own lunch/snack. No trash cans; plan on bringing your trash home.

What to Bring: Bag lunch and drinks. Don't forget the sunscreen, sunglasses, camera, and cash for parking.

Follow-Up Activities: 1) Nature programs such as nature walks, wildflower hikes, bird walks, and Saturdays on the Farm for Kids (ages 6–10) series 10am–12pm. 2) Birthday parties. 3) Summer camps. 4) Cultural programs and concerts throughout the year.

Old Borges Ranch (Ages 4+)

(925) 942-0225; 1035 Castle Rock Road, Walnut Creek, CA 94598
<http://walnut-creek.org/header.asp?genericId=1&catId=4&subCatId=246>

Description: This working cattle ranch is now home to a ranger station and animals including goats, sheep, pigs, and chickens. It has a child's fishing pond, a play area, and an amphitheater on the grounds. This ranch gives us a glimpse of how folks lived in the old West, with historical displays of turn of the 20th century artifacts.

Hours: *Ranch Area:* Daily 8am to dusk. *Visitor Center:* Sat: 1–4pm, first Sunday of each month: 12 noon–4pm. History tours 4th Sunday of each month at 2pm — meet at the Hanna Grove Activity Area parking lot.

Cost: Free.
Bathrooms: Yes.
Facilities: Dirt paths, baby carrier recommended.
Food: No. Picnic tables available.
What to Bring: Picnic lunch, sunscreen, sunglasses, and hat. If you're attending Heritage Day, don't forget to bring $5/family cash for shuttling from Northgate High School at 435 Castle Rock to the ranch.
Follow-Up Activities: 1) *Heritage Day* on the 2nd Saturday in June from 10am–5pm has music, cowboys, horse rides, Indians, crafts, and food. 2) Living history programs are available to groups to learn about the ranching experience; reservations required.

McClellan Ranch Park (Ages 3 +)

(408) 777-3149; 22221 McClellan Road, Cupertino, CA 95014
<www.cupertino.org/just_visiting/what_to_do/index.asp>
<http://clubs.ca4h.org/santaclara/rollinghills>

Description: This hidden park will surprise you. It is used frequently by professional photographers for portraits because of the beautiful diffused lighting afforded by the trees. This preserve is home to a Junior Nature Museum; Community Gardens; the Headquarters of the Audubon Society, Santa Clara County chapter; and the Rolling Hills 4-H Club. The Junior Nature Museum has some snakes, turtles, and insects, depending on the season. It is also the site for after-school and nature classes sponsored through the Cupertino Parks and Recreation Department. Community organic garden plots are available for city residents of Cupertino. Groups can sign up for tours of the farm buildings and the Junior Museum. This preserve is also a good place for bird watching. The Rolling Hills 4-H Club 5-18 raises rabbits, chickens, sheep, pigs, and cattle. The 4-H Club has many child-led projects such as Web design, raising rabbits, or any other project in which the child is interested.
Hours: Tues–Sat: 10am–2pm, or later depending on activity. Call ahead to confirm hours and for the latest events. Tues–Fri: avail. for group tours.
Cost: Free.
Bathrooms: Yes.
Facilities: Strollers OK, but not on the trails.
Food: No.
What to Bring: Sunscreen and sunglasses.

Follow-Up Activities: 1) Wildlife Education Day in early October from 10am–2pm with talks on bats, crafts for kids, and insect collection displays. Call the Audubon Society at (408) 252-3747 for details. 2) To find out events happening at the Junior Nature Museum, e-mail <Barbarab@cupertino.org> to subscribe to her electronic newsletter. 3) Check Cupertino Parks and Recreation for after-school classes.

San Francisco Zoo (All Ages)
Family Farm at the Children's Zoo
(415) 753-7080; One Zoo Road, San Francisco, CA 94132
<www.sfzoo.org>

Description: At the Family Farm, get involved with animal care by feeding the animals their breakfast (10:45 am, weekends year-round, and every day during the summer). Grooming and hoof care of farm animals at 1pm on weekends throughout the year, and every day during the summer. At the hatchery, help collect eggs, feed, and water chicks (11am–noon, weekends and during the summer). You can also help feed the ducks in the pond. There are goats, sheep, miniature horses, ponies, a pig, ducks, and chickens.

Hours: *Daily:* 10am–5pm 365 days a year, including Christmas and Thanksgiving days. *Children's Zoo:* 11am–4pm. During the *summer* (Memorial Day–Labor Day), Children's Zoo 10:30am–4:30pm. *Feedings* for lions & tigers at 2pm (daily except Mondays), penguins at 3pm Fri–Wed and 2:30pm on Thur. *Meet the Keeper* talks at the Children's Zoo for meerkats & prairie dogs are at 2pm, *Insects in Action* are at 2:30pm, and *Native American Animals* are at 3:15pm & 3:45pm on weekends year-round and daily during the summer.

Cost: $11/adult, $8/youth (12–17) or senior (65+), $5/child (3–11), free/child 2 & under. $3/ride on Little Puffer train, $2/2 Dentzel Carousel rides (free for standing adults).

Bathrooms: Yes, throughout the park.

Facilities: Stroller friendly.

Food: Cafés throughout the park.

What to Bring: Jacket, even in the summer, because San Francisco can be foggy and cold. Don't forget the sunscreen, hat, sunglasses, and camera.

Follow-Up Activities: Many classes offered for children ages 3+, and family classes and workshops. Week-long summer day camps, camp outs, and morning bike tours as well as special programs for Scouts and "Close Encounters" for school groups. See entry in the following Zoos & Wildlife Museums section.

Slide Ranch (All Ages)

(415) 381-6155; 2025 Shoreline Highway (HWY 1), Muir Beach, CA 94965 <www.slideranch.org>

Description: This ranch is located off Hwy 1 by Muir Beach, with beautiful views of the Pacific Ocean. The ranch has an animal area, an organic garden, an observation beehive, and access to trails and tide pools. Time your visit with the *Family Farm Days* or special event days such as *Spring Fling* in April, *Sheep to Shawl* in March, *Ocean Exploration* in May includes a tide pool visit, and the *Harvest Celebration* in mid-October. Hands-on activities allow interaction with farm animals during these special events; farm animals are not available for hands-on interaction except during special event days. Preregistration required; plan your outing in advance to avoid disappointment. The *Sheep to Shawl* event features a shearing demonstration and wool carding, spinning, and weaving. Check Web site for current events.

Hours: 10am–4pm.

Cost: Free. Event days cost extra. For example, *Harvest Celebration Event:* $15/person in advance, $20/person at the gate, $60/family 4+, free/child 2 & under.

Bathrooms: Portables only.

Facilities: Stroller friendly on the ranch, but not on the trails.

Food: No, unless specified.

What to Bring: Picnic lunch and drinks. Dress warmly as the coast can be foggy and cool, even in the summer. If you plan on visiting the beekeeping workshop, dress in heavy clothes, gloves, and boots.

Follow-Up Activities: 1) Special programs and events throughout the year. Once on the Web site, click on "Programs & Events," then "Family Program" for details on events. 2) Summer camps for kids 6 & up. 3) School programs.

Tilden Nature Study Area & Little Farm (Ages 2+)
Tilden Regional Park

(510) 843-2137 Swimming at Lake Anza; (510) 524-6773 Merry-Go-Round; (510) 527-0421 Pony Ride; 600 Canon Drive, Berkeley, CA 94708 Wildcat Canyon Road & Grizzly Peak Boulevard entrances, Berkeley, CA <www.ebparks.org/parks/tilden.htm>; Botanical Garden: <www.nativeplants.org>; <www.redwoodvalleyrailway.com> Train;

Description: This beautiful park, nestled in the Berkeley hills, offers a Little Farm with animals, a pony ride circle (*temporarily closed* for renovation in 2006), a carousel, a train, and a botanic garden sprinkled throughout the expansive park. The Little Farm offers family programs and camps for kids throughout the year. The Botanical Garden offers tours and lectures year-round. Look on the Web site for maps before heading there.

Hours: 8am–10pm unless posted otherwise. *Little Farm:* 10am-5pm *Trains:* 11am–6pm weekends and holidays year-round. Open weekdays during the summer until Labor Day weekend from noon to 5pm. *Merry-Go-Round:* 11am–5pm weekends, holidays, and on weekdays during spring and summer breaks. After Labor Day, the Merry-Go-Round is open on weekends 11am–5pm. *Pony rides (temporarily closed for renovation):* 11am–5pm on weekends and 11am–4pm daily during the summer (June 14–Labor Day). *Lake Anza:* 11am–6pm from late March through early October. The lake is open for fishing year-round. *Botanical Garden:* 8:30am-5pm year-round, but closed on major holidays.

Cost: Free parking. *Lake Anza Swim Area:* $3.50/person ages 16–61, $2.50/1-15, free/child 1 & under. *Merry-Go-Round:* $1/ride or $10/13-ride ticket book. *Steam Train:* $2/ride or $8/5-ride family ticket. *Pony ride:* $3/ride or $25.50 for 10 rides.

Bathrooms: Yes, at steam train, carousel, Lake Anza, and the Botanic Garden Visitor Center. Lake Anza has changing rooms.

Facilities: Stroller friendly.

Food: Snack stands at Lake Anza and Merry-Go-Round.

What to Bring: Picnic lunch, sunscreen, sunglasses, and drinks.

Follow-Up Activities: Naturalist programs through the visitor center and the botanical garden. Visit the Web site for program and event information: <www.ebparks.org/events.htm>. See Chapter 2: Plant Kingdom— Gardens & Arboretums for details on the park's Botanical Garden.

Zoos & Wildlife Museums

Learning about animals helps us appreciate the circle of life, so beautifully illustrated in Disney's *Lion King*. Animals help us learn to respect animal habitats and the beautiful world we've inherited. They help us appreciate that we each have a special place on earth.

If you have a little one who loves the zoo and animals, consider purchasing a membership from one of the zoos since one membership provides free or reduced admission to other zoos locally and across the country. For example, Happy Hollow Zoo, Oakland Zoo, Coyote Point Museum and Zoo, and the San Francisco Zoo all have reciprocal memberships. This means membership in one zoo allows free admission for the zoo chosen and reduced admission to all the other local zoos on the list. Membership costs are different depending on the zoo. Research the "reciprocal" list and the prices to determine which membership provides the best value for you. Don't forget to take parking fees into consideration as these fees add up rather quickly. The one you choose will be the one sending the detailed mailings with class and event information. Keep reciprocal memberships in mind for museums and other facilities, too.

The Bay Area Science Alliance Web site provides a calendar of events for many science-related family events and exhibits in the Bay Area <www.basa.info/cs/basa/cal/20>.

California Academy of Sciences (Ages 3+)
Golden Gate Park
(415) 321-8000; 55 Concourse Drive, San Francisco, CA 94118 (Reopens 2008); *Temporary Location:* 875 Howard Street, San Francisco, CA 94103
<www.calacademy.org>

Description: The California Academy of Sciences, which consists of the Natural History Museum, Steinhart Aquarium, and Morrison Planetarium, is where your child can learn about the earth, the oceans, and the universe. It also has a dinosaur skeleton (T-Rex) and an Insect Room with an exhibit of butterflies and moths, to show how camouflage and mimicry can be used to fool one's enemies. See the respective entries under Steinhart Aquarium and Morrison Planetarium (closed for renovation) for more detailed information for each and the full entry in Chapter 4: Science & Technology Museums.

Coyote Point Museum (Ages 2+)

(650) 342-7755; 1651 Coyote Point Drive, San Mateo, CA 94401
<www.coyoteptmuseum.org>

Description: Located on the edge of the San Francisco Bay, the museum is in Coyote Point Park, which has a marina and a bay beach. The museum has exhibits on ecosystems found in the Bay Area, the water cycle, the weather, and recycling and trash. Outside of the main museum building, there are river otters, foxes, coyotes, snakes, and a wonderful walk-through aviary. The museum also has a live see-through beehive with a great exhibit demonstrating how bees dance to communicate where flowers can be found. Don't miss the animal feedings and talks.

Hours: Tues–Sat: 10am–5pm. Sun: noon–5pm. Closed Mondays. *Fox feeding:* daily at 11:30am. *River Otter feeding:* daily at 12:15pm. *Animal Talks:* weekends at 2pm at the Wildlife Amphitheater.

Cost: $5 parking, $6/adult, $4/senior or child (13–17), $2/child (3–12), free/child 3 & under. *Free admission on the first Wednesday of each month,* excludes groups of 10 or more. Free admission for teachers with ID.

Bathrooms: Yes.

Facilities: Stroller friendly.

Food: Drinks & snacks only. Picnic tables outside the museum.

What to Bring: Cash for parking and picnic lunch.

Follow-Up Activities: 1) Birthday parties. 2) Family programs covering topics such as volcanoes, earthquakes, hurricanes, geography, and gardening. The museum even has storytime and toddler programs. See "Calendar" icon on the Web site. 3) Classes for preschoolers through middle school students. Topics include insects, animals, birds of prey, habitats, and native Californians. They also provide classes for homeschoolers. Check the Web site for more detailed information.

Happy Hollow Park & Zoo (Ages 2+)

(408) 277-3000; 1300 Senter Road, San Jose, CA 95112

<www.happyhollowparkandzoo.org>

Description: The park has a small zoo, including a petting zoo with interesting and rare animals, a rides area perfect for preschoolers, a puppet show, and play areas. The rides and puppet show are included with the price of admission. When my daughter was three and four years old, we came at least every other week spring–fall.

Hours: Daily: 10am–5pm. *Summer* (July–August): 10am–6pm. *Puppet Show:* Mon–Fri: noon & 2pm, Sat & Sun: noon, 2pm & 4pm. Summertime can be quite crowded with summer camps that have field trips here. *Winter:* Rides and park are closed, but the zoo is open.

Cost: *Parking:* $6/car when kiosk is attended (typically in the summer). There is a 50% discount on parking for military personnel/veterans (with ID), seniors, the disabled, and members with 10-visit or annual parking passes. *Admission:* $6/person (2–64), $5.50/senior (65–74) & disabled, free/person under 2 or over 74. *Every 2nd Tuesday, admission is only $1*; however, parking fee is charged. $40/10 visit pass or $80/year parking pass good for any San Jose regional park.

Bathrooms: Yes, but no changing stations.

Facilities: Stroller friendly. Stroller rentals by the main entrance.

Food: Café. You may also bring your own food to the park. There are picnic tables by the rides and food concession areas.

What to Bring: Cash for parking, sunglasses, sunscreen, and plenty to drink during hot weather. The kids can work up quite a thirst running around. Consider bringing a picnic lunch and picnic gear. Don't forget to bring a few quarters for the petting zoo, to buy food for the animals.

Follow-Up Activities: 1) Classes year-round for tots to older kids, but advanced registration and additional fees are required. Summer camps on puppetry and the zoo for kids ages 3–9. "Zoofaris" are sleepovers for kids ages 7+. Check Web site for additional class information: <www.hhpz.org/edu/progs.php>. 2) Also at Kelly Park are the Japanese Friendship Garden and History Park, San Jose with a wonderful Trolley Barn filled with antique trolleys and cars. The trolley runs on weekends. See respective entries for details in Chapter 2: Plant Kingdom—Gardens & Arboretums section and Chapter 9: Historical Outings—History Parks & Museums.

Lindsay Wildlife Museum (Ages 2+)

(925) 935-1978; 1931 First Avenue, Walnut Creek, CA 94597
<www.wildlife-museum.org>

Description: Although small, this wonderful museum focuses on native California wildlife and natural history. It has exhibits on birds of prey: hawks, owls, eagles, falcons, etc. It also features foxes, bobcats, raccoons, reptiles, amphibians, and more. There is an eagle or bobcat feeding or a stage presentation of a wild animal on a daily basis. Call for details before your trip. There is a discovery room for young children. The museum is surrounded by gardens and Larkley Park with play structures and picnic areas.

Hours: *School Year* (Sept 16–June 14): Wed–Fri: noon–5pm, Sat & Sun: 10am–5pm. Closed Mon–Tues. *Summer* (June 16–Sept 3): extended hours. Wed–Sun: 10am–5pm.

Cost: $7/adult, $6/senior, $5/child (2–17), and free/child under 2.

Bathrooms: Yes.

Facilities: Stroller friendly.

Food: No. Picnic area in adjacent park.

What to Bring: Picnic lunch, sunscreen, sunglasses, and drinks.

Follow-Up Activities: 1) Preschool classes for children ages 2½ and 3½. There are also classes for various age ranges through age 12. 2) Summer camp for children ages 4–12. Check the "Just for Kids" page on the Web site for current information. 3) Adult classes, trips, and tours are also available in the "Programs" section of the Web site. Some of the classes have included an introduction to bird watching, wetland animals, a tarantula hike, and family travel programs. 4) Birthday parties. 5) Programs for homeschoolers. 6) Tours for Scout groups ages 6–12.

Marin WildCare (Ages 2+)

(415) 453-1000; 76 Albert Park Lane, San Rafael, CA 94901
<www.wildcarebayarea.org>

Description: WildCare is a rehabilitation hospital and environmental education center located in San Rafael. Animals that can't be returned to the wild are on display in the courtyard. There are hawks, brown pelicans, cormorants, and other birds. The museum has taxidermied animals on display including a bobcat, mountain lion, grizzly bear, and golden eagle. Although the center is small, it offers a variety of classes and educational programs, a gem for locals.

Hours: *Natural History Museum:* 9am-5pm daily. *Courtyard:* 9am–5pm daily. Pool bird feeding: 12:30pm & 4:30pm. Raptors on the glove: Tues & Sat: 3-5pm.

Cost: Free.

Bathrooms: Yes.

Facilities: Stroller friendly.

Food: No.

What to Bring: Picnic lunch.

Follow-Up Activities: 1) Tours available for preschoolers, Scouts, and school groups weekdays: 9:30am–2:30pm. Presentations last 75 minutes. During the summer, tours available only on Wed. 2) Field trips available for school groups K-grade 6. These half-day trips help kids learn about geology and nature. Visit Web site for details. 3) Nature camps for preschoolers & up throughout the year.

Museum of Vertebrate Zoology (Ages 4+)

(510) 642-3567; 3101 Valley Life Sciences Building, UCB, Berkeley, CA 94720 <http://mvz.berkeley.edu>; <www.berkeley.edu/map>

Description: The museum's huge collection of taxidermied animals is for research purposes, and as such is normally closed to the public. The only exception is Cal Day, the annual U.C. Berkeley open house in mid-late April. Don't miss this event as the museum puts out an impressive display along with live animals to see and touch. See Cal Day in Chapter 10: Seasonal Events.

Hours: 9am-4pm in mid-April for Cal Day.

Cost: Free.

Bathrooms: Yes.

Facilities: Stroller friendly.

Food: No.

What to Bring: Camera, jacket, cash for parking & food.

Follow-Up Activities: As part of the Berkeley Natural History Museums, there are many online resources for teachers and students interested in living and extinct flora and fauna of California. Visit <http://bnhm.berkeley.edu/index.php> for lesson plans and other resources.

Oakland Zoo (All Ages)

(510) 632-9525; 9777 Golf Links Road, Oakland, CA 94605
<www.oaklandzoo.org>

Description: Oakland Zoo features animals from various environments, including the African savanna (including elephants, which are becoming increasingly rare in zoos), tropical rain forest, and Australian outback. The recently renovated children's zoo offers a fruit bat exhibit, a bug house to learn about insects, a petting zoo (no feeding), underwater viewing portals to see alligators close up, and exhibits for otters and lemurs. The lower park has a separate entrance (to the right of the main entrance) with rides and a mini-roller coaster for little ones. However, these rides are not included with park admission and require additional ticket purchase. Don't miss the train and aerial tram for a beautiful view of the Bay Area.

Hours: Daily 10am–4pm. Rides open at 11am. Closed Thanksgiving, Christmas, and during inclement weather. *Tram ride* open weekends at 11am. *Wildlife Theater*, an educational animal show for kids is at 11:30am & 1pm on Sat & 11:15am & 12 noon on Sun. Check the Animal Feeding schedule at the gate.

Cost: $6/parking fee. Zoo admission: $9.50/person ages 15–54, $6/child (2–14) and seniors (55+). Parking is free on the first Monday of each month, excluding holidays. Rides cost $1–$2 each (train & roller coaster rides cost $2/ride. A package of tickets offers a slight discount.

Bathrooms: Yes.

Facilities: Stroller friendly.

Food: Café. You may also bring a picnic lunch.

What to Bring: Sunscreen, hat, sunglasses, camera, plenty to drink, and cash for parking and rides at the lower park.

Follow-Up Activities: 1) Family events such at "Boo at the Zoo" for Halloween, "Family Sundown Safari," and classes for children throughout the year. Check Web site for most current information. 2) Birthday parties. 3) Summer camps for pre-K to grade 12. Registration begins in March. 4) Sleepovers for Scouts, families, and youth groups.

Pacific Grove Museum of Natural History (Ages 2+)

(831) 648-5716; 165 Forest Avenue, Pacific Grove, CA 93950

Description: The museum has wonderful drawers full of sea shells, sea shell fossils, rocks and gems, and a fabulous display of the birds of northern California. This museum is the place to go if your child is learning to identify birds. There is a nice variety of bird eggs, and the exhibits are well labeled. There's also an exhibit dedicated to the native Indians of the Monterey area. Just a short drive from the Monterey Bay Aquarium, and a stroll from Lovers' Point in Pacific Grove, this little museum is well worth a visit.

Hours: Open Tues–Sat: 10am–5pm.

Cost: Free.

Bathrooms: Yes.

Facilities: Stroller friendly.

Food: No. Restaurants close by in downtown Pacific Grove and at Lovers' Point.

Palo Alto Junior Museum & Zoo (Ages 2+)

(650) 329-2111; 1451 Middlefield Road, Palo Alto, CA 94301
<www.cityofpaloalto.org/community-services/museum-index.html>

Description: Although the zoo is small, there's a very nice collection of animals, including a blue-tongue skink, bats, sharks, baby rats, and interesting birds. The museum has very high quality intereactive exhibits that are age appropriate for preschoolers and up. In the past exhibits have explained simple machines, animation, and basic mechanical physics (friction, velocity, momentum, etc.)

Hours: *Museum*: Tues–Sat: 10am–5pm. *Zoo*: Tues–Sat: 10am–4:30pm, Sun: 1–4pm. Closed Monday.

Cost: Free. Donations appreciated.

Bathrooms: Yes.

Facilities: Stroller friendly.

Food: No.

What to Bring: Picnic lunch. There's a park with a play structure just behind the museum, perfect for a picnic.

Follow-Up Activities: A wide range of science classes is offered through the Palo Alto Parks and Recreation Department. Check the Palo Alto *Enjoy!* Catalog at <www.paenjoy.org> for details.

Randall Museum (Ages 2+)

(415) 554-9600; 199 Museum Way, San Francisco, CA 94114
<www.randallmuseum.org>

Description: Part of the San Francisco Recreation & Parks Department, this gem perched atop Corona Heights offers a panoramic view of San Francisco. The gardens have wonderful sculptures on display. The museum has exhibits on science, nature, and art. There's a display of animals native to California including birds and snakes, an insect exhibit, a small petting zoo, and a see-through beehive. There's also a theater with live performances. Check the Web site under "Classes & Activities" for special events, performances, and classes. The Golden Gate Model Railroad is housed in the basement of the museum; open Sat 10am–4pm.

Hours: Tues–Sat: 10am–5pm. Closed Sunday & Monday. On Saturdays, there are *Family ceramics:* 10:30–11:30am; *meet the animals:* 11:15am–12pm; *animal feeding:* 12pm; and *drop-in workshops for art and science projects:* 1–4pm.

Cost: Free. Workshops require a small fee.

Bathrooms: Yes.

Facilities: Stroller friendly.

Food: No.

What to Bring: Picnic lunch, camera, and cash for workshop fee.

Follow-Up Activities: 1) Classes, camps, and workshops for toddlers & older. Classes include art, ceramics, woodworking, robotics, cosmology, etc. 2) Birthday parties organized by the Buddy Club. For additional info on birthday parties, call: (510) 236-7469. 3) Don't miss Bug Day at the end of May, Family Halloween Fest in October, and Holiday Craft Day in December.

Ringling Brothers and Barnum & Bailey Circus (Ages 3+)

(415) 421-TIXS San Francisco, (510) 762-2277, (650) 478-2277
<www.ringling.com> or <www.ticketmaster.com>

Usually performs at Oakland Arena, Cow Palace, and San Jose Arena.

Description: Circuses are great fun. They are one of the ways to actually see these animals in action, albeit artificially since they have been extensively trained. But it's a treat to see tigers, horses, elephants, and acrobats performing gravity defying stunts. Arrive 90 minutes before the show to

meet the animals up close in the center circle; it is included with the price of admission. *Note:* Clowns can be scary for little ones. You may want to gauge your child's reaction to a clown before taking him to the circle.
Hours: Comes around to local Bay Area arenas once a year, usually in August. Tickets go on sale in July. Check Web site for current schedule and ticket information.
Cost: Varies, usually between $13–$80 per seat, depending on seating and date. Check Web site for most current information.
Bathrooms: Yes.
Facilities: Not stroller friendly.
Food: Hot dogs, candy, sodas, etc.
What to Bring: Camera—if you go early, you can visit with the clowns and other performers before the show begins. There, you have a great opportunity to take pictures with the performers and the animals. Bring cash for food, souvenirs, and parking.

Safari West (Ages 3+)

(707) 579-2551; (800) 616-2695; 3115 Porter Creek Road, Santa Rosa, CA 95404
<www.safariwest.com>

Description: Situated in the beautiful rolling hills of Santa Rosa bordering Calistoga, this nature preserve & zoo for endangered animals provides opportunities to view animals in various habitats. Guided tours by knowledgeable naturalists provide in-depth knowledge of the animals featured, including many types of antelope, giraffes, Cape buffalo, zebras, and exotic birds in the aviary. 2½ hours long, the tour has two parts. The first 2 hours take place in a safari vehicle; the last half hour is a walk to see the birds, cheetahs, and lemurs firsthand. Time your visit in the morning during the spring or summer, if possible. Many babies are born then, and they tend to be more active in the morning.
Schedule: Spring and fall tour times: 9am, 1pm, 4pm. Winter tour times: 10am & 2pm. Call for tour reservations.
Cost: $62/adult, $28/child. Free for children under 3.
Bathrooms: Yes, at the entrance.
Facilities: Not stroller friendly.
Food: Restaurant on site, but prior reservations are required. Lunch: $15/adult, $12/child. Dinner: $25/adult, $15/child. Deli for drop-ins features drinks and snacks. If you are planning to eat lunch at the deli, arrive at least an hour prior to the start of the 1pm tour.

What to Bring: Sunscreen, hat, sunglasses, comfortable clothes and shoes, camera, and binoculars. Dress very warmly if going in the winter.

Follow-Up Activities: Take a virtual tour on the Web site to see the types of animals you will learn about. The Petrified Forest is a few short miles down the road, and Old Faithful Geyser is a bit farther in Calistoga.

San Francisco Zoo (All Ages)
(415) 753-7080; 1 Zoo Road, San Francisco, CA 94132
<www.sfzoo.org>

Description: The San Francisco Zoo is probably my favorite Bay Area zoo because it has such a variety of activities appropriate for little ones. These include the Family Farm at the Children's Zoo, the Insect Zoo, the Little Puffer Train, and Dentzel Carousel. The new African Savanna is a prominent and wonderful addition to the zoo, with zebras, giraffes, ostriches, storks, cranes, and more all living together in a very natural looking environment. In the summer (from Memorial Day to Labor Day), Wildlife Theater features animal shows. The Koret Animal Resource Center has eagles, falcons, and other birds of prey perched on the lawn. Animal feeding time is also great fun. See what lions, tigers, and penguins eat every day. The Insect Zoo is a great place to watch a beehive and learn about bugs.

Hours: Daily:10am–5pm. 365 days a year, including Christmas Day and Thanksgiving Day. Children's Zoo: 11am–4pm. During the summer (Memorial Day–Labor Day), the Children's Zoo has slightly extended hours 10:30am–4:30pm. Here is the feeding schedule. Confirm on <www. sfzoo.org/events/calendar.shtml>, then "Special Animal Encounters."

Daily schedule:
- Big Cats in the Lion House: 2pm daily (closed Mondays).
- Penguins at Penguin Island: 2:30pm daily.
- Binnowee Landing (feed parakeets, cockatiels, and colorful eastern rosellas with feedsticks): additional $2/person entry fee.

Daily during the summer:
- Hatchery Tour: 11:15am (incubating eggs & chicks) @ Family Farm.
- Parrot Encounter: 1-1:45pm @ Nature Theater in Children's Zoo,
- Wetlands Lab: 1-3pm @ Children's Zoo,
- Meerkats and Prairie Dogs: 2pm @ Children's Zoo,

- Life on the Farm: 2pm @ Family Farm in Children's Zoo.
- Incredible Insects in Action: 2:30pm @ Children's Zoo.

Cost: $5/parking lot. Street parking is free. *Free admission on the first Wednesday of each month.* $11/adult, $8/youth (12–17) or senior (65+), $5/child (3–11), free for children 2 & under. Little Puffer Train and carousel rides cost $2/person. See Trains section for more details on train and carousel. Discounted admission for San Francisco residents: $9/adult, $4.50/youth (12–17) or senior (65+), $2.50/child (3–11), free/child 2 & under. Stroller rental available.

Bathrooms: Yes, renovated restrooms throughout the park.

Facilities: Stroller friendly.

Food: Cafés throughout the park. For the menu: <www.sfzoo.org/pdf/Leaping_Lemur_Menu.pdf>.

What to Bring: Jacket, even in the summer, because San Francisco can be foggy and cold. Don't forget the sunscreen, hat, sunglasses, camera, and binoculars. Bring some dollar bills to feed the birds at Binnowee Landing, and other small bills to purchase tickets for the train & carousel rides.

Follow-Up Activities: 1) They've got great classes for kids 18 months & up. See Web site: <www.sfzoo.org/education/classes.shtml>. **2)** Spring, summer, and winter camps for ages 4+. **3)** Birthday parties & sleepovers.

Santa Cruz Natural History Museum (Ages 2 +)
(831) 420-1168; 1305 East Cliff Drive, Santa Cruz, CA 95062
<www.santacruzmuseums.org>

Description: This museum has wonderful children's exhibits. It has a bit of everything, from fossils and bees to the Ohlone Indians who lived in this area years ago. There's a touch pool with starfish and sea anemones. Kids can learn about the animals that lived in the Santa Cruz area and their natural habitats. The cement whale on the front lawn is a favorite climbing spot for kids.

Hours: Tues–Sun: 10am–5pm.

Cost: $2.50/adult, $1.50/seniors (60+), free/youth <18.

Bathrooms: Yes.

Facilities: Stroller friendly.

Food: No. Two restaurants within a couple of blocks' walk.

What to Bring: Picnic lunch, sunscreen, and sunglasses. This museum is very close to the beach; bring beach gear if you want to go to the beach afterward.

Follow-Up Activities: 1) Close to Natural Bridges State Park, Seymour Marine Discovery Center, and Santa Cruz Beach Board Walk. 2) Summer camps for kids ages 8–10. 3) Docent-led school tours from preschool to 6th grade are available with 4 weeks' notice. Times available: Tues–Fri at 9am, 10:15am, 11:30am, 12:45pm, and 2pm.

Directions: On the one-way street next to the museum, the street parking on the side closest to the museum is by permit. Stop in at the front to ask for a permit to park there.

Wild Things Animal Rentals Inc. (Ages 3+)

(831) 455-1901; (800) 228-7382; 400 River Road, Salinas, CA 93908
<www.wildthingsinc.com>

Description: Wild Things' business is show business for animals. Its animals are trained for appearances on TV, movies, pictures, calendars, and live performances. Its animals were models for Disney's *Lion King*, *Tarzan*, *Aladdin*, etc. Fortunately for us, we can visit the facility to learn about these amazing animals.

Hours: One-hour-long daily tours at 1pm. Additional tour at 3pm in June, July, & August. Closed Thanksgiving & Christmas.

Cost: $10/adult, $8/child 14 & under. Family annual pass: $55/2 adults & 2 kids, unlimited visits.

Bathrooms: Yes.

Facilities: Stroller friendly.

Food: No.

What to Bring: Picnic lunch, camera, sunscreen, and sunglasses.

Follow-Up Activities: 1) Special nighttime tours around Halloween, Christmas, & Valentine's Days. Reservations required; call (831) 455-1901 ext. 3. 2) Spring & summer safari day camps for kids ages 7+. "Roar & Snore" is a sleepover from Friday night to Saturday morning. 3) Educational programs for schools.

Nature Preserves

Nature preserves allow us the opportunity to view wildlife in their natural habitat. Bird watching, tide pooling, visiting the northern elephant seal, and whale watching allow us to view wildlife in their natural habitat here in the Bay Area.

California is on the migratory path of many birds. Bird watching can be a bit tricky to the novice. Since I am a novice, I looked for resources that will help in the identification of birds. Here are some resources that I found very useful.

1) *Local Birds of the San Francisco Bay Area: "Quick Guide"* to commonly seen local birds instantly identifies backyard-trail and shore-water birds. This is a quick reference laminated foldout card that's easy to carry along on a bird watching trip. It is 5.5" x 6.5" and very thin with color illustrations and separate sections for shore, backyard, and trail birds commonly found in the Bay Area.

2) *Birding at the Bottom of the Bay: A Birder's site guide from Santa Clara Valley Audubon Society, Third Edition.* This book provides information on where and when to go for bird watching trips in the local area. You can purchase this book directly by mail from the Santa Clara Valley Audubon Society: SCVAS, 22221 McClellan Road, Cupertino, CA 95014 or by credit card by calling (408) 252-3747.

3) You can also purchase the laminated card and the book from the Wild Bird Center, (408) 358-9453, 792 Blossom Hill Road, Los Gatos, CA 95032; or at the San Carlos store: (650) 595-0300, 926 El Camino Real, San Carlos, CA 94070. The Web site is: <www. wildbirdcenter.com>

4) Santa Clara Valley Audubon Society has bird watching trips that are open to members. Membership costs $15/year. Check the Web site <www.scvas.org> in the "calendar" & "Kids' Calendar" sections for trips and events. Annual Wildlife Education Day in October. The society is located at the McClellan Ranch site in Cupertino: 22221 McClellan Road, Cupertino, CA 95014. (408) 252-3747.

5) Many naturalist programs at the Nature Preserves and Parks with Visitor Centers also provide docent- or naturalist-led bird watching walks. These include Baylands, Elkhorn Slough, Arastradero, Sunol,

Lindsey Wildlife Museum, Point Reyes National Seashore, California Academy of Sciences, and Crissy Field.

For bird watching trips, don't forget to bring your binoculars and your bird identification card!

Elkhorn Slough Reserve in Moss Landing, Baylands Nature Preserve in Palo Alto, Point Reyes National Seashore, and Hawk Hill in the Marin Headlands provide wonderful bird watching opportunities.

Elkhorn Slough and Baylands are wetlands and salt marsh environments. This environment provides a transition zone between the freshwater and saltwater of the bay and ocean. The wetlands serve as a diverse habitat for wildlife, from migrating birds to sharks, crabs and shrimp, marine worms, and microscopic algae known as diatoms. The ecology lab inside the Lucy Evans Interpretive Center located at the Baylands and the Visitor Center at Elkhorn Slough have microscopes to view microscopic life that inhabits these environments.

Año Nuevo State Reserve and Point Reyes are breeding grounds for the northern elephant seal. Point Reyes National Seashore also provides opportunities to view birds, elk, whales, and other wildlife.

Año Nuevo State Reserve (Ages 5 +)

(650) 879-0227, New Years Creek Road, Pescadero, CA 94060
(650) 879-2025 Reserve office: 8:30am– 3:30pm
(800) 444-4445 Guided Walk Reservations open 9am-5pm weekdays & 9am-3pm weekends. (Required between December 15 and March 31. Reservations open in late October for individuals; and now can be booked online.)
<www.parks.ca.gov/default.asp?page_id=523>

Description: Located between Santa Cruz and Half Moon Bay, Año Nuevo is the largest breeding colony in the world for northern elephant seals. Come see their mating ritual and the seal pups from December to March. Tours require visitors to hike for about 3 miles. Review information prior to calling for reservations: <**www.parks.ca.gov/pages/523/files/**100006ElephantWalk.pdf>. You may reserve up to 56 days in advance.
Hours: During the breeding season (December–March), access to the Reserve is open only for guided walks. The walks last 2.5 hours and the

hike is about 3 miles. They depart every 15 minutes 9:15 am–2:30 pm.
Cost: $6/car parking fee, $5/person, free/child 3 & under.
Bathrooms: Yes, at the Visitor Center.
Facilities: Not stroller friendly.
Food: Picnic tables next to the Visitor Center.
What to Bring: Drinks/water bottles, warm jacket, picnic lunch, binoculars, and very comfortable walking shoes for the hike.

Arastradero Preserve (Ages 4+)

(650) 329-2423; 1530 Arastradero Road, Palo Alto, CA
(½ mile west of Page Mill Road)
<www.arastradero.org>
<www.city.palo-alto.ca.us/community-services/nat-arastradero.html>

Description: Located in the Palo Alto foothills, Arastradero Preserve is an open space preserve with a lake where wildlife abounds, including many varieties of birds such as bluebirds, wrens, chickadees, flycatchers, and even barn owls. The lake is a 20-minute walk from the parking lot.
Hours: Open daily from 8am to sunset.
Cost: Free parking.
Bathrooms: Portables until visitor center is built.
Facilities: Jogger stroller ok.
Food: No.
What to Bring: Sunglasses, sunscreen, picnic lunch, drinks, binoculars, and bird identification card.
Follow-Up Activities: Nature programs through the Palo Alto Parks and Recreation Department. Check the Palo Alto *Enjoy!* Catalog under the "For Everyone" section or call (650) 329-2423. Past classes have included "Nesting Birds at Arastradero Preserve" and "Ethnobotany Walk," a program that explains how the Ohlone people used plants for food, shelter, basketry, and medicine.

Baylands Nature Preserve (Ages 4+)

(650) 329-2506; 2775 Embarcadero Road, Palo Alto, CA
<www.cityofpaloalto.org/community-services/pk-baylands.html>
<www.abag.ca.gov/bayarea/baytrail/vtour/map3/access/Btpalto/Btpalto.htm>

Description: The Baylands Nature Preserve and Shoreline Lake are prime bird watching areas, with 150 species of wild birds, including some endangered species. There is a duck pond on your way to the Interpretive Center with different species of ducks and other birds. Learn about wetlands/salt marshes as habitats for diverse wildlife at the Lucy Evans Baylands Nature Preserve Interpretive Center. Plan on visiting the Preserve on the weekend so you can take advantage of the slide show, educational video, and nature walks with expert naturalists who can enrich and add depth to your experience. While on a docent-led walk on a November Saturday afternoon, we saw black-necked stilts, dowitchers, and sandpipers, along with the ubiquitous seagulls.

Hours: Closed Mondays. Tues–Fri: 2–5pm. Don't miss the ecology lab: open in the afternoons. Weekends: 1–5pm. On weekends, educational videos: 1 and 4pm, slide show on salt marsh life: 2pm, and nature walks with naturalists: 3pm. *Note: The naturalist may be the only staff at the Visitor Center; when the naturalist is conducting the nature walk at 3pm, the Visitor Center is temporarily closed.*

Cost: Free.

What to Bring: Binoculars, sunscreen, sunglasses, water bottles, and bag lunch if you're planning to eat here. Dress in layers, as it can be windy. Wear good walking shoes that you don't mind getting muddy.

Bathrooms: Yes, inside the Interpretive Center. Portable bathrooms are located at the very end of the road.

Facilities: Stroller friendly. However, if you're planning to go on the nature walks with the naturalist, consider using a baby carrier or backpack instead.

Food: No, but picnic tables available.

Follow-Up Activities: 1) Plan ahead and register for one of the weekend programs such as "Fall and Winter Birding at the Baylands" and "Mysteries of the Mud Workshop" through the Palo Alto Parks and Recreation Department. These programs are free. For program details, see <www.paenjoy.org> for the Palo Alto *Enjoy!* Catalog's "Open Space" or "Everyone" section. 2) 2-week session nature summer camps for $110. 3) *Environmental Volunteers*, a group of wonderful docents who provide science and environmental education to school groups at the Baylands, can be reached at: (650) 961-0545 or by mail at 3921 E. Bayshore Road, Palo Alto, CA 94303-4326. 4) Consider visiting Shoreline Lake in Mountain View, just a few miles off Highway 101, before your visit to Baylands Nature Preserve. You can have a wonderful day trip by first visiting Shoreline Lake. Take a quick look inside the Rengstorff House, go on a paddleboat ride, and have lunch at the Lakeside Café in the morning. After lunch, visit the Baylands Natural Preserve and learn about the diverse animals and marine life that call the salt marshes home.

Bolinas Lagoon Preserve – Audubon Canyon Ranch

(415) 868-9244; 4900 Highway One, Stinson Beach, CA 94970
<www.egret.org>

Description: Best known for its heron and egret nesting grounds, the preserve is open to the public only during the heron and egret season. Guides are stationed at various points of the preserve to answer visitor questions. They provide binoculars and telescopes at strategic viewing spots. At the primary viewing area, there's a binder full of pictures and information about the mating and nesting habits of these birds. Visit during different times of the season to view the phases and different behaviors. Call ahead to see which phase the birds are exhibiting.

Hours: Open only during the heron and egret nesting season (from the 2nd weekend in March through the 2nd weekend in July) on weekends and holidays: 10am–4pm. Open Tues-Fri. 2-4pm by appointment only.

Cost: Free, but donations appreciated.

Bathrooms: Yes.

Facilities: Stroller friendly.

Food: No, but picnic tables are available.

What to Bring: Sunscreen, sunglasses, binoculars, and picnic lunch. Don't forget to wear comfortable walking shoes.

Follow-Up Activities: Free school programs for 4th and 5th graders are available to elementary schools. Call for reservations.

Don Edwards San Francisco Bay National Wildlife Refuge (Ages 4+)

Visitor Center & Newark Slough Learning Center: (510) 792-0222;
9500 Thornton Avenue, Newark, CA 94560
Environmental Education Center: (408) 262-5513; 1751 Grand Boulevard, Alviso
<http://desfbay.fws.gov> (Directions)

Description: The Don Edwards San Francisco Bay National Wildlife Refuge is dedicated to preserving the wetlands and wildlife around the San Francisco Bay. The refuge is on the Pacific Flyway for migratory birds and is home to some endangered species such as the California clapper rail bird. The refuge has two sites for visitors. The Visitor Center in Newark is a great starting point for beginning bird watchers as the exhibits help identify the birds most readily seen in the area, and the location provides opportunities to view birds just outside the doorstep. The upstairs discovery center has activities for kids as well as two huge salt crystals. The Newark site has exhibits of how salt is made in the salt ponds previously owned by Cargill Salt. The Environmental Education Center is located in Alviso. Both the Visitor Center and the Environmental Education Center have interpretive programs and guided walks. Visit the Web site under "Activity Schedule" for events information. The Bay Area Science Alliance Web site lists events as well.

Hours: *Visitor Center:* Tue–Sun 10am-5pm, closed national holidays. *Learning Center:* Mon–Fri: 8am–4pm. *Environmental Education Center:* Mon–Fri: 7am-4:30pm, call to verify. Weekends: 10am–5pm. Closed all national holidays.

Cost: Free, even the fieldtrips are provided to schools free!

Bathrooms: Yes.

Facilities: Stroller friendly.

Food: No.

What to Bring: Sunscreen, sunglasses, binoculars, and picnic lunch. Visit Web site for map and directions; the refuge is not covered by Internet mapping programs.

Follow-Up Activities: 1) Both centers offer programs for field trips. 2) Special events: Migratory Bird Day in May and Open House in October. 3) Cargill Salt's salt ponds are now part of the Refuge. Salt Pond tours held at Bayfront Park in Menlo Park and presentations geared for ages 12 and older are conducted by docents. Reservations required. Visit Web site's "Activity Schedule" for program and tour schedule. Virtual tour of the salt ponds and production process, salt ponds history, and information about salt on Cargill's Web site: <www.cargill.com/sf_bay>.

Elkhorn Slough Reserve (Ages 3+)

(831) 728-2822; 1700 Elkhorn Road, Watsonville, CA 95076
<www.elkhornslough.org>

Description: Elkhorn Slough, the largest remaining coastal wetlands in the state, is considered one of the premier bird watching sites that attract many visitors from all over the country. It is a haven for almost 300 varieties of birds including owls, woodpeckers, hawks, falcons, pelicans, jays, warblers, grebes, and more. Elkhorn Slough Rookery in the north marsh is a nesting site for great blue herons and great egrets, which nest in the treetops of Monterey Pines here in the spring (late January–early March). The Visitor Center has educational exhibits and microscopes to view the microscopic life that lives in the slough and the mud flats. For close-up pictures of microscopic life, such as the diatom (microscopic plants that live in the water and form the base of the food chain), check out the Web site's "Under the Scope" section <www.elkhornslough.org/micro2.htm>.

Hours: The Reserve and Visitor Center are open Wed–Sun: 9am–5pm. Docent tours and nature walks on weekends at 10am and 1pm. Early bird walk on first Sat of the month at 8:30am.

Cost: Visitor Center is free. Entrance fee for the reserve: $2.50/adult 16 and older.

Bathroom: Yes.

Facilities: Stroller friendly.

Food: No.

What to Bring: Binoculars. Dress warmly and wear walking shoes.

Follow-Up Activities: *Elkhorn Slough Safari Nature Tours* offers naturalist guided tours on a pontoon boat of the slough. It provides the opportunity to view sea otters, seals, migratory birds, and shorebirds up close. Minimum age is 3 years old. Cost: $28/adult, $20/child 14 & under, and $26/senior 65+. Visit <www.elkhornslough.com> for schedules and reservations or call: (831) 633-5555. Special focus tours available; see Web site for current schedule. Departures from Harbor District lot off Sandholt Road in Moss Landing.

Hawk Hill (Ages 4+)
(415) 331-0730
~2 miles west of Golden Gate bridge on Conzelman Road, Marin Headlands, CA
<www.ggro.org>

Description: On a clear day, Hawk Hill and the Marin Headlands provides breathtakingly beautiful views of the Golden Gate Bridge, San Francisco Bay, and the San Francisco skyline. Even if you are not interested in birds, this site is well worth a visit if the weather is cooperating. However, if you have an interest in birds of prey, then it's a don't miss outing in September & October. In the fall, falcons, eagles, hawks, and vultures migrate and pass by the Golden Gate. The Golden Gate Raptor Observatory tracks the migration of these birds of prey, banding some birds to follow their migration routes. See Web site for weather, map, & directions.

Hours: *Hawk Talk* on September & October weekends at 12 noon; "banding" demonstration at 1pm with usually a banded raptor release. Rain or fog cancels.

Cost: Free.

Bathroom: Portables only.

Facilities: Not stroller friendly; wear walking shoes. Steep, but short climb up the hill from street parking.

Food: No.

What to Bring: Jacket, sunscreen, picnic lunch, binoculars, and camera.

Midpeninsula Open Space Preserve (Ages 4+)
(650) 691-1200; 330 Distel Circle, Los Altos, CA 94022
<www.openspace.org>

Description: This organization acquires and maintains open space and provides information on 26 preserves with almost 50,000 acres of land along the peninsula, from San Carlos to Los Gatos. Click on the "Preserves" button on the Web site to locate the 26 preserves. There are many nature programs for families throughout the preserves.

Hours: Open all year from sunrise to ½ hour after sunset. Visit the Web site and look under the "Great Activities" button on the top bar, then "Calendar of Activities" for current events, times, and dates.

Cost: Free.

Bathroom: Yes.

Facilities: Stroller friendliness varies based on the preserve.

Food: No.

What to Bring: Sunscreen, picnic lunch, binoculars, and camera.

Point Lobos State Reserve (All Ages)
(831) 624-4909; 3 miles south of Carmel, Highway 1, Carmel, CA
Mailing Address: 1 Box 62, Carmel, CA 93923
<http://pt-lobos.parks.state.ca.us>
Trail Map: <http://pt-lobos.parks.state.ca.us/map/TrailMap.html>

Description: This gorgeous park is rich not only in scenic beauty but also in the diversity of wildlife and cultural history. Wildlife includes birds, land mammals, marine life such as seals and otters, and monarch butterflies. The reserve has been home to American Indians, Chinese, Japanese, and Portuguese whalers. Learn more about this rich heritage from tours and the wonderful Web site.

Hours: 9am–5pm. Last admission ½ hour prior to closing. Extended hours until 7pm during Daylight Savings time. Museum tours (Whalers Cabin & Whaling Station Museums) are open as staffing permits, usually 11am–3pm. Ranger- or docent-led nature walks, cabin tours, and slide programs require advanced reservation by groups or school groups.

Cost: $8 parking fee/car, $4/car with senior, $3 disabled discount

Bathroom: Yes.

Facilities: Stroller friendly only along paths.

Food: No.

What to Bring: Sunscreen, sunglasses, picnic lunch, binoculars, and camera. Dress warmly and wear walking shoes.

Follow-Up Activities: The Web site is worth perusing, as it has a wealth of information on the natural and cultural history of this beautiful reserve.

Point Reyes National Seashore (Ages 3 +)
<www.nps.gov/pore/home.htm>;
<www.nps.gov/pore/planyourvisit/rangerprograms.htm>

Description: Point Reyes National Seashore provides a treasure trove of experiences. These include learning about the Miwok Indians at Kule Loklo, a replica coast Indian village[1]; watching birds, marine life, elephant seals, whales, and tule elk in their natural habitat; and learning about maritime history, environment, and marine fossils at the Kenneth C. Patrick Visitor Center and the Lighthouse Visitor Center. This park has multiple facilities with their own hours, exhibits, and special programs. There is no entrance fee at the park, but check Web site for shuttle bus fees and instructions from December to mid-April when roads may be closed to cars.

For wildlife viewing, try to visit the park when the rangers are conducting their naturalist programs. However, if you are unable to attend during these workshops, you can take self-guided tours. Don't forget your binoculars!

[1] See Chapter 9: Historical Outings—Native American Indians section for Kule Loklo.

Here's a list of where to go: *Abbots Lagoon*: Best bird watching site during fall and winter for shorebirds, waterfowl, sparrows, hawks, and osprey. *Drakes Estero:* Largest harbor seal breeding colony in Point Reyes. *Elephant Seal Overlook:* Breeding colony of elephant seals can be observed from January through March 15. During this season, docents provide information, binoculars, and spotting scopes from 11am–4pm on weekends and holidays. *Five Brooks Pond:* Watch green-backed herons, grebes, hooded mergansers, and ring-necked ducks. See bats in the early evening feeding on insects. Tule elk, found only in California, can be seen at *Tule Elk Preserve* at Tomales Point. From July–September, docents are available on weekends to answer questions and explain their life cycle. *Lighthouse:* View turkey vultures, ravens, hawks, and even peregrine falcons. The colony of murres can be seen on the rocks north of the lighthouse during their spring and summer nesting season. This is also a good place to watch the gray whale migration from January through early May. Mid-January is the peak of the southern migration and mid-March is the peak of the northern migration. Late April & early May bring the calves & moms closer to shore. Visit the Web site for more specific information about these locations, directions, and maps: <**www.nps.gov/pore/planyourvisit/maps.htm**>. Here are the Point Reyes visitor centers:

Bear Valley Visitor Center

(415) 464-5100; Bear Valley Road, Olema, CA

Hours: Mon–Fri: 9am–5pm, Sat/Sun & Holidays: 8am–5pm. Closed Christmas Day.

Description: Exhibits on ecosystems and cultural heritage of the park. It has a weather station, seismograph, and touch table. Kule Loklo, the replica Miwok village, is a short ½ mile walk from the Bear Valley Visitor Center. See the "Native American Indian" section in Chapter 9: Historical Outings for more information on Kule Loklo.

Bathrooms: Yes, at the Visitor Center.

Facilities: Stroller friendly.

Food: No.

Kenneth C. Patrick Visitor Center

(415) 669-1250; Drakes Beach: Sir Frances Drake Boulevard

30 minutes from Bear Valley Visitor Center

Hours: *All Year:* Weekends & Holidays: 10am–5pm. Closed Mon–Fri & Christmas Day. *Summer (Memorial Day to Labor Day only):* Fri–

Tues, 10am–5pm.

Description: Exhibits on 16th century maritime exploration, marine fossils, and marine environments. A 250-gallon saltwater aquarium highlights life from Drakes Bay. A minke whale skeleton hangs from the ceiling.

Bathrooms: Yes, and showers, too.

Food: Picnic tables and barbecues. Drakes Beach Café is located next door.

Follow-Up Activities: Labor Day Sunday Sand Sculpture Contest each year from 9am–3:30pm. Registration held at the Visitor Center starting at 9am. Judging begins at 1pm. Awards at 3:30pm. Call (415) 464-5100 to verify and for more information.

Lighthouse Visitor Center

(415) 669-1534; **Point Reyes Headlands, end of Sir Frances Drake Boulevard** 45 min. from Bear Valley Visitor Center. There is a ½ mile walk (mostly uphill) from the parking lot to the Lighthouse Visitor Center.

Hours: Thur–Mon: 10am–4:30pm. Closed Tues, Wed, & Christmas Day. Weekends 1:30pm Jan-March, ranger led programs to watch gray whale migration. Meet at Lighthouse shuttle stop if shuttle is operating; otherwise, meet at the Lighthouse Visitor Center.

Description: Exhibits on whales, wildflowers, birds, and maritime history.

Bathrooms: Yes.

Facilities: Not stroller friendly—has stairs.

Food: No.

Point Reyes Historic Lighthouse

(415) 669-1534; **½ mile from the parking area down some 300 steps**

Description: The equipment building shows how the fog signal was used at Point Reyes. The historic lighthouse has exhibits on the history of the light and the keepers. The lens room includes the original clockworks and a 130-year-old first order Fresnel lens in working condition.

Hours: Thur–Mon: 10am–4:30pm, weather permitting. Lens room open only 2:30pm-4pm, staff & weather permitting. Closed Tues & Wed. Closed when wind speeds exceed 40 miles per hour. Lighthouse history evening programs on the first and third Saturday each month April–December. Reservations required. Call (415) 669-1534 between 10am–4:30pm.

Follow-Up Activities:

Naturalist Programs on the Weekends with the Park Rangers:

Wonderful programs on the weekends cover a variety of topics. They include Kule Loklo Walk and Work Days, whale watching from the Observation Deck and learning about whales and their migration, elephant seal watching and learning about their life cycle at the Elephant Seal Overlook, whales and wildflowers, Habitat Restoration Workdays, lighthouse history, and more. These programs are based in different facilities. Visit the Web site for more detailed information: <www.nps.gov/pore/planyourvisit/rangerprograms.htm>. Alternatively, from the home page of Point Reyes, select the "Plan Your Visit," then "Guided Tours," and "Ranger Guided Programs."

Educational Programs at Point Reyes:

Junior Ranger Program: There are 2 programs. One provides a study of the lighthouse. The other explores the Coast Miwok Indians' history and culture. For more information on the program, visit either the Bear Valley Visitor Center or the Lighthouse Visitor Center.

Summer Nature Science Camps for kids ages 7–16. Different sessions and age groupings with 4-day sessions for kids 7–9, 5-day camps for kids 9–11 and 10–12, and a 6-day camp for teens 13–16. Camp activities: canoeing, tide pooling, backpacking, bird and mammal observation, night hikes, storytelling, arts and crafts, etc. Registration begins in January. For detailed information on the camps, visit the Web site: <www.ptreyes.org/camp>.

Richardson Bay Audubon Center (Ages 4+)

(415) 388-2524; 376 Greenwood Beach Road, Tiburon, CA 94920
<www.tiburonaudubon.org>

Description: Perched on the edge of San Francisco Bay overlooking Tiburon, this beautiful site provides a place to view birds and learn about nature. Join naturalists on weekends to learn about birds and other animals.

Hours: Mon–Sat: 9am–5pm.

Cost: Free.

Bathrooms: Yes.

Facilities: Stroller friendly for some parts. Baby carrier recommended.

Food: No.

What to Bring: Jacket, sunscreen, sunglasses, camera, and picnic lunch.

Follow-Up Activities: 1) Adventure Camps during school breaks for ages 4+ filled with art, science, and hands-on activities. 2) Field trips for schools, scouts, parent groups, etc. for grades pre-K through 6. 3) Birthday parties.

Nature & Visitor Centers

Shorebird Nature Center (Ages 4+)
Berkeley Marina
(510) 981-6720; 160 University Avenue, Berkeley, CA 94710
<www.ci.berkeley.ca.us/marina/marinaexp>

Description: Time your visit with the Berkeley Bay Festival for the most enriching experience. During the school year, it is geared to school groups with programs on animals and low-tide. Summer marine biology camps offered to students ages 5–16. They also offer boating, canoeing, & sailing classes during the summer.

Hours: Open to the public: 1–5pm. Tues–Fri: 9am–5pm. Mornings are devoted to classroom programs.

Cost: Free.

Bathrooms: Yes.

Facilities: Stroller friendly.

Food: Nearby restaurants at the Berkeley Marina.

What to Bring: Cash for food, jacket, sunscreen, and sunglasses.

Follow-Up Activities: 1) Saturday programs for families include a tour of the Nature Center and the marina. 2) Birthday parties at the Adventure Playground where kids can build, paint, and play with recycled materials. **Adventure Playground** (for ages 7+; younger if accompanied by adult) is open Sat & Sun from 11am–5pm and Mon–Fri 9am-5pm. Rain closes. 3) Marine biology summer camps on the rocky shore and marina environment for ages 5–16. Registration starts early May. Other summer programs available on boating and related topics. 4) *Berkeley Bay Festival* in May from 12noon to 5pm. This festival features free sailboat rides, mini-tours by Hornblower Yachts, dockside tours of many boats, food, music, hands-on activities, a freshwater aquarium, a traveling *Insect Discovery Lab* with insects from around the world, and a portable planetarium to see the stars. The Insect Discovery Lab is an outreach program offered to schools and other groups by the Center for Ecosystem Survival: <www.savenature. org> or (415) 648-3392. It is located at 699 Mississippi, Suite 106, San Francisco, CA 94107. 5) Low-tide and animal (birds, fish, bay scientist) programs available for both school and other groups to learn about the marine environment.

Crab Cove Visitor Center (Ages 3+)
(510) 521-6887; 1252 McKay Avenue, Alameda, CA 94501
<www.ebparks.org/parks/crab.htm>

Description: There is a small exhibit area with a few small animals and some pelicans. Visit during a naturalist program on the weekend to have an enriching experience. During low tides, the mudflats are exposed. The mudflat is a very rich environment for intertidal animals, including small crabs and shrimp, marine worms, and microscopic life. Nearby, there's a pond. It's a nice walk to Crown Beach where we've sighted pelicans. Crown Beach hosts an annual Sand Castle contest in June.
Hours: Wed–Sun: 10am–4:30pm. Naturalist programs schedule on the weekends: <www.ebparks.org/events.htm>.
Cost: $6 parking fee. Most programs are free or require a small fee. Some require preregistration.
Bathrooms: Yes.
Facilities: Stroller friendly.
Food: No.
What to Bring: Binoculars, cash for parking, and picnic lunch.
Follow-Up Activities: 1) Shorebird watching, low tide and minus tide explorations, marine life and land mammal nature programs conducted on weekends. 2) Classes for 3- to 5-year-olds and for 6- to 8-year-olds. There are also camps during school breaks. Program offering changes with the season. Regular attendance throughout the year will provide quite a wonderful series of science classes. 3) Birthday parties.

Crissy Field Center, Presidio (Ages 4+)
(415) 561-7690; Hotline: (415) 4-Crissy; Weekend workshops & classes: (415) 561-7752; Family & kids programs: (415) 561-7765
Presidio: 603 Mason Street, San Francisco, CA 94129
<www.crissyfield.org>; <www.crissyfield.org/center>

Description: This open space and Visitor Center is now a part of the Golden Gate Recreation Area. The Visitor Center has a computer media lab, library, arts workshop, urban ecology lab, and many programs for children and adults. Check Web site for open lab schedule & family fun schedule. Also offered are summer camps, walks, workshops and classes, and special events.

Hours: Wed–Sun: 9am–5pm. *Center Café:* open only when the center is open. *Warming Hut Café:* (415) 561-3042, open daily 9am–5pm.

Cost: Varies from free to small fee, depending on the program.

Bathrooms: Yes.

Facilities: Stroller friendly.

Food: Two cafés, see hours above.

Follow-Up Activities: 1) Parent & tot class on Fridays at 10am, Super Saturdays at 10am for variety of family programs. Check Web site for details. 2) Summer camps for children ages 6–13. 3) School programs. 4) The *Kids and Families* programs include art projects, ecology of the wetlands, bird watching, etc. Check schedule to see when the learning labs are open (media/computer lab to model the weather and explore whales, birds, and the Australian Great Barrier Reef and its inhabitants). There are field trips such as whale watching and guided tours of the Bay Model Museum, etc. These weekend programs are usually for children ages 5+.

Hayward Shoreline Interpretive Center (Ages 3+)

(510) 670-7270; (510) 881-6700 Reservations;
4901 Breakwater Avenue, Hayward, CA 94545
<www.haywardrec.org/hayshore.html>

Description: Hayward Shoreline Interpretive Center provides an introduction to San Francisco Estuary's ecology. The Interpretive Center has exhibits, programs, and activities showcasing the natural and human history of this area. Join the naturalist on a weekend program to help enrich your family's experience.

Hours: Sat & Sun: 10am–5pm. School groups can visit Wed–Fri, with advanced reservations. Office closed Mon & Tues.

Cost: Free for the Interpretive Center, but fee varies with the naturalist program selected.

Bathroom: Yes.

Facilities: Stroller friendly.

Food: No.

What to Bring: Picnic lunch, cash for programs, and jacket.

Follow-Up Activities: 1) Naturalist programs on the weekends. Once at the Web site, click on "Facilities," then "Hayward Shoreline Interpretive Center" for naturalist program schedule. 2) Summer camp for preK–6th grades. 3) May Day celebration of spring and the May Pole Dance in May. For the above activities, see the "Quarterly Brochure" on the Web site listed under the "Program" icon. These programs are offered as part of the Greater Hayward Area Recreation and Park Foundation. The parks and recreation catalog, "Quarterly Brochure," lists the classes, programs, summer camps, etc. that are available at the Sulphur Creek and Hayward Shoreline Interpretive Centers.

Big Basin Visitor Center & Rancho Del Oso Nature & History Center (All Ages)
Big Basin Redwoods State Park Visitor Center
(831) 338-8860; 21600 Big Basin Way, Boulder Creek, CA 95006 via Hwy 9/236
<www.santacruzstateparks.org/parks/bigbasin>; <www.bigbasin.org>
Rancho Del Oso at Big Basin Redwoods State Park
(831) 427-2288; 3600 Highway #1, Davenport, CA 95017
<www.santacruzstateparks.org/parks/rancho/>;
<www.parks.ca.gov/default.asp?page_id=863>

Description: *Big Basin Redwoods State Park* has a gorgeous redwood grove with a very easy trail that's perfect for little ones and strollers. Although a bit more out of the way, it's well worth the drive. This beautiful park rivals Muir Woods without the crazy crowds. The Visitor Center has exhibits on the natural and cultural history of the area. There are many naturalist programs on weekends. Follow directions on Web site; Internet mapping software directions not the best route. *Rancho Del Oso* has nature and cultural history walks on weekends.

Hours: *Big Basin:* Park open 6am-10pm; visitor center: daily 9am–5pm; Redwood Trail 1-hour guided walk March through November: Sat & Sun at 11am & 2pm. *Rancho del Oso:* Sat & Sun 12–4pm. *Guided nature walks:* every Saturday of the month: 1–3:30pm. *Cultural history tours:* every 2nd Sun of the month: 1–2pm.

Cost: $6 parking fee at Big Basin. Free parking (donation suggested) at Rancho.

Bathrooms: Yes.

Facilities: Big Basin: stroller friendly. Rancho: stroller friendly only at the Visitor Center. Some trails are fine with a buggy.

Food: General store at Big Basin open 10am-4pm. No food available at Rancho.

What to Bring: Picnic lunch, binoculars, comfortable walking shoes, sunscreen, sunglasses, and lots of bottled water to drink.

Follow-Up Activities: *Rancho:* 1) Annual bird count walk in late December/early January time frame from 8am–noon and again at 1pm–4pm. 2) Programs on mushrooms and fungus with a mycologist (fungus expert) during the rainy season.

Redwood Grove Nature Preserve (Ages 4+)

(650) 941-4276; 482 University Avenue, Los Altos, CA 94022
<www.ci.los-altos.ca.us>, select recreation & activity guide;
<www.redwoodgroveprograms.com>

Description: This small preserve is located in a residential area of Los Altos. It has a small creek, a grove of redwoods, and a small nature center. The nature center has some small animals, including a turtle, a rabbit, a guinea pig, a frog, and an iguana. There's a play table with some fossils, sand, and a brush, for children to play being at an excavation site. The real treasure is Naturalist Keith Gutierrez, who provides age-appropriate and mesmerizing talks that kids love.

Hours: Open for scheduled programs only.

Cost: Varies, depending on the program.

Bathroom: Yes.

Facilities: Stroller friendly.

Food: No. Picnic tables.

What to Bring: Binoculars for bird watching and picnic lunch.

Follow-Up Activities: 1) Birthday parties for ages 4–11 with music, games, animal visit, and nature walk. Program lasts approx. 1 hour and can be conducted indoors in case of rain. 2) School and scouting groups have special programs available: Learning about Nature (preschooler–2nd grade), Ohlone Indians (2nd grade), Gold Rush program (3rd grade), and an overnight program for scouts. 3) After-school classes and summer camps. Sign up through the Los Altos Parks and Recreation Department.

Sulphur Creek Nature Center (Ages 3+)

(510) 881-6747; 1801 D Street, Hayward, CA 94541
<www.haywardrec.org/sulphur_creek.html>

Description: This nature center has exhibits of coyotes, foxes, opossums, hawks, owls, and a variety of reptiles and amphibians. It also has a changing hands-on display featuring selected animal groups. Best of all, there's a pet lending library that rents hamsters, guinea pigs, rats, and mice for a week for young children to experience the responsibility of caring for a pet. There is a discovery room dedicated to the watersheds and creeks as a habitat for plants and animals. Nature & weekend classes for families (toddlers & up). After your visit, spend some time by the creek, and enjoy a picnic. You'll be amazed at what your kids will find!

Hours: Tues–Sun: 10am–4:30pm; Grounds open until 5pm. Closed Mondays.

Cost: Free.

Bathrooms: Yes.

Facilities: Gravel pathways. Baby carrier or backpack recommended.

Food: No.

What to Bring: Sunglasses, sunscreen, and picnic lunch.

Follow-Up Activities: 1) School and scout groups have access to wildlife education programs. 2) Naturalist programs and classes for children 1–12. See the Greater Hayward Area Recreation and Park Foundation in the Parks and Recreation Section for contact information. The parks and recreation catalog, "Quarterly Brochure," lists the classes, programs, summer camps, etc. available at the Sulphur Creek and Hayward Shoreline Interpretive Centers. 3) Annual Wildlife Fair in early June (10am–4pm) for $5/person, free/child 3 & under. Activities based on a nature theme include crafts, music, face painting, storytelling, and games. 4) Birthday parties.

Sunol Regional Wilderness (Ages 3+)
Sunol Visitor Center

(925) 862-2601; Southeast end of Geary Road, Sunol, CA
<www.ebparks.org/parks/sunol.htm>

Description: This gorgeous preserve is home to eagles, bobcats, mountain lions, and tule elk. The Little Yosemite area is a scenic two-mile hike from the Visitor Center; there's a sandstone outcrop with fossils embedded, the remnants of an ancient sea floor.

Hours: *Park:* 7am–dusk. *Visitor Center:* Sat & Sun: 10am–4:30pm.

Cost: $5 parking fee seasonal, weekends & holidays.

Bathrooms: Yes.

Facilities: Stroller friendly on some trails.

Food: No.

What to Bring: Binoculars, sunscreen, sunglasses, picnic lunch, water, and comfortable walking shoes.

Follow-Up Activities: 1) Naturalist programs on the weekends. These include wildflower hikes, geology walks, science for little tykes, Ohlone and the old ways workshops, etc. Check Web site under Naturalist Programs for details. Call for reservations. 2) Niles Depot Train Station is close by.

Fossil Sites

We can learn about geological history from the fossils that have been found. Math Science Nucleus' Natural History Museum has mammoth, sabertooth cats, and cave bear fossils of bone fragments found in the Fremont area in the 1940s. Sunol Regional Wilderness and Seacliff State Beach have sea life fossils and conduct guided walks to explain the formation and history of these fossils. The Petrified Forest in Calistoga features petrified trees initiated by a volcanic erutpion millions of years ago.

Math Science Nucleus' Natural History Museum (Ages 5+)

(510) 790-6284; 4074 Eggers Drive, Fremont, CA 94536
<www.msnucleus.org/gordon>

Description: This small museum features ice age fossils found in the Fremont area by a group of young boys. The boys found fossils from mammoths, sabertooth cats, and giant cave bears. Besides the fossil room, there's an exhibit of animal specimens found in the local area, tools used by Native Indians, rocks and the rock "life cycle," and the rarely seen fossils of diatoms and single celled protozoans which may be viewed through microscopes. There's a small table for "fossil dig" play. Free science curriculum for grades K–12 offered on the Web site.

Hours: Mon–Fri: 9:30am–4:30pm.

Cost: $2/person, $5/family of 4.

Bathrooms: Yes.

Facilities: Stroller friendly.

Food: No.

Follow-Up Activities: 1) Birthday parties. 2) Afterschool science & math classes. 3) Science summer camps.

Mount Diablo State Park (All Ages)

(925) 837-2525; (925) 837-6119 Summit Center

Mount Diablo Scenic Boulevard, Danville, CA or North Gate Road, Walnut Creek

<www.mdia.org>; <www.parks.ca.gov/default.asp?page_id=517>;

For map & directions:<www.mdia.org/parkmap.htm>

Description: Summit Visitor Center displays the natural and cultural history of Mount Diablo. The walls of the visitor center are made of fossil-embedded sandstone. The Mitchell Canyon Interpretive Center has exhibits on the wildlife, geology, and plants of the park. The best times to visit are spring and fall. Winter provide opportunities to see the rare snow fall at the mountain peak in the Bay Area. Be sure to call for park conditions prior to your trip. For more information on park geology, visit the site: <www.mdia.org/geology.htm>. The entrances to the park are from Walnut Creek or from Danville. See Web site for map & directions.

Hours: Park open 8am—sunset. *Summit Visitor Center*: daily 10am–4pm. *The Mitchell Canyon Interpretive Center*: weekends and some holidays 10am–2pm in the winter and 8am–4pm in the summer.

Cost: $4 park entry fee.

Bathrooms: Yes.

Facilities: Stroller friendly.

Food: No.

What to Bring: Picnic lunch, water, binoculars, sunscreen, sunglasses, camera, and comfortable walking shoes.

Follow-Up Activities: 1) Many ranger-guided walks such as wildflower hikes, fossil walks, etc. For event schedule, visit this Web site: <www.mdia. org/events.htm>. 2) Star gazing parties on select Saturday evenings. Call (925) 837-2525, then press "4" and "#" for recorded information on most current star gazing parties. The Mt. Diablo Astronomical Society's Web site: <www.mdas.net>.

Petrified Forest (Ages 5+)

(707) 942-6667; 4100 Petrified Forest Road, Calistoga, CA 94515
<www.petrifiedforest.org>

Description: Meander through the forest trail showcasing redwood trees that have been turned to stone as a result of minerals (silica) that have replaced the old wood cells. Naturalist-guided walk explains the process of petrification and how the volcanic eruption more than 3 million years ago caused the petrification of the forest. The oldest petrified tree was estimated to be 2,000 years old at the time of the vulcanic eruption.

Hours: Open daily 9am–7pm. *Winter:* 9am–5pm. Naturalist-guided meadow walk on Saturdays at noon and Sundays at 11am.

Cost: $6/adult, $5/senior or junior (12-17), $3/child (6-11). 15% discount coupon on Web site.

Bathrooms: Yes.

Facilities: Stroller friendly.

Food: No.

What to Bring: Picnic lunch, water, sunscreen, sunglasses, camera, and comfortable walking shoes.

Follow-Up Activities: Safari West and Old Faithful Geyser are nearby.

Seacliff State Beach (Ages 5+)

(831) 685-6442; (831) 685-6444 Visitor Center; (800) 444-7275 Reservations;
201 State Park Drive, Aptos, CA 95003
<www.parks.ca.gov/default.asp?page_id=543>
<www.santacruzstateparks.org/parks/seacliff/index.php>

Description: Fossils are embedded in the cliffs along the edge of the beach. This is also a good beach to hunt for seashells. Check with the Visitor Center for exact times and dates of naturalist programs.

Hours: 8am–sunset. *Fossil Walk* scheduled on select Sundays at noon. Visitor Center has programs on the weekends geared toward families.

Cost: $6 parking fee.

Bathrooms: Yes, with showers throughout the beachfront.

Facilities: Stroller friendly off the beach.

Food: Snack bar.

What to Bring: Beach gear, sunscreen, sunglasses, picnic lunch, and cash for parking and food.

Follow-Up Activities: Naturalist programs for families on weekends.

Sunol Regional Preserve (Ages 3+)
(925) 862-2601; Southeast end of Geary Road, Sunol, CA
<www.ebparks.org/parks/sunol.htm>

Description: Sandstone outcrop with embedded fossils. Geology walks are sometimes scheduled on the weekend. Check the Web site for current times and dates: <www.ebparks.org/events.htm>. See full entry for details in Chapter 1: Animal Kingdom—Nature & Visitor Centers section.

Museum of Paleontology (Ages 5+)
University of California, Berkeley
(510) 642-1821; 1101 Valley Life Sciences Building, Berkeley, CA 94720
<www.ucmp.berkeley.edu>

Description: This research museum is the official state repository for all fossils found in California. Unfortunately, due to space and budget constraints, very little of the collection is available for public viewing. On display at the lobby of the ground floor are *Tyrannosaurus rex* and *pteranodon* mounts, and a few displays of California fossils and dinosaur material. On the second floor, there are additional displays, mostly of the evolution of the dinosaurs into birds. Plan your visit for Cal Day in April when the university opens its doors to visitors offering hands-on, kid friendly activities and tours that cover a huge range of topics (music, art, anthropology, engineering, chemistry, paleontology, and more).

Hours: *During the semester the building is open:* Mon–Thur: 8am–10pm, Fri: 8am–5pm, Sat: 10am–5pm, Sun: 1–5pm. *Holiday and Summer* Hours: visit Web site and look under the "Biosciences & Natural Resources Library:" <www.lib.berkeley.edu/AboutLibrary/hours.html#Branches>. Cal Days are usually on a weekend day, in early April every year. For most current Cal Day information: <www.berkeley.edu/calday>.

Cost: Free.

Bathrooms: Yes, in the building.

Facilities: Stroller friendly.

Food: No. Cafeterias and restaurants available on and off campus, but may be a bit of a walk.

What to Bring: Cash for parking and food. Don't forget the camera or video camera with film and batteries.

Follow-Up Activities: 1) This museum's hidden treasures are its extensive on-line exhibits. The virtual exhibits in the "History of Life" section include information about phylogeny (the "tree of life"), geology, and evolution: <www.ucmp.berkeley.edu/exhibits>. 2) Dinosaurs, dinosaurs, dinosaurs, ... and birds? Visit the dinosaur on-line exhibit: <www.ucmp. berkeley.edu/education/dinolink.html>. 3) Docent- led tours are available to schools and groups with a maximum of 25 people per group. For more information on the tours & scheduling, visit: <www.ucmp.berkeley.edu/ about/docent.php>.

Directions: Map and directions to reach UC Berkeley: <www.berkeley. edu/map>. Map of the Valley Life Sciences Building at UC Berkeley: <http://ib.berkeley.edu/admin/facilities/vlsb>.

Marine Life

There are many kinds of marine life besides fish. These include mammals that live in the sea such as sea lions, otters, whales, and dolphins. We can visit aquariums, tide pools, and nature preserves and take whale watching cruises. To learn "How fish hear sounds," visit University of Rhode Island's Discovery of Sound in the Sea's Web site: <www.dosits.org/animals/produce/2f.htm>.

Aquariums & Marine Life Centers

Aquarium of the Bay (All Ages)
1-888-SEA-DIVE (732-3483); (415) 623-5300
Pier 39, Beach Street & The Embarcadero, San Francisco, CA 94133
<www.aquariumofthebay.com>

Description: This walk-through aquarium features the marine life of San Francisco Bay. Behind-the-scenes tours present information on what the divers wear to keep warm, how the aquarium keeps the water clean, where the water comes from, what happens when the fish get sick, and how they prepare food for the fish.

Hours: Mon–Fri: 10am–6pm, Sat & Sun: 10am–7pm. Closed Christmas

Day. *Summer extended hours:* 9am–8pm. *Behind the Scenes Tours (~40 min.):* Fri, Sat, Sun, & Mon starting at noon, 2pm, & 5pm. For reservations (which are recommended): (415) 623-5376. *Feeding Schedule:* Bat Ray Feeding: Tues, Thur, & Sun: 11:30 am; Grab a Bite (narrated): Tues, Thur & Sun: 3pm; Seven Gill Shark feeding: Thur & Sun: 1:30pm. Call (415) 623-5333 for cruise schedules.

Cost: $12.95/adult, $6.50/child (3–11), $6.50/senior 65+, free/child under 3. Family rate for 2 adults & 1 or 2 children: $29.95. Behind-the-scenes tour: $25/person. Yearly family membership: $65 (2 adults & 2 children). Combination packages including aquarium admission and a bay cruise with the Gold and Blue Fleet: $19/adult, $11/child, and $15/senior. Visit the Web site for a $2 off coupon. Internet advanced ticket purchases also get a discounted rate.

Bathrooms: Yes.

Facilities: Stroller friendly.

Food: No, but plenty available close by at Pier 39.

What to Bring: Cash for parking, jacket, camera, and sunglasses.

Follow-Up Activities: 1) Birthday parties and sleepovers offered. 2) For school groups, tours are led by a naturalist. For feeding schedule, birthday party information, sleepovers, and special events schedule, select the "Programs" button on the top toolbar once you've entered the Web site.

Marin Mammal Center (Ages 2+)

(415) 289-7335; Marin Headlands, 1065 Fort Cronkhite, Sausalito, CA 94965
(Reopens Fall 2007)
<www.tmmc.org>

Description: Located in the beautiful Marin Headlands just north of the Golden Gate Bridge, the Marin Mammal Center is a rehabilitation hospital and environmental education center with a branch at Pier 39, Fisherman's Wharf, San Francisco. Animals that are being rehabilitated are on display in the hospital. As such, the number and species of animals vary depending on the season. Spring is the best time to see seal pups while summer and fall are the best time to see sea lions. The "Current Patient Report" on the Web site shows which animals are in residence on a daily basis.

Hours: Daily 10am–4pm. Closed Thanksgiving, Christmas, and New Year's Days.

Cost: Free, but donations appreciated.

Bathrooms: Yes.
Facilities: Stroller friendly.
Food: No.
What to Bring: Jacket, camera, sunscreen, and sunglasses.
Follow-Up Activities: 1) Beach, Marin Headlands Visitor Center, Hawk Hill, and Bay Area Discovery Museum are close by. 2) Programs for schools (K-12) and other groups. Sea lion program at Pier 39, San Francisco.

Monterey Bay Aquarium (All Ages)
(831) 648-4800; 886 Cannery Row, Monterey, CA 93940
<www.montereyaquarium.org>

Description: This aquarium is deservedly world famous, visited by people from all over the world and featured in a *Star Trek* movie. There are many exhibits of the different environments within Monterey Bay. *The Kelp Forest* exhibit shows the interaction between fish and the kelp forest. *The Splash Zone* is a wonderful exhibit for toddlers to elementary school age children with its colorful coral reef animals and interactive displays; it has an interactive educational water play area for little ones. Don't miss the little *tank of sea dragons*, cousins of sea horses. There are *many touch pools*: one at the Splash Zone exhibit for toddlers, a set down stairs on the first floor with bat rays, and one in the *Rocky Shore* exhibit. There is an *Outer Bay* exhibit with speedy tunas and relaxing jellyfish. When the tunas take off, the burst of speed is absolutely breathtaking. The *Jellies: Living Art Exhibit* has more graceful and serene jellies along with gorgeous glass art. Don't miss the animal feedings at the *Otter, Penguin, and Kelp Forest Exhibits*. The courtyard/outside decks of the aquarium provide gorgeous views of the Monterey Bay and telescopes for viewing otters, sea lions, and other wildlife on the bay.

Hours: 10am–6pm daily. *Summer (May 28-Sept. 5) and holiday hours:* 9:30am–6pm. Closed Christmas Day. Daily *sea otter feeding:* 10:30am, 1:30pm, 3:30pm. Feeding at the *Kelp Forest Exhibit:* 11:30am & 4pm. *Penguin feeding* at the Splash Zone: 10:30am & 3pm. *Outer Bay feeding:* Sat. & Sun., Tues. & Thur. at 11am.

Cost: *Parking fees:* depend on the lot or street metered parking. Bring quarters for metered parking on the street. Park at Cannery Row Parking Garage <www.monterey.org/parking/crgmap.html> on Wave Street, between Hoffman Ave and Prescott Avenue. *Admission:* $21.95/adult, $19.95/student (age 13–17) with student ID or senior (age 65+), $12.95/

child (age 3–12) or disabled. *Membership:* $100/year includes 2 adults and children or grandchildren ages 3–12. *Discount Membership*: $45/year per individual, excludes children. Only seniors 65+ and students with ID qualify. Consider purchasing a family membership. Just coming to the aquarium twice will equal the cost of the membership if you have 2 adults and at least one child age 3 or older. One great benefit of membership is the members' entrance. The members' entrance bypasses long admission lines on busy summer weekends. You also get 10% off merchandise at the stores and discounts on special programs.

Bathrooms: Great bathrooms with baby changing tables.

Food: Wonderful cafeteria, restaurant, and snack bar with hot entrees and fabulous ocean views.

What to Bring: The coast can be windy and foggy in the summertime, so be sure to bring a sweatshirt/jacket just in case. You can bring a picnic lunch and eat outside on the deck, if you'd like. Bring quarters if you're considering metered street parking (more economical, but less flexible).

Follow-Up Activities: 1) Past exhibits are now availabe for viewing on the Web site. These include Monterey Canyon & the Deep Sea, Seahorses, Shark: myth & mystery. 2) Numerous programs for schools (toddlers through 12th grade, scouts, youth groups, homeschoolers, and teachers). 3) Aquarium adventures programs for families and kids include an *Underwater Explorers'* program to scuba in the great tide pool just outside the aquarium, and a *Science Under Sail* program for ages 10+ to work alongside an aquarium naturalist on a research sailboat. 4) There's a *Student Oceanography Club* for students 11-14 years old to learn about marine science and conservation that meets twice a month. 5) There's a trail along the coast directly in front of the aquarium that takes you past Pacific Grove to Asilomar State Beach. Lovers' Point Park and the adjacent beach are located in Pacific Grove, just a short drive away. If you have more time, consider renting bikes or just strolling down the trail. *Adventures by the Sea* rents bikes (831) 372-1807. You can access the trail just outside of the aquarium at the intersection of Wave Street and David Avenue. At that intersection, Wave becomes Ocean View Blvd. This is a very scenic coastal drive. In fact, we always leave the aquarium by this route and take Route 68 back to meet up with Hwy 1. Sometimes we catch the sunset along the way.

Directions: *Getting There:* Get maps and directions from the aquarium's own Web site. *Come back the scenic way via coastal drive along Ocean View*

Blvd. to Pacific Grove: If you parked at the Cannery Row Parking Garage on Wave Street, between Hoffman and Prescott Avenue, then as you exit the parking structure at Hoffman, turn left onto Hoffman. Make an immediate left onto Wave Street. Wave Street becomes Ocean View Blvd. Follow Ocean View Blvd along the coast. After Asilomar State Beach, Ocean View Blvd. becomes Sunset Drive/Route 68. Follow signs for Route 68. Turn Right onto Forest Ave/Route 68 to meet Hwy 1. Take Hwy 1 North to come back to the Bay Area.

Seymour Marine Discovery Center (Ages 2 +)
Long Marine Labs at U.C. Santa Cruz
(831) 459-3800; 100 Shaffer Road, Santa Cruz, CA 95060
<www2.ucsc.edu/seymourcenter>

Description: This is a small center with quality exhibits and an excellent touchpool staffed with knowledgeable docents that's well worth visiting if you're in the Santa Cruz area. Hourly site tours are available from 1–3pm daily on a first-come, first-served basis. Sign up at the admissions desk. On select Thursdays & Sundays, there's a Mammal Research Tour (75 minutes) starting at 2:15pm, which provides insight on Long Marine Lab's scientists' research on dolphins, sea lions, seals, and blue whales. Advanced reservations are required, as space is limited to 12 participants. Check the Web site's "Learning Programs: Visitor" page or call (831) 459-3799 for the schedule.

Hours: Tues–Sat: 10am–5pm, Sun: noon–5pm, closed Monday.

Cost: *Free admission on the first Tuesday of each month.* $6/adult, $3/student or senior (60+), $4/youth (4–16), free/child (3 and under).

Bathroom: Yes.

Facilities: Stroller friendly.

Food: No.

What to Bring: Picnic lunch, sunglasses, and jacket.

Follow-Up Activities: 1) There's an annual Father's Day guided tide pooling trip that requires advanced booking. Call Terri, the office manager, at (408) 459-3800 for information and reservations. **2)** Ocean Explorers: marine science weekly summer camps for children ages 7–14. Select "Learning Programs" then "Youth Programs" once you've entered the Web site's home page.

Six Flags Discovery Kingdom (Ages 2+)
Formerly Marine World
(707) 643-6722; 1001 Fairgrounds Drive, Vallejo, CA 94589
<www.sixflags.com/parks/discoverykingdom>

Description: This is a combination theme park, animal park, and marine life showcase. See animals in action in their wildlife theater shows and watch them do tricks and stunts. There are sea lion, bird, dolphin, killer whale, tiger, and elephant shows. Hand-feed the giraffe at the giraffe feeding dock. Walk through the Butterfly Habitat with 500 free-flying butterflies from all over the world, and learn about the life cycle of the butterfly. Ride an elephant at the Elephant Encounter. Visit hand-raised animal babies from tiger cubs to monkeys. The best time to visit these babies is in the morning during the late spring. Don't miss the lorikeets at the Lorikeet Aviary where you can hand-feed these beautiful birds their nectar. The teenagers and older youths will welcome the thrill rides and water rides located throughout the theme park. Little ones will enjoy the Looney Tunes Seaport area with carousel, interactive water play, miniature train, and other rides designed for those 54" and under, accompanied by an adult.

Hours: Closed November through February. *March:* Weekends: 10am–8pm. *April:* Fri–Sun: 10am–8pm. *April 14-27:* Mon–Sun: 10am–8pm. *May:* Fri–Sun: 10am–9pm. *June–August:* Open daily. *September–October:* Open weekends only. Hours may vary. Check the Web site or call to verify times.

Cost: $15/parking. $49.99/general admission, $29.99/child 48" & under, free/child 2 & under. Save $10 if purchased online. *Season Passes:* $69.99/individual. Season passes valid in 18 Six Flags Theme Parks nationwide. $19.99/Seafari Pass voucher which includes 5 "extras" like dolphin, sea lion, lorikeet feeding, giraffe, and elephant rides. $14.99 extra per person for a "flash pass," which can come in handy on crowded summer weekends with long lines for certain thrill rides. These passes allow you to bypass the long lines, with a total limit of 7 rides for each pass. Sometimes there are 50% discount promotions on the Web site under "Special Promotions" as well as buy-one/get-one general admission free coupons from local grocery stores. *Sea Lion Training Session* ($99.99/person for ages 6+) and *Dolphin Discovery* ($149.99/person minimum height 48"+) require advance reservations by calling (707) 556-5274. *Sunset Safari* ($99.99/person) require advanced reservations by calling (707)

556-5436 (or same day sign-ups at Guest Relations on a space available basis). Many of the pony rides, elephant rides, etc. also cost extra. Plan on bringing extra cash for these rides and programs.

Bathrooms: Yes.

Facilities: Lockers, stroller & wheelchair rental. Stroller friendly, but strollers are not allowed inside shows, rides, and exhibits, so plan accordingly. Many rides require a minimum of 42 inches in height.

Food: Yes. Outside food is not allowed, except for baby food.

What to Bring: Swimsuit/change of clothes if you're planning to go on a water ride or have the kids play in the water works area. Don't forget your sunscreen, sunglasses, hat, and lots of extra cash for parking, food, and animal rides.

Follow-Up Activities: Summer Seafari Camp for kids ages 5–12.

Steinhart Aquarium (All Ages)
California Academy of Sciences, Golden Gate Park

(415) 321-8000; 55 Concourse Drive, San Francisco, CA 94118 *(Reopens fall 2008); Temporary Location:* 875 Howard Street, San Francisco, CA 94103 <www.calacademy.org/aquarium>

Description: The Steinhart Aquarium includes exhibits on a living coral reef, tropical sharks, seahorses, a touch pool, a fish roundabout, reptiles and amphibians, and a penguin colony. The new aquarium will have exhibits on rainforests, the California coast, the swamp, coral reef, Costa Rican butterfly canopy with free-flying birds and butterflies, penguins, and African environments. See full entry in the Science Museum section under California Academy of Sciences.

Hours: 10am–5pm. Third Thursdays of the month: open until 9pm with only $5 general admission. *Free admission first Wednesday of each month.* African Penguin feeding: 11am & 3:30pm daily. Fish feeding & coral reef caretaking: 2pm Mon. & Wed. Snake feeding: 2pm Friday.

Tide Pools

Tide pooling is best done in the spring and summer, when there's a longer period of time to view the tide pools when tides are at their lowest. This is a wonderful and fun outing, but must be done with care. Please keep in mind that you will be walking over slippery rocks and doing some rock climbing to view these tide pools. The terrain can be very slippery. Babies in backpacks are not advised because you can really hurt yourself or the baby should you slip and fall. I would definitely recommend visiting with 2 adults if you have a little one younger than 5 years old. It's helpful to have an extra pair of hands to help the little one navigate the rocks.

Learn how to read the tide charts from Coyote Pointe Museum's Web site on tide pools: <www.coyoteptmuseum.org/education/tide_info.htm>. For more specific geographic tide information, go to <http://ceres.ca.gov>, then select "CalOCEAN." In the "Information Indexes" box, click on the "Coastal Counties" under the "By Geographic Area" section, find your county, and click on the "Tides and Ocean Currents" link in the "Coastal Conditions" box. Tide tables available from Crab Cove Visitor Center.

Remember, tide pool animals are delicate. So step carefully, and don't remove them from their niche. Collecting animals is prohibited. Leave them the way you found them, so repeat visits will be just as awesome and wonderful as this visit. Help your children learn to be stewards of the wonderful tide pool habitat.

Asilomar State Beach (Ages 3+)

(831) 646-6440; Sunset Drive, Pacific Grove, CA
Conference Center: 800 Asilomar Boulevard, Pacific Grove, CA 93950
<www.parks.ca.gov/default.asp?page_id=566>; <www.visitasilomar.com>

Description: This beautiful, scenic beach is right off Sunset Drive in Pacific Grove. During low tide you can do tide pooling here. The Asilomar Conference Center, (831) 372-8016, is located just across Ocean Boulevard, within a short walk of the beach. There's a gift shop and restaurant.
Hours: 8am–5pm.
Cost: Free.
Bathrooms: Yes, at the Conference Center, a bit of a walk from the beach.
Facilities: Not stroller friendly on the beach.
Food: Not on the beach. Conference Center has a restaurant.
What to Bring: Sunscreen, sunglasses, jacket, and comfortable shoes with good traction.

Directions: For map and directions, go to the California State Parks Web site listed above, and select "Location/Maps" in the right-hand column.

Agate Beach County Park (Ages 3+)

(415) 499-6387; (415) 507-2818

End of Elm Road at Ocean Parkway, Bolinas, CA
<www.co.marin.ca.us/depts/pk/main/pos/pdagatebch.cfm>

Description: Located within the Duxbury Reef State Marine Sanctuary, Agate Beach provides almost 2 miles of shoreline for tide pooling during low tide. No collecting allowed.

Hours: Dawn to dusk.

Cost: Free. No parking fee.

Bathrooms: Portables only.

Facilities: Not stroller friendly.

Food: No. Bolinas or Pointe Reyes Station is the closest for food.

What to Bring: Picnic lunch, sunscreen, sunglasses, hats, and jacket. Don't forget to wear shoes with good traction; rocky shore can be very slippery.

Follow-Up Activities: For naturalist- and ranger-led walks information in Marin, visit <www.marinopenspace.org>, then select "Walks."

Fitzgerald Marine Reserve (Ages 3+)

(650) 728-3584; California & North Lake Streets, Moss Beach, CA 94038
<www.eparks.net> select Parks, then Fitzgerald; <www.fitzgeraldreserve.org>

Description: This reserve is rich in marine life diversity along the rocky reef habitat. During low tides, marine life can be seen in the ten habitats found along the 3 miles of the Reserve's coastline. For groups of 10+, reservations are required with San Mateo County Parks: (650) 363-4021.

Hours: Daily: 8am–5pm. Open later, depending on season.

Cost: Free.

Bathrooms: Yes.

Facilities: Not stroller friendly.

Food: No. Picnic tables by the entrance.

What to Bring: Wear walking shoes with good traction (rocky shore is very slippery), sunscreen, sunglasses, extra change of shoes/clothes, beach gear, and sand toys.

Follow-Up Activities: 1) On weekends, during low tide, a roving naturalist will provide information about the marine life found here. Call ahead of time to see when these programs are scheduled. 2) "Jr. Ranger" camp for children 9–13 years old in the summer. See Web site for details and registration: <www.fitzgeraldreserve.org>.

Natural Bridges State Beach (Ages 3+)

(831) 423-4609; 2531 West Cliff Drive, Santa Cruz, CA 95060
<www.santacruzstateparks.org>
<www.parks.ca.gov/default.asp?page_id=541>
Tide information: <www.santacruzwharf.com> select "Tides."

Description: During low tide, the tide pools at the northern end of the beach are wonderful to view. There are sea anemones, mussels, sea snails, starfish, and a few hermit crabs. It does require some rock climbing. We went with our one-year-old in a baby backpack carrier. While doable, it's not recommended for your safety because of the slippery rocks.
Hours: 8am–sunset. Visitor Center open most weekends and some weekdays. Call to verify hours.
Cost: $6 parking.
Bathrooms: At the beach and at the visitor center. There are also changing rooms and outdoor showers to wash off the sand.
Facilities: Not stroller friendly at the beach.
Food: No. Picnic tables.
What to Bring: Sunscreen, sunglasses, extra change of clothes and shoes, beach gear, and sand toys. Wear comfortable shoes that provide good traction. Climbing the rocks can be very slippery.
Follow-Up Activities: 1) Monarch butterflies are in residence in the winter. See Chapter 3: Bees, Butterflies, & Bugs for details. 2) Close to the Seymour Marine Discovery Center and Wilder Ranch State Park, an historic dairy ranch of the 1900s.

Whale Watching Cruises

California's coastline is on the migratory path of many species of whales. Whale watching can be done year-round. From December to April, California gray whales are in our waters; from May to October, humpbacks, orcas (killer whales), minkes, and blue whales are passing through. Dolphins, otters, seals, and other marine life can be seen as well during a cruise.

Whale-watching cruises depart from San Francisco, Half Moon Bay, Santa Cruz, and Monterey. They vary in price and trip duration. Some operate year-round, while others only operate in the winter. Some have food onboard, while others provide no food at all. Some have the facilities to accommodate all ages, while other companies have minimum age requirements or at least age recommendations. If you have any doubts about bringing a little one on a cruise, call the companies and speak with them directly, to make sure all your concerns are addressed before you make reservations and commit to a cruise.

Dress warmly and in layers, regardless of the season. Consider bringing warm gloves and a scarf. Wear flat shoes with good traction. Don't forget your sunglasses, sunscreen, hat, camera with film, video camera and battery backups, and binoculars. If you get seasick, consider purchasing non-drowsy over-the-counter medication, and check with your doctor.

Chardonnay Sailing Charters (Recommended Age: 8+)
(831) 423-1213; 790 Mariner Park Way, Dock FF, Santa Cruz, CA 95062
<www.chardonnay.com>

Description: This company provides many cruises on Monterey Bay, departing from Santa Cruz. These cruises include whale-watching, fireworks on July 4th, ecology tour, and many others. Naturalist onboard provides narration and answers questions on whale watching cruises.

Schedule: January–March, tours to see California gray whales. June-August: humpback whales. The whale-watching cruises are three hours in length and depart on Saturday and some Sunday mornings. Visit Web site for cruise schedule.

Cost: $51/person.

Bathrooms: Yes.

Facilities: Not stroller friendly.

Food: Yes.

Chris' Whale Watching Trips (Ages 8+)

(831) 375-5951; 48 Fisherman's Wharf, Monterey, CA 93940
<www.chriswhalewatching.com>

Description: In the past, this company's focus was fishing trips. It now offers whale watching trips year-round. The Web site has pictures and descriptions of marine life. Pictures of the fleet are on the Web site as well. The company is recommended by *Sunset Magazine*.

Schedule: Daily trips with 2-hour narrated tours December–April. May–November trips last 3 hours and cost a bit more. Reservations may be made online.

Cost: December–April: $22/adult, $15/child. May–November: $30/adult, $20/child.

Bathrooms: No.

Facilities: Not stroller friendly.

Food: No.

Monterey Bay Whale Watch (All Ages)

Departs from Sam's Fishing Fleet

(831) 375-4658; 84 Fisherman's Wharf #1, Monterey, CA 93940
<www.montereybaywhalecruise.com>

Description: Marine biologist accompanies each trip. *December-April*: gray whales and dolphins. *May–mid-December*: humpback whales, blue whales, and dolphins.

Schedule: *December 16-April 30*: daily 10am & 1:30 pm departures, 3-hour-long trips. Weekends & holidays: additional 7:30am trip. *May–mid-December*: Daily morning trips depart at 9am and return between 1 and 2pm, 4- to 5-hour trips. Daily May 1–October 31 & weekends Nov.1–Dec. 15: afternoon trips leave at 2pm & return by 5–6pm. Check Web site for tour schedule and availability.

Cost: *December 16–April 30:* $32/adult, $21/child 12 and under, free/child 3 & under. *May–mid-December*: Morning trips cost $43/adult, $33/child 12 and under, free/child 3 & under. Afternoon 2pm trips: $34/adult, $23/child 12 and under, free/child 3 & under. Monterey Bay Aquarium employees, staff, and members qualify for a 20% discount. Show membership card at check-in.

Bathrooms: Yes.

Facilities: Stroller friendly, but too crowded to allow on weekends. Baby carriers recommended.

Food: Yes, but you can still bring your own food and drinks.

Monterey Whale Watching (Min. Age: 3+)

(831) 372-2203, (800) 979-3370; (212) 209-3370
96 Old Fisherman's Wharf #1, Monterey, CA 93940
<www.montereywhalewatching.com>

Description: *Expectant moms and children under 3 are not allowed on these whale watching trips.* Marine biologist- or naturalist-narrated tours.

Schedule: Daily departures at 10am & 1pm. Whale watching trips last 2½ to 3 hours.

Cost: Daily $34.95/adult, $24.95/child under 12.

Bathrooms: Yes.

Facilities: Stroller friendly.

Food: Snacks and drinks. You're welcome to bring your own picnic lunch.

Oceanic Society
(Min. Age: 7-12 ~ note min. age on trip info.)

Adults must accompany those 15 and under.
(800) 326-7491; (415) 474-3385 for reservations and further details.
Fort Mason QRTS 35, San Francisco, CA 94123
<www.oceanic-society.org>

Schedule: Whale cruises with expert naturalists departing from San Francisco (8 hours), Half Moon Bay (3 hours), and Bodega Bay (3 hours). *December–mid-May:* Half Moon Bay departures at 9am & 1pm mostly on weekends with an occasional Friday departure. From Bodega Bay, weekend departures in March & April only. *May–December:* Farallon Islands trips depart from San Francisco. Boat departs at 8am with check-in at 7:30am on Sat & Sun. Tours go rain or shine! Bring your own food and drinks. Visit Web site for departure dates & cost information.

Cost: For Half Moon Bay: $38/adult & senior (60+), $35/youth (7–15) for weekends; and $35/person on the rare Friday departure. For trips to Farallon Islands (8 hours): $88/person. For Bodega Bay: $45/person. Online reservations now available.

Sanctuary Cruises (All Ages)

(530) 778-3444; (831) 643-0128; (831) 917-1046 only for last minute reservations; Moss Landing Harbor, "A" Dock, Moss Landing Road, Moss Landing, CA
<www.sanctuarycruises.com>

Description: Gray whales are migrating in the winter. Cruise representative said that the best time to whale watch is when the humpback whales are migrating, because these whales put on a good show. The boats don't fish, and smoking is not allowed onboard. Look on the Web site under "Whale Watching," then "Whales & Dolphins by Season" to see what animals you'll see in each season. This company provides whale watching cruises for Seymour Marine Discovery Center and the Monterey Bay Aquarium.

Schedule: Tue–Sun & holiday Mondays. March–June: departures at 9:30am. July-Feb: departures at 10:30am. Reservations required.

Cost: 3- to 5-hour whale-watching trips are $42/adult, $32/child 3-12, $6/child under 3. Check the Web site for discounts. Monterey Bay Aquarium members receive 10% discount. Identify affiliation at time of reservation & bring membership card with you.

Bathrooms: Yes.

Facilities: Stroller friendly.

Food: Food available onboard. You may want to bring your own lunch or crackers to help counteract seasickness. You can also purchase one-time-use cameras and rent the Relief Band to counteract seasickness. Advice on how to prepare against seasickness is on the Web site.

Chapter 2
Plant Kingdom

In this age of technology, children often get shortchanged in their understanding of biology. Apples and carrots come out of a bag that Mommy brought home from the grocery store. The plants that produce them have become completely detached. Even as an adult, I had never seen a pineapple plant until I went to Hawaii. I had always imagined that pineapples came from something like a palm tree. Farms, orchards, gardens, and arboretums help us make the connection between the product and the producer. Where do apples come from? Is it from a plant, a shrub, or a tree? Do carrots grow on trees, too? This section provides information on organic gardens, flower gardens, botanical gardens, arboretums, farms, and orchards.

Here are some gardens to put the apples back on the apple tree, the grapes on the vine, and the artichokes on the plant.

Organic Gardens

Ardenwood Farm (All Ages)
(510) 796-0663; 34600 Ardenwood Boulevard, Fremont, CA 94555
<www.ebparks.org/parks/arden.htm>
<www.fremont.gov/recreation/ardenwoodpark>
See full entry in Chapter 1: Animal Kingdom—Farms section.

Children's Discovery Museum (All Ages)
(408) 298-5437; 180 Woz Way, San Jose, CA 95110
<www.cdm.org>
See full entry in Chapter 4: Science & Technology Museums.

Copia (Ages 4+)
The American Center for Food, Wine & the Arts
(888) 512-6742; (707) 259-1600; 500 First Street, Napa, CA 94559
<www.copia.org>

Description: Copia is a food museum, art gallery, and organic garden, all dedicated to food and wine. The food museum has wonderful interactive exhibits featuring the way people make, eat, and think about food as well as the customs and cultures relating to food. This unique center also has a restaurant (Julia's Kitchen) and cafe, along with a fabulous organic kitchen garden. Here's a place that'll cater to your love of good food and wine, while letting your kids learn about plants we use daily in our kitchens. This extensive garden has fruit trees & vines, kitchen herbs, many varieties of vegetables, and even plots dedicated to the varieties of wines. I love to visit in the spring to see all the trees flowering. The art gallery is dedicated to art related to food and wine as well. There are wine tasting, food, and garden tours to suit your time and budget.

Hours: Wed-Mon: 10am–5pm. Closed Tuesdays. *Wine Tasting:* Daily 11am-4pm complimentary wine tasting at the mezzanine wine bar featuring the winery of the week. Wine Tasting 101 class daily at 10:15am & Thur-Sun at 1pm ($15/person). *Garden Group Tour:* 30-minute private, preset tour time ($10/person). The 60-minute private tour includes a taste of the harvest ($28/person). *Food Classes:* 25-minute classes w/ tasting daily at 11am & 3:15pm, topic changes monthly. Check Web site for many more tours & classes.

Cost: $5/adult, $4/senior (62+, students w/ ID), free/child 12 & under. Sonoma & Napa County residents: half price on Wednesdays.

Bathrooms: Yes.

Facilities: Strollers not recommended.

Food: Yes.

Follow-Up Activities: 1) Look for special events for families featured throughout the year. 2) Summer concerts on Thursdays at 7:30pm. Doors open at 5:30pm; seating on a first-come, first-served basis. $25/ticket. Check Web site for performance schedule.

Cupertino Community Gardens (All Ages)
(408) 777-3149; 22221 McClellan Road, Cupertino, CA 95014

See McClellan Ranch Park in Chapter 1: Animal Kingdom—Farms.

Emma Prusch Farms (All Ages)
Community Gardens: Cornucopia & El Jardin.
(408) 793-4165; <www.sjcommunitygardens.org>
See full entry in Chapter 1: Animal Kingdom—Farms. See the list of
community gardens in San Jose Community Gardens entry below.
Bathrooms: Portables in the field.

Hidden Villa (All Ages)
(650) 949-8650 ; 26870 Moody Road, Los Altos Hills, CA 94022
<www.hiddenvilla.org>
See full entry in Chapter 1: Animal Kingdom—Farms section.

San Jose Community Gardens (All Ages)
<www.sjcommunitygardens.org>
These gardens are assigned to San Jose residents on a first-come, first-
served basis, allowing residents to grow a wide range of plants from vegetables, flowers, herbs, and fruits organically. The plots range from 10' x
10' to 20' x 30.' Call (408)793-4165 for additional information if you'd
like to start your own plot.

- Alviso (N. 1st & Tony P. Santos)
- Berryessa (Flickinger & Doxey)
- Bestor Art Park (S. Six and Bestor)
- Calabazas (Blaney & Danridge)
- Cornucopia (S. King & Story) (Emma Prusch Farm park)
- Coyote (Tully at Galveston)
- El Jardin (S. King & Story) (Emma Prusch Farm park)
- Green Thumb (Rhoda & Roewill)
- Hamline (Hamline & Sherwood)
- Jesse Frey (Alma & Belmont)
- La Colina (Allegan Circle)
- Laguna Seca (Manresa & Bayliss)
- Latimer (Latimer & Hamilton Ave)
- Mayfair (Kammerer and Sunset)
- Nuestra Tierra (Tully & La Ragione)
- Rainbow Center Community Garden (Rainbow Drive &
  Johnson Avenue)

- Wallenberg (Curtner & Cottle)

U.C. Santa Cruz Farm & Garden (All Ages)
CASFS, U.C. Santa Cruz

(831) 459-3240; 1156 High Street, Santa Cruz, CA 95064
<http://zzyx.ucsc.edu/casfs/community/tours.html>; <www.lifelab.org>

Description: This organic garden and farm is open year-round. There are kids' tours with hands-on activities in the new Garden Classroom from April–June & in the fall from the Life Lab Science Program.

Hours: Daily: 8am–6pm. *Kids Tours* for school groups: Tues, Thur, & Fri April–early June & in the fall. Call (831) 459-2001 to schedule a tour.

Cost: Free.

Bathrooms: Yes.

Facilities: Stroller friendly.

Food: No.

Follow-Up Activities: 1) Harvest Festival at the Farm: an annual celebration at the farm with hayrides, food, music, tours, and kids' events. Held usually on Saturday in early October 11am–5pm. Free for members and kids 12 and under, $5 for nonmembers. Check calendar of events for current info: <http://zzyx.ucsc.edu/casfs/community/calendar.html>. 2) Spring & summer camps through Life Lab. 3) Tours for preschoolers, elementary schools, and middle schools through Life Lab.

Gardens & Arboretums

Bonfante Gardens Family Theme Park (All Ages)

(408) 840-7100; 3050 Hecker Pass Highway, Gilroy, CA 95020
<www.bonfantegardens.com>

Description: The theme park was built specifically to showcase the circus trees with their intricate trunk designs that were created with grafting techniques. This park is beautifully landscaped with gardens intermingling with the rides and attractions. There are waterfalls, ponds, and gardens of orchids and camellias. Don't miss the Monarch Garden at the back of the park to view example of banana trees, mango trees, and a plant that existed in the time of the dinosaurs. The theme park provides the best combination of transportation examples. There are paddle boat and other boat rides, replica antique cars of the 1920s and 1950s, a mini-train that goes around the perimeter of the park, a monorail through the Monarch Garden, a restored antique 1920s carousel, and a mini-air balloon ride. Check Web site for height requirements for attractions.

Hours: Closed in the winter. Open April: 10am–5pm. Hours vary based on the season. Visit the Web site or call for current information.

Cost: $8 parking fee. *Online Discount Admission:* $27.99 online pricing only/person (all ages). *Gate Admission:* $39.99/person 7-64, $29.99/child 3-6 or senior 65+. *Season Passes:* $59.99/person (4+ people), $69.99 (3 or fewer people). Season passes from Bonfante Gardens also include parking. Parking pass for the season is available for $20. *Discounts:* Discounted tickets available from Walgreen's and local corporations. AAA (Automobile Association of California) members: $5 discount/person (up to 6 people). Paramount's Great America sells a season pass (VIP) that includes free admission to Bonfante Gardens.

Bathrooms: Yes, but baby changing stations are outside the bathrooms.

Facilities: Day use lockers available. Stroller friendly.

Food: Many cafés to choose from (from burgers and hot dogs to Mexican food).

What to Bring: Sunscreen, sunglasses, hat, cash for food and drinks, quarters for locker use, extra change of clothes for water play and perhaps swimsuits for the little ones (Splash Gardens), extra pair of shoes or water shoes for getting wet.

Follow-Up Activities: 1) Educational programs for groups and school field trips relate to trees, water management, the life cycle, agriculture, and nature. Jr. Horticulture Day provides plant-based science to local schools for free. On Jr. Horticulture Day, students learn about the water cycle and composting and participate in a garden scavenger hunt. Schools from farther afield may participate for a small per-student fee. 2) In September, there are Walk in the Gardens days, which provide nature and gardening workshops. Rides are closed during these days. 3) Special camp nights for scouting groups. Check Web site under "Programs."

Conservatory of Flowers (All Ages)
Golden Gate Park
(415) 666-7001; Physical location: John F. Kennedy Drive, San Francisco
Admin: 501 Stanyan Street, San Francisco, CA 94117
<www.conservatoryofflowers.org>

Description: This beautifully restored glass conservatory is a well-known landmark of San Francisco's Golden Gate Park. The collection includes tropical, aquatic, and potted plants. In a recent special exhibit, the Conservatory brought in multiple species of butterflies so visitors may enjoy butterflies flying all around them. Check Web site for current exhibits.

Hours: Tues–Sun: 9am–5pm, last entry is at 4:30pm. Closed Mondays. Open major holidays.

Cost: $5/adult; $3/youth 12-17, seniors 65 & over, and students with ID; $1.50/child 5–11; free/child 4 and under. *Free first Tuesday each month.*

Bathrooms: Located outside next to the Conservatory building.

Facilities: Stroller friendly.

Food: No. Picnic on the lawns outside. No food allowed in the Conservatory.

What to Bring: Picnic lunch, blanket to sit on, and sweater in case of cool weather.

Follow-Up Activities: 1) Programs for elementary school groups. 2) Stow Lake, Strybing Arboretum and Botanical Garden, and the De Young Museum are located within Golden Gate Park.

Filoli Gardens (Ages 5+)
(650) 364-8300 x507; 86 Cañada Road, Woodside, CA 94062
<www.filoli.org>

Description: This is a gorgeous formal garden and mansion. The best time of year to visit is in April when almost everything (tulips, camellias, dogwoods, rhododendrons, and too many others to list) in the gardens is in bloom, except the roses.

Hours: Closed November–mid-February. Open mid-February–October. Tues–Sat: 10am–3:30pm, Sun: 11am-3:30pm, last admission at 2:30pm. Saturday morning nature hikes at 10am last 2½ hours. Orchard tour on select days. House & garden tours are available on a reservation basis.

Contact <tours@filoli.org> or call (650) 364-8300 x507 for reservations.
Cost: $12/adult; $5/student w/ ID, youth 5–17; free/child 5 & under.
Bathrooms: Yes.
Facilities: Stroller friendly.
Food: Small café at main entry building. Picnics not allowed at Filoli.
Edgewood Park or Pulgas Water Temple is ¼ mile north on Cañada
Road.
What to Bring: Sunscreen, sunglasses, camera, and picnic lunch.
Follow-Up Activities: 1) Bring a picnic and lunch at Pulgas Water Temple
to let the kids run and get out their energy. 2) Annual East Egg Hunt
event. 3) In early December, annual Children's Parties ($65/adult, $25/
child). These feature a magician, a puppeteer, a clown, Peninsula Girls
Choir, and visits with Santa and Mrs. Claus. 4) Family programs feature
plants and nature on weekends. 5) School programs include house and
garden tours, native plants & Ohlone ways, and hikes in the Filoli Nature
Preserve. 6) *David C. Daniels Nature Center* is close by at Alpine Road
& Skyline Blvd, Woodside, CA. (650) 691-1200. Its Web site is <www.
openspace.org>; select "Great Activities," then "Daniels Nature Center."
The nature center is open April–mid-November: Sat & Sun 11am–4pm.
School program, "Spaces & Species: Exploring Natural Communities," is
offered during the week. There's a hands-on lab with microscopes to view
microscopic pond life, wildlife skulls, and animal pelts that children can
touch. On the edge of Alpine Pond, the center features the habitat and
food web of the pond.

Gamble Garden (All Ages)

(650) 329-1356; 1431 Waverley Street, Palo Alto, CA 94301
<www.gamblegarden.org>

Description: In the middle of a residential neighborhood, this serene
garden is fun to stroll through. There are flowering annuals, perennials,
herbs, and vegetable beds.
Hours: *Office & House:* Mon–Fri: 9am–noon. *Gardens* open daily during
daylight hours. *Guided Tour:* Available Mon–Fri with 4 weeks advanced
reservation for groups of 8 or more.
Cost: Free. Guided tours: $5/person with min. $40/group. Holiday
Teas: $15/person. The Children's Puppet Shows in December: $10/per-
son.
Bathrooms: Yes.

87

Facilities: Stroller friendly.
Food: No.
Follow-Up Activities: 1) Garden tours for children to help them learn about plants and bugs that live there. Minimum of 5 kids per group. Call to schedule a tour. 2) Summer camps offered in collaboration with the Palo Alto Junior Museum & Zoo. 3) Community Day in early October from 11am–3pm is free. Activities include vintage tractor rides for kids, leaf prints, hunt for the longest earth worms, and learning about the life cycle and migration of monarch butterflies. 4) Children's Puppet Shows designed for children ages 3–6 are in early December. There are only three performances. $10/person. Call to reserve. 5) Children's holiday tea parties in December for kids ages 6+. $15/person. Reserve early to avoid disappointment.

Gardens at Heather Farms (All Ages)

(925) 947-1539; Office: (925)947-1678; Eudcation Office: (925)947-6712
1540 Marchbanks Road, Walnut Creek, CA 94598
<www.gardenshf.org>

Description: These beautiful gardens include a children's garden, a sensory garden with fragrant herbs, a butterfly garden with milkweed plants for monarch butterflies, a rose garden overlooking the park, a composting demonstration area, a water conservation garden, and a native plants garden. For a virtual tour, visit the Web site: <www.gardenshf.org/GardenStroll.html>.
Hours: Daily sunrise–sunset. Office Hours: Mon–Fri 9am-1pm.
Cost: Free.
Bathrooms: Yes.
Facilities: Stroller friendly.
Food: No. Snack bar is located at the Clarke Memorial Swim Center.
What to Bring: Sunscreen, sunglasses, picnic lunch, and swimming gear if you plan on swimming at the pool.
Follow-Up Activities: 1) Docent-led tours available to groups. Tours cost $4/person with a minimum of $30/group. 2) School programs for kindergarten through 5th grades. Call (925) 947-6712 for additional information and reservations. 3) Located in the same park, the Clarke Memorial Swim Center has an Olympic sized pool, a diving pool, and a shallow wading pool. It is located at 1750 Heather Drive, Heather Farm Park, Walnut Creek. *Recreational swimming:* Mon–Fri: 1–4pm, Sat & Sun:

12pm–4:45pm. Extended summer hours. Check Web site <**www.wal-nutcreekrec.org**>; then select "Aquatics." *Cost:* $4.25/adult, $3.75/child 7–17, $3/child 6 & under. Phone: (925) 943-5856.

Hakone Gardens (Ages 3+)
(408) 741-4994; 21000 Big Basin Way, Saratoga, CA 95070
<www.hakone.com>

Description: Nestled in the Saratoga foothills, these serene gardens include hiking trails and gardens with a koi pond. The garden's designers planned different displays throughout the seasons. Spring brings blooming wisteria and cherry. Summer has flowering water lilies, while autumn brings red, orange, and golden leaves.

Hours: Mon–Fri: 10am–5pm, weekends: 11am–5pm. Closed New Year's & Christmas days. *Guided Tours:* Available by appointment only.

Cost: $4/adult admission, $3.50/student w/ ID or senior, free/child under 5.

Bathrooms: Yes.

Facilities: Not stroller friendly. Bring baby in baby carrier.

Food: No. Picnic tables available.

What to Bring: Picnic lunch, camera, and cash for parking.

Follow-Up Activities: 1) Classes on flower arranging, tea ceremony, art, yoga, etc. available. Check Web site under "Calendar," then "Classes" to find current offering. Most of these classes cater to adults. **2)** Close to Sanborn Park where the Youth and Science Institute has a Visitor Center.

Japanese Friendship Garden, Kelly Park (All Ages)
(408) 277-2757; 1300 Senter Road, San Jose, CA 95112
<www.sjparks.org>

Description: This beautiful garden is located within walking distance of Happy Hollow Zoo and Park and the History Park, San Jose at Kelly Park. There are two gardens, an upper garden and a lower garden. Each garden has its own koi pond. Meandering paths and curved bridges provide a nice respite from the crowds and noise of Happy Hollow.

Hours: Daily 8am–sunset.

Cost: Free entrance to the garden. Parking fee: $6 on weekends and daily from Memorial Day to Labor Day.

Bathrooms: Portables just outside the gate of the garden.
Facilities: Stroller friendly, except in a couple of steep sections.
Food: No. Picnic tables.
What to Bring: Picnic lunch and drinks. Quarters to buy food to feed the koi. Cash for parking. Don't forget the sunscreen, sunglasses, camera, and hat.
Follow-Up Activities: Happy Hollow Park and Zoo and History Park, San Jose are also within Kelly Park.

Japanese Tea Garden (All Ages)
Central Park, San Mateo
(650) 522-7440; 50 East 5th Avenue, San Mateo 94403
<www.cityofsanmateo.org> then Departments, Parks & Rec, then Parks Directory

Description: This cozy Japanese Tea Garden was designed by the landscape architect of the Imperial Palace of Tokyo.
Hours: Weekdays: 10am–4pm, weekends: 11am–4pm.
Cost: Free.
Bathrooms: Yes, by the playground.
Facilities: Stroller friendly.
Food: No. Picnic tables and nearby restaurants.
What to Bring: Picnic lunch, sunscreen, sunglasses, and plenty to drink.
Follow-Up Activities: Bianchi Railway and a children's playground are also located within Central Park. See Chapter 6: Transportation Favorites—Trains for information on Bianchi Railway.

Japanese Tea Garden (Ages 3+)
Golden Gate Park
(415) 752-4227; (415) 752-1171 Teahouse;
Tea Garden Drive & Martin Luther King Jr. Drive, San Francisco, CA 94118

Description: One of the most beautiful Japanese Tea Gardens in the Bay Area, this is a large garden with a waterfall and koi pond. There's also a teahouse for snacks and tea, of course.
Hours: 9am–4:45pm (6pm, depending on season). Call prior to visit to confirm.
Cost: $4/adult, $1.5/senior 65+ w/ ID or child 6–12, free/child under 6. Free admission Mon, Wed, & Fri from 9am-10am only.
Bathrooms: Yes.

Facilities: Stroller friendly.

Food: Teahouse has a few Japanese snack items and tea.

What to Bring: Jacket, cash for entry and teahouse, and quarters for metered parking and to purchase food for the fish.

Follow-Up Activities: The De Young Art Museum is around the corner, and the Strybing Arboretum is just across the street. The Conservatory of Flowers is also located within Golden Gate Park.

Luther Burbank Home & Gardens (All Ages)

(707) 524-5445; Santa Rosa Avenue & Sonoma Avenue, Santa Rosa, CA 95404 <www.lutherburbank.org>

Description: This was the home of Luther Burbank, a world renown horticulturist. He developed more than 800 new varieties of plants, including the Shasta daisy, Santa Rosa plum, pluots, and the russet potato, among many others. The garden and greenhouse show examples of his work. The home tour gives a glimpse of how he lived and the environment he worked in. Burbank was friends with Jack London, Thomas Edison, Henry Ford, and Hellen Keller. There's a picture of Burbank, Edison, and Ford together in the living room of the little cottage his wife lived in after his death. The Web site has a virtual tour of the gardens as well as background information and pictures. Vitual Museum site: <http://score.rims.k12.ca.us/activity/LBSite/lobby.html>. Background on famous people: <http://score.rims.k12.ca.us/activity/LBSite/burbankabilia/people.html>.

Hours: Gardens open daily year-round 8am-dusk. Carriage House & Museum: April–October Tues–Sun 10am–4pm. Drop-in guided tours of house, garden, & greenhouse begin each half hour and are offered April–October Tues–Sun 10am–3:30pm.

Cost: Free. Nominal fee for guided tour.

Bathrooms: Restrooms.

Facilities: Stroller friendly.

Food: No.

What to Bring: Sunscreen, sunglasses, camera, and picnic lunch.

Follow-Up Activities: 1) Children's tours of the home & gardens available year-round. Call for information and reservation. 2) Annual Holiday Open House features the home and greenhouse decorated in the Victorian era with arts & crafts table for the kids. First weekend in December 10am-4pm; free admission. 3) Gold Ridge Farm, Luther Burbank's Experimental

Farm is located in Sebastopol. (707) 829-6711; 7781 Bodega Avenue, Sebastopol, CA. Open all year. Docent tours available April–October by appointment. Visit Web site for map & directions: <**www.wschs-grf.pon. net/bef.htm**>.

Overfelt Gardens (All Ages)
Chinese Cultural Garden
(408) 251-3323; 368 Educational Park Drive, San Jose, CA 95116
<www.chineseculturalgarden.org>

Description: This cultural garden is set within Overfelt Gardens in San Jose. The Chinese Cultural garden has examples of Chinese architecture and statues of Confucius, Chiang Kai-Shek, and Dr. Sun Yat-Sen. Before you go, visit the Web site, and select "Tour" to get the background story of these famous Chinese historical figures. Besides being the site of the Chinese garden, Overfelt Garden is worth a visit for it own sake, with ponds serving as home to over-wintering birds that include herons, egrets, and other water birds. A walk around the lakes is a tranquil experience any season.

Hours: Daily 10am to sunset.
Cost: Free.
Bathrooms: Restrooms at the park entrance.
Facilities: Stroller friendly.
Food: No. Picnic tables.
What to Bring: Sunscreen, sunglasses, camera, and picnic lunch.
Follow-Up Activities: 1) The garden hosts a free annual Moon Festival on a Sunday in mid-September from 1-5pm. The festival features lion dancing, Chinese music, arts, dance, games, and poetry as well as arts and crafts and storytelling for kids. Visit Web site and select "Moon Festival" to read about the legend of the Moon Maiden. 2) Elementary school tours available.

The Ruth Bancroft Garden (All Ages)
(925) 210-9663; Office: (925) 944-9352;
1500 Bancroft Road, Walnut Creek, CA 94598
<www.ruthbancroftgarden.org>

Description: This garden has a great collection of succulents, cacti, yucca, and low water consumption plants. It is recognized as a premier private garden that showcases the design possibilities of a water wise garden.

Hours: The garden is revamping its tour schedule for spring 2007. Check the Web site for current information. Open during scheduled tour times. *Docent-led tours:* Mid-July to early-Sept, tours on Fri & Sat at 9:30am and on Sat at 6pm. September–mid-October: Fri & Sat at 9:30am and on Sat at 5pm. November 11–March 31, 2007, tours only on Sat at 10am. Tours are 90 minutes long. Call (925) 210-9663 to make reservations. *Self-guided tours:* mid-July–early Sept: tours on Sat & Sun 6–8pm only, September–mid-October: tours on Sat & Sun 5pm only. From November 11–March 31, 2007, tours only on Sat at 10am. Hours may change. Reservations required for all tours and most events.

Cost: $7/person, free/child under 12. $3/student for school field trips.

Bathrooms: Portables only.

Facilities: Stroller friendly.

Food: No. Picnicking not allowed.

What to Bring: Sunscreen, sunglasses, hat, and cash for entry. Bring picnic lunch and picnic at Heather Farms. See Heather Farms entry in Gardens and Arboretum section.

Follow-Up Activities: Heather Farms and Lindsay Wildlife Museum are close by.

Strybing Arboretum & Botanical Gardens (All Ages)

(415) 661-1316; Golden Gate Park: 9th Avenue, San Francisco, CA 94122
<www.strybing.org>

Description: This is one of the most extensive gardens and arboretums, with plants from South America, New Zealand, Australia, Asia, and South Africa. There's also a California native plants garden and a fragrance garden. The fragrance garden is a kid favorite.

Hours: Open daily. *Weekdays:* 8am–4:30pm. *Weekends and holidays:* 10am–5pm. Free guided walks Mon–Fri at 1:30pm, and weekends at 10:30am & 1:30pm; depart from the bookstore. There are also free guided walks departing from the north entrance (Friend Gate), Wed, Fri, & Sun at 2pm. Free guided walks for school groups, subject to lottery held twice each year.

Cost: Free.

Bathrooms: Yes.

Facilities: Stroller friendly.

Food: No.

What to Bring: Jacket, quarters for metered street parking, sunscreen, sunglasses, and picnic lunch.

Follow-Up Activities: 1) Japanese Tea Garden and the De Young Museum are located within walking distance. 2) Birding and family walks on weekends. For events schedule, select the "Calendar of Events" tab on the home page. 3) School programs for elementary & middle school students. Select the "Education" button on the Web site's home page for information on classes and programs for kids. Call (415)661-1316 ext. 307 for more information.

Sunset Magazine's Gardens (All Ages)

(650) 321-3600; 80 Willow Road, Menlo Park, CA 94025
<www.sunset.com>

Description: This is the magazine's demonstration gardens. The best time to visit this garden is in the spring; however, since the gardens are re-planted 3 times a year, it is nice to visit year-round.
Hours: Mon–Fri: 9am–4:30pm. Closed on holidays and in mid-May.
Cost: Free.
Bathrooms: Yes.
Facilities: Stroller friendly.
Food: No, but you can picnic here.
What to Bring: Picnic lunch, sunscreen, sunglasses, and hat.
Follow-Up Activities: 1) Tours are available for schools, grades 2–5, by reservations only. Call (650) 324-5400 for reservations. 2) Annual Celebration Weekend in mid-May 10am-5pm. Admission is $10/adult, free/child 12 & under.

Tilden Botanic Garden (All Ages)
Tilden Nature Preserve Regional Parks

(510) 841-8732; Wildcat Canyon Road at Shasta Road, Berkeley, CA 94701
<www.nativeplants.org>; <www.nativeplants.org/about.html> for the map

Description: This botanical garden features native California plants, with 10 different sections to display the diversity of the California climate and environment. See full entry under Tilden Park in Chapter 1: Animal Kingdom—Farms.
Hours: 8:30am–5pm. (Open until 5:30pm June–September.) Free tours at 2pm on weekends. Closed New Year's, Thanksgiving, & Christmas.

Cost: Free.
Bathrooms: Yes.
Facilities: Stroller friendly.
Food: No.
What to Bring: Picnic lunch, sunscreen, sunglasses, and hat. Visit Web site for detailed directions.

U.C. Berkeley Botanical Garden (All Ages)

(510) 643-2755; 200 Centennial Drive #5045, Berkeley, CA 94720
<http://botanicalgarden.berkeley.edu>

Description: Set in the Berkeley hills, this huge botanical garden has an extensive collection of plants from various habitats all over the world and from fern grottos to deserts.
Hours: Daily 9am–5pm. Closed 1st Tuesday of each month, Thanksgiving, Christmas Eve, Christmas Day, New Year's Eve, New Year's Day, and Martin Luther King Jr. Day. Free docent-led tours at 1:30pm on Thur, Sat, & Sun.
Cost: *Free first Thursday of each month.* All other days: $5/adult, $3/senior 65+, $1/child 3–17, free/child under 3, UC students free. Parking $.75 for first half hour, $1.50/first hour, then 50 cents/ half-hour thereafter.
Bathrooms: Yes.
Facilities: Only one trail in the canyon is stroller friendly. Bring baby in baby carrier.
Food: No.
What to Bring: Sunscreen, sunglasses, picnic lunch, & cash for parking.
Follow-Up Activities: 1) Educational tours for class groups. 2) Summer camp. 3) Special events & programs. See Web site for current schedule. 4) Close to Tilden Park and Lawrence Hall of Science. See Chapter 4: Science & Technology Museums.

U.C. Santa Cruz Arboretum (All Ages)

(831) 427-2998; 1156 High Street, Santa Cruz, CA 95064
<www2.ucsc.edu/arboretum>

Description: There is a wonderful collection of South African proteas as well as plants from South Africa, Australia, New Zealand, and North America. Also featured are plants native to California and to the nearby islands off the California coast. See Web site for map and directions.
Hours: Daily 9am–5pm. Closed Thanksgiving and Christmas.

Docent-led Tours: First Saturday of each month, at 11am.
Cost: Free. Tour: $3/person.
Bathrooms: Yes.
Facilities: Stroller friendly.
Food: No, but you can picnic here.
What to Bring: Sunglasses, sunscreen, picnic lunch, and camera.
Follow-Up Activities: Santa Cruz Mission, Natural Bridges State Beach, Seymour Marine Discovery Center, and Santa Cruz Beach Boardwalk are all close by.

Fruit Farms & Orchards

To help prepare little ones, consider reading the picture book *Little Apple: A Book of Thanks* by Brigitte Weninger and Anne Möller for a wonderful introduction to how apples come from the tree and how the tree comes from the apple seed.

The following berry farms along the coast and the fruit farms in Brentwood and Sonoma County allow you to pick your own. Fruit ripens differently based on the micro climate, season, and fruit variety. Below is a general guideline on the approximate harvest times of various fruits available for U-pick. Keep in mind that different varieties of the same fruit ripen at different times. Each variety may last just a few weeks. Call the farms that you're interested in visiting ahead of time to ensure ripeness and availability.

Month	Fruit
May	Cherries, strawberries (no thorns)
June	Nectarines, plums, apricots, blackberries, strawberries, peaches
July	Nectarines, peaches, plums, apricots, raspberries
August	Asian pears
September	Apples
October	Apples, pumpkins
Nov/Dec	Kiwis

Items to Bring With You

1) Cash to purchase the fruit you pick. 2) Containers to hold your picked fruit. Bigger containers for bigger fruit such as apples and peaches, etc. Sealable plastic containers are good choices for berries. If you're planning to pick blackberries or raspberries, consider bringing something to line your car to prevent staining. 3) Gloves for berry picking, especially for raspberries and blackberries. The vines have thorns. 4) Don't forget your sunscreen, sunglasses, and hat. 5) Pack lots of drinks for the return trip. Picking berries in the sun makes for thirsty kids. 6) Handy wipes to clean hands off after picking berries. If you're lucky, there will be a place where you can wash your hands, but it's best to be prepared. 7) A light jacket or sweater if the farm is along the coast, since the coast can be overcast or foggy. 8) You might also want to bring an extra change of clothes and shoes for the kids. Being in the fields can get shoes and clothes muddy. 9) Generally speaking, fruit picking is done in the fields. Strollers don't work very well over bumpy, and sometimes muddy, fields. I would recommend putting babies in baby backpacks or baby carriers. 10) Most farms have portable bathrooms in the fields; some have nice, standard bathrooms by the store or picnic area.

Making Jam with Your Harvest

Jam making is relatively easy and definitely worth the trouble. Homemade jams are very flavorful! If you'd like to make jam, plan on purchasing canning jars and *SureJell* fruit pectin ahead of time, and have lots of sugar on hand. Depending on the fruit, you may also need some lemons. When you get home, load up your dishwasher with the canning jars and wash them while you're preparing the fruit and the jam so they'll be hot and sterile. You need about 5 cups of prepared fruit for a package of *SureJell*. Follow the instructions in the recipe that comes with the *SureJell* packet to make your jam. Use the inversion method and be sure to fill the jar as close to the rim as possible without spilling. This will ensure a tight seal. Plan about 1 to 1½ hours for making jam. It's a tasty treat! This includes preparing your fruit and cooking the jam. This is a great gift idea for Christmas that the kids can give to friends and relatives.

Additional Resources

For a map of the farms in the Santa Clara/Santa Cruz Counties and surrounding area, send a self-addressed stamped envelope to: *Country*

Crossroads Map, Santa Clara County Farm Bureau, 605 Tennant Avenue, Suite H, Morgan Hill, CA 95037. Alternatively you can send your request to Santa Cruz County Farm Bureau, 141 Monte Vista Avenue, Watsonville, CA 95076. The phone number is (408) 776-1684 or (831) 724-1356. The Web site is <**www.sccfarmbureau.org**>.

The *Harvest Trails Map* to farms in San Mateo County can be obtained by calling (650) 726-4485 or sending a self-addressed stamped envelope to San Mateo County Farm Bureau, Harvest Trails Map, 765 Main Street, Half Moon Bay, CA 94019.

Marin County's Marin Agricultural Land Trust's member farms sponsor hikes and tours throughout the year. These tours include Hog Island Oyster Farm, Strauss Dairy, McEvoy Olive Ranch, Clark Summit Farm, Cowgirl Creamery, and many other tours. They also sponsor an annual *Harvest Day at the Farm* in October at Nicasio Valley Farms located at 5300 Nicasio Valley Road, Nicasio, CA. Nicasio Valley Farm is open in October from 10am - 5pm. (415) 662-9100. Free admission. Don't miss these popular programs! Check the "Hikes and Programs" then the "Hikes and Tours" section on MALT's Web site <**www.malt.org/hp/hikestours. html**> for tours, dates, times, and places to meet.

For the *Sonoma County Farm Trails Map*, call 1-800-207-9464 or (707)571-8288 or e-mail your request to: farmtrails@farmtrails.org. The Web site is <**www.farmtrails.org**>. For the Sonoma County harvest calendar: <**www.farmtrails.org/calendar.html**>.

Farther afield, Central Valley farms have *Harvest Trails,* which has information on farms, a harvest calendar, and maps. Visit the Farm Bureau Web site: <**www.stanfarmbureau.com**>, then scroll down to download the *Harvest Trails* map.

Napa, Yolo, and Solano counties have *Napa–Yolano Harvest Trails* on their Web site: <**www.napayolanoharvesttrails.org**>.

The Small Farm Center at U.C. Davis has a wonderful database on its Web site that provides information on California Agri-Tourism farms that are open to the public and those that provide educational experiences.

The Web site is <www.calagtour.org>. Here's a direct link to the database: <www.calagtour.org/AgTour.ASP>.

Coastal Berry Picking Farms

Strawberries work very well for toddlers because they are thornless. Boysenberries and blackberries are fairly easy to pick for little ones. Raspberries definitely require gloves and skill. Part the raspberry plant to look for raspberries in the center of the plant.

Coastways Ranch/Swant Farms (Ages 3+)

(650) 879-0414, (831) 469-8804;
640 Cabrillo Highway (HWY 1), Pescadero, CA 94060
<www.swantonberryfarm.com>

Description: This ranch is now part of Swanton Farms. The ranch has boysenberries, olallieberries, and loganberries. Pumpkin available in October. Kiwi available in November/December. Christmas trees available in November/December, starting the day after Thanksgiving. Call to verify availability. Visit Web site for map and directions.
Schedule: Blackberries season: late May–July 9am–5pm.
Cost: $2/pound for blackberries.
Bathrooms: Portables.
Food: No.

Emile Agaccio Farms (Ages 3+)

(831) 728-2009; 4 Casserly Road, Watsonville, CA 95076

Description: Blackberries and raspberries.
Schedule: Olallieberries season: May–June. Raspberry season: May–July.
Cost: No entrance fee. Olallieberries are around $2/lb and the raspberries are around $2/lb, depending on market conditions.
Bathrooms: Portable restrooms in the fields.
Facilities: Not stroller friendly.
Food: No, picnic tables by the fruit stand.

Gizdich Ranch (Ages 3+)

(831) 722-1056; 55 Peckham Road, Watsonville, CA 95076
<www.gizdich-ranch.com>

Description: Gizdich Ranch has a variety of berries for you to pick: strawberries, boysenberries, olalliberries, and raspberries. In October, apples are available. School groups can tour in Sept/Oct for apple harvest, and pumpkin tours are available in October.

Schedule: Open 9am–5pm (May to July: strawberries; June: boysenberries & ollalieberries; July: blackberries & raspberries; September/October: apples). The Apple Butter Festival on the 3rd Saturday in October has apple butter making and canning as well as hayrides and a pumpkin patch. On Saturdays in September, watch apples juice pressing.

Cost: Prices for berries are ~ $2 per pound. You need cash to purchase the berries you pick and anything else you'd like such as freshly pressed apple juices, lunch, jams, or pies. Cardboard trays are $1.

Bathrooms: Yes. There are portables in the fields and nice bathrooms at the café and picnic area.

Facilities: Not stroller friendly; bring a baby carrier instead.

Food: Café has sandwiches and box lunches. Picnic area is available if you'd like to bring your own lunch. Homemade pies and fresh-squeezed juice are sold at the café. Fresh pressed apple cider is especially good, but be careful of giving the juice to little ones since it is not pasteurized. You can also purchase freshly picked fruit, jam, and honey at the main store.

Directions: Berry farms are located at the corner of Lakeview and Carlton. Look for signs. Watsonville is 20 min. south of Santa Cruz.

Phipps Country Store & Farm (Ages 3+)

(650) 879-0787; 2700 Pescadero Road, Pescadero, CA 94060
<www.phippscountry.com>

Description: In addition to strawberries and blackberries, Phipps Ranch also has a barnyard of animals. These animals include rabbits, goats, geese, chickens, ducks, turkeys, donkeys, pigs, and some exotic birds. Check the Web site before your trip for directions and weather. It is on the coast by Half Moon Bay, and the weather can be foggy and cool.

Schedule: Strawberry season: late April/mid-May–end of September (call to check on season). Olallieberry season: June–July. Boysenberry season: July. Call to confirm availability. Open April–October: 10am–

6pm, November–March: 10am–5pm.

Cost: The strawberries and blackberries are $2/lb. Additional entrance fee: $3/person ages 5–59, free/child younger than 5 or senior 60+.

Bathrooms: Portables.

Facilities: Strollers OK.

Food: No. Picnic lunch OK.

Swanton Farms (Ages 3+)

(831) 469-8804; Hwy 1 & Swanton Road, Davenport, CA 95017
<www.swantonberryfarm.com>

Description: This is an organic strawberry farm where you can pick berries yourself. It also provides farm tours, and large school groups are welcome. Visit Web site for map and directions.

Schedule: Season: late May–July 9am–6pm.

Cost: They range around $1.50/lb. for the berries.

Bathrooms: Portables.

Food: Farmstand has a few snacks, and prepicked fruits for sale.

Webb Ranch Farm (Ages 3+)

(650) 854-5417; Stand: (650) 854-3134; 2720 Alpine Rd., Menlo Park, CA 94025
<www.webbranchfarm.com>; <www.webbranchriding.com>

Description: Raspberries, blackberries, boysenberries, and olallieberries as well as melons, tomatoes, and pumpkins are available for U-pick. For Halloween, there's a haunted house and pumpkin patch. In December, the farm offers Christmas trees. Blue lake green beens, squash, and corn are also available for u-pick. Visit Web site for map and directions.

Schedule: Berry season: June to mid-July from Wed–Sun 10am–5pm. Pumpkin u-pick: October weekends 10am-4pm. Christmas trees: begins day after Thanksgiving. Pony rides begin late May. Hay rides begin early October. Both run on weekends 11am-4pm.

Cost: Pony and hay rides: $5/person. Hay ride free for kids 7 & under with paid adult.

Bathrooms: Portables.

Food: Farmstand has a few snacks and prepicked fruits for sale.

Follow-Up Activities: Riding lessons for kids ages 7–15 in the summer. Call (650) 854-7755 or visit <www.webbranchriding.com>.

Brentwood's Fruit Orchards

Many farms have planted lower-limbed trees that make picking accessible to all, even a toddler. Ladders are generally not necessary.

The Harvest Time Web site provides a comprehensive collection of farms in the Brentwood area. The following farms allow you to pick your own fruit. For an area map of Brentwood farms: <www.harvest4you.com>.

Bacchini's Fruit Tree

(925) 634-3645; 2010 Walnut Boulevard, Brentwood, CA 94513
<www.brentwoodfruit.com>

Description: Apricots (Flavor Giant, Katy, and Poppy), white peaches, plums, cherries, olallie blackberries, pluots, and loquats in late May to early July. Orchard is designed with lower-limbed trees so ladders will not usually be needed.

Hours: Daily in season 8am–4pm. Season opens around Memorial Day weekend. Check Web site for specific dates.

Cost: $1/lb to $3/lb, depending on the fruit.

Bathrooms: Portables.

Food: No.

Canciamilla Ranch

(925) 634-5123; 401 Eureka Avenue, Brentwood, CA 94513 (next to Seko Ranch)

Description: Peaches, nectarines, and plums beginning in late May. Peach varieties available: Spring Gold, Springcrest, and Babcock white peaches. Nectarine varieties available: Juneglo, Fire Bright, Independence, Fantasia, and assorted white nectarines. Plum varieties available: Satsuma and Santa Rosa.

Hours: May–August: Daily 9am–6pm.

Bathrooms: Portables.

Food: Picked fruit, dried fruit, walnuts, and ice cream are for sale. Picnic area available.

DC's Extraordinary Cherries

(925) 516-4495; Marsh Creek Road, Brentwood, CA 94513
(1 mile west of Walnut Blvd)

Description: Cherry varieties available: bing, Utah Giant, Sweet Anne, Rainier (white), and Van. Ladders not needed.
Hours: Memorial Day to mid-June, daily 8am–5pm
Bathrooms: Portables.
Food: No.

The Farmer's Daughter Produce

(925) 634-4827; Marsh Creek Road & Walnut Boulevard, Brentwood, CA 94513

Description: Cherries, apricots, freestone and cling peaches, nectarines, plums, white peaches, and white nectarines are available.
Hours: June to September 1. Mon–Fri: 8am–6pm, Sat: 6am–1pm, Sun: 7am–1pm. Tours and field trips on Tues and Thur with one week advance reservations available.
Bathrooms: Portables.
Food: Fruit and produce stand. Cold drinks available.

Freitas Cherry Ranch

(925) 634-5461; 555 Hoffman Lane, Brentwood, CA 94513
<www.freitasranch.com>

Description: Coral Champagne cherries. Ladders & buckets provided.
Hours: May 14–June, weekends only in season: 8am–5pm. Call to confirm availability.
Cost: $2.50/lb.
Bathrooms: Portables.
Food: No.

The Gerry's Fruit Bowl

(925) 634-3155; Marsh Creek Road and Orchard Lane, Brentwood, CA 94513

Description: *Peaches:* June–Aug.15; *Nectarines:* July. Ten varieties.
Hours: Opens first week of June, weekends & holidays in season: 8am–5pm.
Bathrooms: Portables.
Food: No.

Gursky Ranch Country Store

(925) 634-4913; 1921 Apricot Way, Brentwood, CA 94513
(½ mile west of Fairview Avenue)
<http://home.pacbell.net/roygur/>

Description: Roy and Lynn Gursky own this "pick your own" walnuts orchard. The season is mid-September to December. These walnut trees have been specially grown so that someone in a wheelchair can pick them. The store also sells 10 other kinds of nuts (either in-shell or meats), candied fruits and nuts (from plain to gourmet), honey, garlic items, flavored vinegars, olive oil, soup mixes, fruit butters, preserves, etc. Dried fruits, gift baskets, and boxed selections of other gourmet nut and fruit items are available for purchase.

Hours: mid-September–December: Weekends only 9am-4pm.

Lopez Ranch

(925) 634-4433
Marsh Creek Road, Brentwood, CA 94513; 1¼ miles west of Walnut Boulevard.

Description: Bing and white Rainier cherries, white & Freestone peaches, plums, nectarines, and apples (Mutsu, Granny Smith, and Fuji varieties).
Hours: Open daily late-May through September: 8am–5pm.
Bathrooms: Portables.
Food: No.

Maggiore Cherry Ranch (Ages 5+)

(925) 634-4176; Walnut Boulevard and Balfour Road, Brentwood, CA 94513
(On Walnut Boulevard, ½ mile south of Balfour Road)

Description: Bing, Brooks, and Corral Champagne cherries available May 14–mid-June. Keep in mind that children are not allowed on ladders. Call in advance to confirm availability.
Hours: Daily mid-May to mid-June: 8am–4pm.
Bathrooms: Portables.
Food: No. Picnicking OK.

Moffat Ranch (Ages 5+)

(925) 634-3049; 1870 Walnut Boulevard, Brentwood, CA 94513
(just north of Marsh Creek Road)

Description: Peaches (Suncrest, Faye Elberta, O'Henry, and Elegant Lady) and nectarines (Fantasia and July Red). Bring containers. Most varieties last approximately two weeks. Ladders provided.
Hours: Open daily during season: 8am–5pm mid-July–mid-August.
Cost: ~$1–$1.50/lb, depending on market conditions.
Bathrooms: Portables.
Food: No. No picnicking allowed. ~2 miles to downtown Brentwood.

Papini Farms
(925) 634-6319; 2750 Concord Avenue & Walnut Blvd., Brentwood, CA 94513

Description: Cherries, early variety Springcrest peaches, apricots, nectarines, white peaches, and plums (Santa Rosa & Queen Rosa). Buckets provided for picking and boxes for the fruit. Ladders provided, but ladders are only needed for the cherries.
Hours: Daily late May—mid-July: 8am–4pm.
Cost: ~$1/lb for apricots, peaches, plums, and nectarines, depending on market conditions. ~$1.50 to $2/lb for cherries.
Bathrooms: Portables.
Food: No. No picnicking allowed.

Pease Ranch
(925) 634-4646; Marsh Creek Road, Brentwood, CA 94513
(1 mile west of Hwy 4 or 2 miles east of Vasco Road/Walnut Boulevard)

Description: Cherries (Bing, Rainier, Chinook, Early Burlat, Jubilee, Van, etc.), boysenberries, olallieberries, and loganberries. The best time for the cherries is one week before and one week after Memorial Day. Ladders available, but only for those more than 12 years old due to insurance requirements.
Hours: Open daily May–June: 8am–5pm.
Cost: ~ $1.50/lb for cherries and ~$1.75/lb for berries.
Bathrooms: Portables and hand washing area.
Food: No. Picnics OK and plenty of shade. Juice, soda, and mineral water for sale. ~5 miles to downtown Brentwood.

Pomeroy Farms

(925) 634-3080

Marsh Creek Road, Brentwood, CA 94513; west of Walnut Boulevard

<www.pomeroyfarm.com>

Description: Bing, Brooks, and White Rainier cherries; nectarines; apricots, and peaches. White Rainier and Brooks cherries are located on Marsh Creek Rd. west of Walnut Blvd. (Vasco Rd.). Bing & White Rainier cherries are located on Payne Avenue east of Walnut Blvd. Cherry season starts mid-May to mid-June. Flavorcrest and Springcrest Peaches and nectarines are available late May to June. Patterson and Westley apricots are available mid-May to mid-June at orchard on the east end of Eureka Avenue. See map on Web site for location of orchards.

Hours: May 20 through July.

Cost: NA.

Bathrooms: Portables.

Food: No.

Seko Cherry Ranch

(925) 634-3771; Eureka Avenue, Brentwood, CA 94513; West of Walnut Blvd.

Description: Bing cherries for you to pick. Prepicked Burlat and Mono cherries for sale.

Hours: Season is mid-May to mid-June: 8am–5pm.

Cost: ~$2/lb.

Bathrooms: Portables.

Food: No. No picnicking allowed.

Sharp Ranch

(925) 513-1517; 795 Hoffman Lane, Brentwood, CA 94513

(¾ mile South of Marsh Creek Road)

Description: Bing cherries.

Hours: Season starts mid-May. Open during season Thur–Fri: 8am–4pm or by appointment.

Bathrooms: Portables.

Food: No.

Smith Family Farm

(925) 625-5966; 625-3544; 4430 Sellers Avenue, Brentwood, CA 94513
<www.smithfamilyfarm.com>

Description: Boysenberries, tomatoes (more than 50 varieties), pumpkins, and Christmas trees that you can pick yourself.
Hours: May–November: fruit stand open daily 8am–5pm. On weekends, U-pick boysenberries. Open in December for Christmas trees.
Cost: $5.50/person for the farm tours for school groups.
Bathrooms: Portables.
Food: No.
Follow-Up Activities: Fall Pumpkin Harvest held in October features hayrides, a pumpkin patch, live music, farm animals kids can pet, hay tunnel, scarecrows, a corn maze, and sunflowers. There's a picnic area and a replica of a Coast Miwok Village. Farm tours for school groups are available in April, May, June, and October.

Tidrick Ranch

(925) 634-5115; 1800 Orchard Lane, Brentwood, CA 94513

Description: Bing cherries.
Hours: Memorial Day to mid-June: daily 8am–dusk.
Cost: ~$2/lb.
Bathrooms: Portables.
Food: Hot dogs and snacks only. Picnics OK.

Wolfe Ranch (Ages 5+)

(925) 634-1308; 2111 Concord Avenue, Brentwood, CA 94513;
700 Marsh Creek Road; 164 Payne Avenue (Peaches)
<www.peterwolfe.com>

Description: Cherries (bing, white rainier, and van) from late-May to the early-June. Peaches available from mid-May to late-July. Black friar plums are available for picking at Payne Avenue. Prepicked apricots (blenheim, helena, castlebrite, perfections, patterson), loquats, heirloom tomatoes, and homemade honey for sale. Different orchard locations. Check Web site for current availability and locations/directions.
Hours: Memorial Day to July. Open daily: 8:30am–4:30pm.
Bathrooms: Portables.
Food: No.

Sonoma County's Pick Your Own Farms

Chileno Valley Ranch

(877) 280-6664; (707) 765-6664; 5105 Chileno Valley Rd., Petaluma, CA 94952
<www.chilenobnb.com>

Description: Organic apple varieties include Orin, Pinova, Molly's Delicious, and Jonathan's Pride. Visitors are encouraged to explore the ranch and enjoy the wildlife, gardens, and land of the ranch.
Hours: Closed Dec & Jan. Call to make an appointment to pick apples during apple season.
Cost: $2/lb.
Bathrooms: Portables.
Food: No.

Gabriel Farm

(707) 829-0617; 3175 Sullivan Road, Sebastopol, CA 95472
<www.gabrielfarm.com>

Description: Organic apples available for u-pick. Each visit includes a farm tour explaining the processes of an organic farm and the difference between organic and conventional farms. It also sells prepicked asian pears and persimmons.
Hours: September: by appointment. Times that work best are: Mon & Tues mornings or Wed, Fri, and Sun. Saturdays are okay, too.
Cost: $2/lb. Suggested budget is $20/visit.
Bathrooms: Portables.
Food: No.
Follow-Up Activities: Tours for school and other groups.

Green Valley Chestnut Ranch

(707) 829-3304; 11100 Green Valley Road, Sebastopol, CA 95472
<www.chestnutranch.com>

Description: Organic chestnuts are available in October/November. In the past, open house weekends in early October offered orchard tours, chestnuts u-pick, and sampling of roasted chestnuts. The store also sells chestnut honey, crème, and other chestnut-related items. Bring gloves, chestnut pods are sharp.

Hours: November to December weekend afternoons by appointment.
Bathrooms: Portables.
Food: No.

Hoffman Farm
(707) 226-8938; 2125 Silverado Trail, Napa, CA 94558

Description: Offers Bartlett pears, sugar prunes, peaches, persimmons, quinces, and walnuts.
Hours: August to early-December daily 9am-5pm.
Cost: $2/lb.
Bathrooms: Portables.
Food: No.

Chapter 3
Bees, Butterflies, & Bugs

Insects play an important role in the environment. Butterflies and bees are pollinators that help us farm; ants, earthworms, and termites help us decompose dead plant materials; and spiders and ladybugs help keep other bugs under control.

Kids love bugs. They are fascinated with ladybug beetles, beautiful butterflies and dragonflies, bees, and spiders. Learning about insects and their life cycles provides a wonderful introduction to nature and the world of science.

To learn about insects, visit the Oakland Zoo's Bug House within the Children's Zoo area, the Randall Museum in San Francisco, or the Insect Zoo within San Francisco Zoo's Children's Zoo area. San Francisco Zoo's Insect Zoo has an extensive collection with bees, beetles, millipedes, centipedes, praying mantis, and many other interesting bugs.

Learn how bees make honey, how they dance to communicate, and the important role they play as pollinators. San Francisco Zoo's Insect Zoo, the Randall Museum in San Francisco, and the Children's Discovery Museum in San Jose have see-through beehives. Coyote Point Museum in San Mateo has a wonderful exhibit showing how bees dance to communicate how far away flowers are from their hive.

Visit butterfly habitats at Natural Bridges, in Pacific Grove, and at Point Lobos State Reserve in Carmel to learn about monarch butterflies, their life cycle, and their migration routes. Six Flags Marine World's walk-through Butterfly Kingdom allows you to experience butterflies flying all around. Occasionally, the Conservatory of Flowers in Golden Gate Park has exhibits on pollinators and butterflies.

Butterflies:
Recommended books on butterflies:
- *The Very Hungry Caterpillar* by Eric Carle (for preschoolers).
- *Monarch Magic! Butterfly Activities & Nature Discoveries* by Lynn M. Rosenblatt (for ages 4–12).
- *My Monarch Journal* by Connie Muther (Parent-Teacher Edition) (for grades 1+). This book has detailed time lapse photos of the egg to caterpillar to butterfly stages, as well as areas for students to make observations and guided questions and discussion tips for parents and teachers. Best when used with a live egg to watch through the many stages of the monarch's life cycle.

For monarch butterflies, Natural Bridges Visitor Center provides in-depth exhibits about these special butterflies, their migration routes, their life cycle, their habitats, and much more. Natural Bridges Visitor Center provides easy stroller access between the parking lot, the visitor center, and the grove where the butterflies cluster on the eucalyptus trees. On-site docents are extremely knowledgeable and provide an enriching experience. The only drawback is the distance from the butterflies perched high on the eucalyptus trees, making them rather hard to see. To grow your own butterflies and silkworms, visit <www.insectlore.com> for live insect kits.

Ardenwood Historic Farm in Fremont has butterfly and bird programs on select days in the winter and early spring. See the full entry Chapter 1: Animal Kingdom—Farms for event information.

CityBugs (Ages 4+)
<http://nature.berkeley.edu/citybugs>

The wonderful Web site has links to on-line bug museums, information on insects and spiders, teacher lesson plans, student games and activities, and an "ask the experts" section where you can e-mail your questions to UC Berkeley entomologists. There's also a bank of previously asked questions and answers. It participates in Cal Day at UC Berkeley, held annually in early April. For more details on Cal Day, see the entry in Chapter 10: Seasonal Events. Visit <www.berkeley.edu/calday> for current information on Cal Day.

Essig Museum of Entomology (Ages 4+)

(510) 643-0804; Room 211, Wellman Hall, UC Berkeley, Berkeley, CA 94720
<essig.berkeley.edu>; Map: <www.berkeley.edu/map>

Description: Displays of bees, beetles, butterflies, etc. in the hallway of Wellman Hall. This museum is not generally open to the public. The collection is for research and sharing within the scientific community. However, school groups and individuals may arrange for tours. There are on-line exhibits. It also participates in Cal Day. For current information on Cal Day: <www.berkeley.edu/calday>.

Henry Cowell Redwoods State Park (All Ages)

(831) 438-2396, 335-7077; (831) 335-3174 Mountain Parks Foundation
101 North Big Trees Park Road, Felton, CA 95018
<www.mountainparks.org>; <www.parks.ca.gov/default.asp?page_id=546>

Description: The "Bug Day" event in May 11am–4pm features puppet shows, displays, art projects, etc.

Junior Nature Museum (All Ages)

McClellan Ranch Park in Cupertino has live insects on display. Displays vary week by week, depending on the season and availability. Call prior to visit for details. See entry in Chapter 1: Animal Kingdom—Farms.

Natural Bridges State Beach (All Ages)

(831) 423-4609; 2531 West Cliff Drive, Santa Cruz, CA 95060
<www.parks.ca.gov/default.asp?page_id=541>
<www.santacruzstateparks.org>

Description: The Visitor Center has exhibits on the migration routes and life cycle of the monarch butterfly. The park maintains a milkweed demonstration patch so visitors can view the larvae, caterpillars, and chrysalis. Milkweed is the only plant eaten by the monarch larva (caterpillar). Don't forget to pick up the brochure *The Monarch Butterfly* by the California State Parks. The bookstore located in the Visitor Center is great for children's books on butterflies and other insects. Allow approximately 1 hour for butterfly viewing. Don't forget to pick up your map to the Natural Bridges State Beach at the Visitor Center.

Hours: 8am–sunset. Docent-led tours are available on weekends mid-

October to February at 11am & 2pm. The tours last for ~45 minutes. "Welcome Back Monarchs Day" in October celebrates their migration to the Bay Area. The "Migration Festival" in February signals their departure. Visitor center open most weekends and some weekdays; call to verify its hours prior to visit.

Cost: $6 day use fee.

Bathrooms: Located at the visitor center and by the beach. There are dressing rooms and outdoor showers to wash off the sand.

Facilities: Stroller friendly to butterfly viewing area only.

Food: No. Picnic tables and barbecues are available.

What to Bring: Sweaters and jackets, binoculars for viewing butterflies, and camera or video camera if you'd like. Bring sand toys and beach gear if you're thinking about going to the beach afterward. Don't forget sunscreen. If you go tide pooling here, be prepared to have an extra set of clothes and shoes, as you'll be climbing over some rocks and may get a bit dirty. Be careful of the slippery rocks! See the Tide Pooling section for additional details.

Follow-Up Activities: 1) If it's a warm day, you may want to spend extra time at Natural Bridges Beach and go tide pooling. 2) Consider visiting Seymour Marine Discovery Center, either before or after Natural Bridges, since it's just around the corner. To get there from Natural Bridges, as you're exiting Natural Bridge's entrance, turn left onto Swanton, away from the beach. Make a left onto Delaware. The Seymour Marine Discovery Center entrance is at the end of Delaware. 3) Also, Santa Cruz Beach Boardwalk is close by. If you're thinking about going to Santa Cruz Beach Boardwalk, consider going to Natural Bridges in the morning, then spending the afternoon at the Boardwalk.

Magical Beginnings Butterfly Farms of Los Gatos (All Ages)

(408) 395-5123; (888) 639-9995 Toll free
114 Royce Street, Suite H, Los Gatos, CA 95030
<www.butterflyevents.com>; <www.magicalbeginnings.com>

1) Purchase butterflies for release at birthday parties or other events. 1-2 dozen butterflies cost $95; cost per dozen decreases with increased volume.

2) They sell 19 varieties of milkweed seeds online through <www.butterflyencounters.com>. Milkweed is the sole host plant that butterfly

caterpillars feed on.

3) They sell live insect kits with live catepillars and lady bugs through <www.magicalbeginnings.com> under "Educational Insect Kits."

Monarch Grove Sanctuary (All Ages)

(831) 375-0982; (888) PG-MONARCH
Ridge Road & Lighthouse Avenue, Pacific Grove, CA 93950

Description: Friends of the Monarchs and the Pacific Grove Museum of Natural History have docent programs to guide visitors.

Hours: Always open. During butterfly season from late October through February, docent are stationed at the site. *Weekdays:* noon–3pm. *Sat & Sun:* 10am–sunset. Special docent tours can be reserved in advance for groups. The sanctuary has been reopened since Oct. 2005.

Cost: Free.

Bathrooms: Portables.

Facilities: Stroller friendly.

Food: No.

What to Bring: Binoculars, camera or video camera, warm jacket, and picnic lunch.

Follow-Up Activities: 1) Learn about the migration of the monarch butterflies and their life cycle from the Pacific Grove Museum of Natural History. See entry below. 2) Grow your own caterpillars and other insects with a kit: <www.insectlore.com> 3) Friends of the Monarchs' Web site has detailed information on the monarch's life cycle, migration, and habitat: <www.pgmonarchs.org/fomh.html>, <www.pgmonarchs.org/foml.html>.

Directions: Directions from the Pacific Grove Museum of Natural History Web site: <www.pgmuseum.org> select "Monarchs," then "Map & Directions," for a detailed map to Monarch Grove Sanctuary: <www.93950.com/monarchs.htm>.

Pacific Grove Museum of Natural History

(831) 648-5716; 165 Forest Avenue, Pacific Grove, CA 93950
<www.pgmuseum.org>

Description: The museum has an exhibit on the monarch butterflies. See Chapter 1: Animal Kingdom—Zoos & Wildlife Museums,

Point Lobos State Reserve (All Ages)

Point Lobos State Reserve is also host to wintering monarch butterflies. Ask the guard at the entrance gate to direct you to the butterflies. For full entry, see Chapter 1: Animal Kingdom—Nature Preserves.

Randall Museum (Ages 2+)

(415) 554-9600; 199 Museum Way, San Francisco, CA 94114
<www.randallmuseum.org>

Description: The museum has bug exhibits and a special "Bug Day" in April. See Chapter 1: Animal Kingdom—Zoos & Wildlife Museums.

San Leandro Monarch Tours (All Ages)

(510) 577-6085; **Starts from** Mulford-Marina Branch Library: **13699 Aurora Drive, San Leandro, CA 94577**

Description: Monarch Bay Golf Course is an overwintering site for monarch butterlies. The City of San Leandro conducts docent-led monarch butterfly tours from October through January. School group tour dates available by appointment on Tue & Fri at 10am & 11:30am. Contact <**butterflynaturalist@earthlink.net**> to reserve.

Hours: Saturdays: 11:30 am, 1:30 pm, & 2:30 pm from October through the end of January. Registration not required.

Cost: Free tours on Saturdays for the public. School tours cost $40/group from San Leandro school or $55/group from non-San Leandro schools.

What to Bring: Binoculars, camera or video camera, & warm jacket.

Six Flags Discovery Kingdom (Ages 3+)

(707) 643-6722; 1001 Fairgrounds Drive, Vallejo, CA 94589
<www.sixflags.com/parks/discoverykingdom>

Description: *Butterfly World* inside Six Flags Discovery Kingdom. For full entry, see Chapter 1: Animal Kingdom—Marine Life .

Youth Science Institute – Sanborn Park (Ages 3+)

(408) 867-6940; 16055 Sanborn Road, Saratoga, CA 95070
<www.ysi-ca.org>

Sanborn YSI site has an annual Insect Fair in early May. $5 parking fee.

Chapter 4
Science & Technology Museums

The physical world we live in is fascinating. Science museums provide interactive exhibits to help us learn about the physical world. These museums show us how physical work can be converted into energy and electricity, how the microprocessor works, how the ocean tides work, how the water cycle works on earth, and how the solar system and the universe work. Some of these museums cater to the learning style of very young children, some cater to school age children, and some to adults.

For current museum events in the Bay Area, visit <www.onlyinsanfrancisco.com/calendar>—select "Museums."

How Come? by Kathy Wollard answers many questions from kids such as why the sky is blue, why giraffes have long necks, why bubbles are round, and more (Workman Publishing).

Bay Area Discovery Museum (All Ages)
(415) 339-3900; East Fort Baker: 557 McReynolds Road, Sausalito, CA 94965 <www.badm.org>

Description: The museum has many small buildings where exhibits are housed. A changing exhibit area provides space for exhibits such as the Wizard of Oz, Arthur, Clifford, etc; some of these exhibits also visit the Children's Discovery Museum in San Jose at different times. One of the things that makes this museum unique is the abundance of plays, concerts, and shows. It also hosts annual festivals throughout the year such as the "Chinese New Year Festival," "Asian Pacific Heritage Festival," and "Kwanzaa Celebration." The museum has drop-in art and open ceramic studios; check Web site for times. Many exploration areas for tots as well as their older siblings.

Hours: Closed Monday. *Tues–Fri:* 9am–4pm, *Sat & Sun:* 10am–5pm.
Cost: $8.50/adult, $7.50/ child. Free/child under 1. *Free second Saturday each month for families (free admission 1–5pm).* Web site has information on discounts and discount coupon. AAA, California Alumni, and KQED members receive $1 discount/person, up to 5 people. $1/person discount for Young Audiences Arts Card <www.artscard.info> for up to 2 adults. Entertainment coupon book: free admission for 1 adult when accompanied by child.
Bathrooms: Yes.
Facilities: Stroller accessible only between buildings. Strollers are not allowed inside the buildings.
Food: Yes, although on busy days it's very crowded, and places to sit and eat are limited. It's a good idea to pack a picnic lunch.
What to Bring: Warm jacket and windbreaker, especially in the winter. The museum is laid out as a series of small buildings. To go from area to area, you have to go outside to the next building. It's a good idea to bring a picnic lunch because the café gets overwhelmingly crowded. Don't forget to bring cash for the bridge crossing (free for carpools during commute hours).
Follow-Up Activities: 1) Check the Web site for exhibit and special event schedules. There have been concerts, circus troupes, acrobats, Chinese New Year celebrations, Annual Goblin Jamboree in October, Gingerbread House (build your own) after Thanksgiving & December, and Kwanzaa Celebration (December). 2) Birthday parties. 3) Spring & summer camps as well as classes.

Bay Model Visitor Center (Ages 5+)

(415) 332-3871; 2100 Bridgeway, Sausalito, CA 94965
<www.spn.usace.army.mil/bmvc/>

Description: The Bay Model simulates the San Francisco Bay's and the Sacramento Delta's rise and fall of tides, flow and currents of water, and mixing of freshwater and saltwater. Exhibits on the estuary, wildlife habitats, and geography of the bay as well as the history of a World War II Sausalito shipyard. Workshops for kids (K–college) help students learn about marine mammals and their habitat, bay and delta, oil spills, water quality, tides, water cycle, etc.
Hours: *From Labor Day to Memorial Day:* Closed Sun & Mon. Tues–

Sat: 9am–4pm. *From Memorial Day to Labor Day:* Closed Mon. Tues–Fri: 9am–4pm, Sat & Sun: 10am–5pm.
Cost: Free.
Bathrooms: Yes.
Facilities: Stroller friendly.
Food: No. Picnic tables available.
What to Bring: Picnic lunch, jacket, and cash for crossing the bridge.
Follow-Up Activities: 1) Ranger guided tours for school groups & workshops for teachers available. 2) Special events and weekend docent-guided tours. Check Web site for calendar.

California Academy of Sciences (All Ages)
Golden Gate Park
(415) 321-8000; *Temporary Location:* 875 Howard Street, San Francisco, CA 94103; 55 Concourse Drive, San Francisco, CA 94118 *(reopening 2008)* <www.calacademy.org>

Description: 1) The Academy has a temporary location until 2008 in downtown San Francisco. It remains open to the public. Check the Web site for the latest information on the move back to the permanent location in Golden Gate Park. 2) The Academy of Sciences is a complex of three institutions that includes the Steinhart Aquarium, Natural History Museum, and Morrison Planetarium. The Natural History Museum includes exhibits of dinosaurs, African wildlife, California wildlife, earthquakes, insects, minerals, and changing exhibits. Past exhibits are archived on the Web site. If you've missed the chocolate or dinosaur exhibit, visit the Web site for archived exhibits. The Steinhart Aquarium has exhibits on the living coral reef, tropical sharks, seahorses, reptiles and amphibians, and a penguin colony. There is also a touch pool and a fish roundabout. The planetarium includes shows for young children; however, the planetarium is closed until the permanent location in Golden Gate Park reopens. For more information on the planetarium, see the full entry in Chapter 5: Planetarium & Observatories.

Hours: 10am–5pm every day of the year. Third Thursday of the month: open until 9pm; 5pm-9pm, $5/person admission. On Saturday mornings, there's Children's Story Time geared for children from 3–7 years old. Books are chosen from the Biodiversity Center Library based on monthly topics. Tours for all ages scheduled Wed–Fri at 12 noon & 1pm, and on the 1st and 3rd weekends at 10:30am and 11:30am. Check at the information desk upon arrival on available tours.

Cost: *Free admission on the first Wednesday of each month.* $10/adult; $6.50/youth (12–17), student w/ ID, & senior 65+; $2/child (4–11); free/child 3 & under. Annual membership: $60/family. City Pass has 50% admission to the museum but provides admission to 6 attractions in San Francisco. Arts Card holders: $1 discount per child & up to 2 adults. Homeschool days: $1/person. Check Web site for specific days. *Planetarium tickets*: $2.50/adult, $1.25/youth (6–17) & senior 65+. San Francisco residents have additional "Neighborhood Free Days" depending on zip code and proof of residency in the form of a driver's license or utility bill. Check the Web site under "Admission" for the schedule or call (415) 750-7144.

Bathrooms: Yes.

Facilities: Stroller friendly.

Food: Cafe.

What to Bring: Quarters for metered parking and cash for food. Don't forget to bring a jacket, since San Francisco can be a bit cool, even in the summertime.

Follow-Up Activities: 1) Birthday parties. 2) Many educational programs for families and schools. Summer camps for ages 6-16. Visit the Web site <www.calacademy.org/education> and download the brochure for additional information. 2) Homeschool days. 3) Lectures related to current exhibits and research done at the Academy. 4) See Chapter 12: Science and Arts Education—Science & Technology Education for more details of educational offerings.

Chabot Space & Science Center (Ages 5+)

(510) 336-7300; (510) 336-7373 Box Office
10000 Skyline Boulevard, Oakland, CA 94619
<www.chabotspace.org>

Description: Learn about the history of our space explorations; see our planet, our solar system, and the Milky Way. Learn about the sun and the various types of eclipses. There are also traveling exhibits. Discovery Lab is a wonderful hands-on exploration area for younger kids.

Hours: *Regular hours (Sept – July):* Closed Mon & Tue. Wed–Thur: 10am–5pm, Fri–Sat: 10am–10pm, Sun: 11am–5pm. *Telescope viewing* on Fri & Sat. evenings. April–October: dusk–10:30pm (Daylight Savings Time) & November–March: 7:30–10:30pm. Open on certain holidays from 10am–5pm. Closed Christmas Day & Thanksgiving Day. Check Web site for most current schedule.

Cost: *General Admission includes 1 show:* $13/adult, $9/child (3–12), $10/student w/ ID or senior 65+, free/child under 3. *Planetarium or Megadome Theater:* $8/adult, $7/child or senior.

Bathrooms: Yes.

Facilities: Stroller friendly.

Food: Café on site.

What to Bring: Cash for food and planetarium tickets.

Follow-Up Activities: 1) Summer camps. 2) Birthday parties. 3) Techbridge Summer Academy offers summer classes to encourage girls in science and technology fields, <techbridgegirls.org>. 4) Challenger Learning Center provides programs for groups as well as the general public. Programs include simulated space missions. For kids ages 8 to 12, costs $15/adult, $12/youth or senior. Call (510) 336-7421 to make reservations. From the home page, select "Challenger Learning Center," then "Community & Family Missions." 5) Archived online exhibits and resources, including "Ask an Astronomer" on the "Virtual Science Center."

Children's Discovery Museum (Ages 2–10)

(408) 298-5437; 180 Woz Way, San Jose, CA 95110
<www.cdm.org>

Description: This is our favorite children's museum. We find it to be a safe and wonderfully engaging place for children as young as two. It has a permanent exhibit of transportation items including signal lights, an ambulance, a fire truck, and sometimes the Wells Fargo stagecoach. Interactive energy exhibits show how different kinds of work can be turned into electricity to power lights, a fan, and an airplane. There's a sound exhibit for kids to experience rhythm and how sounds "look" on the scope. There's also an exhibit for kids to interact with bubbles. There's a wonderful water play area to experience all kinds of fun with water and balls. There are two art studios, and a little garden open during the summer. The wonderful list goes on. Twice a year, special traveling exhibits such as Arthur's World, Richard Scary's Busy Town, Alice in Wonderland, Wizard of Oz, etc. come to Children's Discovery Museum. Call or check the Web site for the most current exhibit information. Don't miss the shows that correspond to the special traveling exhibit. Check show times under the "Information" icon under "Calendar" on the Web site, usually on weekends. The shows usually ask the studio audience children to volunteer and participate. Don't miss the beehive and the old-fashioned clothes tub and clothesline located in the exhibit area next to the garden entrance. Upstairs, there's a cornhusk doll making station staffed with volunteers to help you create these dolls yourself. The Wonder Cabinet is upstairs for children under 5 to play with sand, art, pretend, and read. Allow 2 hours or more for your trip, depending on the age and attention span of your child. We've arrived at 11am and stayed until closing time. **Hours:** Closed Mondays. Open Tues–Sat: 10am–5pm, Sun: noon–5pm. Check the Web site. Open during some holidays such as Martin Luther King Day.

Cost: *Admission*: $7/child or adult, $6/senior (60+), free/infant under 1 year old. *Show*: $1/person. Purchase the show tickets from the "Post Office" beneath the stairs to the second floor. Cash only for the show tickets. *Parking:* Parking in the city owned lots varies from $3 to $7 per car, depending on the day and whether there are special events close by. If you plan to visit often, consider purchasing the family membership.

Bathrooms: Yes, including a family restroom.

Facilities: Day use lockers. Stroller friendly. ATM located next to the bookstore.

Food: Café.

What to Bring: Camera and cash for parking, lunch, and show. Don't forget a change of clothes since water play can get the kids wet.

Follow-Up Activities: 1) Art and science classes for all ages, including toddlers. 2) Summer camps. For descriptions of classes and schedule, you can call or go to the Web site and select the "Information" icon, then the "Parent/Child Workshop" icon (for ages 2–10), or the "calendar" icon for a full list of classes. 3) Birthday parties.

Directions: For a detailed map of the Children's Discovery Museum and the surrounding area in downtown San Jose, go to the Web site, and select the "Information" icon, then the "Directions & Parking" icon.

Computer History Museum (Ages 14+)

(650) 810-1010; 1401 N. Shoreline Boulevard, Mountain View, CA 94043
<www.computerhistory.org>

Description: Finally, Silicon Valley has a museum dedicated to computing, from the first abacus and slide rule to the very first computers (ILLIAC, JOHNNIAC & Cray) and the Apple One to the Internet today.

The museum documents the history of the microprocessor, the Internet, and the timeline of computer history.

Hours: Wed, Fri, & Sun: 1–4pm, Sat: 11am–5pm. Docent-led tours at 11:30am (Sat. only), 1pm & 2:30pm (Wed, Fri, & Sat); Sunday tour times vary.

Cost: Free.

Bathrooms: Yes.

Facilities: Stroller friendly.

Food: No, but restaurants are across the street.

Follow-Up Activities: An online exhibit and a free lecture series show the history of computing. Special tours can be arranged by calling (650) 810-1038.

Exploratorium (Ages 4+)
Palace of Fine Arts

(415) EXP-LORE; (415) 561-0360; Tactile Dome Reservations: (415) 561-0362;
3601 Lyon Street, San Francisco, CA 94123
<www.exploratorium.edu>

Description: This museum is all about interactive exhibits to demystify science and technology. The hands-on exhibits help the visitor experience and better understand physical forces such as momentum, light and optics, sound, and temperature. Upstairs, the Traits of Life exhibit provides actual examples of how plants use energy from the sun and produce the oxygen we breathe and how proteins are assembled from the code of life, DNA. The Tactile Dome is a whole new experience in touch; it's all done in the dark. It is extremely popular, and requires advanced reservations. All the exhibits are made on site in the workshop. There's a theater that shows videos on various science and art topics to enhance the exhibits. Changing exhibits round out the museum's offerings. Don't miss the Web casts that provide more in-depth explorations and go beyond the walls of the museum. Topics include solar eclipse, mold science: cheese, biology of DNA, etc.

Hours: Closed Mondays. Tues–Sun: 10am–5pm. Closed Thanksgiving Day and Christmas Day. Open on Mondays for holidays such as Martin Luther King, Jr. Day; Presidents' Day; Memorial Day; and Labor Day.

Cost: *Free admission on the first Wednesday of each month.* $13/adult (18–64), $10/student (over 18 w/ ID) or senior, $10/disabled person or youth (13–17), $8/child 4–12, free/child 3 & under. For those over 7 years old, the *Tactile Dome* includes general admission: $16/person. To purchase tickets to the Tactile Dome, call: (415) 561-0362. *Membership:* $80/year for a family of 2 adults & their children under 18. This membership is well worth considering because of its discounted admission to many museums in the Bay Area, including the Tech Museum, Zeum, Lindsay Wildlife Museum, Chabot Space & Science Center, Lawrence Hall of Science, Happy Hollow, etc.

Bathrooms: Yes.
Facilities: Stroller friendly.
Food: Café.
What to Bring: Cash for food purchase.
Follow-Up Activities: 1) Birthday parties for members' children ages 6–12. 2) Programs for schools and other youth groups. 3) Many classes (ages 3+) and summer camps (ages 7–14) offered to children of members. Members' classes typically take place on Saturday afternoons 2–4pm. These classes cost $30/class per child. See entry in Chapter 12: Science and Arts Education—Science & Technology Education for details.

Hall of Health (Ages 5+)

(510) 549-1564; 2230 Shattuck Ave (Lower Level), Berkeley, CA 94704
<www.hallofhealth.org>

Description: Started as an exhibit in the Alta Bates Hospital lobby, it is now a permanent museum sponsored by the Children's Hospital Oakland. Located just across the hall from Habitot Children's Museum, the focus of the museum is health education, helping visitors learn about human body systems, nutrition, puberty, safety, drugs and addiction, and health and the environment. There are hands-on exhibits including body and organ models as well as some medical equipment for kids to play doctor. There is a *Kids on the Block* puppet show focusing on topics such as blindness, Down syndrome, and other conditions to help promote understanding of differences. (On a request basis — call for details.)

Hours: Tues–Sat: 10am–4pm.
Cost: $5/person, free/child under 3.
Bathrooms: Yes.
Facilities: Stroller friendly.
Food: No, but restaurants are in the building and nearby.
Follow-Up Activities: Field trips for groups led by a docent.

Intel Museum (Ages 8+)
Main Lobby, Intel Corporation's Robert Noyce Building
(408) 765-0503; 2200 Mission College Boulevard, Santa Clara, CA 95054
<www.intel.com/museum>

Description: Intel Museum provides the history of the microprocessor and has exhibits showing how transistors and microprocessors work and how computer chips are made. Learn how Silicon Valley got its name. There's a dress up area for visitors to suit up to enter a clean room. A virtual tour is on the Web site.

Hours: *Mon–Fri:* 9am–6pm, *Sat:* 10am–5pm. Closed Sundays & holidays. Check Web site for closure dates.

Cost: Free.

Bathrooms: Yes.

Facilities: Stroller friendly.

Food: No.

What to Bring: No bags or backpacks are allowed inside the museum. There are also no coat check services. Please plan accordingly.

Follow-Up Activities: 1) Tours of the museum available Mon–Fri 10am–4pm. To schedule, call (408) 765-0503. School group tours available for grades K–12. 2) Wonderful Web site provides additional information on how transistors and microprocessors work and how computer chips are designed and made. 3) "Journey Inside" provides multimedia lessons online about computers, circuits and switches, microprocessors, the Internet, etc. 4) "Design and Discovery" is an online curriculum for kids ages 11-15 to learn about engineering, designing, modeling, prototyping, and final presentation of designed products. 5) Intel sponsors two science and technology competitions: *Intel Science Talent Search* and the *Intel International Science and Engineering Fair*, both highly prestigious competitions with significant awards and prizes.

Junior Center of Art and Science (Ages 2–9)
Lakeside Park
(510) 839-5777; 558 Bellevue Avenue, Oakland, CA 94610
<www.juniorcenter.org>

Description: There is a drop-in art studio, a pottery studio, a Nature Room, a woodworking studio, and an exhibit on California Native Americans. The exhibit shows the tools, baskets, food, games, hunting techniques, and housing used by the American Indians. It is designed for schools and is usually reserved for them between 10:30am–2pm. Drop-in art and science activities are for children of all ages, including preschoolers. **Hours:** *September–May*: Tues–Fri: 10am–6pm, Sat: 10am–3pm, *June– August*: Mon–Thur: 8:30am–5:30pm. **Cost:** Free admission. Fee based afterschool and Saturday art, science, and carpentry classes for children ages 5–17. Registration is required. Pottery studio: $7/hr for adults, $5/hr for kids plus cost of the ceramic item. **Bathrooms:** Yes. **Facilities:** Stroller friendly. **Food:** No. **What to Bring:** Dress for mess. **Follow-Up Activities:** 1) After-school and Saturday art, carpentry, and science classes. 2) Birthday parties. 3) Summer camps. 4) School programs available. 5) Special events throughout the year include annual Star Party in October and Earth Day Celebration in April. 6) Next door to Children's Fairyland and Lake Merrit.

Lawrence Hall of Science (Ages 2+)

(510) 642-5132; Centennial Drive, Berkeley, CA 94720; (near Grizzly Peak Blvd.) <www.lhs.berkeley.edu>

Description: Perched high on the Berkeley hills, the Lawrence Hall of Science has a wonderful view of the entire Bay Area, but especially of the Golden Gate Bridge. In the front entrance plaza, there are sculptures of DNA and a humpback whale kids love to climb. Don't miss "Forces that Shape the Bay" in the back courtyard with rides that simulate earthquakes and the simulated Sierra Nevada waterways, which allow kids to control water flow. The Hall is designed as a resource to provide hands-on activities for science and math education. As such, there is a wide range of exhibits including games and puzzles of different countries; changing exhibits featuring the hottest science topics; a Young Explorers Area with puppet theater, blocks, and books; biology and computer labs; and a planetarium. The Biology Lab downstairs has animals you can touch, including a chinchilla, a dove, a frog, a gecko, a lizard, a rat, turtles, and snakes. The Computer Lab is geared for children ages 5 and older, with age-appropriate software. The Planetarium has shows for younger children during daytime hours. There are two shows for children 4–6 years old that are

125

shown on weekends at 1pm. Most Planetarium shows allow only those 6 years or older. Planetarium tickets sold at the Information Desk.
Hours: Daily 10am–5pm. Closed Labor Day, Thanksgiving Day, and Christmas Day. *Biology Lab*: weekends & holidays 1:30–4pm. *Computer Lab:* Saturdays: 12:30–3:30pm. *Planetarium Shows*: weekends & holidays: 1pm, 2:15pm, & 3:30pm. *Flying High*: weekends & holidays: 1pm.
Cost: $9.50/adult (ages 19–61), $7.50/youth (5–18), 62+, disabled person, $5.50/child (3–4), free/child 2 & under. Planetarium show tickets are additional and cost $3/adult, $2.50/child 18 and under, with museum admission. *Free admission on Cal Day*. See Cal Day in Chapter 10: Seasonal Events.
Bathrooms: Yes.
Facilities: Stroller friendly.
Food: Café open until 4pm daily. Menu on the Web site.
What to Bring: Cash for food & machine ticketed parking. Don't forget a jacket, even during the summer, as fog is unpredictable.
Follow-Up Activities: 1) Birthday parties. 2) Scouting events (sleepover & Health Day). 3) Many, many school programs. 4) Look in Chapter 12: Science and Arts Education— Science & Technology Education section under Lawrence Hall of Science for additional information on family workshops, science classes, and summer camps offered. Don't miss Cal Day in April since admission is free to many museum on the U.C. Berkeley campus that day. Special events listed on the Web site, especially during the summer.
Directions: On the Web site under "About," then the "Directions" link.

Lawrence Livermore National Labs' Discovery Center (Ages 9+)

(925) 423-3272; Eastgate Drive, Livermore, CA 94550
(Greenville Road near the Laboratory's Eastgate entrance)
<www.llnl.gov>; Map: <www.llnl.gov/llnl/visiting/directions.jsp#visit>
Description: Located just outside the gates of the Lawrence Livermore Labs, The Center is open to the public, and no badging is required. The Discovery Center has exhibits on the research conducted at the Labs, including research on cancer, lasers, the environment, and historical highlights of the Lab. For kids, the Center has a hands-on energy bike display to show how the bike can be used to power a TV There's also an earthquake display, video, and simulation to explain how earthquakes work.

Hours: Tues–Fri: 1–4 pm & Sat: 10 am–2pm; closed on Lab holidays. Call prior to visit to confirm hours. Weekday mornings are dedicated to school field trips.

Cost: Free.

Bathroom: Yes.

Facilities: Stroller friendly.

Food: No.

What to Bring: Picnic lunch and camera.

Follow-Up Activities: 1) Community day events include "Got Science Saturday" at the nearby Robert Livermore Community Center in Livermore in October with hands-on science activities and demonstrations by lab scientists. Free admission. Visit Web site for current public events: <www.llnl.gov/llnl/community/events.jsp>. 2) "Science on Saturdays" is a free lecture and demonstration series for middle school and high school students, held both in the Tri-Valley and in the Central Valley. See public events Web site in item #1 above. 3) Super Science school field trips for grades 4 and 5 provide a free tour of the Discovery Center along with lab scientist science demonstration for kids on topics such as the states of matter, air pressure, and other topics aligned with the grades 4 and 5 science curriculum. Homechoolers can join in with a scheduled school field trip. For details and reservations, look under "Public Affairs," then "Community," then "School field trips" on <www.llnl.gov/pao/com/school_tours.html> or call (925) 422-0302. 4) New after-school program for Scouts and science clubs include a guided tour of the Discovery Center followed by a visit with a lab scientist and science demo. 5) Around February and March, the Center hosts an annual conference titled "Expanding Your Horizons" for middle school and high school girls to learn about careers in math and science. Expanding Your Horizons is a national network providing conferences nationwide. For a site closest to you, visit <www.llnl.gov/eyh>. 6) The Lab also sponsors an annual science and engineering fair for middle and high school students that is affiliated with the prestigious Intel International Science and Engineering Fair: <http://tvsef.llnl.gov/>.

Mystery Spot (Ages 5+)

(831) 423-8897; 465 Mystery Spot Road, Santa Cruz, CA 95065
<www.mysteryspot.com>

Description: Come see this spot where strange phenomena occur, where tall objects seem short and balls seem to roll uphill. Are these merely optical illusions or strange natural forces? Scientists have brought their students to study this spot.

Hours: *Summer Hours (Memorial Day–Labor Day):* 9 am–last tour at 7pm. *Winter Hours:* 9am–last tour 4:30pm. Reservations highly recommended, and may be made online.

Cost: $5 parking fee/car, $5/person, free/child under 3. Cash or check only for admission, or purchase tickets online.

Bathrooms: Yes.

Facilities: Not stroller friendly; baby carrier recommended.

Food: Snacks only.

What to Bring: Picnic lunch, prepurchased tickets, and cash/check for admission.

NASA Exploration Center (Ages 5+)
NASA Ames Research Center
(650) 604-6274; (650) 604-6497; Moffett Field, Mountain View, CA 94035
<www.nasa.gov/centers/ames/home/exploration.html>;
<www.nasa.gov/centers/ames/home/directions.html> Map

Description: The visitor center shows the research and technology of this world renown organization. There's a wonderful interactive exhibit right in the middle of the center. In 2006, it had an interactive display that allows the user to control air traffic and simulates an airport air traffic control room. Previously, interactive Mars Rovers were the featured attraction, allowing visitors to control the movement of the Rovers by programming their instructions, just as the scientists do. There's also an immersive theater showing panoramic videos of Mars and Saturn. There are even samples of moon rocks brought back by astronaunts. The center is located just outside the main gate of the NASA Ames Research Center, so no badging is required.

Cost: Free.

Hours: Tue–Fri: 10am–4pm. Sat & Sun: noon–4pm. Closed Mondays and federal holidays. Check Web site for current hours.

Bathrooms: Yes.

Facilities: Stroller friendly.

Food: No. Downtown Mountain View is relatively close by with plenty of restaurants.

What to Bring: Sunscreen, sunglasses, comfortable walking shoes, a jacket during cool weather, food and drinks.

Follow-Up Activities: 1)The Sally Ride Science Festival is for girls in grades 5–8. See Sally Ride Science Festival Web site <www.sallyridefestivals.com> for details. 2) The NASA Quest Challenge is for students in grades 5–8. Topics change yearly; in 2006, the challenge was to design and build a model of a Lunar Research Station to live and work on the moon. For current information, visit <http://quest.nasa.gov>. 3) Ames Exploration Encounter is for students in grades 4–6 with hands-on stations exploring physics, flight, space, and earth. To reserve: <http://encounter.arc.nasa.gov> or call (650) 604-1110. Mailing address: NASA Ames Research Center, M/S 226/1, Moffett Field, CA 94035. 4) Robotic Alliance Project provides information on robotics and robotics competitions: <http://robotics.arc.nasa.gov>. 5) The education division has many programs for all levels, K-12 and up and for kids, students, educators, and community groups: <www.nasa.gov/centers/ames/education/index.html>.

Oakland Discovery Center (Ages 6+)

Site 1: (510) 535-5657; East Center: 2521 High Street, Oakland, CA 94601
Site 2: (510) 832-3314; West Center: 935 Union Street, Oakland, CA 94067
<www.oaklandnet.com/parks/facilities/centers_oakland_discovery_e.asp>
<www.oaklandnet.com/parks/default.asp>

Description: This recreation center provides after-school hands-on activities in science and art projects. Activities include woodworking, telescopes, computers, rockets, electro-mechanics, physics, microscopes, and art.
Hours: *Summer:* Tues–Sat: 3–7pm, *September–June:* Tues–Thur: 3–7pm, Fri–Sat: 3–8pm.
Cost: $0.50.
Bathrooms: Yes.
Facilities: Stroller friendly.
Food: No.
What to Bring: Cash for parking.

Stanford Linear Accelerator Visitor Center/Tour (Recommended Age: 11)

(650) 926-2204; 2575 Sand Hill Road, Menlo Park, CA 94025
<www2.slac.stanford.edu/vvc>; <home.slac.stanford.edu/visitslac.html>

Requires photo ID to enter site. See full entry in Chapter 7: How Things Work—Site Tours.

The Tech Museum of Innovation (Ages 7+)

(408) 294-TECH; 201 South Market Street, San Jose, CA 95113
<www.thetech.org>

Description: The Tech Museum focuses on the innovation and technology that has made Silicon Valley world renown. Hands-on exhibits cover a range of topics, from biologically based innovations to microprocessors and robotics to space technologies that help us see and understand the universe better. Don't miss the IMAX Theater with shows that enrich your experience at the museum.

Hours: Tues–Sun: 10am–5pm. Closed Monday, Thanksgiving Day, & Christmas Day. Check Web site for current shows and schedule at the IMAX Theater.

Cost: *Admission:* $8/person includes 1 IMAX show admission. Additional IMAX show: $4/person. IMAX feature film: $10/person.

Bathrooms: Yes.

Facilities: Stroller friendly.

Food: Café Primavera opens ½ hour after the museum opens and closes ½ hour before the museum closes.

What to Bring: Cash for parking and food.

Follow-Up Activities: 1) Summer camp programs on technology offered through Galileo. See entry in Chapter 12: Science & Arts Education—Science & Technology Education. 2) Online exhibits and archives on earthquakes, lasers, color, robotics, DNA, space and the Hubbell space telescope, and other technology topics. 3) Hands-on activities to do at home and in the classroom are online under their "Education," then "Programs" tabs. 4) Yearly Tech Challenge for middle school and high school teams to design and solve real-world problems <http://techchallenge.thetech.org>. 5) Field trips (grades 4–8) and educational programs for schools.

Zeum, Yerba Buena Gardens (Ages 5+)

(415) 820-3320; (415) 247-6500 Carousel
221 Fourth Street, San Francisco, CA 94103
<www.zeum.com>

Description: Zeum is a technology and multimedia museum, combining traveling exhibits with permanent exhibits that demonstrate various forms of media. At Zeum, the visitor can make a music video, create a movie using clay animation, compose a soundtrack, or experiment with digital art.

Hours: *School Year:* Wed–Sun: 11am–5pm. *Carousel Hours:* 11am–6pm. *Summer:* Tue–Sun: 11am–5pm. *Animation Studio and Digital Sound Room* are sometimes reserved for groups until 2:30pm. Call ahead, as these vary day to day.

Cost: $8/adult, $7/students & seniors w/ ID, $6/youth (3–18), free/ child 2 & under. *Carousel:* $3/ticket, 2 rides per ticket. 4th & Mission parking lot for parking.

Bathrooms: Yes.

Facilities: Stroller friendly.

Food: Lots of restaurants nearby.

What to Bring: Cash for parking and food. Park at the Mission & 5th Street Parking Lot: <www.fifthandmission.com>.

Follow-Up Activities: 1) Workshops on weekends include theater workshops. Check the "Events Calendar" icon on the Web site. 2) Plays and exhibit films at the theater. Ticket prices vary, depending on the performance. 3) Birthday parties. 4) Learn about the world of archaeology at <www.dignubia.org>. 5) Lots of attractions nearby, including San Francisco Museum of Modern Art, Cartoon Art Museum, Yerba Buena Gardens, Moscone Center and the Metreon, and the temporary location of the California Academy of Sciences (until 2008).

Chapter 5
Planetariums
& Observatories

The sun, moon, and stars are an everyday part of our lives. Encourage your child's curiosity and help him learn about our solar system, the galaxies, and our universe. Planetariums simulate the night sky to help us visualize the constellations and learn how the sky changes with the seasons. Observatories provide telescopes for us to view the sky directly. It is possible to view the sun, with filtered telescopes to prevent eye damage. Foothill College in Los Altos Hills has a program on Saturday mornings to view the sun.

Cabrillo College Planetarium (Ages 4+)
Natural and Applied Sciences 700 building (below room 706)
(831) 479-6506; 6500 Soquel Drive, Aptos, CA 95003
<www.cabrillo.edu/academics/astronomy>; e-mail: rinolthe@cabrillo.edu

Description: Shows suitable for all ages, from preschool to high school, describe our solar system, how the sky changes as the earth rotates, a few constellations, asteroids, and comets.
Schedule: One-hour show available on Monday afternoons from 1–5pm. Reservations required. Maximum occupancy: 47.
Cost: $50/show per group.
Bathrooms: Yes.
Facilities: Stroller friendly.
Food: No.
What to Bring: Cash for parking: $2 in quarters for ticket machine.
Follow-Up Activities: Look through the *Summer Academy* class schedule for parent and student classes through the college. The Backyard Astronomy course for students in 6–12 grades is offered in the summer

evenings with planetarium as well as telescope viewing at the observatory above Cabrillo College. Additionally, there is a summer whale-watching class and a computer robotics engineering course using Lego® for students in grades 6+. Call the Community Education Office at Cabrillo (831) 479-6331 or visit the Web site and look under the *Summer Academy* catalog: <www.cabrillo.edu/services/extension/summeracademy>.

Directions: For a map of the campus: <www.cabrillo.edu/services/extension> then select "Map & Directions" tab.

Chabot Space & Science Center (Ages 5+)
(510) 336-7300; (510) 336-7373 Box Office
10000 Skyline Boulevard, Oakland, CA 94619
<www.chabotspace.org>

For full entry information, look under Chapter 4: Science & Technology Museums.

Hours: Wed–Thur: 10am–5pm. Fri & Sat: 10am–10pm. Sun: 11am–5pm. *Extended Hours* (some holidays): 10am–10pm. Closed Mon & Tues, Thanksgiving Day & Christmas Day. Check Web site for current schedule prior to visit to avoid disappointment. *Free Telescope Viewing:* Fri–Sat evenings, weather permitting—November to March: 7:30–10:30pm, April to October: dusk–10:30pm.

Foothill Observatory, Foothill College (Ages 3+)
(650) 949-7334; 12345 El Monte Road, Los Altos Hills, CA 94022
<www.foothill.edu/ast/fhobs.htm>

Description: See the solar system, star clusters, nebulae, and even distant galaxies on Friday nights. Each viewing will be different, depending on the season and what's in viewing range. On Saturday mornings, see 2 layers of the sun through safe solar filters. Special viewing events are scheduled when there are eclipses, comets, supernova, etc. Check Web site for these special events.

Hours: Weekly programs. Every Friday night: 9–11pm. Every Saturday morning: 10am–noon. Closed on cloudy days.

Cost: Free for the observatory. Parking is $2 from the parking lot ticket machines. Use parking lot 4.

Bathrooms: Yes.

Facilities: Strollers not recommended.

Food: No.

What to Bring: $2 in quarters for parking permit machines and jackets for evening events.

Directions: Map: <www.foothill.edu/ast/fhmap.htm>.

Minolta Planetarium (Ages 3 +)

(408) 864-8814; De Anza: 21250 Stevens Creek Boulevard, Cupertino, CA 95014 <www.planetarium.deanza.edu> *(Reopens spring 2007)*

Hours: The newly renovated planetarium is located in the back of the campus, by the track and swimming pool area. Shows are on selected Saturday evenings at 7pm September–April. During the school year, there are shows for school groups on weekday mornings. Individual families can attend by saying they're "walk ins" to find out when the next show is scheduled.

Cost: $2 parking at De Anza College. Tickets: $6/adult, $5/child under 12. Ticket purchase starts at 6pm. For field trip groups or "walk-in" shows, admission is $4.50 per person. Bring cash or check for entry fee.

Bathrooms: Yes.

Facilities: Stroller friendly.

Food: No.

What to Bring: 8 quarters for parking permit machines, and cash or check for admission fee. Use Parking Lot E.

Follow-Up Activities: Telescope viewing available after each presentation as the weather permits in the evenings.

Morrison Planetarium (Ages 3 +)
California Academy of Sciences, Golden Gate Park

(415) 321-8000; 55 Concourse Drive, San Francisco, CA 94118 (reopening 2008) <www.calacademy.org/planetarium>

Description: *Due to reconstruction, the planetarium will be closed until the new building is completed in 2008.* Planetarium shows help us better understand the sun, moon, stars, constellations, and planets in our solar system. Special event shows on topics of current interest. One show is on the stars over San Francisco—now versus those 50 years ago. For full entry of the California Academy of Sciences, look in Chapter 4: Science & Technology Museums.

Schedule: Schedule varies, but usually on Sat. & Sun noon–4pm. "Free First Wednesdays" have shows noon–6pm. Check Web site or call for current information.
Cost: $2.50/adult, $1.25/youth or senior.
What to Bring: Jacket and cash for the show.
Follow-Up Activities: 1) Astronomy Day in early May is a special event featuring solar viewing, making a star wheel project, planetarium shows, and other activities.

Rosicrucian Egyptian Museum & Planetarium (Ages 5+)

(408) 947-3635; 1342 Naglee Avenue, San Jose, CA 95191
<www.egyptianmuseum.org>

Description: This museum presents Egyptian culture, history, and view of the afterlife. There's a planetarium with shows focusing on Egyptian culture. See full entry in "History Parks & Museums" in Chapter 9: Historical Outings.
Hours: Mon–Fri: 10am–5pm, Sat–Sun: 11am–6pm. Last admission ½ hour prior to closing. Planetarium shows on Mon–Fri at 2 pm, Sat–Sun: 2 pm & 3:30 pm. Closed on major holidays.

San Jose Astronomical Association (Ages 5+)

(408) 559-1221
<www.sjaa.net>

This organization is a group of amateurs who have star-gazing parties. These are open to the public. Go to the Web site to get the event calendar and meeting details.

UCO/Lick Observatory (Recommended Age 8+)

(408) 274-5061; Top of Mount Hamilton Road, San Jose, CA
<mthamilton.ucolick.org>

Description: Perched on the summit of Mount Hamilton, this site has beautiful views of the entire Bay Area on a clear day. While it is open to visitors on weekdays from 12:30–5pm and on weekends from 10am–5pm, telescope viewing by the public is limited only to a few special days during the summer. The Summer Visitors program is extremely popular and held on a lottery basis to determine who will be able to purchase tickets. The program includes history and astronomy lectures with each viewing. Check the Web site for dates, times, and ticket information. Place yourself on the e-mail list to be notified when the lottery begins.

Schedule: Usually held on a weekend each month from July—September in the evenings at 7:45pm.

Bathrooms: Yes.

Food: No.

What to Bring: Warm jacket.

Follow-Up Activities: On a sunny day, go down the other side of Mt. Hamilton to Livermore. This is a gorgeous drive. Bring a picnic lunch and a good map of the area, including Mt. Hamilton and the Livermore area. Have plenty of gas in the car, and spend a day exploring this "uncivilized" area. Not recommended for families with very young children.

William Knox Holt Planetarium (Min. Age: 4)
Lawrence Hall of Science

(510) 642-5132; Centennial Drive & Grizzly Peak Boulevard, Berkeley, CA 94720
<www.lhs.berkeley.edu/Planetarium>

Description: *A Sky Full of Stars* and *Journey to the Moon* are appropriate for children 4–7 years old, and scheduled at convenient, early afternoon times on weekends. *Journey by Starlight, Colors from Space,* and *Constellations Tonight* are for children ages 6 and up. For full entry information, look under the Science Museum section.

Hours: Shows are presented on weekends, most holidays, and daily during the summer.

Cost: There is an additional fee of $3/adult and $2.50/child ages 18 and under for the planetarium.

Follow-Up Activities: LHS publishes a set of science education books and kits, for home schoolers, teachers, and day care providers. These books and kits are geared for different levels, from preschool through grade 12. Check the Web site under the "Shop" icon.

Chapter 6
Transportation Favorites

Kids love boats, cars, planes, and trains. They love to ride them, play with them, and learn about them. These vehicles come in many shapes and sizes. This chapter has specific sections on each of these types of transportation. A budget tip to keep in mind — on "Spare the Air" days (in the summer), public transportation is free around the San Francisco Bay Area, so free fare on cable cars, buses, ferries, CalTrain, and BART. For specific information when Spare the Air Days are announced by the local media, visit <www.511.org> for details.

Boats

Boats come in a variety of sizes, functions, and materials: from rowboats, canoes, and paddleboats to sailboats, ferryboats, aircraft carriers, submarines, and more. Pick a sunny day and rent a paddleboat or rowboat on one of the many recreational lakes in the Bay Area; take a bay cruise or ferry ride, and enjoy the experience of being on the water. Visit the maritime museums both afloat and on solid ground to experience the range and sizes of boats. For an answer to "Why do boats float?" visit this Web site: <**www.howstuffworks.com/question254.htm**>.

Paddleboat & Canoe Rentals

A wide selection of lakes and parks have inexpensive small boat rentals readily available. Some are open for business solely in the summer while others are open year-round, weather permitting.

Bonfante Gardens Family Theme Park (Ages 3+)

(408) 840-7100; 3050 Hecker Pass Highway (HWY 152), Gilroy, CA 95020
<www.bonfantegardens.com>

Description: One great place to introduce all these modes of transportation for the littlest ones is Bonfante Gardens Theme Park in the foothills of Gilroy, just before Hecker Pass. Originally built and designed for its beautiful gardens and unique circus trees, it has rides that feature boats, trains (both a miniature train and a monorail), vintage cars, and simulated airplane and hot air balloon rides. See full entry in Chapter 2: Plant Kingdom—Gardens & Arboretums.

Hours: Open spring–fall.

Cost: Front Gate Admission: $39.99/adult, $29.99/child 3+, free/child 2 & under. For cost of front gate admission, take photo ID on the first visit and get admission for the season. Online prepurchased ticket: $29.99/ticket. Look for discounts online. AAA discounts also available. You may want to consider a season pass for older preschoolers. Great America has Great America VIP season pass that allows admission to both Great America and Bonfante Gardens. See Great America's Web site: <www2.paramountparks.com/greatamerica/shop/shopping_season_pass.cfm>.

Bathrooms: Yes, throughout the park.

Facilities: Day use lockers. Stroller friendly.

Food: Many concessions throughout the park offering hamburgers, pizzas, Mexican food, etc. Outside food is not allowed in the park. You may bring water and fruit into the park.

What to Bring: Sunscreen, sunglasses, hat or visor, water bottles, and an extra change of clothes and shoes. Don't forget swimsuit, towels, and flip-flops if you're planning to play in the Bonfante Splash Garden.

Lafayette Reservoir (Ages 3+)

(925) 284-9669; 3849 Mt Diablo Boulevard, Lafayette, CA 94549
<www.lafayettechamber.org/pages/reservoir.htm>
<www.ebmud.com/services/recreation/east_bay/lafayette>

Description: Located off Hwy 24, this reservoir has fishing and boating.

Hours: Ranges 6am–9pm, depending on the season; check Web site for current hours.

Cost: $6 park entry fee. Metered parking: $0.50/half-hour with a 2-hour maximum. Rowboats and pedalboats are available for rent on an hourly, half-day, or full-day basis from the activity center. Rowboat and pedal boat rentals: $15/hour, $22.50/90minutes (rowboat only), $25/half day, $35/full day, $30 deposit/paddleboat, $35 deposit/rowboat. Seniors and the disabled get 50% off rentals.

Bathrooms: Yes.

Facilities: Stroller friendly.

Food: No. Picnic tables available.

What to Bring: Quarters for meter parking, cash/check for boat rental, picnic lunch, drinks, hat or visor, sunscreen, and sunglasses. Wear comfortable shoes with good traction. For map & directions: <www.ebmud.com/services/recreation/east_bay/lafayette/directions.pdf>

Lake Almaden (Ages 3+)

(408) 277-5130; Almaden Expressway & Coleman Road, San Jose, CA 95120
<www.sjparks.org>; <www.sjparks.org/Parks/Regional%20Parks/almaden.asp>

Description: Besides boating, this lake has a sandy beach and swim area with lifeguards on duty. Fishing is allowed, too.

Hours: Year-round 8am–½ hour after sunset. Boat rentals and swimming area are open Memorial Day–Labor Day.

Cost: $6 parking fee collected April–September. Pedalboats and kayaks available for rental. Boat rental: $8/ first ½ hour, $12/ first hour, $10/ each additional hour, $4 late fee for each 15-minute increment. Check the Web site: <www.parkhere.org> and select "Park Fees" under "Quick Links" for most current fees.

Bathrooms: Yes.

Facilities: Stroller friendly.

Food: Snack bar. Closed in the winter.

What to Bring: Sunscreen, sunglasses, beach gear, and water bottles.

Lake Chabot (Ages 3+)

Marina: (510) 582-2198; 17600 Lake Chabot Road, Castro Valley, CA 94546
Urban Park Concessionaires: (510) 247-2526
<www.ebparks.org/parks/lakechab.htm>; <www.norcalfishing.com/chabot.html>

Description: Boat tours of the lake are available on weekends and holidays. Fishing is allowed. The marina rents out rowboats, canoes, kayaks, paddleboats, and boats with electric trolling motors.

Hours: *Park* open sunrise to sunset. *Marina & café*: Mon–Thur: 6am–5:30 pm, Fri, Sat, & Sun: 6am–6:30pm. *Tour boat:* Weekends & holidays through October; departing the marina at 11am, noon, 1pm, & 2pm. Call prior to visit for most current tour times.

Cost: $5 parking fee. Daily fishing access permit: $4, 1-day California state fishing license $11.30, California state fishing license $30.45. Boat rental ½ price on Weds. *Boat rentals:* Rowboats, canoes, pedalboats, & kayaks: $20/hour; $40 deposit & photo ID. Extended ½-day and full-day rentals available. Special pricing during weekdays; $16/day on Mondays, half-price rentals Tues–Thur. See Web site for current rates. *Sightseeing boat tour*: $4.25/adult, $2.75/child (12 and under).

Bathrooms: Yes.

Facilities: Stroller friendly.

Food: Lake Chabot Marina Café serves breakfasts, lunches, snacks, and drinks.

What to Bring: Photo ID, sunscreen, sunglasses, hats, and camera.

Lake Cunningham Park (Ages 3+)
(408) 277-4319; 2305 S. White Road, San Jose, CA 95148
<www.lakecunningham.org>; <www.sjparks.org>;
<www.sjparks.org/Parks/Regional%20Parks/LakeCunningham.asp>

Description: This lake has boating, fishing, and sailing in the spring and summer and bird watching in the winter. It is also home to Raging Waters.

Hours: 8am–½ hour after sunset. *Marina:* Spring weekends, daily during the summer (Memorial Day–Labor Day).

Cost: Parking fee: $6 collected on weekends and holidays and daily during the summer through Labor Day. Paddleboats: $12/hour and kayaks: $10/hour. Check Web site for the most current fees: <www.lakecunningham.org>. Sailboats: $15/hour. Must passs a basic skills test.

Bathrooms: Yes, by the marina.

Facilities: Stroller friendly.

Food: Snack bar. Picnic tables.

What to Bring: Photo ID, sunscreen, picnic lunch, sunglasses, change of clothes, and towels in the summer. Binoculars for bird watching in the winter.

Follow-Up Activities: 1) Sailing classes and summer sailing camps are offered; $80 for the week-long sailing camp. Call (408) 277-4319 for additional information. 2) In February and November, "Taking Kids Fishing in Silicon Valley" events are offered for kids ages 5–15. They provide the instruction, rod, and bait, and kids can fish until noon. Check the park's Web site to get current dates. 3) In the winter, Lake Cunningham Park is home to great blue herons, snowy white egrets, white pelicans, and Canadian geese. 3) Raging Waters is located right next door <www.rwsplash.com>.

Lake Del Valle (Ages 3+)

(925) 373-0332; (925) 449-5201; 7000 Del Valle Road, Livermore, CA 94550
<www.ebparks.org/parks/delval.htm>; <www.sunrisemountainsports.com>
<www.ebparks.org/dropdown/boating.htm#DVALLE>
Boat rental: <www.rockymountainrec.com/lakes/lake-delvalle.htm>

Description: In the summer, there are boat tours at the lake 1–2:30 pm. Ticket sales start at 11am at the marina. Tour accommodates a maximum of 23 people. Fishing and swimming are allowed. For kids under age 16, no permits are required. For those 16 and up, a valid CA fishing license and daily fishing access permit are required. These can be purchased at the boating center. Call (925) 248-3474 for additional information.

Hours: 6am–9pm.

Cost: $6 parking fee. Pedalboats, canoes, & rowboats: $10/2 hrs, $7/additional hour, $38/day. All require $50 deposit and photo ID. Motorboats and extended ½- and full-day rentals available at higher cost. *Del Valle Boat Rentals:* (925) 449-5201 or <www.rockymountainrec.com/lakes/lakedelvalle.htm>. Sunrise Mountain Sports has kayak rentals: $15/ hour & up; call (925) 245-9481, or visit <www.sunrisemountainsports.com>.

Bathrooms: Yes.

Facilities: Stroller friendly.

Food: Two snack bars available. East Beach Snack Bar is open from April through September. Rocky Snack Bar is open May–Labor Day.

What to Bring: Sunscreen, sunglasses, swimsuit, and water shoes

Follow-Up Activities: During summer weekends from May to September, the Visitor Center has naturalist programs for all ages on a drop-in basis. Most programs are free. For additional information, call Sunol at (925) 862-2601. For Sunol informations, see Chapter 1: Animal Kingdom—Nature Preserves.

Lake El Estero (Ages 2+)

(831) 375-1484 Boat Rental; (831) 646-3860 Playground; (831) 372-8446 Food
Del Monte Avenue & Camino El Estero, Monterey, CA 93940
<www.monterey.org/rec/locations.html>;
<www.monterey.org/rec/denmenace06.pdf>

Description: The lake and Dennis the Menace Playground are both located at Lake El Estero Park. The lake allows for boating and fishing; it is stocked with rainbow trout, Sacramento perch, and blackfish, etc.
Hours: *Park:*10am–dusk. Closed winter Mondays except on holidays. *Boating* concession: 10am–4pm, with the last boat out at 3:30pm.
Cost: Boat rentals at Lake El Estero cost $8/half hour, $13/hour.
Bathrooms: Yes.
Facilities: Stroller friendly.
Food: Snack bar outside of the Dennis the Menace Playground on Pearl Street. Open 11am–5pm; closed on Tuesdays.(831)372-8446.
What to Bring: Picnic lunch and cash for food and rides.
Follow-Up Activities: *Dennis the Menace Playground* is adjacent to the Lake El Estero Park boating area on Pearl Street. This unusual playground has a steam mini-train, a swinging rope bridge, and a maze.

Lake Elizabeth in Central Park (Ages 2+)

(510) 790-5541; 40000 Paseo Padre Parkway, Fremont, CA 94538
<www.ci.fremont.ca.us/Recreation/Boating>

Description: This is a pretty city park with a swimming lagoon, children's playgrounds, baseball fields, and a 2-mile trail that circles the lake. Be careful of the resident geese, since they can be aggressive.
Hours: Sunrise–10pm.
Cost: Kayaks: $5/½ hour, small paddleboat/canoe: $10/½ hour, large paddleboat: $12/½ hour, El Toro/Topper Sailboat: $15/hour.
Bathrooms: Yes.
Facilities: Stroller friendly.
Food: 3 concession stands located in various parts of the park.
What to Bring: Sunscreen, sunglasses, swim gear, beach towel, and umbrella if you plan to swim in the lagoon.

Lake Merritt Boating Center (Ages 3+)

(510) 238-2196; 568 Bellevue Avenue, Oakland, CA 94610

Gondola Rental: 866-SERVIZIO (866-737-8494)

Boat rentals: <www.oaklandnet.com/parks/programs/boating_boatrates.asp>
Gondola tour: <www.gondolaservizio.com>

Description: In addition to the canoes and rowboats, there are authentic Venetian gondolas for romantic dates and birthday parties. Two separate boat rental concessions operate on this lake. One concession rents out the traditional rowboats, canoes, etc.; the other rents out the gondolas. Information on the gondolas is listed in "Follow-Up Activites" below.

Hours: *Boat rental* closing times reflect when the last boat can leave the dock. *Summer* (Memorial–Labor Day): Mon–Fri: 9am–6pm, Sat/Sun: 10am–6pm; *Fall* (September–October): Mon–Sun: 10:30am–5pm; *Winter* (November–February): Mon–Fri: 10:30am–3:30pm, Sat/Sun: 10:30am–4pm; *Spring* (March–May): Mon–Fri: 10:30am–4pm, Sat/Sun: 10:30am–5pm.

Cost: Rent your own canoes, rowboats, kayaks, or pedalboats. All boat rentals require $10 to $20 deposit. Canoes & rowboats: $8/hour; pedalboats: $8/½ hour, $10/hour; kayaks: $10/hour; El Toro sailboats: $8/hour; Sunfish sailboats: $10/hour; Capri, Hobie, & Catamarans: $15/hour. Sailboats require sailing certificates.

Bathrooms: Yes.

Facilities: Stroller friendly around the lake.

Food: No.

What to Bring: Photo ID, picnic lunch, sunscreen, sunglasses, and rubber-soled comfortable shoes. Dress warmly in winter.

Follow-Up Activities: You can ride gondolas imported from Venice, Italy. Make reservations for the gondola rides online. Hours vary by season. Open summer, seven days a week. Prices range from $45/couple and $10 per additional person for a 30-minute cruise around Lake Merritt. Other packages also available.

San Pablo Reservoir (Ages 3+)

(510) 223-1661; 7301 San Pablo Dam Road, El Sobrante, CA 94803
<www.ebmud.com/services/recreation/east_bay/san_pablo>;
<www.norcalfishing.com> select San Pablo

Description: This is a favorite lake for boating and fishing (well stocked). There is a children's play area and plenty of picnic tables. There's also a bait and tackle shop on site, fish cleaning stations, and a handicap fishing dock.

Hours: Range 6am–9pm, depending on the month. Closed mid-November to mid-February. Open at least 6:30am–5:30pm, with extended hours to 9pm in June and July. Check Web site for specific times.

Cost: $6 park entry fee. Kayaks and rowboats: $12/hour, $24/3–5 hours, $34/day, $35 deposit. Motorboats and other boats available. Specials on Web site.

Bathrooms: Yes.

Facilities: Stroller friendly at the park.

Food: San Pablo Grill serves cooked-to-order breakfast and lunch.

What to Bring: Driver's licence, sunscreen, sunglasses, shoes with good traction, and fishing gear if you want to fish also.

Shoreline Lake Aquatic Center & Sailing Lake (Ages 3+)

(650) 965-7474 Boathouse; (650) 965-1745 Café
3160 N. Shoreline Boulevard, Mountain View, CA 94043
<www.shorelinelake.com>

Description: This is a beautiful park. Although there are no expert naturalists to enrich your knowledge of the wetlands and wildlife, there is plenty to see and do here. *Rengstorff House* is a restored mansion that provides a time capsule of the history of the Santa Clara Valley in the 1880s.

Hours: Open year-round, except during inclement weather. *Spring/Summer* (April–October): 10am–6pm. *Fall/Winter* (November–March): 10:30am–5pm on weekdays and 10am–5:30pm on weekends. The best time to visit the lake area is during the morning if you go on weekends, as this is a popular destination and the marina parking lot and café get very crowded.

Cost: Free parking. Sailboats, paddleboats, rowboats, canoes, windsurfers, kayaks, and bicycles are available for rent. Rentals range from $13/hour to $22/hour, depending on the equipment and the day of the week. Sailing and windsurfing classes are available for older children (9+) and adults.

Bathrooms: Yes.

Facilities: Day use lockers. Stroller friendly.

Food: Lakeside Café is located on the lake and directly next to the boat rental center. Lakeside Café has outdoor seating facing the lake. There are also quite a few restaurants located within the park.

What to Bring: Photo ID, sunscreen, sunglasses, water shoes, and change of clothing and towels just in case you get a bit wet.

Follow-Up Activities: 1) Camp Shoreline is a week-long summer camp for kids ages 6–11, focusing on water activities, including kayaking, rowing, windsurfing, and wildlife. Windsurfing & Sailing Camps are week-long summer camps for kids ages 9–15. 2) Consider visiting Baylands Nature Preserve at the end of Embarcadero Road East in Palo Alto, just a couple of exits north of Shoreline Blvd. off Hwy 101. This would be a nice activity for elementary school age children who enjoy learning about birds and the wetlands habitat. For more information on Baylands, look under the Nature Preserves section.

Stow Lake, Golden Gate Park (Ages 3+)

(415) 752-0347; 50 Stow Lake Drive, San Francisco, CA 94118

Description: Located in beautiful Golden Gate Park, this is a gorgeously landscaped and intimate boating lake, something you'd expect to see in old-fashioned romantic movies. There are many areas to sit and view the beauty of this small lake. Many international visitors visit this lake, so you're likely to hear a variety of different languages spoken here.

Hours: Daily 10am–4pm.

Cost: Pedalboats: $19/hour, rowboats: $14/hour, electric motor boats: $29/hr, $1 deposit. Cash only!

Bathrooms: Yes.

Facilities: Stroller friendly.

Food: Snack bar.

What to Bring: Cash only for boat rental.

Follow-Up Activities: The Japanese Tea Garden and Strybing Arboretum are nearby.

Vasona Lake County Park (All Ages)

(408) 356-2729; 333 Blossom Hill Road, Los Gatos, CA 95032
<www.parkhere.org>

Description: Vasona Lake rents paddleboats and canoes from early spring to early fall. Fishing is allowed. Vasona is directly adjacent to Oak Meadow Park.

Hours: 8am–sunset.

Cost: $6 parking fee. Boat rental fee: $8/first ½ hour, $12/first hour, $10/ each additional hour. For most current information, check the Web site: <www.parkhere.org> and select "Park Fees" under "Quick Links."
Bathrooms: Yes, but good idea to bring towelettes.
Facilities: Stroller friendly.
Food: No. Picnic tables and barbecues.
What to Bring: Sunscreen, hats, photo ID for boat rental, and checkbook or enough cash.
Follow-Up Activities: 1) The Billy Jones Wildcat Railroad, a miniature train, and the carousel are favorites at adjacent Oak Meadow Park in Los Gatos. The Billy Jones Wildcat Railroad Web site: <www.bjwrr.org>. Open daily during the summer but only on weekends the rest of the year. See the Mini-Trains Section for additional information. 2) Sailing classes are offered through the Los Gatos–Saratoga Parks and Recreation Dept. during the summer. Check the Local Parks and Recreation section for additional contact information. 3) The Youth Science Institute has great hands-on science classes for kids from preschool on up. Summer camps and afterschool science classes during the school year are popular. Class schedules are printed in the newsletter on the Web site: <www.ysi-ca.org>. See entry in the Science Education section. In May, the Sanborn YSI site has an annual Insect Fair. $5/vehicle parking. 4) During the Christmas holiday season, see the *Fantasy of Lights* drive-through lights display with music in Vasona Park. These are nightly from the end of November— December, from 6–10pm. *Admission Fees*: *Mon–Thur:* $9/vehicle with 9 or fewer people, *Fri–Sun:* $12/vehicle with 9 or fewer people, *Every Day:* $25/vehicle with 10–19 people, $35/vehicle with 20+ people. For additional information on the *Fantasy of Lights*, call the coordinator at (408) 355-2201 or visit the Web site: <www.parkhere.org> and select "Fantasy of Lights" in "Quick Links."

Cruising the Bay

Seeing the landscape from a boat provides a different vantage point since the view of the skyline is different from the water. Take a boat ride and see the beautiful San Francisco skyline or the Monterey Bay coastline. There are cruise operators such as the Blue and Gold Fleet and the Red and White Fleet. Public ferries operating from departure points throughout the Bay Area run frequently and are very affordable. While ferries may not have tour narration, they provide a wonderful boating experience. If you go, don't forget your jacket, camera, sunglasses, sunscreen, and cash for food and parking. Check Web sites for discount coupons, maps, and schedules, as these items get updated periodically.

Alcatraz Cruises (Ages 5+)

(415) 981-7625; Pier 33, Fisherman's Wharf, San Francisco, CA 94133
<www.alcatrazcruises.com>; <www.nps.gov/alcatraz>; <www.alcatraz.cc>
Virtual Museum: <www.cr.nps.gov/museum/exhibits/alca/overview.html>

Description: This company is affiliated with Hornblower Yachts. Its exclusive province is to ferry visitors to Alcatraz. The only access to Alcatraz Island is through Alcatraz Cruises. There are Kids' Tours available; call for additional information. From late-September to mid-February, go on the Agave Trail for panoramic views of the San Francisco skyline. In April/May, see nesting and egg laying by sea birds; chicks hatch around mid-June. View Brandt's cormorants, snowy egrets, and black crowned night herons from the West Road. Visit Web site for information on parking, maps, schedules, etc. Don't forget to wear comfortable walking shoes.

Schedule: Alcatraz Island closes at 4:30pm during the spring, fall, and winter. In the summer, the island closes at 6:30pm. Early bird cruise departs at 9:30am. Departures every half hour starting from 10:15am to 2:15pm.

Cost: Free admission to the park. Alcatraz Cruise: $10.75/child 5–11, $18.75/adult. Costs include the audio tour. Evening tours at 4:20pm & 5:10pm available seasonally from Thursday to Monday. Island Hopping tours includes Alcatraz & Angel Islands and include a one-hour narrated tram tour on Angel Island: $44.25/adult. To purchase tours without the audio narration, call to purchase tickets — $5 off/adult, $2.50 off/child.

Bathrooms: Yes.

Facilities: Strollers not recommended.

Food: No food available on the island. Snack bar on the boat.

Blue and Gold Fleet (All Ages)

(415) 773-1188; Pier 41, Fisherman's Wharf, San Francisco, CA 94133

Description: This company provides bay cruises; tours to Alcatraz; and ferries to Sausalito, Tiburon, Alameda/Oakland, Vallejo, Angel Island, and Pacific Bell Park during baseball season. The San Francisco Bay Cruise is approximately 1 hour long. There are also land tours to the wine country, Muir Woods, San Francisco, Monterey/Carmel, and Yosemite.

Schedule: See Web site for frequent departure times.

Cost: San Francisco Bay Cruise: $13/child 5–11, $17/youth 12–17, and $21/adult. If you purchase tickets by phone or online, there's an additional $$2.25/ticket convenience charge. However, there's an additional Web site discount of $3/person when purchased online. Tickets available from the Box Office at Pier 41 Fisherman's Wharf, right next to Pier 39. Consider purchasing San Francisco's City Pass <www.citypass.com/san-francisco> for the Bay Cruise tour if you're interested in other attractions in San Francisco within a 7-day period. Check out discount coupons to San Francisco attractions at: <www.destinationcoupons.com>.

Bathrooms: Yes.

Facilities: Stroller friendly.

Food: Snack bars on the boat.

Red and White Fleet (All Ages)

(415) 673-2900, Reservations: (415) 901-5254 ;
Pier 43-1/2, Fisherman's Wharf, San Francisco, CA 94133
<www.redandwhite.com>

Description: The San Francisco Bay Cruise is approximately 1 hour, narrated in 8 languages.

Schedule: See Web site for frequent departure times starting at 10am, approximately every 45 minutes.

Cost: San Francisco Bay Cruise: $13/child 5–11, $17/youth 12–17, and $21/adult. *Bay City Guide* provides online coupons at: <www.sanfranciscoonline.com> select "San Francisco Coupons." Online discounted tickets may be purchased at <www.onlyinsanfrancisco.com>. Select "Visitor," then "Tickets & Tours," then type in attraction name in the search box. The Go San Francisco Card provides admission to 45 top Bay Area attractions for one fixed price. These cards are priced at 1-, 2-, 3-, 5-, or 7-day increments starting at $39/adult & $29/child 12 & under: <www.gosanfranciscocard.com>.

Bathrooms: Yes.

Facilities: Stroller friendly.
Food: Yes.

Ferry Building Line (All Ages)

(415) 901-5253; Ferry Building: Gate E, 1 Ferry Plaza, San Francisco, CA 94105
<www.ferrybuildingline.com>

Description: A new venture of the Red & White Fleet, this cruise provides tour narration via wireless headphones, available in 4 languages. The 90-minute tour allow each passenger to choose between 3 separate tour narratives or alternate between them at will: architecture, Native American, and natural history.
Schedule: See Web site for departure times, which vary by date and season.
Cost: $26/child 5–11, $39/youth 12–17, and $39/adult.
Bathrooms: Yes.
Facilities: Stroller friendly.
Food: Yes.

Bay Area Ferries

Plan to arrive early enough to have time to park, get tickets, and board. Plan at least 20 minutes prior to departure time.

The San Francisco Bay Water Transit Authority is planning additional ferry routes to be implemented in the next few years. These routes include Antioch/Martinez, Richmond, Hercules, Berkeley, Treasure Island, South San Francisco, and Redwood City to San Francisco. For details, visit: <www.watertransit.org>.

Alameda and Oakland Ferry Service (All Ages)

(510) 522-3300; Alameda Dock: 2990 Main Street, Alameda, CA 94501;
Oakland Dock: Jack London Square, Oakland, CA
<www.eastbayferry.com>

Description: This ferry goes between Alameda/Oakland and San Francisco

(Ferry Building and Pier 39), Angel Island, and AT & T Park.

Hours: Closed Thanksgiving, Christmas, and New Year's Day. For schedules, check the Web site: <www.eastbayferry.com/when/when.html>.

Cost: *Parking:* Free parking next to the Alameda terminal. Free parking in the 7-story garage at Washington Street and the Embarcadero, Jack London Square at the Oakland terminal. Validate your parking ticket onboard the ferry for free parking. *Fares:* Between Alameda/Oakland and San Francisco: *One-way fare:* $5.50/adult, $2.75/junior (5–12), $3.25/senior (65+ with ID), $4.25/active military personnel, $3.25/disabled person, $1.25/between Alameda and Oakland, free for children under 5 with an adult. *Round-trip fares* are double the one-way fares. For the best value, ticket books for frequent trips. $45/10-ticket book (5 round trips), $80/20-ticket book (10 round trips), $150/40-ticket book (20 round trips). *Round-trip fares between Alameda/Oakland and Angel Island:* $13.50/adult (19+); $10.50/junior (13–18), seniors (62+), and disabled; $8/child (5–12); free for children under 5. These fares include park admission.

Bathrooms: Wheelchair accessible bathrooms on the first deck.

Facilities: Stroller friendly. You can also bring bikes onboard.

Food: Concession with beverages and snacks.

What to Bring: Sunglasses, jacket, and camera.

Angel Island/Tiburon Ferry (All Ages)

(415) 435-2131; 21 Main Street, Tiburon, CA 94920
<www.angelislandferry.com>

Description: This ferry goes between Tiburon and Angel Island. The company also provides cruises to groups of 25+ to view Alcatraz, the Golden Gate Bridge, Three Bridges, and the Marin shoreline.

Schedule: *May–September:* Mon–Fri: departing Tiburon at 10am, 11am, 1pm, and 3pm. Sat/Sun: hourly 10am–5pm. Mon–Fri: departing Angel Island at 10:20am, 11:20am, 1:20pm, and 3:30pm. Sat. & Sun: hourly 10:20am–5:20pm. *Rest of the Year:* Check Web site. *Sunset Cruises* operate May–October on Fri & Sat evenings from 6:30–8pm.

Cost: Round-trip fare includes Angel Island admission: $10.25/adult or senior, $8/child (5–11), $1/bike. Sunset cruises: $15/adult, $10/child 5–11, free/child under 5 per adult. $150 season passes available for unlimited number of cruises.

Bathrooms: Yes.

Facilities: Stroller friendly on the bigger ferryboat.

Food: No. Snacks available onboard for sunset cruises.

What to Bring: Jacket, camera, sunglasses and sunscreen, dinner picnic for sunset cruises.

Follow-Up Activities: Summer camps on Angel Island through the Belvedere-Tiburon Recreation Department for children 7–12. Call the Belvedere-Tiburon Recreation Department at (415) 435-4355 or <www. btrecreation.org>.

Golden Gate Ferry (All Ages)

(415) 455-2000 Marin County; (415) 923-2000 San Francisco;
(707) 541-2000 Sonoma County;
San Francisco Ferry Building Terminal: foot of Market Street
San Francisco Pier 39: Fisherman's Wharf (ferry docks at nearby Pier 39)
<www.goldengateferry.org>

Description: Golden Gate Ferry provides daily service between Larkspur or Sausalito (Marin County) and San Francisco, and between San Francisco and AT & T Park. Trips last 30 to 50 minutes, depending on the destination and speed of the boat. Most trips take 30 minutes, except between San Francisco and Larkspur on the *Spaulding,* which takes 50 minutes.

Schedule: Check Web site or call for current schedule information. Holiday schedules are different from regular schedules. There is no service on Thanksgiving, Christmas, and New Year's days.

Cost: *One-way fare—Larkspur & Sausalito:* $6.75/adult; $3.35/child (6–18), disabled, or senior (65+); free/child 5 & under (up to 2 kids/paying adult fare). Frequent rider ticket books: $85/20 tickets to Larkspur, $72/20 tickets to Sausalito; not valid for group travel. *AT & T Park*: $7/ person one way. Free/child 5 & under (up to 2 kids/paying adult fare).

Bathrooms: Yes.

Facilities: Stroller friendly.

Food: Snack bar.

What to Bring: Windbreaker, camera, sunglasses, sunscreen, and cash.

Directions: *Larkspur terminal* is located in Marin County at 101 East Sir Francis Drake Boulevard, just east of HWY 101. There are Park and Ride lots and street parking along Sir Francis Drake Blvd. For free parking voucher and conditions for the Marin Airporter parking lot across from the terminal, see Web site for details. *Sausalito terminal* is located in downtown Sausalito, at Humbolt and Anchor streets.

Harbor Bay Ferry (All Ages)

(510) 769-5172; 2 McCartney Drive, Alameda, CA 94502
<www.alamedaharborbayferry.com>;
<www.alamedaharborbayferry.com/transit.php>

Description: Provides commuter service between Alameda and San Francisco (Ferry Building, Gate E) on weekdays only.

Schedule: Runs only during early-morning and late-evening commuter hours. Closed for holidays. Check Web site for holiday schedules.

Cost: *One-way Fare*: $6/person 12+ and under 62, $3/child (5–12), $3.50/senior (62+) or disabled, $4.75/active military, free/child under 5. Kids ride free on Friday afternoons during the summer. $50/book of 10 one-way tickets, $90/book of 20 one-way tickets. Monthly pass: $165/month. Free parking at the Harbor Bay Isle Ferry Landing. Purchase tickets once you board at the snack bar.

Bathrooms: Yes, on lower deck.

Facilities: Stroller friendly.

Food: Food and beverage service onboard, cash or check only.

What to Bring: Jacket, sunglasses, camera, and cash or check for food and parking.

Directions: See Web site for maps. Docks at the San Francisco Ferry Building by the Embarcadero.

Vallejo/Baylink Ferry (All Ages)

(707) 64-FERRY; (877) 64-FERRY; 289 Mare Island Way, Vallejo, CA 94590
<www.baylinkferry.com>

Description: Ferry service between Vallejo Terminal and San Francisco (Ferry Building & Pier 41). Service to Discovery Kingom (Marine World) during the summer between May and Labor Day.

Schedule: Closed on Thanksgiving, Christmas, and New Year's days. Check current schedule on the Web site.

Cost: One-way fare: $11.50/adult (13–64); $5.75/youth (6–12), seniors (65+), and disabled; free/child ages 0–5. Up to 2 kids free/paying adult fare. Day passes, monthly passes, and punch cards also available. Free parking at the Vallejo Ferry Terminal on Mare Island Way. Limited parking in the San Francisco Ferry Building Terminal; additional parking available in the garage across from Pier 39 in San Francisco for a fee on an hourly basis.

Bathrooms: Wheelchair accessible restroom available.
Facilities: Stroller friendly.
Food: Snack bar.
What to Bring: Jacket, sunglasses, camera, and cash.

Whale Watching

Whale-watching cruises depart from San Francisco, Santa Cruz, and Monterey Bay. See the whale-watching section in Chapter 1: Animal Kingdom—Marine Life for additional information.

Maritime Museums

Maritime museums provide firsthand experience with a submarine and gargantuan aircraft carrier. If you ever get the opportunity, it's well worth the trip to experience being in a submarine. Hawaii and many tourist destinations provide submarine tours. It's a wonderful firsthand experience of being underwater and seeing how colors change as the submarine submerges and less sunlight gets through to the deeper water. Although I had intellectually understood the concept and the effect of depth on color light, I truly didn't understand it until I experienced it myself. The experience made a tremendous difference because it was the event and the actual physical sensation of being in an underwater environment that helped me to really "get it." Intellectually understanding and truly understanding with personal experience can be two entirely different things.

San Francisco Maritime National Historic Park (All Ages)

This park is spread out between the new Visitor Center, the Maritime Museum (currently closed for renovation; reopens in 2009), the Library, the boats at Hyde Street Pier, and the *U.S.S. Pampanito*. Although the physical museum building is closed until 2009, the park's programs continue at Hyde Street Pier, so don't discount its programs. It's within walking distance of both Pier 39 and Ghiradelli Square. The Visitor Center opened in August 2003 across from the entrance to Hyde Street Pier at the corner of Hyde and Jefferson Streets in San Francisco.

Visitor Center
(415) 447-5000; 499 Jefferson Street, San Francisco, CA 94109
<www.nps.gov/safr>

Description:
Hours: 9:30am–7pm daily in the summer (Memorial Day–September 30), 9:30am–5pm October 1–Memorials Day).
Cost: Free to the Visitor Center.
Bathrooms: Yes.
Facilities: Stroller friendly.
Food: Nearby restaurants across the way at Ghiradelli Square.
What to Bring: Jacket, cash for parking and lots of quarters for metered parking, and camera.
Follow-Up Activities: Hyde Street Pier is just across the Beach Street.

Maritime Museum (Reopens 2009)
(415) 561-7100; 900 Beach Street, San Francisco, CA 94109
<www.maritime.org>

Description: The beautiful views of the San Francisco Bay and Alcatraz Island from the balcony of this museum are well worth the visit. There's also a sandy beach at Aquatic Park, just steps from the back of the museum. The museum has displays, videos, oral history recreations, interactive exhibits, and models. The Steamship Room provides an exhibit on the evolution from the wind to steam-powered technologies used in boats. Don't miss the demonstrations in the radio room that provide hands-on exhibits of the evolution of communications technology from signal flags to the radios and the use of Morse code.
Hours: 10am–5pm daily. Radio room demonstration on Sundays 1–3pm. Weekend tours start at 12:30pm.
Cost: Free.
Bathrooms: Yes.
Facilities: Stroller friendly only on the first floor. There are stairs to the 2nd and 3rd floors.
Food: Nearby restaurants across the way at Ghiradelli Square.
What to Bring: Jacket, cash for parking and lots of quarters for me-

tered parking, and camera.

Follow-Up Activities: 1) If you're in the mood for the beach directly behind the museum at Aquatic Park, bring some beach gear. Don't expect it to be warm since San Francisco tends to be cool, especially in the summer. 2) Walking distance to Hyde Street Pier, Ghiradelli Square, and cable car terminus. 3) Many special events throughout the year include bird watching walks, historical talks, engineering talks about steam piston technology, concerts, and costumed Living History Days where you get to meet the captain and his wife and learn about life onboard ship. Check the calendar for specific programs: <**www.maritime.org/calendar.htm**>. 3) The Maritime Park Association also sponsors various educational programs such as the submarine school, gold rush prospecting, and boat building through group programs. Scout, YMCA, and school groups can register for these programs that are geared for the elementary grades 4 and up.

Hyde Street Pier

(415) 561-7100; (415) 447-5000; (415) 556-6435 Sea Festival
Hyde Street at Jefferson Street, San Francisco, CA 94109
<www.nps.gov/safr/local/ship.html>;
<www.nps.gov/safr/planyourvisit/outdooractivities.htm>

Description: A short distance from the Maritime Museum, there are 8 ships docked here, ranging from the full-rigged *Balclutha* to steam schooners, tugboats, and a ferry. This collection of ships is a nice sample of the ships in San Francisco Bay at the turn of the 19th century.
Hours: 9:30am–5pm regular hours. *Summer hours* (Memorial Day–September 30): 9:30am–5:30pm. Last admission ½ hour before closing. Closed Christmas Day, New Year's Day, and Thanksgiving Day.
Cost: $5/adult (more than 17 years old); joint individual ticket to Hyde Street Pier and the submarine, *U.S.S. Pampanito*: $10; joint family ticket to Hyde Street Pier and *Pampanito*: $27. *Free boarding once a year on National Public Lands Day at the end of September.*
<www.publiclandsday.org>
Bathrooms: Yes.
Facilities: Limited stroller accessibility; good idea to bring baby in a baby carrier. Stroller accessible on the main decks of the boats, but there are stairs to navigate on the boats.
Food: Nearby restaurants.
What to Bring: Jacket, sunglasses, cash, and camera.

Follow-Up Activities: Living History Days, Festival of the Sea, concerts (Chantey Sings, Sea Music for Kids), Gold Rush lectures, engine room tours, and more are available as special programs. Living History Days are scheduled on select Saturday of each month from 11am–4pm. The engine room tours of the different vessels are on one Sunday a month in the afternoon. The Festival of the Sea is on a Saturday in September from 10am–5pm. The Festival of the Sea has hands-on kids' arts and crafts along with special performances for children, living history shipboard demonstrations, knots, rope making, blacksmithing, and the music and culture of the sea. $5 donation suggested. Events calendar: **<www.nps.gov/safr/planyourvisit/events.htm>**.

Presidential Yacht Potomac (All Ages)

(510) 627-1215 Voice Mail; (510) 627-1502 Recording
Jack London Square: 540 Water Street, Oakland, CA 94607
<www.usspotomac.org>

Description: This yacht is otherwise known as President F.D. Roosevelt's "floating White House" and has hosted many presidential events. It has been restored and provides public cruises on select days. Special event cruises on Mother's Day, Father's Day, July 4th, Veteran's Day, Fleet Week, etc.

Hours: *Dockside Tours:* Wed & Fri: 10:30am–2:30pm, Sun: noon–3pm, with tickets sold 45 minutes before closing. Call (510) 627-1502 to confirm hours prior to your visit. *Two-Hour History Tours* around SF Bay: May–October on select Thursdays & Saturdays at 11am.

Cost: *Dockside Tours:* $7/person ages 13–59, $5/senior 60+, free/child under 13. *Two-Hour Cruises:* $40/person ages 13–59, $35/senior 60+, $30/person for groups of 20+, $20/youth 6–12 years old, free/child 6 and under. You can order tickets by calling 1-866-468-3399 or online from <www.ticketweb.com>.

Bathrooms: Yes.

Facilities: Bring baby in baby carrier.

Food: Nearby restaurants in Jack London Square.

What to Bring: Jacket, sunglasses, cash, and camera.

S. S. Jeremiah O'Brien (Ages 3 +)

(415) 544-0100; Pier 45 Fisherman's Wharf, San Francisco, CA
<www.ssjeremiahobrien.org>

Description: This is an operational World War II cargo liberty ship.
Hours: Daily 9am–4pm. Closed major holidays. On the third weekend of each month, except when the boat is out for a cruise, the ship's engines are operational, and visitors can see how they work. Call to confirm dates, as it may be rescheduled due to holidays. Tours for groups of 10+ are available if reserved three weeks in advance.
Cost: $8/adult, $5/senior, $4/child (6–14), free for military w/ ID and for children under 6. $20/family.
Bathrooms: Yes.
Facilities: Stroller friendly.
Food: Nearby.
What to Bring: Jacket, sunscreen, sunglasses, picnic lunch, and cash for parking and food.
Follow-Up Activities: 1) Cruises throughout the year require advanced reservations. Cost is $150-$175/person, depending on the cruise. During Fleet Week, cruise the bay on board the *S.S. Jeremiah O'Brien.*

U.S.S. Hornet Museum (Ages 8 +)

(510) 521-8448; Pier 3, Alameda Point, Alameda, CA 94501
<www.uss-hornet.org>

Description: This World War II era aircraft carrier, known for its combat record and for its recovery of the Apollo 11 command module, is still operational today. For engine room and other docent-led tours of many parts of the carrier, arrive no later than 1pm to sign up for the tours. Children under 12 are not allowed in the engine room and combat information center. Virtual tour of the boat and photo gallery on the Web site. There's also a flight simulator to experience flying in a Desert Storm mission aboard an F/A 18 Hornet Strike Fighter or flying on a spy mission in a Seahawk from a battleship.
Hours: Daily 10 am–5pm. Last entry at 4pm. *Flight simulator hours:* Wed–Fri: noon–5pm, Sat & Sun:10 am–5pm. Closed Thanksgiving Day, Christmas Day, and New Year's Day.
Cost: $14/adult; $12/senior, military, or students w/ ID; $6/child 5–17, free/child under 5 with paying adult. Flight simulator ride: $5/ride,

$7/both rides. Rides last ~ 6 minutes.

Bathrooms: Yes.

Facilities: Lots of stairs and ladders. Wheelchair accessible, but limited to the main flight deck. If you have a little baby/toddler, be prepared to put your little one in a baby carrier.

Food: No food available except for vending machines on weekends.

What to Bring: Camera, jacket, comfortable walking shoes, cash, picnic lunch, and drinks. No backpacks are allowed onboard; be prepared to check them at the admissions desk.

Follow-Up Activities: 1) Many special events throughout the year. Visit Web site for most current events. 2) *Western Aerospace Museum,* located at Oakland International Airport, North Field, is close by: 8260 Boeing Street, Oakland, CA 94614. (510) 638-7100. For more information, refer to the Airplane Museum section later in this chapter.

U.S.S. Pampanito (All Ages)

(415) 775-1943; Pier 45 Fisherman's Wharf, San Francisco, CA
<www.maritime.org/pamphome.htm >

Description: *The USS Pampanito* (SS-383) is a World War II Balao class fleet submarine that is now a submarine museum and memorial. The Web site features a virtual tour of the submarine, its history, technology, and historical photographs. Special cruises on Father's Day, Fleet Week, etc.

Hours: *Mid-October–May:* Sun–Thur: 9am–6pm, Fri & Sat: 9am-8pm; *End of May–mid-October:* Thur–Tues: 9am–8pm, and Wed: 9am–6pm.

Cost: $9/adult, $5/senior 62+, $4/current military w/ ID, $3/child (6–12), free /child under 6 with an adult. $20/family (2 adults and up to 4 children under 18 years old).

Bathrooms: Public restrooms at the end of the pier.

Facilities: Not stroller friendly. Bring baby in baby carrier.

Food: Many restaurants nearby in Ghiradelli Square, Fisherman's Wharf, and Pier 39. Consider having lunch or dinner at the *Rainforest Café* just a few steps away, next to *Ripley's Believe It or Not!*

What to Bring: Camera, jacket, comfortable walking shoes, cash for food and parking.

Follow-Up Activities: Day programs, sleep-over camp, and "submarine school" programs available. 1) For day tours, the cost is $3/person. Call (415) 561-6662 ext. 30 or (415) 567-4653 to schedule a docent tour. 2) Sleepover program costs $20/person weeknights and $26/person weekends. Group size: min. 25, max. 48. 3) "Submarine school" program provides an opportunity for students to learn the scientific principles behind how submarines work. Cost: $58/child, $31/adult. Call (415) 561-6662 for details. 4) Cable car terminus at Fisherman's Wharf, just a few steps from the Maritime Museum, *USS Pampanito*, and the Hyde Street Pier.

Trains

Both boys and girls seem to have a special love affair with trains. There are mini-trains in the zoos and parks, big steam trains, and commercial trains of CalTrain, Light-rail, and Amtrak. Take a leisurely ride, enjoy the scenery, and expose your child to the sights and sounds of the city or the countryside. This section is divided into mini-trains, big trains, public trains, and railroad museums.

Mini-Trains at Parks & Zoos

Bianchi Railway Co. (All Ages)
Central Park, San Mateo
(650) 340-1520; 50 E. 5th Avenue (at El Camino Real), San Mateo, CA 94402
<www.cityofsanmateo.org/dept/parks/locations/central.html>
Description: Located by the playground off El Camino Real, this small train circles around the track. Central Park also houses a Japanese garden and a botanic garden. The botanic garden is open Tuesday, Thursday, & Sunday 10am–3pm. See Chapter 2: Plant Kingdom—Gardens & Arboretums.
Hours: March–October: Weekends: 11am–3pm (weather permitting). June 15 – August 15: weekdays: 10:30am–12pm. November – February: weekends 11am–1pm (weather permitting).
Cost: $1.25/ride.
Facilities: Stroller friendly.
Food: Snack stand with popcorn, snow cones, sodas, hot dogs, etc.
Stand Hours: 1–3pm on weekdays and 11am–4pm on weekends. Closed

Thursdays.

What to Bring: Picnic lunch, cash for the rides and quarters for metered street parking, sunscreen, and sunglasses.

Bonfante Gardens Theme Park (All Ages)

(408) 840-7100; 3050 Hecker Pass Highway, Gilroy, CA 95020
<www.bonfantegardens.com>

There's a train that goes around the perimeter of the park as well as a monorail in the back of the park by the Monarch Garden. See full entry in Chapter 6: Transportation Favorites—Boats.

Cost: Included with park admission.

Casa de Fruta (All Ages)

(408) 842-9316; 10021 Pacheco Pass Highway, Hollister, CA 95023
<www.casadefruta.com>

Description: Has a miniature train. See full entry in Chapter 10: Seasonal Events.

Hours: Call to confirm train operating schedule: (408) 842-9316. Closed January and February. March–December, hours are generally 7am–9pm. Call ahead to confirm hours.

Cost: *Fun Pass*: $5.49/person includes a ride on the train, one carousel ride, and a bag of popcorn. *Day Pass*: $10.99/person with unlimited rides on the train and carousel for the day. *Annual Pass*: $21.99/person with unlimited rides on the train and carousel. Birthday parties cost $15/child.

Bathrooms: Yes.

Facilities: Stroller friendly.

Food: Casa de Coffee restaurant (open 24 hours), a deli, and a fruit stand for snacks. Casa de Sweets has ice cream, coffees, and pies. Picnic grounds.

What to Bring: Sunscreen, sunglasses, camera, picnic lunch and drinks, and cash for train rides and food purchase.

Follow-Up Activities: For special events, check the Web site calendar. See entry in Chapter 10: Seasonal Events—Civil War Reenactment & Renaissance Pleasure Faire.

Children's Fairyland (All Ages)

(510) 452-2259; 699 Bellevue Avenue, Oakland, CA 94610
<www.fairyland.org>
Cost: Included with park admission. See the full entry in Chapter 8: Art
& Performing Arts—Children's Theater.

Golden Gate Live Steamers Club (All Ages)

Tilden Park Grizzly Peak Boulevard & Lomas Cantadas Road, Berkeley, CA 94708
<www.ggls.org>
Description: Located next to the Redwood Valley Railway, this club is
one of the oldest steam train clubs in the country. The club members built
the trains, which run on coal, diesel, propane, or even car batteries. For a
full description of the park, look in the Tilden Nature Study Area entry in
Chapter 1: Animal Kingdom—Farms.
Hours: Rides on passenger trains on Sundays noon–3pm, weather per-
mitting. Spring and summer open house, usually in May and August.
Check Web site under schedule of events.
Cost: Free.

Kennedy Park (All Ages)

(510) 670-7275; 19501 Hesperian Boulevard, Hayward, CA 94541
<www.haywardrec.org> or e-mail: parkdept@haywardrec.org
Description: This park is home to the Triple Pines Ranch petting zoo, the
miniature train, and a merry-go-round. It has pony rides and a bouncer,
too. There's plenty of picnic areas, a playground, and tennis and horseshoe
courts.
Hours: Open on weekends, most holidays, and school breaks 11:30am–
4:30pm.
Cost: Everyone must have a ticket, including infants and accompanying
adults, on the merry-go-round, Triple Pines Ranch, and train. Tickets sold
at the snack bar. $1.25/ticket for the train, merry-go-round, bouncer, and
petting zoo. The pony ride is $1.50/ride. *Discount* packages available for
train, bouncer, merry-go-round, and Triple Pines Ranch:

Special Tickets	$3.50 for 3–$1.25 tickets (single ticket)
Package A	$25 for 25–$1.25 tickets (single ticket)
Package B	$90 for 100–$1.25 tickets (separate tickets)

Bathrooms: Yes.
Facilities: Stroller friendly.
Food: Snack bar.
What to Bring: Sunscreen, sunglasses, picnic lunch, and cash for rides and food.

Oak Meadow Park/Vasona Park (All Ages)
Billy Jones Wildcat Railroad/ W.E. Mason Carousel
(408) 395-7433; Blossom Hill Road &University Avenue, Los Gatos, CA 95032
Train: <www.bjwrr.org>; Train and Carousel:
<www.los-gatos.ca.us/los_gatos/parks_and_rec/billy_jones_rr/bjwrr.html>
Map:< www.los-gatos.ca.us/los_gatos/gifs/oakmeado.html>;
<www.losgatosca.gov/index.asp?NID=910>

Description: This popular playground has a decommissioned airplane, an old-fashioned fire engine, an operating antique carousel, and a miniature train that loops between Oak Meadow and the adjacent Vasona Lake Park. Don't miss the turnaround at the end of the railroad. After your ride, go to the end of the train tracks and watch how the engine is manually turned around for another trip. During the winter, the ducks are in residence along the creek. Hidden spots along the creek provide wonderful opportunities to watch ducks in the winter months and sometimes ducklings in the early spring.

Hours: Park Hours: 10am–5pm. **Train Hours:** *Spring* (Starting March 15): Weekends 10:30am–4:30pm; *Summer* (June 15 to Labor Day): Daily 10:30am–4:30pm; *Fall* (Labor Day – October 31): Weekends: 10:30am–4:30pm; *Winter* (November 1 – March 14): Weekends 11am–3pm.

Carousel Hours: *Spring* (March 15): Tues–Sun 10:30am–4:30pm; *Summer* (June 15): Daily 10:30am–4:30pm; *Fall* (Labor Day – October 31): Tues–Sun 10:30am–4:30pm; *Winter:* (November 1 – December 1) Tues–Sun: 11am–3pm & (January 2 – March 14): weekends 11am–3pm.

Cost: $5/car parking fee during the summer. *Train:* $1.50/ride, Group rate: $1/ticket for 50+ tickets. *Carousel:* $1.50/ride. Group rate: $1/ticket for 50+ tickets. Free/child 2 & under.

Bathrooms: Yes, located across from the carousel.

Food: On weekends, the kiosk next to the train station is open for snack foods such as icees, popsicles, popcorn, and hot dogs.

What to Bring: Cash for the carousel, miniature train, and snacks. Picnic lunch, sunscreen, sunglasses, and camera.

Follow-Up Activities: 1) Paddleboat and canoe rentals are available at adjacent Vasona Lake Park during the summer. There's a pathway that leads to Vasona Lake Park via the footbridge next to the train station and carousel area. 2) The train has special events during Halloween and Christmas: *Haunted Forest* and *Phantom Express Train* (in the evening), *Holiday Train of Lights,* and Christmas *Fantasy of Lights* drive-through in the adjacent Vasona Lake Park. See Vasona Lake entry for more information on the *Fantasy of Lights.*

Oakland Zoo (All Ages)
(510) 632-9523; 9777 Golf Links Road, Oakland, CA 94605
<www.oaklandzoo.org>

Description: C.P. Huntington miniature train, a replica of a Civil War era train, goes through the zoo and provides a panoramic view of the Bay Area from the Oakland hills.

Hours: Daily 10am–4pm in the rides area (to the right of the main zoo entrance).

Cost: $2/ride. There's a package of tickets for a slight discount.
See the full Oakland Zoo entry in Chapter 1: Animal Kingdom—Zoos & Wildlife Museums.

Redwood Valley Railway (All Ages)
Tilden Regional Park
(510) 548-6100 Steam train; (510) 562-PARK Park;
Grizzly Peak Boulevard & Lomas Cantadas Road, Berkeley, CA 94708
For maps: <www.ebparks.org/parks/tilden.htm>;
Steam train: <www.redwoodvalleyrailway.com>

Description: Located at the farthest corner of the park, a ride on this steam train provides beautiful views of the Berkeley hills. The Golden Gate Live Steamers Club is located toward the back of this area. (See Train Museum section later in this chapter). Tilden Park is also home to a beautiful carousel, Lake Anza, and a botanic garden. The Lawrence Hall of Science is a short drive away via Centenial Drive & Grizzly Peak Blvd. For a full description of the park, look in the Tilden Nature Study Area entry in Chapter 1: Animal Kingdom—Farms.

Hours: *Winter* (September–May): Weekends: 11am–6pm. *Summer* (June 14–Labor Day): Weekends: 11am –6pm, Mon–Fri: noon–5pm. Closed

Thanksgiving and Christmas days.

Cost: No parking fee, $2/ride. $8/5-ride family ticket (can be shared between family members), free/child under 2.

Bathrooms: Yes.

Facilities: Stroller friendly.

Food: Snack bar concession.

What to Bring: Cash, jacket, camera, and picnic lunch.

San Francisco Zoo (All Ages)

(415) 753-7080; 1 Zoo Road, San Francisco, CA 94132
<www.sfzoo.org>

Cost: Little Puffer steam train: $3/ride. Dentzel Carousel: $2/ride (free for adult standing with the child on the carousel). See the full San Francisco Zoo entry in Chapter 1: Animal Kingdom—Zoos & Wildlife Museums.

What to Bring: Cash, jacket, camera, and picnic lunch.

Traintown (All Ages)

(707) 938-3912; (707) 996-2559
20264 Broadway (Hwy 12), Sonoma, CA 95476
<www.traintown.com>

Description: Besides the trains and the rides, there is a small petting zoo with llamas, sheep, goats, and ducks.

Hours: *June 1–Labor Day:* daily 10am–5pm; *September 1–May:* Fri–Sun: 10am–5pm. Not all rides open on Fridays. Trains run every ½ hour. Open major holidays except Thanksgiving and Christmas.

Cost: Train fare: $3.75/ride; rides on merry-go-round, ferris wheel, etc. are $1.75 per ticket. You can purchase a book of 8 tickets for $10.

Bathrooms: Yes, but no baby changing stations.

Facilities: Stroller friendly.

Food: Yes.

What to Bring: Sunscreen, sunglasses, picnic lunch, cash, and camera.

Big Trains

Ardenwood Historic Farm (All Ages)

(510) 796-0663; (510) 791-4196 Patterson House
34600 Ardenwood Boulevard, Fremont, CA 94555
<www.ebparks.org/parks/arden.htm>; <www.spcrr.org>

Description: The horse-drawn train operates on special event days with costumed brakemen and drivers. The blacksmiths demonstrate how to shape iron and steel into boxcar parts. The carpenters make mortise and tenon joints to repair cars. Laborers lay track and the mechanics repair the brakes. See full entry in Chapter 1: Animal Kingdom—Farms.

Hours: From April to mid-November, the horse-drawn train runs on Thur, Fri, & Sun 10am–4pm. Closed in the winter from mid-November through March.

Cost: Train ride is included with admission of $5/adult, $4/senior, $3/child, free/child 3 & under.

Follow-Up Activities: Historic Rail Fair is over Labor Day weekend and Haunted Train is in mid/late October. Check events calendar at: <www.fremont.gov/recreation/ardenwoodpark> or <www.spcrr.org>.

Niles Canyon Railway & Museum (All Ages)

Pacific Locomotive Associations Museum

(925) 862-9063; (408) 249-2953 Reservations
Sunol Depot: 6 Kilkare Road, Sunol, CA 94586
Niles Station: 37001 Mission Boulevard, Fremont, CA 94536
<www.ncry.org>; Niles: <www.nilesunity.com/?section=557>

Description: This was part of the first transcontinental railroad. There are steam and skunk trains.

Hours: 1st and 3rd Sundays of each month for the months of January to March, and October. Every Sunday during the months April to September. Sunday operations 10am–4pm. Check Web site for specific dates and departure times. Allow 90 minutes for round trip. Closed most of November and all of December. Holiday trains in December are in the evening. For holiday trains, check Web site by August to get advance tickets. Tickets sell out early.

Cost: Donation request: $10/person 13+, $8/seniors, $5/child (ages 3-12), free/child under 2. Holiday trains (Holiday Train of Lights with

Santa) $12 for 3 years old and up.

Bathrooms: Portables by the parking lot only.

Facilities: Very limited wheelchair access. Baby carrier or umbrella stroller highly recommended.

Food: Snacks only onboard. Some cafés and restaurants close by.

What to Bring: Sunscreen, sunglasses, picnic lunch, cash, and camera.

Follow-Up Activities: 1) Holiday Train of Lights (train is lit up with beautiful lights) with Santa is in late November and December. Tends to sell out early and require reservations. Tickets go on sale in September. After Christmas, there's no Santa onboard. In the past, it ran Wed, Fri–Sun, with 4:30pm and 7pm departures. These rides may be purchased from Pacific Locomotive Association at (408) 249-2953, online, or at the Sunol depot. 2) Spend a few minutes in the museum to see the collection of old steam and diesel trains.

Railtown 1897 State Historic Park (All Ages)

(209) 984-3953; (916) 445-6645 Recording; 5th & Reservoir Streets, Jamestown
P.O. Box 1250, Jamestown, CA 95327
<www.californiastaterailroadmuseum.org>, <www.railtown1897.org>
<www.parks.ca.gov/default.asp?page_id=491>

Description: These steam and diesel trains have been featured in Hollywood productions such as "Little House on the Prairie," "High Noon," and "Back to the Future." See the train engines used as movie props in the Roundhouse. For train aficionados only, the Roundhouse tour provides insight into the technology of steam engines, how to put new wheels on the train, how the turntable operates, and how replacement parts for the trains were made in the machine shop.

Hours: Railtown Depot Store & Visitor Center: daily April–October: 9:30am–4:30pm, daily November–March: 10am–3pm. Closed Thanksgiving, Christmas, and New Year's days. Steam trains: Hourly departures 11am–3pm on weekends April–October, which run a six mile loop for ~40 minutes. In November, trains operate only on the weekend after Thanksgiving on Fri–Sun departing hourly from 11am–3pm. Roundhouse tours start at 10:10am and depart hourly, with the last tour departing at 3:10pm. Call ahead to confirm times and costs. Check Calendar of Events for special events and days of operations.

Cost: Free park admission. *Guided Roundhouse Tours*: $2/adult, $1/youth 6–12, free for children ages 5 & under. *Steam Train Rides*: $8/adult, $3/

youth (ages 6–17), free for children ages 5 & under.

Bathrooms: Yes, at the depot.

Facilities: Stroller friendly in the park, not on the train. You can leave the stroller with the cashier at the Depot Store.

Food: No. Picnic tables.

What to Bring: Picnic lunch, drinks, sunscreen, sunglasses, and camera.

Follow-Up Activities: 1) For special events such as Autumn Festival in October, check the Web site events calendar. 2) Close to Columbia State Historic Park, a working historic town preserved from the 1850s Gold Rush era. See Chapter 9: Historic Outings—Gold Rush.

Roaring Camp Railroads (All Ages)
(831) 335-4484; Graham Hill Road, Felton, CA 95018
<www.roaringcamp.com>

Description: Nestled in the Santa Cruz mountains and surrounded by redwoods, Roaring Camp Railroads provides a beautiful ride through the redwoods on a big steam train or a visit to Santa Cruz Beach Boardwalk.

Hours: Redwoods Train: *Jan–Feb:* weekends 12:30pm departure, *March–mid-June:* weekend departures at 11am, 12:30pm, & 2pm; weekday departure only at 11am. *Memorial Day weekend* departures at 11am, 12:15pm, 1:30pm & 2:45pm. *Mid-June–mid-August:* daily departures at 11am, 12:30pm, 2pm & 3:30pm. *Late-August–late-October:* 11am departure on weekdays, weekend departures at 11am, 12:30pm, & 2pm. *November–December:* weekend departures at 11am, 12:30pm, & 2pm. Some special schedules on select days. Call to confirm costs and train departure times prior to visit. **Beach Train:** Trains typically make two runs each way when the train is operational. In the summer, trains run daily. In the spring and fall, trains typically run only on the weekends. In December, the Santa Cruz holiday lights train travels within Santa Cruz and does not go to Roaring Camp. Advanced tickets must be purchased.

Cost: $6 parking fee. Steam trains through the redwoods: $18/adult, $12/child 3–12, free/child under 3 years old. Beach trains: Require 3 hours round trip. Beach trains go between Felton and Santa Cruz Beach Boardwalk ($20/adult, $15/child 3–12, free/child under 3 years old).

Bathrooms: Yes, at the depot.

Facilities: Stroller friendly in the park.

Food: Café on site. Picnic tables available.

What to Bring: Sunscreen, hat, sunglasses, picnic lunch, and water.

Follow-Up Activities: 1) Lots of special events: annual Civil War reenactment over Memorial Day weekend, Thomas the Train, Great Train Robbery reenactments, 1880s Harvest Fair in October (showcases old-fashioned crafts such as spinning, weaving, candle making, and pumpkin carving), and Pioneer Christmas in mid-December. Check the Web site for event calendar. 2) Adjacent to the Henry Cowell Redwoods State Park. (Official entrances are far apart, but there's a walking path that connects the two parks. See map: <www.roaringcamp.com/pdfs/mountain.pdf>.)

Public Trains

Depending on your location, it might be more accessible for you to ride the commuter trains and light-rails during noncommute times.

Cable Cars, San Francisco (Ages 4+)

(415) 673-6864; San Francisco, CA
<www.sfcablecar.com>; Bell ringing: <www.sfmuni.com/cablecar>

Description: This world-famous symbol of San Francisco is well worth a visit, even for locals who have never taken a trip. It's a wonderful experience. There are two lines originating at Powell & Market Streets: the Powell–Mason line and the Powell–Hyde line. The Powell–Mason line runs from Powell and Market to Bay Street at Fisherman's Wharf. The Powell–Hyde line goes to the Ghiradelli Square end of Fisherman's Wharf. The third line goes along California Street from the Embarcadero through Chinatown to Van Ness & California. For a route map: <www.sfcablecar.com/routes.html>. I recommend the age minimum be at least 4 because care must be taken on the cable car; please use your best judgment. Note also that the extreme popularity of the cable cars, especially during tourist season and on weekends, can be very challenging, with very long lines. The best time to attempt this is in the early morning on weekends. You may also want to take the taxi to go back to the originating station due to crowds.

Hours: Runs frequently daily with special weekend and holiday schedules. Check the Web site <www.sfmuni.com/cablecar> for schedule information for San Francisco cable cars. For light-rail, trolley bus, and buses at:

<transit.511.org> select "Schedules & Route Maps," then select "MUNI (SF)" in the "Transit Providers" box, then page down and select name of the route.

Cost: $3/person one way. Free for children under 5. You may also consider purchasing a day pass ($9/person), which allows you to ride on streetcars, buses, and cable cars. The 3-day pass: $15, and the 7-day pass: $20.

Bathrooms: No.

Facilities: Not stroller friendly.

Food: No. Restaurants nearby at the termini: Fisherman's Wharf, Ghiradelli Square, and Downtown San Francisco.

What to Bring: Jacket, sunglasses, camera, cash (exact fare), & food.

Follow-Up Activities: 1) Cable Car Bell Ringing Competition event has the gripmen ring out melodies on the cable car bells. It is held on a Thursday early in July. For current information, call in June to confirm. This event is held at Union Square at noon. Free to the public. For additional information, visit <www.sfmuni.com/cablecar>. 2) Visit the cable car museum to better understand how the cable system works. See Cable Car Museum entry in the Train Museums section.

California Trolley & Railroad (Trolley Barn) (All Ages)

(408) 287-2290; History Park San Jose: 1600 Senter Road, San Jose, CA 95112
<www.ctrc.org>

Description: Operational historic trolleys run on the weekend afternoons. The Trolley Barn houses a wonderful collection of antique trolleys and cars, definitely worth a visit for the train lover. Small model train on the side of the Trolley Barn. See full entry in Chapter 9: Historical Outings. Select "Trolleys & Trolley Barn" under the "Projects" tab on Web site's landing page.

Hours: Thur–Mon: 9am–4pm. Closed Tues & Wed.

Light-Rail (MUNI Light-Rail) (All Ages)

(415) 673-6864; San Francisco, CA
<www.sfmuni.com>; <www.sfmta.com/historic>

Description: There are 6 light-rail lines. The *N-Judah line* goes from the CalTrain Station on 4th & King to Ocean Beach via Judah Ave. The *J-Church line* goes from the Embarcadero via Church to Glen Park. *The*

L-Taraval line goes from the Embarcadero to San Francisco Zoo. The *M-Ocean View line* goes from Embarcadero to Balboa Park via St Francis Circle, Stonestown, and San Francisco State University. The *K-Ingleside line* goes between Embarcadero and Balboa Park via Junipero Serra and Ocean and San Francisco City College. The *F-Market & Wharves line* goes between Castro and Fisherman's Wharf through downtown. Check Web site for route map and schedules:

Hours: For schedules, see: <www.sfmuni.com/php/routelist.php>.

Cost: $1.50/adult; 50 cents/senior 65+ w/ ID, youth (5–17), or disabled person; free/child 4 & under.

Bathrooms: None onboard.

Facilities: Not all stations are stroller friendly; plan accordingly.

Food: No.

What to Bring: Exact fare required. Subway turnstiles require coins.

Light-Rail (Santa Clara VTA Light-Rail, San Jose)
(408) 321-2300; San Jose, CA
<www.vta.org>; <transit.511.org>

Description: The light-rail in Silicon Valley operates between downtown Mountain View through Sunnyvale and Santa Clara to the edge of Milpitas and south through downtown San Jose to Santa Teresa. Visit the Web site for a route map with more specific information on stations: <www.vta.org/schedules/lr_interactive_map/lrBusMap.html>.

Hours: Operates 24 hours a day and seven days a week. See Web site for specific schedules.

Cost: Single-ride tickets: $1.75/adult, $1.50/youth 5–17, $0.75/senior or disabled person. Look online for discounts & passes.

Bathrooms: None onboard.

Facilities: Wheelchair accessible. Umbrella stroller highly recommended.

Food: Not onboard. Plan accordingly.

What to Bring: Exact fare. Drivers do not give change. Ticket vending machines do not provide change in nickels or dimes.

Follow-Up Activities: Historic Trolley Service operates late-November–late-December on Saturdays only 2:30pm–10pm. These trolleys provide free service between Paseo de San Antonio and San Jose Civic Center stations. Historic trolleys do not have wheelchair access. <www.vta.org/schedules/SC_920.html>. From VTS's home page, select "Schedules, Maps, & Fares," then "Light-Rail Schedules," then "Historic Trolley (920)."

CalTrain
1(800) 660-4287
<www.caltrain.com>

Description: CalTrain services the San Francisco peninsula between San Francisco and Gilroy. 1) Consider taking a short trip from the Mountain View station to the San Jose Arena station; walk about 2 blocks to Arena Green with a carousel, playground, and concessions. The Arena Green Children's Carousel costs $1/ride. Children under 12 ride *free on second Tuesday of each month*. Hours vary seasonally, but it is open at least: Tues–Sun: 11am–5pm. During the summer, it is also open on Mondays and has extended hours: 10am–7pm. For the most current information, call (408) 999-6817 for carousel operation information or see the Web site <**www. grpg.org/ArenaGreen.html**>. For the Park Rangers at the Guadalupe River Park & Gardens Visitor Center: (408) 277-5904. The *Children's Carousel* is located at Autumn and Santa Clara Streets, directly across from the San Jose Arena on Autumn Street. 2) Alternatively you can take a short trip between the Mountain View station and Palo Alto California station. The Mountain View Evelyn Ave station is in downtown Mountain View, just a short block to Castro Street with its many restaurants and shops. The Palo Alto California station also has many restaurants and shops and a neighborhood park nearby. Bowden Park is located at 2380 High Street/Alma Street at Oregon Expressway, about two blocks away from the California Station.

Hours: For stations, schedules, and fares, visit the Web site.

Cost: Fares depend on distance. See Web site for more information. For example, between San Francisco 4th St and King station to Lawrence station in Sunnyvale, the one-way fare is $6.75 and the trains run approximately every ½ hour, with more frequent departures during the evening commute between 5 and 6pm.

Bathrooms: At some stations.

Facilities: Wheelchair accessible from most stations. Umbrella stroller or baby carrier is highly recommended.

Food: No, none onboard.

What to Bring: Picnic lunch, snacks, water bottles, cash for fare and food.

Follow-Up Activities: For those able and willing to walk a bit, CalTrain's San Francisco terminus is close to the Modern Art Museum and the Yerba Buena Gardens, about 6–7 city blocks from King and 4th Street, in the direction of Market Street.

BART (Bay Area Rapid Transit)

(510) 236-2278 Richmond/El Cerrito
(510) 465-2278 Oakland/Berkeley/Orinda
(415) 989-2278 San Francisco/Daly City
(650) 992-2278 South San Francisco/San Bruno/San Mateo
(925) 676-2278 Concord/Walnut Creek/Lafayette/Antioch/Pittsburgh/Livermore
(510) 441-2278 Hayward/San Leandro/Fremont/Union City/Dublin/Pleasanton
<www.bart.gov>

Description: BART is a public transportation system that extends from Milbrae through San Francisco to the East Bay. It now also has a transfer point from Caltrain to the BART system at Milbrae. Amtrak <www.amtrak.com> can also be connected to the BART system at the Richmond station. Use the trip planner on the Web site to help you navigate the BART system and to find out how much fare you will need.

Hours: *Mon–Fri:* 4am–midnight, *Sat:* 6am–midnight, *Sun & Holidays:* 8am–midnight. BART trains generally run every 15 to 20 minutes.

Cost: Fares vary depending on distance. Here's an example of a one-way adult fare: From Fremont station in Fremont to the Downtown San Francisco Powell Street Station, the fare is $5. Children under 5 ride for free. Tour BART with an excursion fare, which allows you to ride for 3 hours for $4.65/person; however, you must enter and exit from the same station. You can purchase discounted tickets. Children 5 to 12 years old can get a 62.5% discount; tickets must be purchased in advance online or from select stations. See Web site for details.

Bathrooms: At some stations.

Facilities: There are elevators available, but many stations require assistance of the station agent, who can be reached via the white courtesy phones. Use a baby carrier or umbrella stroller that is light and can be easily folded up. Access to the station is most convenient on the escalators.

Food: No. Some stations may have street vendors outside.

What to Bring: Tickets can be purchased from ticket machines. These machines will accept cash: from coins, $1, $5, $10, and $20 bills. Up-to $4.95 in change is made by the ticket machines. Some stations have ticket machines that will accept credit cards. If you're planning on a long ride, consider bringing some reading materials or things for your little ones to do during the ride.

Follow-Up Activities: If you take BART to the Powell Street Station in downtown San Francisco, consider taking the cable car to Fisherman's

Wharf, Ghiradelli Square, or Hyde Street Pier. See the Cable Car entry for more navigation details. This will be a long day, considering the lengths of the trips both on BART and on the cable car. I do not recommend this outing for younger children unless someone will meet you with the car at one of these destinations to drive home.

Train Museums

Golden Gate Model Railroad Club (All Ages)
Located in the basement of the Randall Museum
(415) 346-3303; 199 Museum Way, San Francisco, CA 94114
<www.ggmrc.org>

Description: There's an HO scale model railroad layout with trains from 1938–1955 as well as modern trains. These model trains have freight and passenger cars. See the Randall Museum entry in Chapter 4: Science & Technology Museums.
Hours: Sat: 11am–4pm. Look for special "Junior Engineer Days" when kids can help drive the model trains.
Cost: Free.

Golden State Model Railroad Museum (All Ages)
(510) 234-4884; 900-A Dornan Drive, Point Richmond, CA 94801
<www.gsmrm.org>

Description: This model railroad museum has N, HO, and O scale layouts of model trains on display. *Scale* refers to the proportion of the model size to the actual real size of trains. These model railroads display California scenery and use models of trains from many eras, from traditional steam engines to the most modern diesels.
Hours: Trains run April–December: Sunday noon–5pm. Open, but trains not operating: Saturdays noon–5pm, Wednesdays 11am–3pm. Open on Memorial Day, July 4, and Labor Day. Closed January–March.
Cost: Sundays: $3/adult, $2/senior or child under 12, $7/family. Free admission on Saturdays & Wednesdays, but model trains will not be operating.
Bathrooms: Yes.

Facilities: Stroller friendly.
Food: No.
What to Bring: Picnic lunch and cash for entry.

Golden Gate Railroad Museum (Ages 6+)
(415) 822-8728; <www.ggrm.org>

Description: Unfortunately it lost its lease, and must relocate. Most of the collection of authentic period trains including steam trains, passenger, freight, and commuter trains has been moved to the Niles Canyon museum. Once a new site is found, it will be posted on the museum's Web site.

San Francisco Cable Car Museum (Ages 5+)
(415) 474-1887; 1201 Mason Street, San Francisco, CA 94108
<www.cablecarmuseum.org>; <www.sfcablecar.com/barn.html>

Description: This museum shows how the cable system works. A video show of the San Francisco cable car system plays every 17 minutes. Best of all, the underground cable system can be viewed during its operation here at the museum.
Hours: *April–September:* Daily 10am–6pm, *October –March*: Daily 10am–5pm. Closed Easter Sunday, Thanksgiving, Christmas, and New Year's Day.
Cost: Free.
Bathrooms: Yes.
Facilities: Stroller friendly via Washington Street.
Food: No.
What to Bring: Jacket and cash for parking.
Follow-Up Activities: The Web site shows how cable cars work in the "Cable Car Heritage" section. Don't miss the annual Cable Car Ringing Competition usually held in July — see the "Cable Car Heritage" section on Web site for details and dates.

South Bay Historical Railroad Society (All Ages)
(408) 243-3969; 1005 Railroad Avenue, Santa Clara, CA 95050
<www.sbhrs.org>

Description: This museum is dedicated to the preservation and renovation of the historic Santa Clara Depot. The museum is a complex of historic buildings that gave this organization life. Besides operational scale model railroads on display, there are railroad artifacts, railroad signaling equipment, and right-of-way maps. There's also a library with a collection of railroading books and videos. Perhaps the best part of this museum is its proximity to the Union Pacific Santa Clara freight yard, where both freight and commuter trains can be seen and heard.

Hours: *Tues:* 6–9pm. *Sat:* 10am–3pm.

Cost: Free.

Bathrooms: Yes.

Facilities: Stroller friendly.

Food: No, restaurants across the street.

Follow-Up Activities: 1) Open House & Model Railroad Show in April and first weekend in November on both Sat & Sun: 10am–5pm. $5/ adult, free/child. 2) *Great American Train Shows:* All shows are 10am–4pm, $7/adult & free/child 12 and under. Discount coupon available online. Check Web site <gte.ciadvt.com> or <www.greattrainexpo.com> for current information and show schedule. Train show schedule:

• March   Cow Palace, Daly City.
• November   Alameda County Fairgrounds, Pleasanton.

These shows tour the U.S. with the largest model railroad displays.

Tiburon Railroad–Ferry Depot Museum (All Ages)

(415) 435-1853; 1920 Paradise Drive, Tiburon, CA 94920
<www.landmarks-society.org> select "Landmarks"

Description: This is a small museum with model train displays and historical exhibits of the old Tiburon trains.

Hours: Open April to October. Wed & Sun: 1–4pm.

Cost: Free. Donation appreciated.

Bathrooms: No, public restroom ½ block away.

Facilities: Stroller friendly.

Food: No, nearby restaurants.

What to Bring: Cash for parking, picnic lunch, sunscreen, and sunglasses. Recommends parking at 1550 Tiburon Boulevard, Tiburon.

Follow-Up Activities: Close to the Bay Area Discovery Museum in Sausalito and the Tiburon/Angel Island Ferry. See entries under Chapter 4: Science & Technology Museums, Chapter 6: Transportation Favorites—Boats: Ferries.

Western Railway Museum (All Ages)

(707) 374-2978; 5848 State Highway 12, Suisun, CA 94585
<www.wrm.org>

Description: This museum has 50 historic railcars on display as well as train rides on operational streetcars and interurban electric trains. The rides are unlimited with admission. In the second half of October, the Pumpkin Patch Festival includes unlimited train rides, hay rides, a hay bale fort, arts and crafts, live music, a petting zoo, and a pumpkin to take home.

Hours: *Year-round:* Sat & Sun: 10:30am–5pm. *Summer extended days* (Memorial Day to Labor Day): Wed–Sun: 10:30am–5pm. Pumpkin patch trains in late October run every half hour starting at 10am. Closed major holidays. Check Web site for specific holidays closed.

Cost: $10/adult, $9/senior 65+, $7/child (2–14). Pumpkin patch trains: $12/adult, $11/senior, $9/child (2-14).

Bathrooms: Yes.

Facilities: Stroller friendly.

Food: Café with hot dogs, ice cream, drinks, and snacks.

What to Bring: Cash, sunscreen, sunglasses, and camera.

Follow-Up Activities: Santa Trains run on the weekends in December prior to Christmas.

California State Railroad Museum (All Ages)
Out of Area

(916) 445-7387 **Business Office**; (916) 323-9280 **Museum Front Desk**
(916) 445-6645 **Recording**; 111 "I" Street, Sacramento, CA 95814
<www.californiastaterailroadmuseum.org>

Description: Located in Old Sacramento, this is considered to be one of the finest railroad museums in North America. The museum is housed in a complex of historic buildings with restored, authentic trains on display, as well as an operating steam train visitors can ride. There are changing exhibits such as the *Toy Trains on Parade* with a million-dollar toy train collection. Don't miss the *Evidence of a Dream* video documenting the importance of the railroad to California's growth and development. Docent-led tours follow the video. Tours last 30–40 minutes. Group tours can be scheduled in advance. For families, self-guided tours are available, with docents stationed throughout the museum to share their knowledge and answer questions. **Hours:** Daily 10am–5pm. *Train rides:* Every weekend April–September: Depart on the hour (11am–5pm) from the Central Pacific Railroad Freight Depot/Public Market in Old Sacramento for a 40-minute trip, just two blocks south of the Railroad Museum on Front Street. *Evidence of a Dream* video shown hourly, on the hour. The video lasts approximately 20 minutes.

Cost: *Museum Admission:* $8/adult, $3/youth 6–17, free/child 5 & under. *Train Tickets:* $8/adult, $3/youth 6–17, free/child 5 & under. *Free on Sacramento Museum Day:* <www.sacmuseums.org/museumday.html>

Bathrooms: Yes, but not on the trains!

Facilities: Stroller friendly, except on certain exhibits due to stairs and in narrow openings on passenger trains. Leave strollers by the ticket office.

Food: Silver Palace restaurant located in the Central Pacific Railroad Passenger Station, one block from the main entrance of the museum. Other restaurants are nearby.

What to Bring: Sunscreen, sunglasses, camera, and cash for food and parking. Plan to arrive with at least 20 minutes to spare to allow time to purchase tickets and to board.

Follow-Up Activities: 1) Visit Old Sacramento where this museum is located. This state park harkens back to the days of the Gold Rush. For additional information, see the Old Sacramento entry in Chapter 9: Historical Outings—Gold Rush. 2) For special events such as *Gold Rush Days* on Labor Day weekend, *Spookomotive* Halloween trains, and *Santa's Yuletide Express* in December, check the Web site. 3) For school field trips, call for free entry by reserving with Reserve America at (866) 240-4655. School tours led by docents require a nominal fee. Different programs available directed at specific objectives. 4) Watch for the next Railfair, a grand celebration of railroads and railroad history to be held when the new Railroad Technology Museum opens, expected in 2007/2008 timeframe. See Web site for current events. 5) For more railroad and Gold Rush history, look up information from the California State Railroad Museum Web site under "Explore & Learn": <www.csrmf.org/doc.asp?id=15>.

Directions: Public garage parking is located on I street entrance to Old Sacramento, and metered parking (limited to 90 minutes) is available.

Airplanes

Mankind has been fascinated with flight: from the days of Greek myths and the story of Icharus and Daedulus, to the Renaissance and Leonardo da Vinci's models, to the first planes invented by the Wright Brothers, to today's supersonic jets and space shuttle. Of course, flight has to be experienced by taking a ride. Before taking the first trip with your little one, consider visiting the airport just to familiarize your child with the hustle and bustle. There are three international airports and numerous municipal airports in the Bay Area. Visit the aviation museums for the history of flight and historic aircraft. Best of all, attend an air show to see these wonderful machines in action.

For an answer to "How Do Planes Fly?" visit the following Web sites: <www.howstuffworks.com> then search for airplanes or <www.allstar.fiu.edu/aero/fltmidfly.htm>

Airports

Oakland International Airport
(510) 563-3300; 1 Airport Drive, Oakland, CA 94621
<www.flyoakland.com>

Bathrooms: Yes.
Facilities: Stroller friendly.
Food: Yes.
What to Bring: Cash for parking and cart.
Follow-Up Activities: Western Aerospace Museum and the *U.S.S. Hornet* are nearby.

San Jose International Airport (SJC)
(408) 277-4SKY; 1661 Airport Boulevard, San Jose, CA 95110
<www.sjc.org>

Terminal A: 2077 Airport Boulevard, San Jose, CA 95110

International: 2065 Airport Boulevard, San Jose, CA 95110
Terminal C: 1661 Airport Boulevard, San Jose, CA 95110
Kidport, an aviation-themed play area, is located in the Main
Lobby by the Information Booth.

San Francisco International Airport (SFO)
(650) 821-8211;
Hwy 101 SF International Airport exit, South San Francisco, CA 94128
<www.flysfo.com>

Hours: The San Francisco International Airport is now home to many
exhibits featuring the arts, history, cultures, and sciences throughout the
airport. Visit <www.sfoarts.org> for current exhibits and locations. The
Aviation Museum, dedicated to the history of commerical aviation, is located within the International Terminal. AirTrain is a free service that
helps people navigate between the terminals, garages, and BART. It runs
two separate lines and provides a great way to tour the airport while enjoy-
ing free train rides for the kids. It runs frequently, 24 hours per day, every
day. Visit Web site, select "Airport Guide," then "Getting Around SFO,"
then "AirTrain" for the AirTrain routes map.
Bathrooms: Yes.
Facilities: Stroller friendly.
Food: Yes.
What to Bring: Cash for parking and cart.
Follow-Up Activities: The Aviation Library & Museum is located within
the international terminal on the "Departures" level, next to the escalators. It is free and open Sun–Fri 10am–4:30pm. No tickets or boarding
passes are needed. Closed Saturdays & holidays. The phone number is
(650) 821-9900 during open hours, and (650) 821-6700 during nonopen
hours. Directions/map on Web site: <www.sfoarts.org>, select "Library &
Museum" tab, then "Directions."

Watsonville Airport (Ages 8+)
(831) 728-6075; 100 Aviation Way, Watsonville, CA 95076
<www.watsonvilleairport.com>

Description: This small municipal airport has some wonderful events for
plane enthusiasts. 1) May–November, on the first Saturday of each month
10am–1pm, the Experimental Aircraft Association Chapter 119 sponsors

the Young Eagles Flight Rally [held at 60 Aviation Way, (831)479-7986] and gives *free* airplane rides to youths ages 8–17. There's a short preflight class explaining the theory of flight, a safety inspection of an aircraft, then a 20-minute flight around the Watsonville–Santa Cruz area. Release forms signed by parents required. 2) *Watsonville Fly-In & Air Show* on Memorial Day Weekend every year. 3) *Airport Open House* in October. See Web site for events.

Cost: Free, except for the Fly-In & Air Show. See Air Shows section for more details.
Bathrooms: Yes.
Facilities: Stroller friendly.
Food: Yes.
What to Bring: Cash for food.

Air Shows

California International Air Show (All Ages)
1-888-845-SHOW; (831)754-1983
Salinas Airport: 30 Mortensen Avenue, Salinas, CA 93905 (off of Highway 101)
<www.salinasairshow.com>; <www.airshownetwork.com>

Description: This weekend-long air show features military aircraft such as the U.S. Air Force Thunderbirds (and sometimes the Blue Angels), the Stealth fighter, antique aircraft, and acrobatics. The Friday evening show has a fireworks display.
Schedule: September/October weekend starting at 9am. Flying events start at 11am. Visit Web site for most current information.
Cost: $8 parking. Purchase tickets online. Price ranges from $15-$27/adult dependent on seat & time purchased. $11-$24/child 6-12, free/child under 6. Premium box seats available at higher cost.
Bathrooms: Yes.
Facilities: Stroller friendly.
Food: Yes.
What to Bring: Sunscreen, sunglasses, camera, and cash for parking and food. Airshow runs rain or shine, so be prepared.

Fleet Week in San Francisco (All Ages)

(650) 599-5057; Marina Green: Scott Street and Marina Boulevard, Pier 39, Beach Street & The Embarcadero, San Francisco, CA 94133

<www.military.com/Content/MoreContent1?file=main>

<www.airshownetwork.com> Annual show schedule posted in January.

<www.fishermanswharf.org/Events.htm>

Description: Fleet Week includes air shows and the Parade of Ships sponsored by the Navy. The Blue Angels are usually the star attraction. Tours of ships for ages 4+. Read security requirments on Web site prior to outing.

Schedule: The event takes place usually on a weekend in early October along the San Francisco waterfront from the Ferry Building on Fisherman's Wharf to Marina Green. The schedule of events usually includes a *Practice Air Show* on Friday afternoon at the Municipal Pier/San Francisco waterfront. *Parade of Ships* usually is on Saturday morning from 11am–noon, with the best view at Marina Green. *Air Shows* (415) 487-6453 on both days noon–5pm, with the Blue Angels flying at 3pm. Pier 39 (415) 705-5500, Ghiradelli Square, Marina Green, The Cannery (415) 771-3112, and Muni Pier have entertainment scheduled on Sat & Sun.

Cost: Free along the waterfront, but premium seating can be purchased through the Air Show Network at the Web site above or by calling (800) 367-5833. Entertainment listed above is free except for food and parking. For discount coupons to businesses and attractions at Fisherman's Wharf, visit Fisherman's Wharf's Web site under "Discount Coupons."

Bathrooms: Yes.

Facilities: Stroller friendly.

Food: Yes.

What to Bring: Sunscreen, sunglasses, camera, cash for parking and food, and a jacket (San Francisco can be foggy and cold, even in the summer).

Pacific Coast Dream Machines (All Ages)
Half Moon Bay Airport

(650) 726-2328; Hwy 1, 5 miles North of Hwy 92, Half Moon Bay, CA

<www.miramarevents.com>

Description: Static displays of 2,000 driving, flying and working machines including classic cars, army tanks, antique motorcycles, military aircraft, Model-T cars, steam tractors and other farm equipment, race cars, and show planes. Helicopter and biplane rides are available at additional cost. Live music and food booths.

Schedule: Last Sunday in April: 10am–4pm. Check Web site 3 weeks prior to the event for details. The show was cancelled in 2006.

Cost: $15/adult, $5/senior 65+ or youth 5–14, free/child 4 & under. Parking included with admission. Tickets available at the gate only.

Bathrooms: Yes.

Facilities: Stroller friendly.

Food: Yes.

What to Bring: Sunscreen, sunglasses, camera, cash for parking and food, and jacket. The coast can be foggy and cold, even in the summer.

Vertical Challenge Helicopter Show (All Ages)
San Carlos Airport—Hiller Aviation Museum
(650) 654-0200; 601 Skyway Road, San Carlos, CA 94070
<www.hiller.org>

Description: Besides performing flying feats, the air show exhibits the full range and use of helicopters, from military to life saving functions. Attractions include helicopter rides; Otto the Clown helicopters; ShowCopters demonstrating formation maneuvers and the helicopter's versatility; search and rescue helicopter demonstrations; and firefighting, police, and emergency helicopters. There is also a pyrotechnics show from Canada. During the show, ride a helicopter for $40/person.

Schedule: Event occurs in mid-June, with ticket sales starting June 1 at the Hiller Aviation Museum, 9am–5pm. Two air shows: 11:30 am morning air show and a different air show at 2pm. Each show is one hour long.

Cost: $15/adult, $10/youth (5–17) or senior 65+, free/child 4 & under.

Bathrooms: Yes.

Facilities: Stroller friendly.

Food: Yes.

What to Bring: Sunscreen, sunglasses, camera, and cash for food.

Watsonville Fly-In & Air Show
(831)763-5600; Watsonville Airport: 100 Aviation Way, Watsonville, CA 95076
<www.watsonvilleflyin.org>

Description: See daredevils stunts and aerobatics, military fly-bys, and military aircraft displays. Get a close-up view of antique aircraft, helicopters, military planes, and homemade aircraft. Friday night performance features fireworks.

Schedule: Every Memorial Day Weekend.

Cost: $4 parking. Advance tickets: $10/adult, $4/child 6–12, $8/senior 60+ or military, $25/family (2 adults & 2 kids) for 1 day. Prices at the gate: $15/adult, $5/child 6–12, $10/senior 60+ or military w/ ID. Purchase tickets online.

Bathrooms: Yes.

Facilities: Stroller friendly.

Food: Yes.

What to Bring: Sunscreen, sunglasses, camera, cash, and parking.

Wings Over Wine Country Air Show
Pacific Coast Air Museum
(707) 575-7900 Museum; (707) 566-8380 Hotline;
2230 Becker Boulevard, Santa Rosa, CA 95403
<www.pacificcoastairmuseum.org>

Description: Antique, military, and modern day aircraft perform fly-bys and stunts. Best of all, visitors can climb aboard and see antique and military aircraft close-up.

Schedule: Weekend in mid-August, 9am–4pm.

Cost: $15/adult @ gate, $13/adult in advance, $10/senior 65+, $5/child 6-12, free/child 5 & under, free/active military with ID.

Bathrooms: Yes.

Facilities: Jogger stroller friendly. Baby carrier recommended.

Food: Yes.

What to Bring: Sunscreen, sunglasses, camera, and cash for food and parking.

Aviation Museums

Hiller Aviation Museum (Ages 4+)
(650) 654-0200; 601 Skyway Road, San Carlos, CA 94070
<www.hiller.org>

Description: The museum chronicles one hundred years of flight, with vintage aircraft, airplane models, prototypes of future aircraft, and pictures. Avitor, the first "aeroplane," was developed here in the San Francisco Bay Area. We get the word airplane from this first "aeroplane," coined by its British inventor who was living in San Mateo at the time. The Restoration Shop shows restoration projects in progress. Docent-led tours and school field trips are available with at least 3 weeks advanced reservations. Don't miss the virtual exhibits on the Web showing different aircraft through the years, including the Flying Platform.

Hours: Daily 10am–5pm. Call prior to visit; occasional closure due to special events.

Cost: $9/adult, $6/senior 65+ or youth (5–17), free/child under 5. Get a $1 discount coupon from the Web site.

Bathrooms: Yes.

Facilities: Stroller friendly.

Food: Restaurants next door.

What to Bring: Picnic lunch or cash for food.

Follow-Up Activities: 1) Offers a Young Eagles program for children 8–17 to fly over San Francisco Bay for free on the third Saturday of each month from 11am–1pm at the San Carlos Airport. A legal guardian must sign the registration form. The flights are in a registered airplane flown by a licensed pilot. See Web site for details. 2) Many special events offered by the museum, including the air show in June. Visit the Web site for current events schedule. 3) Week-long Aviation Day Camp in the summer is available for children in grades 2–5.

U.S.S. Hornet Museum (Ages 5+)

(510) 521-8448
Pier 3, Alameda Point, Alameda, CA 94501 (Atlantic Avenue and the Bay)
<www.uss-hornet.org>

Description: WW II-era aircraft carrier known for its combat record and recovery of the Apollo 11 command module. Current displays include only a few planes, but aircraft from the 1940s through the 1960s, including dive bombers and torpedo planes, will be added as restoration work on the vessel continues. Visiting this aircraft carrier is truly an "event" or an "experience" because these humongous ships at the dock require your presence to fully appreciate their awesome size. Just driving onto the dock and seeing the ships looming above is an awesome experience. It's also a bit of a thrill to get to the boat as you go up the catwalk onto

the main deck. Tours take you to all parts of the boat, from flight simulators and navigation to the top deck where the planes lift off and land. My then 5-year-old daughter said, "This is cool!" Overnight parties for scouts, school groups, corporate events, and birthday parties are available.
Hours: Daily 10am–5pm. Closed Thanksgiving, Christmas, and New Year's Days. Tours start at 11am; arrive before 1pm to sign up. Children under 12 are not allowed into the engine room and the combat information center. Last admission is at 4pm.
Cost: $14/adult; $12/senior, student, or military w/ ID; $6/child 5–17; free/child 4 & under.
Bathrooms: Yes.
Facilities: Wheelchair accessible through the elevator in the back of the boat, but access is limited. Stairs and ladders throughout the boat. Strollers not recommended.
Food: No.
What to Bring: Jacket, camera, and cash. No backpacks are allowed onboard—check bags at entrance.
Follow-Up Activities: Western Aerospace Museum at the Oakland Airport is close by.

Western Aerospace Museum (Ages 6+)
(510) 638-7100; 8260 Boeing Street, Oakland, CA 94614
<www.westernaerospacemuseum.org>

Description: This collection has historically significant planes including a flying boat (extra $2 for a tour), a plane similar to Amelia Earhart's, and a former NASA vertical take-off Harrier jet. There are many model airplanes and some large model ships as well as a few planes that youngsters can board and experience with adult supervision.
Hours: Wed–Sun: 10 am–4pm. Flying boat open for boarding only on Sunday. Closed Monday and Tuesday.
Cost: $9/adult, $8/senior, $7/youth 13–18 or military, $5/child 6–12, free/child 5 & under.
Bathrooms: Yes.
Facilities: Ströller friendly.
Food: No, area with tables and soft drinks. Deli nearby.
What to Bring: Picnic lunch.
Follow-Up Activities: *U.S.S. Hornet* is close by.

Wings of History Air Museum (Ages 5+)

(408) 683-2290; Mailing address: PO Box 495, San Martin, CA 95046
12777 Murphy Avenue, San Martin, CA 95046;
<www.wingsofhistory.org>

Description: Many gliders and an exact replica of the 1903 Wright Flyer built by the Wright brothers are on display.

Hours: Tues & Thur: 11am–3pm, Sat & Sun: 11am–4pm.

Cost: Free. Requested donation of $5/adult, $3/child.

Bathrooms: Yes.

Facilities: Stroller friendly.

Food: No. Picnic lunch OK. Restaurants are nearby in Morgan Hill.

What to Bring: Picnic lunch. Sunscreen, sunglasses, camera, and cash for food if you're planning to visit the Cinco de Mayo event.

Follow-Up Activities: Annual open house event in May at the South County Airport in San Martin is the best time to visit. The event has hot air balloons, display of vintage model airplanes, antique cars and model Ts, steam and diesel trains, and Young Eagles free rides program for kids 8–17. Food is available during the special event.

Cars

From the first wagons and carriages to today's cars and trucks, automotive history has evolved. Want to see how cars are made? The New United Motor Manufacturing plant in Fremont, a joint venture between Toyota and General Motors, will show you. For a selection of vintage cars, visit the Blackhawk Museum in Danville or attend the classic car shows. Your child is fascinated with fire trucks? Visit the Fire Truck Museum in San Francisco, or take a tour of San Francisco in an antique red fire truck. Need for speed? Visit Malibu Grand Prix for a taste of race car driving.

Blackhawk Museum (All Ages)

(925) 736-2280; 3700 Blackhawk Plaza Circle, Danville, CA 94506
<www.blackhawkmuseum.org>

Description: The museum is located in Blackhawk Plaza with its beautiful water fountains and man-made creek, home to resident ducks. The automotive museum provides an extensive and exquisite collection of vintage cars, providing examples of cars as they evolved through the years, starting with carriages, the Model-T, and all the cars along the way. Affiliation with the Smithsonian Institute provides another source for high-quality changing exhibits.

Hours: Wed–Sun: 10am–5pm. Closed Thanksgiving, Christmas, and New Year's days. *Docent-led tours* are available on weekends at 2pm. Tours last approximately one hour, included with paid admission.

Cost: $8/adult, $5/student with ID or senior 65+, free/child 6 & active military. Scheduled school, youth, & disabled persons groups are free.

Bathrooms: Yes.

Facilities: Stroller friendly.

Food: No, but restaurants in the plaza. You can also bring a picnic lunch and picnic on the lawn.

What to Bring: Cash for food.

Follow-Up Activities: 1) Tours for groups and school field trips are available. 2) Annual Open House in August. 3) Car shows and special events throughout the year. See Web site calendar for events information.

Bonfante Gardens Family Theme Park has a ride featuring antique 1920s and 1950s vintage cars.

Children's Discovery Museum in San Jose has a real ambulance, an old-fashioned fire truck, and an antique car for children to sit in and explore.

Hillsborough Concourse d'Elegance (All Ages)
Classic Car Show and Carnival at Crocker Middle School
(650) 344-2272; 2600 Ralston Avenue, Hillsborough, CA 94010
<www.hillsboroughconcours.org>

Description: Sponsored by the parents of Hillsborough public schools, this event is a fundraiser for the schools. The show exhibits 200 select vintage, classic, and exotic cars representing various historic periods. There's also a parade of classic cars winding along the coast and Woodside before arriving at Hillsborough. The family carnival includes entertainment and food for the whole family. See schedule and map with free parking loca-

tions and shuttles on the Web site.
Schedule: First Sunday in May, 10am–4pm. Confirm on Web site.
Cost: $10/adult, $5/youth 5–15, free/child 5 & under.

History Park, San Jose at Kelly Park has antique automobiles on display at the Trolley Barn.

Malibu Grand Prix and Malibu Castle (See height requirements)

(650) 366-6463; 340 Blomquist Street, Redwood City, CA 94063
<www.malibugrandprix.com>

Description: This entertainment complex includes miniature golf, batting cages, an arcade, and a mini-racing track with smaller scale "race" cars. The driving course accommodates go-carts, one-seater cars, and two-seater cars.
Hours: *Summer:* Mon–Sun: 10am–midnight. *Fall:* Mon–Thur: noon–9pm, Fri: noon–11pm, Sat: 10am–11pm, Sun: 10am–9pm. The *minimum height requirements* are 3'6" for car passenger, 4'8" for go-cart rider, and 5' for Grand Prix driver with a valid driver's license.
Cost: *One-seater & go-carts*: $4/1 lap, $14.95/4 laps, $18.95/6 laps, $24.95/10 laps. *Two-seaters*: Add $2 for each of the above prices for the one-seater, except it is $5/1 lap.
Bathrooms: Yes.
Facilities: Strollers not recommended.
Food: Yes.
What to Bring: Plenty of cash, sunscreen, and sunglasses.

Jack London Square (All Ages)

1 (866) 295-9853;
Jack London Square: Broadway & Water Street, Oakland, CA 94607
<www.jacklondonsquare.com>

Description: Jack London Square has many events throughout the year, including car and boat shows such as the annual Strictly Sail Pacific in April <www.sailamerica.com> and the Fall Boat Show in September. The July 4th celebration features fireworks and a free concert.

NUMMI (Min. Age: 10)
(New United Motor Manufacturing)
(510) 498-5649; (510) 498-5765; 45500 Fremont Boulevard, Fremont, CA 94538
<www.nummi.com>

See Chapter 7: How Things Work—Site Tours.

Oak Meadow Park in Los Gatos has an antique fire truck.
See Chapter 6: Transportation Favorites—Trains.

Palo Alto Concours D'Elegance, Classic Car Show
(650) 961-5444; Stanford University: Sand Hill Rd. & Pasteur Dr., Stanford, CA
<www.paconcours.com>

Description: Sponsored by the Palo Alto Lions Club for charity, this car show includes exhibits of race cars, vintage cars, cars from private collections, military cars, hot rods, and a working miniature engine by the Bay Area Engine Modelers on display. Food and drinks are available at the show. See the map on the Web site.

Schedule: Late June Sunday, 7am–4:30pm.

Cost: $25/person, free/child 12 and under.

San Francisco Fire Department Museum (All Ages)
(415) 563-4630; 655 Presidio Avenue, San Francisco, CA 94115
<www.sffiremuseum.org>

Description: Displays antique fire vehicles previously used by the fire department, including horse-drawn steamers, hand pumps, trucks from the 1800s, a fire bell, a fire alarm, and the fire department's history and memorabilia.

Hours: Thur–Sun: 1–4pm.

Cost: Free.

Bathrooms: No. Fire department next door has one, but not always available.

Facilities: Stroller friendly.

Food: No, nearby.

Follow-Up Activities: 1) Antique fireboats are docked at Pier 22½ at Embarcadero and Harrison Streets. For pictures and information of the fireboats, visit: <www.sffiremuseum.org/fireboats.html>. 2) Visit Web site to learn about the great fires of San Francisco, including the 1906 earthquake and fire.

San Francisco Fire Department Stations (Ages 5+)

You can visit fire stations throughout the city by arranging visits through the administrative office (415) 558-3403. For stations closest to you, visit their Web site: <www.ci.sf.ca.us/fire>. In fact, many city fire departments will accommodate station visits by groups. Call your local station to request a visit.

San Francisco Fire Engine Tours (All Ages)
The Cannery, Fisherman's Wharf

(415) 333-7077; 2801 Leavenworth Street, San Francisco, CA 94133
<www.fireenginetours.com>;
<www.thecannery.com>; <www.delmontesquare.com>

Description: Ride an old-fashioned shiny red fire engine for a 75-minute tour of the Presidio, Fort Point, Sausalito, Fort Baker, and over the Golden Gate Bridge.

Schedule: Tours leave daily at 1pm, except on Tues. On certain days, there are additional tours at 11am, 3pm, & 5pm. Tours depart from The Cannery, located at Courtyard Level, Beach Street and Columbus. Advanced reservations are required.

Cost: $40/adult, $30/teen, $25/child 12 & under.

Bathrooms: None onboard. Bathrooms located at The Cannery.

Facilities: Some strollers can fit into the truck to be stowed. It's best to leave the stroller in the car in the parking garage across the street.

Food: No, nearby restaurants.

What to Bring: Cash for parking, warm jacket, sunglasses, and camera.

Follow-Up Activities: Birthday party and charters offered.

San Jose Fire Department (Min. Age: 5)
Office of Public Education

(408) 277-2878; 170 W. San Carlos Steet, San Jose, CA 95113
<www.sjfd.org>; <www.sjfd.org/PubEd/index_pubed.htm>

Description: Station tours and other community education programs available. Complete the request form on the Web site and return it at least

3 weeks in advance. Only children 5 and older may visit. *Do not bring strollers and children under 5 years old*; the fire stations are not childproof and may be dangerous for children under 5.

Towe Auto Museum in Old Sacramento has vintage cars on display. See entry in Chapter 9: Historical Outings—Gold Rush under Old Sacramento.

Chapter 7
How Things Work

Many companies and organizations provide tours of their facilities to show the public how they make their products. These tours are usually free or are very affordable. They provide the company with free publicity and the public with knowledge of the processes involved in making the products we see and use every day. Help your child learn about how things work. Stanford University's Alliance for Innovative Manufacturing has a Web site with virtual tours of "How Everyday Things Are Made": <http://manufacturing.stanford.edu/>. Tours on airplanes, cars, candy, clothes, and packaging as well as processes such as die casting, molding, and assembly.

Site Tours

Basic Brown Bear Factory (Ages 3 +)
1-866-5BB-BEAR; (415) 409-2806; 2801 Leavenworth Street, San Francisco, CA
<www.basicbrownbear.com>

Description: Learn how the teddy bear got its name and the process of making a teddy bear from designing to cutting to stuffing and cleaning. Each child can make his own bear. Groups: minimum $12 purchase/person required.

Hours: Mon–Sat: 10am–6pm, Sun: 11am–6pm. Hourly tours daily until 1 hour prior to closing. Reservations required for groups of 8 people or more. Call ahead for available times.

Cost: $12 for the smallest bear. Prices vary depending on the size of bear and clothing purchased. $20/child for birthday party.

Bathrooms: Yes.

Facilities: Stroller friendly.

Food: No, nearby restaurants.

Cowgirl Creamery (Age 3 +)

(415) 663-9335; 80 Fourth Street, Pt. Reyes Station, CA 94956
<www.cowgirlcreamery.com>

Description: Watch cheese being made through a glass window. Call to find out the cheese making schedule. Or take the tour on Fridays to learn how cheese is made. Tours also offered through Marin Agricultural Land Trust's hikes and tours programs: <www.malt.org>.

Hours: Wed–Sun: 10am–6pm. Group tours held on Fridays at 11:30am last for 25 minutes. Call for reservations.

Cost: $3/person for group tours.

Federal Reserve Bank Tour, San Francisco (Ages 12 +)

(415) 974-3252; 101 Market Street, San Francisco, CA 94105
<www.frbsf.org/federalreserve/tours.html>
<www.federalreserveeducation.org> For High School & College level info.

Description: The highlight of this free tour is the fabulous currency exhibit, which encompasses the first notes of the 13 colonies, the gold standard notes, and today's currency. During the tour, visitors learn how to distinguish counterfeit bills, play a video game to learn about interest rates and inflation, watch a video depicting the history of currency, and learn about the basic structure of the federal reserve and its role in the economy. There's lots of history and fascinating facts to learn. Federal buildings now requires this tour to be conducted after a security check.

Hours: Access to the exhibit is limited to the hour-long tours, which take place every Friday at 12 noon on a drop-in basis. Bring identification with you. To avoid disappointment, allow ample time to find parking and to walk to the bank. For groups, the federal reserve offers personal finance training as well as tours. Group tours for high schoolers and above available Monday through Thursday at 9:30am or 1:30pm; call in advance for reservations.

Follow-Up Activities: Don't miss the FedVille online town with games and activities designed especially for kids ages 9–12 to learn about money: <www.frbsf.org/education/fedville>. For more online money facts, history, and information, visit: <www.frbsf.org/federalreserve/money/index.html>. For educational exhibits on-line produced by the U.S. Treasury: <www.treas.gov/education>. Take a virtual tour of the main Treasury Building in Washington D.C. The Web site for kids, <www.treas.gov/kids>, has links to the U.S. Mint, Bureau of Engraving and Printing, and more. For U.S. Mint history: <usmint.gov/historianscorner> or <usmint.gov>.

Fortune Cookie Factory (All Ages)
(510) 832-5552; 261 12th Street, Oakland, CA 94607
<www.chinese-fortune-cookie.com>

Description: See how fortune cookies are made.
Hours: Mon–Fri: 10am–3pm for groups of less than 10 people. Self-tour. Guided tour only for groups of 10 people or more; call for reservations.
Cost: $1/person. You also get a bag of cookies.
Bathrooms: Yes.
Facilities: Stroller friendly.
Food: Restaurant next door.

Golden Gate Fortune Cookie Company (All Ages)
(415) 781-3956; 56 Ross Alley, San Francisco, CA 94108
<www.chinese-fortune-cookie.com>

Description: See how fortune cookies are made.
Hours: 9am–12am (midnight).
Cost: Free tour with a free sample. $3/bag of cookies.
Bathroom: Yes.
Facility: Stroller friendly.
Food: No. Nearby restaurants.

Jelly Belly Factory Tour (All Ages)
(800) 953-5592; One Jelly Bean Lane, Fairfield, CA 94533
<www.jellybelly.com>

Description: Walking tour shows the candy making process. Tour lasts ~40 minutes. During the tour, you'll see amazing examples of mosaic and sculpture art composed entirely of Jelly Belly beans. There's even a portrait of President Reagan and other famous celebrities. Besides jelly beans, the factory also makes gummi candy, chocolates, and taffy. There's an exhibi-

tion kitchen where hand-dipped chocolates are made in front of visitors. Free tasting at the end of the tour lets the visitor try more than 50 different flavors of Jelly Belly beans. Virtual tour on Web site.
Hours: Visitor Center open daily 9am–5pm. Tours operate 9am-4pm and run every 15 minutes; reservations not needed. Closed Thanksgiving, Christmas, New Year's, and Easter Sunday. Check Web site to verify dates and hours, especially during the holiday season prior to your trip. On weekends, only videos show the candy making process since the workers have the weekend off.
Cost: Free.
Bathrooms: Yes.
Facility: Stroller friendly.
Food: Jelly Belly Café. Open 11am–3pm. There're plenty of picnic tables, if you want to bring a picnic.
Follow-Up Activities: Special events during October with "Halloween Swamp Tour" and "Munchkin Masquerade;" "Jelly Belly Tree Lighting Ceremony" and "Photos with Santa" after Thanksgiving; and "Brunch with Santa" in early December. Call event reservations at (707) 399-2266 in early November. Reserve early to avoid disappointment.

Levi Strauss Visitor Center
(415) 501-6000; 1-800-USA-LEVI; 1155 Battery Street, San Francisco, CA 94111
<www.levistrauss.com/Heritage/OurArchives.aspx>

Description: Although the factory tours have been discontinued, there is a Visitor Center on Battery Street. See exhibits of jeans styles, video booths running a video on old advertisements, and a video on how jeans were made.
Hours: Mon–Fri: 9am–6pm; Sat & Sun: 10am-5pm.
Cost: Free.
Bathrooms: Yes.
Facilities: Stroller friendly.
Food: No.
Follow-Up Activities: Company history archive online:
<www.levistrauss.com/Heritage>.

Marin French Cheese Company (All Ages)

(800) 292-6001 x12; (707) 762-6001; 7500 Red Hill Road, Petaluma, CA 94952
<www.marinfrenchcheese.com>

Description: See how Camembert and Brie cheeses are made during this factory tour. The Web site has a collection of recipes using these cheeses.
Hours: 8:30am–5pm. *Tours:* daily 10am–4pm, dependent on staff availability. Call to verify. Reservations required for groups of 10 or more.
Cost: Free.
Bathroom: Yes.
Facilities: Strollers can be left at the store. Baby carrier recommended.
Food: Deli and gift store.
What to Bring: Picnic lunch and drinks. Don't forget the sunscreen and sunglasses during the summer.

Mee Mee Bakery (Ages 5+)

(415) 362-3204; 1328 Stockton Street, San Francisco, CA 94133
<www.meemeebakery.com>

Description: Located within San Francisco's Chinatown, this bakery makes the Shangri-La brand of Chinese fortune cookies as well as other Chinese baked goods. Custom cookie orders are $15/100 cookies.
Hours: Daily 8am–6pm. Call for a tour appointment.
Cost: Free.
Bathrooms: No.
Facilities: Not stroller friendly.
Food: Fortune cookies and chinese pastries. Food nearby in Chinatown.
What to Bring: Cash for parking.

Monterey Bay Chocolates (All Ages)

(831) 899-7963; 1291 Fremont Boulevard, Seaside, CA 93955
<montereybaychocolates.com>

Description: See how more than 100 types of chocolates are made.
Hours: Mon–Fri: 10am–6pm, Sat: 10am–5pm; closed Sundays except for some extended hours during holidays. Tours available during weekdays, but depend on availability of Verne Ricketts. Free samples of the chocolates at the chocolate buffet. See the movie at <www.earthflix.com/stories/chocolate_01.php>.

Cost: Free.
Bathrooms: Not open to the public.
Facilities: Stroller friendly.
Food: No, restaurants across the street.
What to Bring: Picnic lunch and drinks.

Mrs. Grossman's Sticker Factory (Recommended Age: 5+)

(800) 429-4549; (707) 763-1700; 3810 Cypress Drive, Petaluma CA 94954
<www.mrsgrossmans.com>

Description: Take a tour and learn how stickers are made. The Visitor Center features a video showcasing how Mrs. Grossman started her company from the first heart sticker. There are displays of all the stickers ever made by Mrs. Grossman on the walls. At the end of the tour, stickers and postcards are provided for kids to decorate. Sticker art classes available. Check Web site for the map and calendar of events.
Hours: *Store:* Mon–Fri: 9am–5:30pm. *Tours:* September through first week of June: Mon–Fri: 9:30am, 11am, 1pm, and 2:30pm. *Summer & Holiday Tours:* Mon–Fri: 9am–3pm, starting on the hour. Check Web site for specific holiday dates. Reservations are required.
Cost: $3/person (age 3+).
Bathrooms: Yes.
Facilities: Strollers OK in the store, but not on the tour.
Food: Vending machines with snacks only. Dining room and picnic tables outside.
What to Bring: Camera, picnic lunch, and drinks.

NUMMI (Min. Age: 10+)
(New United Motor Manufacturing)

(510) 498-5649; 45500 Fremont Boulevard, Fremont, CA
<www.nummi.com>; Map/directions: <www.nummi.com/direct_loc.html>

Description: Take a 75-minute tour and learn about the car manufacturing process. It is appropriate only for children ages 10 and up. For younger children, visit the Web site for an online tour to learn about the process. Cameras or cell phones with cameras are not allowed.
Hours: Free tours offered Mon–Fri: 10:15am for youth groups and 8:15am or 9am for adult groups. Reservations required (510) 770-4008

or book online.

Cost: Free.

Follow-Up Activities: Virtual tour: <www.nummi.com/web_tour.html>.

Oakdale Cheese & Specialties (Ages 5+)

(209) 848-3139; 10040 Hwy 120, Oakdale, CA 95361
<www.oakdalecheese.com>

Description: Learn how cheese is made with the tour and educational video. This site also features a petting zoo and picnic area. The company also makes brownies and cheesecakes.

Hours: Daily 9am–6pm.

Cost: Free tours. Groups more than 10 require advanced reservations. Company requests $0.50/child to provide feed for the animals.

Bathrooms: Yes.

Facilities: Stroller friendly.

Food: French bread and cheese are available from the bakery and gift shop.

What to Bring: Picnic lunch and drinks.

Port of Oakland (All Ages)

(510) 627-1188; Jack London Square, 530 Water Street, Oakland, CA 94607
<www.portofoakland.com/communit/serv_tour.asp>

Description: Take an hour-long tour around the Oakland harbor to learn how Oakland contributes to our region's economy and the maritime operations of massive cranes constantly loading and unloading container ships from around the world. Reservations for groups up to 50 required at least 3 days in advance.

Schedule: Third Thursday of each month from May through October. Reservations begin in April. Departures at 10:30am & 1pm; boarding begins 30 minutes prior.

Cost: Free.

Bathrooms: Yes.

Facilities: Stroller friendly.

Food: Snacks available for purchase.

What to Bring: Picnic lunch, cash for parking and food, camera, and windbreaker. Breezes on the ferries can be cool, even in the summer.

Follow-Up Activities: The *U.S.S. Potomac* is located at the next dock.

Practicum Kids (Ages 6–9)

(510) 573-2211

<www.practicumkids.com>

Description: Summer camp offered through Fremont's Recreation Services Department <www.ci.fremont.ca.us/Recreation> and *Ohlone for Kids* show kids how things work in local businesses and factories. Tours have included Bank of America, Barnes and Noble Booksellers, Kaiser Permanente, Raley's Supermarket, Fremont Police Department, and even a TV station. Workshops on entrepreneurship and how the city council works are offered through the Ohlone For Kids program. Ohlone for Kids is a program of Ohlone College in Fremont. Registration for the summer camps begins in March. Visit Web site **<www.ohloneforkids.com>** or call (510) 659-6090.

Scharffen Berger Chocolate Maker (Min. Age: 10)

(510) 981-4050; (510)843-6000 cafe; (800) 930-4528 **Retail orders**

914 Heinz Avenue, Berkeley, CA 94707

<www.scharffenberger.com>

Description: Learn about chocolates, how and where cocoa beans are grown, their history, and how they are made. Tours last approximately 1 hour and include chocolate tasting. Vitual tour available on the Web site. Tours can be reserved online.

Hours: 10am–5pm. Mon, Tues, & Thur: 10:30am, 12:30pm, 1:30pm, 2:30pm, and 3:30pm tours. Wed & Fri: 10:30am, 12:30pm, 1:30pm, and 3:30pm tours. Sat: 10:30am, 11:30am, 12:30pm, 1:30pm, 2:30pm, and 4:30pm tours. Sun: 11:30am, 12:30pm, 2:30pm, 3:30pm. Reservations required and can be made on the Web site. Walk-ins available only if there is space. Arrive 10 minutes prior to the start of the tour.

Cost: Free for public tour. Private tour: $35 with max. of 35 people; call (510) 981-4066 to arrange for private tour.

Bathrooms: Yes.

Facilities: Wheelchair accessible.

Food: Cafe at the factory open 11am to 3pm.

What to Bring: Wear closed-toe shoes for saftey.

Stanford Linear Accelerator Tour (Recommended Age: 11+)

(650) 926-2204; 2575 Sand Hill Road, Menlo Park, CA 94025
<home.slac.stanford.edu/visitslac.htmls>; <www2.slac.stanford.edu/vvc>

Description: Visitor Center has displays on the forefront of particle physics programs of the laboratory. Children under 11 may come with parents, but it is recommended that children be older due to the complexity of the information presented. The Web site has information and a virtual tour on the linear accelerator and how it works; the particle detectors and how they work; and how electron beams and synchrotron x-ray technologies are used in medical, biological, and industrial applications.

Hours: *Visitor Center:* Mon–Fri: 8am–5pm. *Tour Schedule:* Tours conducted several times a week for the public, generally at 10am and 1pm. Tours last approximately two hours. Advanced reservations required and can be made on the Web site. Groups can call to select the best times available; some evening tours.

Cost: Free.

Bathrooms: Yes.

Facilities: Wheelchair accessible.

Food: Available at the cafeteria next to the auditorium. Reservations must be made in advance.

What to Bring: Photo ID or passport at the gate. Cameras OK.

U.S. Geological Survey (Recommended Age: 8+)

Western Region Center, Menlo Park

(650) 853-8300 Operator; (650) 329-4390 Recording; (650) 329-5392 Speaker and Tour requests; 1-888-ASK-USGS
345 Middlefield Road, Menlo Park, CA 94025
<http://openhouse.wr.usgs.gov>; Events: <http://online.wr.usgs.gov/calendar>;
Map: <http://online.wr.usgs.gov/kiosk/mptour.html>

Description: 1) *Tours* of the facility are available to groups of 10–20. Larger groups can be accommodated by splitting into separate tour groups. Tours last approximately 1 hour. The first 30 minutes are spent on earthquakes, followed by 30 minutes at the Information Center with explanations on how to read topographic maps and the products in the Info Center. The tour can be extended with a self-guided tour that directs the visitor to a collection of rocks (including the second largest rock found in Antarctica) and globes, as well as the library. For tour reservations, call the tour co-ordinator. 2) The *Open House* provides a very rare opportunity to see the inner workings of the USGS, to talk to the scientists, and to see the latest research and exhibits. It occurs only every three years, due to lack of funding. There's food and live music at this event. There are exhibits and hands-on activities for kids, including free gold panning. Activities include touring the USGS laboratories, learning how maps are made, watching educational videos, and learning about science and nature. You can learn to identify rocks, experience the rock hardness scale with different types of rocks, and see which rock can float. There are also exhibits on earthquakes where children 11 and under can ride a simulated earthquake and experience the earth scope to learn how it detects earthquakes. See exhibits on volcanoes and landslides, as well as the ecosystem of the mudflats and the San Francisco Bay.

Hours: Open House should be in 2009, 2012, etc. The event is usually held in early or mid-May. It's open to the public on Sat–Sun 10am–4pm. Schools have a special preview day on the Friday prior, 9am–3pm, by invitation only. Call for Schools Preview Day at (650) 329-4477.

Cost: Free.

Bathrooms: Yes.

Facilities: Stroller friendly.

Food: Snack bars and concessions at the Open House event only.

What to Bring: Sunscreen, sunglasses, camera, and cash for food.

Follow-Up Activities: 1) *Ask-a-Geologist* by e-mail: <ask-a-geologist@usgs. gov>. 2) The Learning Web at <education.usgs.gov> has lots of information on a huge range of science topics for students, teachers, and explorers.

Whole Foods (All Ages)

<www.wholefoods.com>

(510) 649-1333	3000 Telegraph Avenue, Berkeley, CA 94705
(408) 371-5000	1690 S. Bascom Avenue, Campbell, CA 95008
(408) 257-7000	20830 Stevens Creek Boulevard, Cupertino, CA 95014
(650) 559-0300	4800 El Camino Real, Los Altos, CA 94022
(408) 358-4434	15980 Los Gatos Boulevard, Los Gatos, CA 95032
(415) 381-1200	414 Miller Avenue, Mill Valley, CA 94941
(831) 333-1600	800 Del Monte Center, Monterey, CA 93940
(650) 326-8676	774 Emerson Street, Palo Alto, CA 94301

(707)762-9352	621 E. Washington, Petaluma, CA 94952
(650) 367-1400	1250 Jefferson Streeet, Redwood City, CA 94062
(415) 618-0066	399 4th Street, San Francisco, CA 94107
(415) 674-0500	1765 California Street, San Francisco, CA 94109
(650) 358-6900	1010 Park Place, San Mateo, CA 94403
(415) 451-6333	340 Third Street, San Rafael, CA 94901
(925) 355-9000	100 Sunset Drive, San Ramon, CA 94583
(707) 575-7915	1181 Yulupa Ave, Santa Rosa, Ca 95405
(707) 829-9801	6910 McKinley St., Sebastopol, CA 95472
(925) 274.9700	1333 E. Newell, Walnut Creek, CA 94596

Description: This grocery store chain specializes in providing organic and environmentally friendly products whenever possible. Tours are catered to the specific group. There is no minimum number of participants, but the maximum is 20 per group. For young children in kindergarten or pre-school, adult chaperones of one adult for every three kids are requested. The tours cover the various departments of the store and how organic methods are used to produce the products. For example, in the fish department learn how fish can be farm raised; in the dairy department, learn how butter is made; and in the meat department, learn what makes an organic chicken different from a "regular" chicken. At the end of the tour, take home goody bags with stickers, crayons, and a booklet for the children.

Hours: At the Los Gatos location, tours can be booked on Tues or Thur at 11am. Call to confirm with the store closest to you. Ask to speak with the marketing coordinator and make a reservation.

Cost: Free.

Bathrooms: Yes.

Facilities: Stroller friendly.

Food: Yes.

For factory tours outside of the Bay Area:

<factorytoursusa.com>

Chapter 8
Art & Performing Arts

Art

"I am enough of an artist to draw freely upon my imagination. Imagination is more important than knowledge. Knowledge is limited. Imagination encircles the world." —Albert Einstein (1875–1955)

"Every child is an artist. The problem is how to remain an artist once he grows up."
—Pablo Picasso (1881 – 1973)

"Creativity is allowing yourself to make mistakes. Art is knowing which ones to keep."
—Scott Adams, *The Dilbert Principle*

Art is a language we can all understand; it doesn't need to be translated. Many people assume that young children find art museums boring. However, young children react to art, especially to modern art. They react to the colors, the shapes, and to abstract art with their vivid imaginations. While children may not react to art the way we might, encouraging their reactions as they see the art and providing exposure to art help children see the world in new ways. It stimulates their creativity and encourages their imagination. Young children love to do art. They love to make sculptures with their Playdough®, paint pictures, and make drawings. As they grow, they'll become more sophisticated. The Bay Area Children's Discovery Museum in Sausalito, Children's Discovery Museum in San

Jose, Habitot Children's Museum in Berkeley, and Randall Museum in San Francisco have drop-in art areas for children. The free Cantor Arts Center is a hidden gem, and the Stanford campus and shopping center are close by. This section focuses on drop-in art outings. For art classes, see Section II, Chapter 12: Science & Arts Education.

The Young Audiences Arts Card gives $1, 10%, or even 50% discount on admission for cardholders of participating museums and organizations. To sign up, visit <www.artscard.info>.

Ceramics & Drop-In Art Outings

The following are studios where you can create one-time art projects.

Art-Gecko Creative Studio (Ages 2+)
(925) 680-2500; 1720 Linda Drive, Pleasant Hill, CA 94523
<www.artgeckostudio.com>

Description: Art-Gecko is a drop-in based art studio offering ceramic and wood painting. It also offers projects in mosaics, stepping stones, spin art, and clay. Project costs vary and are in addition to the studio fee. Camps, birthday parties, and ceramic clay classes are available as well.
Hours: Mon-Thurs: 10am–8pm, Fri: 10am–9pm, Sat: 10am–7pm, Sun: 11am–7pm.
Cost: $6.95/child 12 & under, $8.95/adult. Project continuation: $5 studio fee. Discounts on select days. Check Web site for offers.

Brush Strokes Studio (Ages 7+)
(510) 528-1360; 745 Page Street, Berkeley, CA 94710
<www.brushstrokesstudio.com>

Description: Paint your own pottery. Birthday parties, art camps throughout the year, after-school classes for kids ages 7–12.
Hours: *Weekdays:* 11am–8pm. *Weekends:* 11am–6pm.
Cost: $6/person. *Parties:* $23/child for a 2-hour party. Ceramic pieces range from $3 to $40 per item.

Color Me Mine

<www.colormemine.com>

(510) 521-8893; Alameda Towne Centre, 2205 South Shore Center, Alameda, CA 94501

<www.alameda.colormemine.com>

Hours: Mon–Sat: 10am–9pm, Sun: 11am – 6pm.

(650) 756-2706; 445 Westlake Shopping Center, Daly City, CA 94015
<www.dalycity.colormemine.com>

Hours: Sun–Thur: 10am–8pm, Fri and Sat: 10am – 9pm.

(510) 226-6983; 43301 Mission Boulevard, Fremont, CA 94539
<www.fremont.colormemine.com>

Hours: Mon–Sat: 10am–8pm, Sun: 11am – 7pm.

(650) 328-4486; 602 Santa Cruz Avenue, Menlo Park, CA 94025
<www.colormeminemenlopark.com>

Hours: Mon–Tues: 11am–8pm, Wed–Sat: 11am–9pm, Sun: 11am–6pm.

Cost: $5/hour per person studio fee.

(408) 865-1833; Westgate West Shopping Center, 5337 Prospect Road, San Jose, CA 95129

<www.sanjose.colormemine.com>

Hours: Sun: 11am–5pm, Mon–Sat: 11am–8pm.
San Rafael Town Center, 994 Fourth Street, San Rafael, CA 94901
<www.sanrafael.colormemine.com>

Hours: Fri–Sat: 10am–9pm, Sun–Thur: 10am–8pm.

(925) 280-2888; 1950 Mt. Diablo Boulevard, Walnut Creek, CA 94596
<www.walnutcreek.colormemine.com>

Hours: Mon–Fri: 11am–9pm, Sat–Sun: 11am–5pm.

Description: This franchise "paint your own" pottery studio has locations throughout the Bay Area, the United States, and the world. Birthday parties and classes for all.

Cost: Costs vary from location to location but are in this range: $5–$7/child 12 & under, typically $6/child, $9-$10/adult studio fee. Cost of pieces range from $2 to $70, depending on the item. Some studios charge a glazing fee as well. See Web sites for special discount nights, frequent visitor cards, etc. Classes offered as well.

Habitot Children's Museum (Ages 1–6)

(510) 647-1111; 2065 Kittredge Street, Berkeley, CA 94704

<www.habitot.org>

Description: This small museum is wonderful for the toddler and pre-school set. There are separate play areas dedicated to various types of play: a little fire engine structure and a train playtable, a little market and kitchen area, and a pretend play dress-up area. There is a drop-in art studio with a ceramic clay play table, a water play area, and a book nook for quiet time and reading.

Hours: Tues & Fri: 9:30am–5pm, Wed: 9:30am–1pm, Thur: 9:30am–7pm, Sat: 10am–5pm, Sun: 11am–5pm only from October 1 to March 31. Closed Sundays April 1 to September 30. Closed Mondays, New Year's Day, Easter, July 4, Labor Day, Thanksgiving Day, and Christmas.

Cost: $6/child, $5/adult, 10% discount to the disabled and seniors. *Visit Web site for free admission days throughout the year.*

Bathrooms: Yes.

Facilities: Stroller friendly once inside the building, but getting inside the building is a bit tricky. There's a side door that allows easier access to the museum. Call prior to your visit to get directions on stroller navigation.

Food: No, but restaurants nearby in the same building.

What to Bring: Cash for parking. Parking structure is across the street.

Follow-Up Activities: 1) Carpentry, art, music, dance, and literacy classes, as well as camps for the very young child. 2) Birthday parties. 3) Hall of Health is just across the hallway.

Palo Alto Art Center (Ages 18 months +)

(650) 329-2366; 1313 Newell Road, Palo Alto, CA 94303

<www.cityofpaloalto.org/community-services/ac-generalinfo.html>

Schedule: Family Days scheduled throughout the year provide hands-on art activities. Visit <**www.cityofpaloalto.org/community-services/ac-events.html**> for schedule. The Center has a gallery, with docent-led tours. The Center also offers art classes and camps through the Palo Alto Recreation *Enjoy!* catalog.

Hours: *Gallery:* Tues–Sat: 10am–5pm, Sun: 1pm–5pm, Thursdays: open until 9pm.

Cost: Free Family Days. Gallery: suggested $1 donation.

Petroglyph (Ages 4+)

<www.petroglyph.com/studios.htm>

Los Gatos:
(408) 395-6278; 37 N. Santa Cruz Avenue, Los Gatos, CA 95030
Hours: Mon–Thur: 10am–9pm, Fri & Sat: 10am–10pm, Sun: 10am–7pm.

Santa Cruz:
(831) 458-4278; 125 Walnut Avenue, Santa Cruz, CA 95060
Hours: Mon–Thur: 10am–8pm, Fri & Sat: 10am–10pm, Sun: 10am–7pm.

Willow Glen:
(408) 971-4278; 1140 Lincoln Avenue, San Jose, CA 95125
Hours: Mon–Thur: 10am–9pm, Fri & Sat: 10am–10pm, Sun: 10am–7pm.

Description: This is a ceramic studio where you can paint your own ceramic. Purchase a premade piece of pottery, then paint the piece (paint is provided). The studio fires the piece and you come back to pick it up in 24 hours. Takes a bit of time and patience, but it's lots of fun.

Cost: $9.75/adult, $7/child under 12 flat rate, plus cost of the ceramic piece you want to paint.

Bathrooms: Yes.

Facilities: Stroller friendly. Kid friendly. Even has a TV to occupy little ones while you work.

Food: Nearby restaurants.

Laurel Street Arts (Ages 18 months+)

(650) 591-1005; 733 Laurel Street, San Carlos, CA 94070
<www.laurelstreetarts.com>

Description: Drop-in art studios for ceramic painting, mosaics, and glass crafts.

Hours: Mon–Thur: 10am–7pm, Fri/Sat: 10am–9pm, Sun: noon–5pm.

Cost: *Painting & Mosaic Studio Fees:* $8/adult, $5/senior or child 14 & under. *Return Paint Fee:* $3/day to finish project. Includes paint materials, glazing, & firing. *Glass Lab Fee:* $8/day. Ceramic pieces range in cost from $3 to $75. Glass material is also additional. See Web site for discounts and special offers.

Bathrooms: Yes.

Facilities: Stroller friendly.
Food: Restaurants next door.
What to Bring: Wear clothes that can get messy from art activities.
Follow-Up Activities: 1) Birthday parties 2) Summer camps. 3) School & Scout groups. 4) Classes.

Museum of Children's Art (MOCHA) (Ages 18 months+)

(510) 465-8770; 538 Ninth Street, Oakland, CA 94607
<www.mocha.org>

Description: Small museum with an art scavenger hunt. Friendly staff. Appropriate for the preschooler. Drop-in art studios for children more than 18 months old features a different theme each week. Also special programs during school holidays.
Hours: *Gallery:* Tues–Fri: 10am–5pm, Weekends: Noon–5pm. *Drop-in Studio:* Tues–Fri: 10am–5pm. *Family Wrokshop:* Weekends: Noon–5pm.
Cost: *Gallery:* free. *Drop-in studio:* $5/child. *Family Workshop:* $5/child.
Bathrooms: Yes.
Facilities: Stroller friendly.
Food: Restaurants next door.
What to Bring: Wear clothes that can get messy from art activities.
Follow-Up Activities: 1) Birthday parties. 2) Classes. 3) Art camps.

Museums

For the older child (elementary school age) who is mature enough to appreciate the finer museums, there are some great museums to visit. Some of the museums have developed activity books for children to help involve them in the art collections; ask at the information desk.

Asian Art Museum (Ages 4+)

(415) 581-3500; 200 Larkin Street, San Francisco, CA 94102
<www.asianart.org>

Description: The new facility is a rehabilitation of the former San

Francisco Main Library building. This museum's permanent collection of Asian art spans the centuries and includes countries such as Japan, China, India, Iran, and Korea. The museum provides insight into these countries' cultures.
Hours: Closed Mondays. Tues–Sun: 10am–5pm. Thur: open until 9pm.
Cost: $12/adult, $8/senior, $7/youth 13–17, free/child 12 & under. Thur after 5pm: $5/person. *Free first Tuesday of each month.*
Bathrooms: Yes.
Facilities: Stroller friendly.
Food: Yes.
What to Bring: Jacket and cash for food and parking.
Follow-Up Activities: Check Web site calendar for family programs and events. The *Asia Alive* program has hands-on activities and artist demonstrations. Gallery tours at 11am, 1pm, and 2 pm.

Berkeley Art Museum & Pacific Film Archive (Ages 8+)

(510) 642-0808 Main; 2626 Bancroft Way, Berkeley, CA 94704
(510) 548-4366 Café; 2621 Durant Avenue, Berkeley, CA 94704
(510) 642-5249 Film; 2575 Bancroft Way, Berkeley, CA 94704
<www.bampfa.berkeley.edu>

Description: The Berkeley Art Museum provides exhibits on contemporary and avant garde art, as well as historical, international, and Asian art. There are changing exhibits throughout the year. The Pacific Film Archive has more than 6,000 films and videos on archive, including international, silent, animation, and classic films. The theater shows some of these films. See the Web site for a schedule of performances.
Hours: Wed–Sun: 11am–7pm.
Cost: $8/adult; $5/youth 13–17, senior 65+, disabled person, or non-UC student; free/child 12 & under or UC students, faculty, and staff members. *Free first Thursday of each month. Free admission on Cal Day in April.* See Chapter 10: Seasonal Events.
Bathrooms: Yes.
Facilities: Stroller friendly.
Food: Yes.
What to Bring: Cash for food and parking.
Follow-Up Activities: Guided tours are generally on Thursdays at 12:15pm and 5:30pm and Sundays at 2pm. Check the calendar for cur-

rent schedule. School groups can take self-guided tours with advanced reservations by calling (510) 642-5188.

Cantor Arts Center (Ages 4+)
Stanford University
(650) 723-4177; Lomita Drive & Museum Way, Stanford, CA 94305
<museum.stanford.edu>

Description: This art museum is located on the beautiful Stanford University campus. It has a wonderful collection, with exhibits on Ancient Mediterranean (Rome & Greece), African, Egyptian, and Native American cultural artifacts. There are also Asian ceramics and paintings, European and American paintings, and modern abstract sculptures and paintings. This museum has one of the most extensive collections of Rodin bronze sculptures displayed in the outdoor garden and the indoor gallery. To see a more extensive collection of Rodin sculpture, you'd probably have to visit the Rodin Museum in Paris, France. Visitors can also tour the beautiful Stanford Memorial Church, the Stanford campus with its collection of modern sculpture, and the Rodin collection with a docent.

Hours: Wed–Sun: 11am–5pm, Thur: 11am–8pm. Closed Monday, Tuesday, & holidays. *Rodin tours:* Wed: 2pm, Sat: 11:30am, Sun: 3pm (meet at the main lobby). *General tours* on the weekends at 1pm. *Outdoor Sculpture Walk:* First Sunday of each month at 2pm. *Changing Exhibit Tours:* Thursdays at 12:15pm & weekends at 2pm. *Memorial Church Tour:* Fridays at 2pm. Advanced registration required for group tours (at least 6 weeks in advance).

Cost: Free admission. Parking fee required on weekdays until 4pm. Free parking after 4pm on weekdays and all day on weekends.

Bathrooms: Yes.

Facilities: Stroller and wheelchair friendly. However, the stroller access is located by the café entrance at the back of the building next to the outdoor Rodin sculpture garden.

Food: Café features organic food and drinks. Little ones may find the fare a bit too "gourmet" for their tastes. Bring a bag lunch for your child if your child likes select foods.

What to Bring: Bring quarters and dollar bills for parking, as needed.

Follow-Up Activities: Art classes and camps for children.

Cartoon Art Museum (Ages 4+)

(415) CAR-TOON (227-8666); 655 Mission Street, San Francisco, CA 94105
<www.cartoonart.org>

Description: Exhibits on the history of cartoon art and its evolution from animation, comic strips, comic books, editorial cartoons, magazine cartoons, and underground cartoons. Some parts of the gallery are not appropriate for children. However, there is a great gallery of children's favorites and familiar Disney cartoons.

Hours: Closed Monday. Tues–Sun: 11am–5pm. *"Pay what you wish" day is on the first Tuesday of each month.* Closed New Year's Day, Easter, July 4, Thanksgiving, and Christmas.

Cost: $6/adult, $4/student or seniors, $2/child 6–12, free/child <5.

Bathrooms: Yes.

Facilities: Stroller friendly.

Food: No, but restaurants close by.

What to Bring: Cash for parking and food.

Charles M. Schulz Museum (Ages 3+)

(707) 579-4452; 2301 Hardies Lane, Santa Rosa, CA 95403
<www.schulzmuseum.org>

Description: This museum is dedicated to the art of *Peanuts* comic strip creator, Charles Schulz. You'll find a *Snoopy* labyrinth outside, in front of the museum, the nursery wall mural painted by Charles Schulz in his Colorado house, a drop-in art studio for cartooning, and video shows noon–4pm. Don't miss the back courtyard with holograms of *Peanuts* characters above the bird bath. On the second Saturday of each month, 1pm–3pm, meet the cartoonist-in-residence and watch the artist at work to learn more about cartooning art from a professional.

Hours: Weekdays: 11am–5pm, Sat & Sun: 10am–5pm. Closed Tuesdays. During the summer (Memorial Day to Labor Day), they're open on Tuesdays also. Closed New Year's, Easter Sunday, July 4, Thanksgiving, Christmas Eve, and Christmas Day.

Cost: $8/adult, $5/youth or senior, free/child under 4.

Bathrooms: Yes.

Facilities: Stroller friendly.

Food: No. Food available across the way at the Empire Ice Arena.

Follow-Up Activities: Classes & camps are offered.

De Young Museum (Ages 3+)

(415) 863-3330
Golden Gate Park, 50 Hagiwara Tea Garden Drive, San Francisco, CA 94118
<www.thinker.org/deyoung>

Description: This completely renovated museum reopened back at its Golden Gate Park home in late 2005. The collection includes American paintings, sculpture, and decorative arts; art from Africa, Oceania, and the Americas; textiles and fashions; and European tapestries.

Hours: Tues–Sun: 9:30am–5pm. Closed Thanksgiving, Christmas, & New Year's days. Docent-led tours on a drop-in basis; see Web site for schedule <www.famsfdocents.info>. On Saturday mornings 10:30am–12pm, there are drop-in art workshops taught by professional artists for children 3½–12 years old. For members' children, the museum offers these same workshops in the afternoon, 1:30pm–3pm.

Cost: $10/adult, $7/senior 65+, $6/youth 13–17 & college students with ID, free/child 12 & under. Free for San Francisco students with ID. *Free admission on the first Tuesday of each month. Tickets may be used on the same day for free admission to the Legion of Honor, and vice versa.*

Bathrooms: Yes.

Facilities: Stroller friendly.

Food: Café.

What to Bring: Cash for food and parking.

Follow-Up Activities: 1) Free docent-led art tours for school groups with at least 8 weeks notice. Call (415) 750-3522 for reservations. 2) Advanced Placement Art History class is offered to Bay Area high school students. Free. 3) Children's Theater for school groups grades K–3 at the Florence Gould Theater at the Legion of Honor Museum on Wednesday or Friday mornings at 10am. See Web site under "Education" for the registration form.

Legion of Honor (Ages 3+)

(415) 863-3330; Lincoln Park: 100 34th Avenue, San Francisco, CA 94121
<www.thinker.org/legion>

Description: Situated in serene Lincoln Park overlooking San Francisco Bay, this gorgeous museum has an extensive collection of fine European painting and decorative arts as well as ancient art including Greek, Roman, Egyptian, and Mesopotamian sculpture, pottery, and metalwork.

The museum also offers an extensive collection of French & English porcelain and "works in paper" spanning 600 years. These include works by Kandinsky, O'Keefe, Rembrant, and Gaugin.

Hours: Closed Monday. Tues–Sun: 9:30am–5pm. Docent tours offered; visit Web site calendar for tour times. Organ concerts on weekends at 4pm, included with admission.

Cost: $10/adult, $7/senior 65+, $6/youth 12–17, free/child 12 & younger. Special exhibits cost extra. *First Tuesdays of the month are free. Tickets may be used on the same day for free admission to the De Young Museum and vice versa.*

Bathrooms: Yes.

Facilities: Stroller friendly.

Food: Café.

What to Bring: Cash for food.

Follow-Up Activities: Florence Gould Theater hosts concerts, plays, operas, and lectures.

Napa Valley Museum (Ages 4+)

(707) 944-0500; 55 Presidents Circle, Yountville, CA 94599
<www.napavalleymuseum.org>

Description: Although small, this museum has a quality art exhibit and great displays of the history and natural resources of the Napa Valley. The interactive and multimedia "California Wine: The Science of an Art" exhibit, which details the steps of wine making, will fascinate wine lovers.

Hours: Wed–Mon: 10am–5pm. Closed Tuesdays.

Cost: $4.50/adult, $3.50/senior 65+ or student w/ ID, $2.50/youth 7–17, free/child 6 & under.

Bathrooms: Yes.

Facilities: Stroller friendly.

Food: No.

Follow-Up Activities: Copia is close by.

Oakland Museum of California (Ages 4+)

(510) 238-2200; 1000 Oak Street, Oakland, CA 94607
<www.museumca.org>

Description: This museum is dedicated to California. It has permanent exhibits on the history of California, the natural sciences of California,

and Californian art including sculptures, paintings, photographs, prints, and decorative arts. For prehistoric beast lovers, the museum worked on a mastodon (ice age animal resembling an elephant) exhibit. For the virtual exhibit online at <www.museumca.org/mastodon>. In fact, the virtual exhibits are extensive, including California's Gold Rush, California's underground caves, and a library of sound files from California's wildlife.
Hours: Wed–Sat: 10am–5pm. Sun: 12–5pm. Closed Mondays and Tuesdays. First Friday of each month: open until 9pm. Closed on New Year's Day, July 4, Thanksgiving Day, and Christmas Day. Visit Web site for holiday hours.
Cost: $8/adult, $5/senior 65+ or student w/ ID, free/child under 6 years old. *Free second Sunday of each month.*
Bathrooms: Yes.
Facilities: Stroller friendly.
Food: Café—great food!
What to Bring: Cash for food.
Follow-Up Activities: 1) For special family events, visit the calendar of events page: <www.museumca.org/cal-public/calendar.cgi>, then select "Kids and Family Events" for a listing. Usually has Lunar New Year Celebration in February. 2) Children's theater performances by East Bay Children's Theater: <www.childrens-theatre.org>.

San Francisco Museum of Modern Art (Ages 4+)
(415) 357-4000; 151 Third Street, San Francisco, CA 94103
<www.sfmoma.org>

Description: Collections include modern art paintings and sculptures, architecture and design, media arts, and photography. The Koret Visitor Education Center has video clips focused on artists, hands-on activity for kids, and multimedia kiosks with interview clips and footage of studio artists represented in the museum's collection.
Hours: Closed Wed. *Fri–Tues:* 11am–5:45pm, *Thur:* 11am–8:45pm. *Summer* (Memorial Day–Labor Day): museum opens at 10am, still closed on Wednesday. The Museum is closed on July 4, Thanksgiving, Christmas, and New Year's Day. Daily tours at 11:30am, 12:30pm, 1:30pm, and 2:30pm. Additional tours Thursday nights at 6:15pm & 7:15pm.
Cost: $12.50/adult, $8/senior 62+, $7/students w/ ID, free/child under 12. *Free the first Tuesday of each month. ½ price every Thursday evening 6–9pm.*

Bathrooms: Yes.
Facilities: Stroller friendly.
Food: Café.
What to Bring: Cash for food and parking.
Follow-Up Activities: For family programs and the scheduled monthly family studio with docent-led tour and hands-on art activities, visit <www.sfmoma.org/education/edu_inthemuseum_fprog.asp>. Programs are included with museum admission.

San Jose Museum of Art (Ages 4+)
(408) 271-6840; (408) 294-2787; 110 South Market Street, San Jose, CA 95113
<www.sjmusart.org>

Description: This museum focuses on contemporary art, including ceramics sculpture, abstract and realist paintings, and new media art.
Hours: Tues–Sun: 11am–5pm. Closed Mondays, Monday holidays, Thanksgiving, Christmas, and New Year's Day. Drop-in tours offered daily at 12:30pm & 2:30pm.
Cost: $8/adult, $5/senior or student, $2 discount for San Jose Library cardholders, free/child 6 & under. It will validate parking in lots displaying the "Pv" sign, with nominal purchase at museum store or cafe.
Bathrooms: Yes.
Facilities: Stroller friendly.
Food: Café.
What to Bring: Cash for food and parking. Visit <www.sjdowntown-parking.com> for parking information.
Follow-Up Activities: 1) For school groups, the museum offers the "2-Part Art," which includes a tour and a 60-minute long art workshop. 2) The museum is part of the San Jose Safari Summer Day Camp offered through the Friends of Guadalupe River Park & Gardens. 3) Look for the "Family Art" weekend for art workshops.

Santa Cruz Museum of Art & History (MAH) (Ages 3+)
(831) 429-1964; 705 Front Street, Santa Cruz, CA 95060
<www.santacruzmah.org>

Description: The Museum of Art & History focuses on contemporary art and the history of Santa Cruz County. A permanent exhibit, *Where the*

Redwoods Meet the Sea, provides a glimpse into the lives and culture of the Ohlone Indians who lived in this area.

Hours: Tues–Sun: 11am–5pm. First Friday of each month: 11am–6pm. Closed on Mondays. Family Art Saturdays offer art workshops monthly. Call (831) 429-1964 x 20 or e-mail education@santacruzmah.org to pre-register. Age appropriateness and cost vary by workshop. Visit Web site for schedule and details <**www.santacruzmah.org/4_events.html**>. Family Festivals take place in May & October, with music, storytelling, hands-on activities, and tours, all for free.

Cost: $5/adult; $2/youth 12–17, $3/students (18+) or senior (62+); free/child 12 & under. *Free admission on the first Friday of each month.*

Bathrooms: Yes.

Facilities: Stroller friendly.

What to Bring: Picnic lunch.

Follow-Up Activities: School tours must sign up during two periods: mid-August to mid-October or December through January. Call the receptionist at (831) 429-1964 ext. 10 to schedule the tour.

Triton Museum of Art (Ages 4+)

(408) 247-3754; 1505 Warburton Avenue, Santa Clara, CA 95050
<www.tritonmuseum.org>

Description: Exhibits works by California artists. Art tours given by docents can be arranged in advance for both contemporary art and Native American art. Call (408) 247-9352 for art tour reservations.

Hours: Fri–Wed: 11am–5pm, Thursdays open until 9pm.

Cost: Free.

Bathrooms: Yes.

Facilities: Stroller friendly.

Food: No.

What to Bring: Picnic lunch.

Follow-Up Activities: 1) Provides classes for children and adults taught by professional artists and in many media. 2) Free Family Art Days include art activities, live performances, and hands-on guided tours. Visit Web site for schedule. 3) Summer art camps for children—see the museum's calendar for most recent events.

Galleries

Art galleries are wonderful to visit. Best of all, they feature contemporary artists, the visits are free, and you can learn about the art and the artists firsthand from the galleries! There are three specific galleries I'd like to suggest for outings: Carmel Art Association's gallery, the Rodrigue Studio, featuring the Blue Dog Gallery; and the Lynn Lupetti Gallery. The Rodrigue Studio and the Lynn Lupetti Gallery are very close to each other and provide an easy entrée into the world of art galleries because the art is so fun and approachable. Both of these galleries are wonderful for children. They are located by the Carmel Public Library and within a short walk of Carmel Beach at the bottom of Ocean Ave. For a more complete listing of galleries in the Carmel/Monterey area, visit: <www.monterey-carmel.com/galleries.htm>.

Carmel Art Association (Ages 3+)
(831) 624-6176; Dolores Street between 5th & 6th, Carmel, CA 93921
<www.carmelart.org>

Description: This gallery features a collection of art from local artists.
Hours: 10am–5pm daily.
Bathrooms: Yes.
Facilities: Stroller friendly.
Food: Nearby restaurants.

Lynn Lupetti Gallery (Ages 3+)
(831) 624-0622; PO Box 5776, Carmel, CA 93921
6th Avenue between Dolores & Lincoln, Carmel, CA
<www.lynnlupettigallery.com>

Description: Lynn Lupetti paints magical and imaginary landscapes with children and animals.
Hours: 10am–5pm, daily.
Bathrooms: Public restrooms diagonally across from the Public Library.
Facilities: Stroller friendly.
Food: Nearby restaurants.

Rodrigue Studio (Ages 3+)
Blue Dog Gallery
(831) 626-4444; P.O. Box 8-3214, Carmel, CA 93921
On 6th Avenue between Lincoln & Dolores, Carmel, CA
<www.georgerodrigue.com/index2.htm#>

Description: Famous for his Blue Dog paintings of his dog in various poses with brightly colored landscapes. The dog is usually painted blue in the paintings, hence the name.
Hours: 10am–6pm daily.
Bathrooms: Public restrooms are across the street at the Public Library.
Facilities: Stroller friendly.
Food: Nearby restaurants.
Follow-Up Activities: *Why is Blue Dog Blue?* written by the artist, George Rodrigue, and Bruce Goldstone is a fun, colorful children's book explaining why the dog is blue.

Music

"Music is a moral law.
It gives a soul to the universe,
wings to the imagination,
a charm to sadness,
and life to everything."
—Plato

Music is the universal language that speaks to our souls. We are all inherently musical. We can all appreciate and understand music. Help your children develop their innate musical appreciation by finding concerts or musical performances that they can relate to and understand. It's hard to separate music from other performing arts since music is such an inherent part of musicals, dance, etc. There are many touring shows such as *The Wiggles, Dragon Tales, Annie, Sound of Music, Disney on Broadway,* and *Disney on Ice* that are very approachable for children. Please refer to the Theater Performances section for more outing ideas. In this section, I will focus on purely musical performances.

The holidays are a great time to introduce musical performances by attending traditional family concerts such as *Peter and the Wolf* and ballets like the *Nutcracker*. For very young children, the *Nutcracker* or musicals may be more suitable because the activity of the performers and visual spectacle will better engage their attention. For information on *Nutcracker* performances, see the Ballet Performances section later in this chapter.

In this section, you will find symphonies and orchestras that cater to families, free concerts, local youth symphonies or orchestras, and a music museum—the Beethoven Museum.

Family Concerts

Cal Performances (Ages 4+)
(510) 642-9988; UC Berkeley: 101 Zellerbach Hall #4800, Berkeley, CA, 94720
<www.calperfs.berkeley.edu>

Description: 1) Family Fare Series provides deeply discounted tickets (50%) for children 16 and under. Search under "CalPerformances Presents," then "Family Fare" once on the Web site for event schedule and prices. 2) The *SchoolTime* program provides school groups an opportunity to see an hour-long performance of the same artists as the regular season during the school day for only $4/ticket. Programs are appropriate for grades K–12. Series opens for registration in August for the following school year. On the Web site, select "Education & Community Programs," then "K–12 Educational Initiatives," then "SchoolTime." In-classroom enrichment programs also provided.

Deck the Halls (Ages 3+)
San Francisco Symphony, Davies Symphony Hall, San Francisco
(415) 864-6000; 201 Van Ness Avenue, San Francisco, CA 94102
<www.sfsymphony.org>

Description: This is a family oriented concert designed for kids ages 3–10 with Christmas carols. The post-show party includes arts and crafts and refreshments. See San Francisco Symphony below.

Schedule: Early December with only 2 performances.

Cost: $27 per person. Check Web site for most current information.

Follow-Up Activities: 1) The Symphony also offers a "Music for Families" program on Saturday afternoons designed for kids ages 7+. It's a great way to introduce the world of symphonies to young kids. For kids 12 & under, tickets are half-price. 2) There is a "Concert for Kids" program with the Children's Concerts series targeted for K-grade 3 during weekday mornings in April and the Youth Concerts series for grades 4-9 during weekday mornings in early May. Cost is only $3.50/person. For each series, educational docents visit the classroom upon request. For addtional information, call (415) 503–5500 or e-mail <CFK@sfsymphony.org>. 3) College students can subscribe (with a group of friends even) to the symphony for half-price! 4) For 100 talented and lucky young orchestral musicians, the San Francisco Youth Symphony provides preprofessional training with world renown guest artists who in the past have included Isaac Stern, Yo-Yo Ma, and Michael Tilson Thomas. Besides all that, it's tuition free! 5) There are also "Open Rehearsals" on Wednesday mornings at 10am with prerehearsal talks at 9am. Check Web site for schedule and to buy tickets.

Fremont Symphony Orchestra (Ages 5+)
Ohlone College, Fremont
(510) 794-1659; P.O. Box 104 Fremont, CA 94537
Smith Center: 43600 Mission Boulevard, Fremont, CA 94539
<www.fremontsymphony.org>

Description: The performances are held at Jackson Theater at the Gary Soren Smith Center for the Fine and Performing Arts, Ohlone College. Family Concert series for ages 5+ on Sunday afternoons. Check the Web site for current schedule under "Musical Treats."

Cost: $12/adult, $6/child

Le Petit Trianon (Ages 5+)
(408) 995-5400; 72 North Fifth Street, San Jose, CA 95112

Mountain View Center for the Performing Arts (Ages 3+)
(650) 903-6000; 500 Castro Street, Mountain View, CA 94039
<www.mvcpa.com>

Description: Provides wonderful family entertainment including plays, musicals, concerts, etc. Parking available in basement underneath the Performing Arts Center. Follow signs to the "Civic Hall" parking.

Music for Minors (Concerts for kids) (All Ages)
(650)237-9130; 883 N. Shoreline Boulevard, C120, Mountain View, CA 94043
<www.mfm.org>

Music at Kohl Mansion (Ages 3+)
(650) 762-1130; 2750 Adeline Drive, Burlingame, CA 94010
<musicatkohl.org>

Description: Provides daytime Children's Concerts and Friday evening Family Concerts—an introduction to chamber music for children and their families. The Pocket Opera group presents introductions to opera for young children.
Cost: $5/person for the Children's Concerts. For Family Concerts, single tickets: $18/adult, $10/youth under 16, $30/1 adult & 2 youths. Series subscription available.

Peter and the Wolf (Ages 4+)
San Francisco Symphony, Davies Symphony Hall
(415) 864-6000; 201 Van Ness Avenue, San Francisco, CA 94102
<www.sfsymphony.org>

Description: This is a holiday favorite and a wonderful way to introduce young children to the symphony. After Prokofiev's *Peter and the Wolf*, there's a performance of Christmas carols and a sing-along. Before you come to the symphony, it's a good idea to read the story of *Peter and the Wolf* together and watch the video. This helps prepare your child and enriches his first symphonic experience. Consider watching the 30-minute ballet video, *The Royal Ballet School in Prokofiev's Peter and the Wolf*, with choreography by Matthew Hart and Narrator Anthony Dowell. Distributed by BBC and RM Arts. There's also a wonderful picture book, *Peter and the*

Wolf, by Russian artist Vladimir Vagin (Scholastic Press) which retells the story. Plan to arrive at least 30 minutes early to allow time for parking and seating. Traffic to downtown San Francisco can be quite challenging, so allow enough time to get there without being stressed.

Schedule: Only 2 performances in early December. Visit the Web site or call for specific times and dates.

Cost: Varies, depending on seating.

Bathrooms: Yes.

Food: Snacks only. California Pizza Kitchen (415) 436-9380, or <www.cpk.com> at 524 Van Ness Avenue and McAllister Street is within a short walk of Davies Symphony Hall. Nearby are also a few fast food places, including McDonald's.

What to Bring: Opera glasses or binoculars and cash for parking and food. Dress warmly, as San Francisco can be windy and foggy.

Follow-Up Activities: 1) *Carnival of the Animals* by Camille Saint-Saens is a humorous musical piece that will captivate your child. Composed as a musical joke, it quickly became so popular that it is now considered his masterpiece. The children's book of the same title by Barrie Carson Turner and Sue Williams provides a guide to understanding the composition. The book comes with a CD. It introduces instruments and provides explanations and illustrations for each track on the CD. 2) The San Francisco Symphony has a wonderful music Web site for kids: <www.sfskids.org>. It introduces kids to musical instruments. There is also a music lab to help kids learn about rhythm, pitch, tempo, and dynamics. It even has a *Performalator* to let you play tunes like *Twinkle Twinkle Little Star* and a *Composerizer* to assemble your own tune using preset measures of music.

Villa Montalvo (Ages 2+)
(408) 961-5800; 15400 Montalvo Road, Saratoga, CA 95071
<www.villamontalvo.org>

Description: Features family theater with wonderful performances of puppet shows, fairy tales, plays, musicals, and concerts.

Free Concerts

Ghiradelli Square, Golden Gate Park, and Yerba Buena Gardens in San Francisco, and Jack London Square in Oakland have regularly scheduled events throughout the year that include musical performances. Visit San Francisco Convention and Visitor's Bureau Web site <onlysf.sfvisitor.org> and Jack London Square's Web site <www.jacklondonsquare.com/events-frame.html> or call 1(866) 295-9853 for event schedule.

Don't forget to check with your cities and local public libraries because they provide free public concerts usually during the summer, as special holiday events, or as part of arts and wine festivals. Free summer concerts are usually sponsored by the city and usually take place at the civic center plazas or city parks. Parks and Recreation Department catalogs usually announce free concerts.

Community Concerts (East Bay)
<www.communityconcerts.com>

Provides a list of concerts in the East Bay, including free concerts.

Community School of Music & Arts (Ages 3+)
(650) 917-6800; 230 San Antonio Circle, Mountain View, CA 94040
<www.arts4all.org>

Description: Provides free "Concerts 4 Kids" on Sundays at 2pm and "Family Concerts" on Sundays at 4pm. Check Web site for schedule. Offers art and music lessons.

Memorial Park Amphitheater (Ages 4+)
(408) 777-3120;
Memorial Park: Stevens Creek Boulevard & Anton Way, Cupertino, CA 95014
<www.cupertino.org/event_calendar>

Description: Located at the corner of Mary Ave and Stevens Creek Boulevard, across from De Anza College. Summer performances on Thursdays 6–8pm. No concerts July 4—fireworks on De Anza College grounds.

Linden Tree Children's Recordings and Books (All Ages)

(650) 949-3390; 1-800-949-3313; 170 State Street, Los Altos, CA 94022
<http://lindentree.booksense.com/NASApp/store/IndexJsp>

Description: *Family Concert Series:* During the summers, Linden Tree offers free concerts titled *Wednesdays in the Courtyard* on Wednesdays at 10am. Contact Linden Tree for concert schedule. Admission is a donation of a new book for literacy programs. Special events are often advertised in *Bay Area Parent* magazine and *San Jose Mercury News.*

Music at Noon Series (Ages 3+)
Center of Performing Arts Recital Hall, Santa Clara University
(408) 554-4429; (408) 554-4015
Franklin and Lafayette Streets, Santa Clara, CA 95050
<www.scu.edu/cpa>; <www.scu.edu/cpa/events/musicatnoon.cfm>

Schedule: Music at Noon Series is held on Wednesdays at noon. Visit Web site for calendar, map, and directions.

San Francisco Conservatory of Music (Ages 5+)

(415) 864-7326 (SFCM); 50 Oak Street, San Francisco, CA 94102
<www.sfcm.edu>

Description: Provides free concerts and low-cost events. Check Web site for concert and events schedule.

San Francisco Youth Arts Festival (All Ages)
De Young Museum
Golden Gate Park, 50 Hagiwara Tea Garden Drive, San Francisco, CA 94118
Youth Arts Program/Festival Contact only:
(415) 750-8630; 20 Cook Street, San Francisco, CA 94118
<www.sfyouthartsfestival.org>

Description: In early June, the week-long Youth Arts Festival features visual art exhibits. Don't miss the opening day with music and dance performances along with kids' entertainment including jugglers, clowns, and face painting. See Web site for event times and details.

Sigmund Stern Grove Festival (All Ages)

(415) 252-6252; 19th Avenue & Sloat, San Francisco, CA
Mail: 44 Page Street, Suite 600, San Francisco, CA 94102
<www.sterngrove.org>

Description: High-quality performances in the past have featured the San Francisco Symphony, San Francisco Ballet, and San Francisco Opera, as well as the Russian National Orchestra. A brand new *The Wolf and Peter* by Jean-Pascal Beintus premiered in the 2002 season. *The Wolf and Peter* is a "sequel" to Prokofiev's *Peter and the Wolf.* Free kids' education days during the week. Register online on May 1.

Schedule: Sunday afternoons at 2pm, mid-June through mid-August. Preconcert talks are usually held at 12pm on select concerts. Check the Web site for current schedule starting May 1. You can request to be on the mailing list to get information for next season's events.

Tapestry Arts Festival (All Ages)

(408) 494-3590; Admin: 255 North Market Street, Suite 124, San Jose, CA 95110
<www.tapestryarts.org>; <www.sjdowntownparking.com> parking

Description: This annual event held on the streets of downtown San Jose has attracted hundreds of thousands of visitors. This festival celebrates the visual and performing arts, with a special section, Creativity Zone, devoted to interactive kids' art activities. There are hundreds of artists showcasing their work, and music performers entertaining visitors on multiple stages. This fundraiser provides seed money to neighborhood schools and the community for arts education. See Web site for maps.

Schedule: Annually over the 3-day Labor Day weekend, 10am-6pm.
Cost: Free.
Bathrooms: Yes.
Facilities: Stroller friendly.
Food: International food booths.
What to Bring: Sunglasses; sunscreen; cash for food, drinks, souvenirs, and shopping.

U.C. Berkeley's Noon Concert Series(Ages 10+)
Hertz Hall at U. C. Berkeley

(510) 624-4864; Near College Avenue & Bancroft Way, Berkeley, CA
<music.berkeley.edu>; <music.berkeley.edu/noon.html>; <www.berkeley.edu/map>

Description: Concerts held at Hertz Hall, U.C. Berkeley on Wednesday and Fridays: 12:15pm–1pm. Doors open for seating at 11:55am. Check concert schedule on Web site.

Yerba Buena Gardens Festival (All Ages)
At Esplanade of Yerba Buena Gardens
(415) 543-1718 Arts & Events; 760 Howard Street, San Francisco, CA, 94103
<www.ybae.org>

Description: Events include music, art, dance, theater, puppet shows, festivals, children's programs, and special events. The music variety is comprehensive, including jazz, classical, opera, and international music. The San Francisco Symphony and the San Francisco Opera perform here. Dance includes ballet performances by the Smuin Ballet and the San Francisco Ballet School. Festival and concerts highlight Italian, Filipino, Native American, and African American cultures. Picnic style lawn seating is available. There are plenty of restaurants nearby, but picnics are allowed and encouraged. Picnic blankets can be no larger than 8' x 8'.
Schedule: Annual festival from May through October with a hundred performances and events, all free. See the Web site for details on individual events, dates, and times.

Youth Symphonies & Local Musical Groups

For older children who are able to sit through more challenging musical pieces, there are many local youth orchestras, community symphonies, and musical groups that provide lower cost concerts to the community.

California Youth Symphony
(650) 325-6666; Office: 441 California Avenue #5, Palo Alto, CA 94306
<www.cys.org>

Concerts held at Flint Center, Cupertino and San Mateo Center for Performing Arts.

El Camino Youth Symphony

(650) 327-2611; 2439 Birch Street, Suite 3, Palo Alto, CA 94306
<www.ecys.org/calendar.html>

International Russian Music Piano Competition

(408) 927-7686; PO Box 20246, San Jose, CA 95120
<www.russianmusiccompetition.com>; Email: russianmusiccomp@yahoo.com

Description: Annual piano competition held in June features musicians ages 6 to 30 from all over the world. The winners' concert, the final event, held on a Saturday, showcases Russian folk music, art songs, dancing, and the winner of the annual competition. Performances take place at Le Petit Trianon in San Jose (72 North 5th Street, San Jose, CA). To purchase tickets or to get more information, visit Web site.

Irving M. Klein International String Competition
California Music Center

(415)282-7160; 3260 Harrison Street, San Francisco, CA 94110
<www.kleincompetition.org>

Description: Annual strings international competition held in early June in San Francisco. The competition and final concert are open to the public. Select "Competition," then "Schedule" for dates and times on the Web site.

Oakland Youth Orchestra

(510) 832-7710; Alice Arts Center, 1428 Alice St., #202M, Oakland, CA 94612
<www.oyo.org>

Peninsula Youth Orchestra

(650) 325-7967; 1091 Industrial Way #208, San Carlos, CA 94070
<www.peninsulayouthorchestra.org/pyohome.htm>

Palo Alto Chamber Orchestra

(650) 856-3848; 4000 Middlefield Road, #M-1, Palo Alto, CA 94303

Ragazzi Boys Chorus

(650) 342-8785; 20 N. San Mateo Drive, Suite 9, San Mateo, CA 94401
<www.ragazzi.org>

This Bay Area boys choir also trains boys to sing. Visit the Web site for concert schedule.

San Francisco Symphony Youth Orchestra (Recommended Ages: 12+)
Davies Symphony Hall

(415) 864-6000; 201 Van Ness Avenue, San Francisco, CA 94102
<www.sfsymphony.org>

San Jose Symphony Youth Orchestra

(408) 885-9220; 595 Park Avenue, Suite 302, San Jose, CA 95110
<www.sjys.org>

Santa Cruz Chamber Players

(831) 425-3149; 10707 Soquel Drive, Aptos, CA 95003
<www.scchamberplayers.org>

Steinway Society of the Bay Area

(408) 295-6500; Le Petit Trianon, 72 North 5th Street, San Jose, CA 95112
<www.steinwaythebayarea.com>

Music Museum

Ira F. Brilliant Center for Beethoven Studies & Museum (Ages 13+)
Dr. Martin Luther King Jr. Library, San Jose State University

(408) 808-2058 or -2059; Library: 150 E. San Fernando Street, San Jose, CA
(Cross Street: 4th Street); Mail: One Washington Square, San Jose, CA 95192
<www.sjsu.edu/depts/beethoven>

Description: This center is devoted to the life and works of Ludwig van Beethoven. It has the largest collection of Beethoven materials outside of Europe. It has sponsored exhibits, concerts, and piano competitions. Plan ahead to attend the lectures and concerts.

Hours: Mon–Tues, Thur: 11am–6pm, Wed: 11am–8pm, Fri: 11am–5pm and Sat: 1pm–5pm. Confirm prior to visit by calling or visiting the Web site. Closed most federal holidays.

Cost: Free admission. Tickets to concerts and other events vary.

Follow-Up Activities: Most concerts are performed at the Concert Hall at San Jose State University. The annual Young Pianists' Beethoven Competition is in the Spring. It has been in April in recent years. These competitions are open to the public and are inexpensive. Check Web site for events schedule and cost: <www.sjsu.edu/depts/beethoven/events/events.html>.

Ballet Performances

The *Nutcracker*, usually performed during the holiday season, is another wonderful way to introduce young children to dance, music, and musical theater. The *Nutcracker* is probably the easiest ballet for children to appreciate with its toys, toy soldiers, and battle bewteen the Nutcracker and the Mouse King. Other ballets that are harder to find, but with equally beautiful music and still approachable for children, are *Sleeping Beauty*, *Swan Lake*, and *Giselle*. Prior to attending the ballet, read the corresponding stories from children's picture books to help prepare your child to understand the ballet and the music. These ballets have toured the Bay Area at the San Francisco Ballet and at CalPerformances in U.C. Berkeley. Ballet performances can be expensive, but they're worth it. If you get the rare opportunity to watch world class ballet by the Bolshoi and the Kirov ballet companies, don't miss it!

These ballets are fairly long, usually approximately 2½ to three hours, with intermission approximately halfway through the ballet. Consider the attention span and interest of your child in deciding whether to attend. My daughter loved the *Nutcracker* and *Sleeping Beauty*; she was hooked.

Although it was a bit of a challenge to keep a four-year-old from wriggling during the last hour of the performance, she was so enthralled with *Sleeping Beauty* that she requested *Swan Lake* and *Giselle*. It probably helped that she'd seen Disney's *Sleeping Beauty* multiple times and loved to sing with it. The *Barbie in the Nutcracker* and *Barbie of Swan Lake* videos can also be used to introduce your child to these ballets.

For the most current Bay Area dance performance events in ballet and modern dance, visit this Web site: <www.baydance.com>.

Nutcracker Ballet at the San Francisco Ballet (Ages 4+)
War Memorial Opera House
(415) 865-2000; Performs at: 301 Van Ness Avenue, San Francisco, CA
<www.sfballet.org>

Description: A holiday favorite and a great way to introduce children to ballet and the fine arts. This ballet is about a little girl, Clara, who receives a nutcracker from her uncle, who is believed to be a magician. When the Mouse King attacks the nutcracker, Clara comes to the nutcracker's rescue. They are whisked away to a magical land where they are entertained by dancers from around the world. The music is engaging and the costumes are sumptuous. To help prepare your child, read the *Nutcracker* story prior to attending the performance. The SF Ballet Web site has the *Nutcracker* story and history of the ballet. The *Barbie in the Nutcracker* video is a great way to introduce children to the story, even though it is a different version of the traditional *Nutcracker* story. If you're new to ballet, check out San Francisco Ballet's "Ticketing FAQs" section on its Web site. Detailed directions and map are in the "Transportation & Parking" section under the "Performances" tab of the Web site.

Schedule: December. Select *Nutcracker* family performances provide opportunities to take pictures with *Nutcracker* characters for the first 500 kids. Cookies and milk are provided during intermission.

Tickets: Prices vary depending on date/times and seating. Price ranges from $50 to $150 per seat. Standing room only tickets are $18/person, on sale only on the day of the performance.

Bathrooms: Yes.

Food: Snacks only. The Opera Café located at the very bottom level of the

Opera House is open for meals for certain performances; call for reservations at (415) 861-8150. California Pizza Kitchen is located within walking distance at 524 Van Ness Ave (McAllister Street is the cross street). Phone (415) 436-9380 or visit <www.cpk.com>.

What to Bring: Opera glasses (or you can rent them there), cash for parking and snacks, and a camera if you're attending the Sugar Plum Party following the performance.

Other Nutcracker Performances

Ballet San Jose (Ages 3+)
Center for the Performing Arts
(408) 288-2800; 255 Almaden Boulevard, San Jose, CA 95113
<www.balletsanjose.org>

Schedule: In the 2nd half of December with Sat & Sun performances at 1:30pm and 7:30pm. Children's matinee features a shorter, hour-long performance. In addition to the *Nutcracker*, there is a children's ballet performance series. See Web site for current performances.

Cost: Price per ticket ranges from $25 to $78, depending on age, seating, and performance times. Tickets go on sale in mid-September.

Berkeley City Ballet (Ages 3+)
(510) 841-8913; Tickets: (510) 642-9988; 1800 Dwight Way, Berkeley, CA 94703
<www.berkeleycityballet.org>

Berkeley Ballet (Ages 3+)
Julia Morgan Center for the Arts
(510) 843-4689; 2640 College Avenue, Berkeley, CA 94704
<www.berkeleyballet.org>; <www.juliamorgan.org>

California Ballet (Ages 3+)
Dean Lesher Regional Center for the Arts
(925) 943-7469; 1601 Civic Drive, Walnut Creek, CA 94596

Contra Costa Ballet Centre (Ages 3+)
Dean Lesher Regional Center for the Arts
DLRCA: (925) 943-SHOW (7469); 1601 Civic Drive, Walnut Creek, CA 94596
(925) 935-7984;
Contra Costa Ballet: 2040 North Broadway, Walnut Creek, CA 94596
<www.dlrca.org>; <www.contracostaballet.org>

Diablo Ballet (Ages 4+)
(925) 943-1775; P.O. Box 4700, Walnut Creek, CA 94596
<www.diabloballet.org>

Description: Performs at Dean Lesher Regional Center for the Arts &
Zellerbach Hall at U.C. Berkeley.

Marin Ballet (Ages 4+)
Marin Center Veterans' Memorial Auditorium
Marin Center: 10 Avenue of the Flags, San Rafael, CA 94903
(415) 453-6705; 100 Elm Street, San Rafael, CA 94901
<www.marinballet.org>; <www.marincenter.org>

Description: Performed at the Veterans' Memorial Auditorium in the
Marin Center.

Marin Dance Theatre (Ages 4+)
Marin Center Veterans' Memorial Auditorium
Marin Center: 10 Avenue of the Flags, San Rafael, CA 94903
(415) 499-8891; One St. Vincent Drive, San Rafael, CA 94903
<mdt.org>; <www.marincenter.org>

Description: Costs $16 to $35/seat. Teddy Bear Tea Party following performance costs $8/person.

Ronn Guidi's Nutcracker (Ages 4+)
Paramount Theatre
Ronn Guidi's Foundation: 2626 Harrison Street, Oakland, CA 94612
Paramount Theatre: (510) 465-6400; 2025 Broadway, Oakland, CA
<www.rgfpa.org>; <www.paramounttheatre.com>

Description: Nutcracker is performed at the Paramount Theater in the
2nd half of December. Purchase tickets from Paramount Theater. Sweet
Dreams Party after the Saturday matinee. Tickets range $15–$50.

Pacific Theater Ballet (Ages 3+)
Mountain View Center for the Performing Arts
(650) 903-6000; 500 Castro Street, Mountain View, CA 94039
<www.pacificballet.org>; <www.mvcpa.com>

Schedule: Late November or early December.

Peninsula Ballet Theatre (Ages 3+)
San Mateo Performing Arts Center
(650) 340-9448; Peninsula Ballet Theatre: 126 Second Avenue, Suite 206, P.O. Box 1804, San Mateo, CA 94403;
San Mateo Performing Arts: 600 North Delaware Street, San Mateo, CA 94401
<www.peninsulaballet.org>

Description: Performs in early December. Tickets cost $6 to $60, depending on age, seating, and performance time.

Peninsula Youth Ballet (Ages 3+)
San Mateo Performing Arts Center
(800) 595-4849; 600 North Delaware Street, San Mateo, CA 94401
<www.pyb.org>

Description: Performs in late November, early December. Offers a separate Clara's Tea Party after the performance. Tickets cost $15 to $35 depending on seating and age.

San Jose Dance Theater (Ages 3+)
San Jose Center for the Performing Arts
(408) 286-9905; 255 Almaden Boulevard, San Jose, CA 95113
<www.sjdt.org>

Schedule: Early December with matinee and evening performances.
Cost: Ranges from $18 to $45, depending on seats.
Description: Danced by children with adult guest dancers. Candy Kingdom ($10) and backstage tours ($5) also available.

Santa Clara Ballet (Ages 3+)
Santa Clara Convention Center
(408) 881-0879; 5001 Great America Parkway, Santa Clara, CA 95054

Schedule: Early December with matinee and evening performances.
Cost: $18 to $28.50.

Santa Cruz Ballet Theater (Ages 3+)

(831) 477-1606; 2800 S. Rodeo Gulch Road, Soquel, CA 95073
Santa Cruz Civic Auditorium: 307 Church Street, Santa Cruz, CA 95060
<www.scbt.org>

Schedule: Mid-December with matinee and evening performances.
Cost: $12 to $30.

Smuin Ballet (Ages 3+)

(415) 495-2234; 300 Brannan Street, Suite 407, San Francisco, CA 94107
<www.smuinballet.org>

Description: Performances held in various venues in the Bay Area. Check Web site for performance schedule, location, and ticket information.

South Valley Ballet/Morgan Hill Dance Center (Ages 3+)
Ann Sobrato High School Theatre

(408) 776-1661; 401 Burnett Avenue, Morgan Hill, CA 95037
Morgan Hill Dance Center: 40 East 4th Street, Morgan Hill, CA 95037
<www.morganhilldance.com>

Schedule: In mid-December with matinee and evening performances.
Cost: $20/seat.

Valley Dance Theatre (Ages 3+)
Livermore High School Performing Arts Theatre

Livermore High School: 600 Maple Street, Livermore, CA
(925) 243-0925; 2247 Suite B, Second St., Livermore, CA 94550
<www.valleydancetheatre.com>

Schedule: In mid-December with matinee and evening performances.
Cost: $13 to $18/seat. Sugar Plum Tea: $25/person.

Western Ballet (Ages 3+)

Mountain View Center for the Performing Arts (The Mountain View Ballet Company and School)

(650) 968-4455; 914 N. Rengstorff Avenue, Mountain View, CA 94043
<www.westernballet.org>; <www.mvcpa.com>

Description: The dancers are from the Western Ballet School. The choreography and performance are wonderful. "The Land of the Sweets Party" provides an opportunity to meet some of the dancers and have cookies and treats.

Schedule: Early December with matinee and evening performances.

Cost: $22.50/adult, $18.50/child. Land of the Sweets Party: $7/person. To purchase tickets, contact the Mountain View Center for the Performing Arts at (650) 903-6000 or online: <www.mvcpa.com>.

What to Bring: Camera, if you're planning to attend the party.

Children's Theater

Theater helps bring favorite stories to life and inspires the imagination. There is a huge selection of companies and venues that provide family theater. There are Broadway tours that are appropriate for children. Many performing arts centers have special family programs. A huge number of community groups provide children's theater, sometimes by children for children. There are also puppet shows and plays at Children's Fairyland, Happy Hollow Park & Zoo, and Children's Discovery Museum in San Jose as well as the Bay Area Children's Museum in Sausalito. For current shows and discounts all around the Bay Area, visit <www.theatrebayarea. org>.

Develop your child's love of reading and explore the world through stories. Reading with your child develops listening skills, increases attention span and concentration, broadens vocabulary, and nurtures the imagination.

American Musical Theatre of San Jose (Ages 3+)
The Center for the Performing Arts
(408) 453-7108; (888) 455-SHOW; 255 Almaden Boulevard, San Jose, CA 95113
<www.amtsj.org>

Bay Area Storytelling Festival (Recommended Ages: 9+)
Kennedy Grove Regional Recreation Area, El Sobrante, CA
<www.bayareastorytelling.org>

For mapping on the Internet Web sites, use San Pablo Dam Road & Castro Ranch Road, El Sobrante, CA. In mid-May, this two-day weekend festival brings storytellers from around the state and country. The genres include fables, fairy tales, and many other types of stories. May not always be appropriate for children. For school groups in grades 3 to 6, they offer a field trip day on the Friday prior.

Best of Broadway
(415) 551-2000; (415) 551-2050
<www.bestofbroadway-sf.com>
For a current list of shows: www.bestofbroadway-sf.com/goldengate.html

Description: Brings the "Best of Broadway" series to San Francisco. Many Broadway musicals are appropriate for children, including Disney's *Beauty and the Beast* and *Lion King, Annie, My Fair Lady, The Sound of Music,* and *Peter Pan.*
Venues:

> Orpheum Theater: 1192 Market Street, San Francisco, CA
> Golden Gate Theater: 1 Taylor Street, San Francisco, CA
> Curran Theater: 445 Geary Street, San Francisco, CA

Broadway by the Bay
San Mateo Performing Arts Center
(650) 579-5565; 600 North Delaware Avenue, San Mateo, CA 94401
<www.broadwaybythebay.org>

Description: Past performances included *Singing in the Rain, Sound of Music,* and *West Side Story.* Single ticket prices: $21–$42 depending on seats and age.

Bus Barn Stage Company
Los Altos Youth Theater
(650) 941-0551; 97 Hillview Avenue, Los Altos, CA 94022
<www.busbarn.org>

California Shakespeare Festival/California Shakespeare Theatre Midsummer Stage (Ages 7+)
(510) 548-9666 Box Office;
Bruns Amphitheater: 100 Gateway Boulevard, Orinda, CA 94563
Administration: 701 Heinz Avenue, Berkeley CA 94710
<www.calshakes.org>

Description: Performs Shakespeare plays in an outdoor amphitheater in the hills between Berkeley and Orinda, off Highway 24. Grounds open 2 hours prior to the performance, and picnics are encouraged. There is also a cafe on site. Student matinees and outreach programs for East Bay schools and year-round classes & camps for youths, teens, and adults are offered.

Children's Discovery Museum (All Ages)
(408) 298-5437; 180 Woz Way, San Jose, CA 95110
<www.cdm.org>

Description: Features plays, concerts, story telling, etc. on the weekends. Plays are $1 per person plus general admission. Check the Web site for the calendar.

Children's Fairyland (Ages 2–10)
(510) 452-2259; 699 Bellevue Avenue, Oakland, CA 94610
<www.fairyland.org>

Description: Bring your toddler's nursery rhymes to life by visiting Children's Fairyland in Oakland and enrich your child's reading experience. This is a great little park where the rides and exhibits are built around nursery rhymes, fables, and stories. Don't miss the "Magic Key," which can be rented for $2, to hear stories at the exhibits. The Puppet Shows are "must see." Live shows are performed by kids through the Children's Fairyland Theater. See the Web site for current schedules. The park also has a small carousel and a mini-train.

Hours: *Spring* (April 19–June 11): Wed–Sun: 10am–4pm. *Summer* (June 12–September 4): weekdays: 10am–4pm, weekends: 10am–5pm. *Fall* (September 6–October 29): Wed–Sun and holidays: 10am–4pm. *Winter* (November 3–mid-April) as weather permits: Fri–Sun and holidays: 10am–4pm.

Cost: $6/person includes unlimited rides. Free/child under one.

Bathrooms: Yes.

Facilities: Stroller friendly.

Food: Yes. Bring your own picnic lunch, but no glass bottles allowed.

What to Bring: Your favorite nursery rhyme book to bring the stories alive.

Follow-Up Activities: 1) In late October, costume parades and costumed fairy tale characters celebrate Halloween at Fairyland's "Jack O'Lantern Jamboree." Hours are 11am–7pm. Admission is $7/person, all ages. Check the Web site or call for current dates/times. 2) If your 8- to 10-year-old likes to perform, Fairyland has a free one-year Children's Theater training program. Summer Performing Arts Day Camp is also available for ages 5–11.

Children's Musical Theater, San Jose (Ages 6+)
Montgomery Theater
(408) 288-5437; 1401 Parkmoor Avenue, San Jose, CA 95126
Montgomery Theater: 291 S. Market Street, San Jose
<www.cmtsj.org>

City Lights Theater Company of San Jose
(408) 295-4200; 529 S. Second Street, San Jose, CA 95112
<www.cltc.org>

Description: Discounted tickets to student groups of 10 or more at $10/ticket. For single tickets, students with valid ID can get tickets for $15 each. Study guides and TalkBack discussions follow the second Sunday of each performance. Call for details.

Coastal Repertory Theatre

(650) 726-0998; (650) 569-3266 Single Tickets; (650) 726-9208 Season Tickets
1167 Main Street, Half Moon Bay, CA 94019
<www.coastalrep.com>

Description: Performances as well as drama classes for kids ages 4 through 18 are offered. Call (650) 726-0267 for information about classes.

Disney on Broadway

<www.disneyonbroadway.com>

Beauty and the Beast, High School Musical, Mary Poppins, Tarzan, The Lion King, Aida, and other musicals tour throughout the United States. Visit Web site for the most current information.

Disney on Ice (All Ages)

<www.disneyonice.com>

To check for most current Disney stories translated into ice skating performances, visit the official Web site.

Douglas Morrisson Theatre (All Ages)

(510) 881-6777; 22311 North Third Street, Hayward, CA 94541
<dmtonline.org>

Description: Plays, musicals, and concerts.
Hours: Tues–Fri: 12:30pm–5:30pm for information. *Show times*: Thur, Fri, & Sat: 8pm, Sun: 2pm.
Cost: *Musicals:* $22/adult, $14/junior (under 18), $18/senior (over 50). *Plays:* $18/adult, $12/junior (under 18), $16/senior (over 50). *Concerts:* $12/adult, $6/junior (under 18), $10/senior (over 50). Season subscription packages are also available.
Follow-Up Activities: 1) New program with discounts for school groups along with backstage tours, discussion guides, and discussions with the cast and director. 2) Theater camp and voice classes offered. 3) Stage props, furniture, set pieces, and costumes are available for rental; visit <www.dmtrentals.org> for collection. Rental Department is open Mon–Fri: 10am–4pm by appointment only.

Heritage Theatre
408) 866-2700; 1 West Campbell Avenue, Campbell, CA 95008
<www.ci.campbell.ca.us/heritagetheatre>

Hillbarn Theatre & Conservatory
(650) 349-6411; 1285 E. Hillsdale Boulevard, Foster City, CA 94404
<www.hillbarntheatre.org>

Julia Morgan Center for the Arts
(510) 845-8542; Box Office: (925) 798-1300
2640 College Avenue, Berkeley, CA 94704
<www.juliamorgan.org>;

Kids on Broadway
(831) 425-3455; P.O. Box 3461, Santa Cruz, CA 95063
<www.kidsonbroadway.org>

Performs at Louden Nelson Community Center, located at 301 Center Street, Santa Cruz, CA 95060.

Lyric Theatre of San Jose
(408) 986-9090; Box Office: (408) 986-1455;
430 Martin Avenue, Santa Clara, CA 95050
<www.lyrictheater.org>

Performs light opera and operettas year-round at various venues. Example: Gilbert & Sullivan's *H.M.S. Pinafore*.

Marin Center
(415) 499-6800; 10 Avenue of the Flags, San Rafael, CA 94903
<www.marincenter.org>

Menlo Players Guild
(650) 322-3261; PO Box 301, Menlo Park, CA 94026
<www.menloplayersguild.org>

Performs Shakespeare and other pieces. Shakespeare Festival in the park in the summer. The Menlo Players Guild performs at various venues on the peninsula.

Mountain View Center for the Performing Arts
Tickets: (650) 903-6000; Administration: (650) 903-6565
500 Castro Street, Mountain View, CA 94039
<www.mvcpa.com>

This performing arts center features many local theater and dance companies, as well as visiting troupes. Visit the Web site for the calendar of events and to purchase tickets.

Peninsula Youth Theatre
(650) 988-8798; 2500 Old Middlefield Way, Mountain View, CA 94043
<www.pytnet.org>

Quality Children's Theater. Performs at the Mountain View Center for the Performing Arts and Cubberley Theatre. During the summer from late June to mid-August, free Children's Theater in the Park series perform on Fridays at 6:30pm. Performances at the outdoor Parkstage next to Pioneer Park. Each production is 45 minutes. You may bring a picnic dinner and blanket.

Theatre Works
Admin. (650) 463-1950; Tickets: (650) 463-1960 (11am–5pm)
<www.theatreworks.org>
Performs at the Mountain View Center for the Performing Arts and Lucie Stern Theatre in Palo Alto. Offers student matinees at $10/ticket. Matinees include study guide, post-show discussion with cast, and preparatory workshop in the classroom with actors from the show.

Napa Valley Opera House
(707) 226-7372; 1030 Main Street, Napa, CA 94559
<www.napavalleyoperahouse.org>

Palo Alto Players
(650) 329-0891; 1305 Middlefield Road, Palo Alto, CA 94301
<www.paplayers.org>
Performs at the Lucie Stern Theatre in Palo Alto.

Pleasanton Playhouse

Studio Theatre: (925) 462-2121; 1048 Serpentine, #309, Pleasanton, CA 94566
Amador Theatre: (925) 484-4486; 1155 Santa Rita Road, Pleasanton, CA
<http://pleasantonplayhouse.com>

San Jose Repertory Theater

(408) 367-7255; 101 Paseo de San Antonio, San Jose, CA 95113
<www.sjrep.com>

Student matinees on Wednesdays. Backstage tours, study guides, and artist in the schools are available for school groups with advance registration. There are also job shadowing opportunities for middle schoolers and early high schoolers. Call Education Director at (408) 367-7291. Acting camps for kids ages 7–16 during the summer.

Santa Clara Players

(408) 248-7993; 1900 Don Avenue, Santa Clara, CA 95050
<www.scplayers.org>

Performs at the Triton Museum of Art's Hall Pavilion. Free summer series with readings. Call to make reservations to the summer series.

Saratoga Civic Theater

(408) 868-1249; 13777 Fruitvale Avenue, Saratoga, CA 95070

Saratoga Drama Group
(Saratoga Civic Theater)
Box Office: (408)266-4SDG (4734)
P.O. Box 182, Saratoga, CA 95071
<www.saratogadramagroup.com>

West Valley Light Opera
(408) 268-3777; P.O. Box 779, Los Gatos, CA 95031
<www.wvlo.org>

Festival Theatre Ensemble

(800) 838-3006 Tickets; (408) 996-0635;
708 Blossom Hill Road, #121, Los Gatos, CA 95032
<www.festivaltheatreensemble.org>

Performs plays by Shakespeare at Oak Meadow Park, Los Gatos on July

& August evenings at 8pm. Tickets are $20/adult, $14/child 17 & under or senior 60+.

Shady Shakespeare Company
Sanborn-Skyline County Park
(408) 298-0649; 483 N 15th Street, San Jose, CA 95112
Sanborn Park: (408) 867-9959; 16055 Sanborn Rd., Saratoga, CA 95070
<www.shadyshakes.org>

Performs plays by Shakespeare at Sanborn-Skyline County Park, Saratoga on August & September evenings for free. Parking is $5/vehicle. Bring low back chairs & blankets. Dress in layers. Snack concession.

Shakespeare in the Park (Free)
<www.sfshakes.org/park/index.html>

1) Free performances held at various venues throughout the Bay Area. In the past, performed in Pleasanton, Cupertino, Oakland, San Francisco, and San Mateo. Performances are in the summer, from July to early October. Visit Web site for dates, locations, maps, and directions. 2) Shakespear on Tour program brings these free programs to school and libraries. Call (415) 558-0888 to schedule a program. 3) Sponsors the Bay Area Shakespeare Camps for children ages 7–18 to learn acting and perform Shakespeare's works. These summer camps are located throughout the Bay Area: San Francisco, Oakland, Cupertino, Los Altos, Pleasanton, Pacifica, Berkeley, Danville, Walnut Creek, San Jose, etc. For more information on the camps, call (415) 558-0888 or (800) 978-PLAY.

Shakespeare Santa Cruz
UCSC Theater Arts Center & Festival Grove
UCSC Ticket Office: (831) 459-2159
Performing Arts Center, 1156 High Street, Santa Cruz, CA 95064
<shakespearesantacruz.org>

Season: July & August. Tickets available in May. Beyond the summer Shakespeare season, other plays around the holiday season.

Stage One Theatre
Newark Memorial High School
(510) 791-0287; 39375 Cedar Boulevard, Newark, CA 94560
<www.stage1theatre.org>

Sunnyvale Community Center Theatre
(408) 733-6611; 550 E. Remington Drive, Sunnyvale, CA 94087
<http://sunnyvale.ca.gov/Departments/Parks+and+Recreation/Recreation/Performing+Arts+Center/>

California Theater Center and Sunnyvale Community Players use the Sunnyvale Community Center Theatre.

California Theater Center
(408) 245-2978; P.O. Box 2007, Sunnyvale, CA 94087
<www.ctcinc.org>, E-Mail: boxoffice@ctcinc.org

Sunnyvale Community Players
(408) 733-6611; P.O. Box 60399, Sunnyvale, CA 94088
<www.sunnyvaleplayers.org>

U.C. Santa Cruz Theater Arts MainStage
Theater Arts Center
(831) 459-2159; UCSC Main address: 1156 High Street, Santa Cruz CA 95064
Theater Arts Center: Located off Meyer Drive inside Campus. See map:
<www.events.ucsc.edu/tickets>; Map: <http://maps.ucsc.edu/cdtheaterarts.html>

Villa Montalvo
(408) 961-5800; Box Office: (408) 961-5858;
15400 Montalvo Road, Saratoga, CA 95071
<www.villamontalvo.org>
Features Family Theater showcasing puppet shows, fairy tales, and musicals in an intimate theater with beautiful surroundings. Park and gardens also open for hikes. Call prior to visit to confirm hours. Weather or events may lead to park closure.

Wells Fargo Center for the Arts
(707) 546-3600; 50 Mark West Springs Road, Santa Rosa, CA 95403

Yerba Buena Center for the Arts Theater
(415)978-2700; Tickets: (415)978-2787;
701 Mission Street, San Francisco, CA 94103
<www.yerbabuenaarts.org>; <www.ybca.org/calendar>

Young Performers Theatre (Ages 3+)
Fort Mason Center
(415) 346-5550; Building C, Room 300, San Francisco, CA 94123
<www.ypt.org>

Kids' shows and classes for kids 3 and older. Birthday parties.
$9/adult and $6/child.

Ticketmaster's Upcoming Family Events:
<www.ticketmaster.com/section/family?tm_link=tm_home_a_family>
Or www.ticketmaster.com.

Once you're at the site, select the "Family" icon across the top bar, and
then select the location to "N. California/N. Nevada" to see a list of up-
coming events. These events include children's TV shows that tour such
as *The Wiggles*, *Dragon Tales*, and *Barney*. It also sell tickets to *Disney on
Ice*, *Champions on Ice*, etc.

Web Site Links for Theaters in California
<www.curtainrising.com/usa/sanfrancisco.php>

Web Sites for Additional Events in the Bay Area
A selection of events and happenings in the San Francisco Bay area
<www.scaruffi.com/travel/sfoevent.html>
<www.theatrebayarea.org/whatsplaying/prod_rslt.jsp?genre=9&thispage=kids>

Children's Events

Our public libraries and children's bookstores are wonderful resources. Local libraries and bookstores have story times and other events geared toward families. These include sing-along concerts; arts and crafts; lectures; and special events such as puppet shows, magic shows, animal visits, storytime, plays, and much more. Even the *Nutcracker* ballet and the Dickens Christmas Fair have performed excerpts at these venues during the holiday season.

Library Events

In addition to special family events, many libraries have book clubs for kids and summer reading programs to encourage reading and literacy. These summer reading programs have reward programs such as discounts and free merchandise to a large selection of attractions and merchants.

Bay Area Library Web Site Links
<www.bayarealibraries.com/libraries.htm>

Alameda County Public Libraries
Fremont Main Library
(510) 745-1400; (510) 745-1421 Children's Services;
2400 Stevenson Boulevard, Fremont, CA 94538
<www.aclibrary.org> Branch locations

Berkeley Public Library
(510) 981-6100; 2090 Kittredge, Berkeley, CA 94704
<berkeleypubliclibrary.org> for branch locations & events

City of Mountain View Public Library
(650) 903-6337; 585 Franklin Street, Mountain View, CA 94041
<www.mountainview.gov/city_hall/library>

Contra Costa County Library
(800) 984-INFO within Contra Costa County only
(925) 646-6434 outside of Contra Costa County
<www.ccclib.org>; www.contra-costa.lib.ca.us>
<www.contra-costa.lib.ca.us/libinfo/branch.html> for 25 branch locations
<www.ccclib.org/youth/kid.html> for kids' events

Livermore Public Library
(925) 373-5500; 1188 South Livermore Avenue, Livermore, CA 95030
<www.livermore.lib.ca.us> for 3 branch locations & events

Los Gatos Public Library
(408) 354-6891; 110 East Main Street, Los Gatos, CA 95030
<www.library.town.los-gatos.ca.us>
Select "Kids Page" then "Children's Programs" for events including ventriloquists, sing-alongs, storytellers, etc.

Marin County Free Library
(415) 499-6056; 3501 Civic Center Drive, #427, San Rafael, CA 94903
<www.co.marin.ca.us/library> for all 11 branches, locations & hours.

MARINet (includes other Marin Public Libraries)
<www.co.marin.ca.us/depts/lb/main/branches.cfm>
Covers Marin County libraries, including city and town independent libraries: Belvedere Tiburon, Larkspur, Mill Valley, San Anselmo, San Rafael, Canal, and Sausalito. Select "Events & Classes," then "All Library Events" for an events calendar; don't miss the "Special Events for Kids" section.

Oakland Public Library
(510) 238-3134; 125 14th Street, Oakland, CA 94612
<www.oaklandlibrary.org> 17 branch locations throughout Oakland
<www.oaklandlibrary.org/Calendar.html#kids> Kids' events.

Palo Alto City Libraries
(650) 329-2436; 1213 Newell Road, Palo Alto, CA 94303
<www.city.palo-alto.ca.us/library> for branch locations
<www.city.palo-alto.ca.us/library/news-events/events.html> for events

Palo Alto Children's Library (Reopens 2007)
(650) 329-2134; 1276 Harriet Street, Palo Alto, CA 94303
<www.city.palo-alto.ca.us/library> for news & reopening date.

Peninsula Library System
<www.plsinfo.org> 35 locations; <www.plsinfo.org/library/calendar.asp> events.
Serves S. San Francisco, Daly City to Redwood City, and Woodside.

San Francisco Public Library
(415) 557-4400; Main Branch: 100 Larkin Street, San Francisco, CA 94102
<http://sfpl.lib.ca.us/> branch locations; <sfpl.lib.ca.us/news/events.htm> events

San Jose Public Library
Dr. Martin Luther King Jr. Main Library
(408) 277-4846; 180 W. San Carlos Street, San Jose, CA 95113
<www.sjlibrary.org> for 18 branch locations

San Leandro Public Library
(510) 577-3971; Main Library: 300 Estudillo Avenue, San Leandro, CA 94577
<www.ci.san-leandro.ca.us/sllibrary.html> for 2 branch locations

Santa Clara City Library
Central Park Library
(408) 615-2900; 2635 Homestead Road, Santa Clara, CA 95051
<www.library.ci.santa-clara.ca.us>
<www.library.ci.santa-clara.ca.us/calendar/kids/kids-calendar.html>

Santa Clara County Libraries
<www.santaclaracountylib.org> with links to each of these libraries.
<www.santaclaracountylib.org/kids/kidssites.html> Links to Kids' sites.
Serves Alum Rock, Campbell, Cupertino, Los Altos, Saratoga, Milpitas, Morgan Hill, and Gilroy libraries.

Santa Cruz County Public Libraries
(831) 420-5700; 224 Church Street, Santa Cruz, CA 95060: Central Library
<www.santacruzpl.org> with links to each of these libraries.

Includes Branciforte, Capitola, Central, Garfield Park, Live Oak, Aptos, La Selva Beach, Boulder Creek, Felton, & Scotts Valley branch libraries.

SNAP Public Libraries
Solano, Napa and Partners Library Consortium
<http://snap.lib.ca.us/>; <solanolibrary.com>
Includes Solano County (9 branches), Napa City-County libraries as well as Benicia, Dixon, and St. Helena public libraries.

Sonoma County Libraries
<www.sonomalibrary.org> with links to each of these libraries.
Includes Central Santa Rosa, Cloverdale, Guerneville, Healdsburg, Northwest Santa Rosa, Petaluma, Rincon Valley, Rohnert Park-Cotati, Sebastopol, Sonoma Valley, and Windsor libraries.

Sunnyvale Public Library
(408) 730-7300; 665 W. Olive Avenue, Sunnyvale, CA 94086
<www.ci.sunnyvale.ca.us/library>

Store Events

Barnes and Noble
<www.bn.com>; <http://storelocator.barnesandnoble.com>

Barnes and Noble has simplified the process to find store events. On its home page, select "Find an in-store event near you" below the "Search" box. Then type in your zip code and click on the "Find Events" button. This should bring up a listing of events of stores closest to you.

Borders Books
<www.bordersstores.com>

Once you've entered the Web site, select the "Store Locator" icon, enter your zip code, then select (click on) the store(s) closest to you. This will bring up store-specific events, addresses, hours, and maps. Different stores have different events. Some stores have more family oriented programs, so look at a few store close to you.

Linden Tree Children's Recordings and Books

(650) 949-3390; (800) 949-3313; 170 State Street, Los Altos, CA 94022
<http://lindentree.booksense.com/NASApp/store/IndexJsp>

Family Concert Series, free sing-alongs for children. Admission is a new book to donate to literacy programs.

The Wooden Horse

(408) 356-8821; 796 Blossom Hill Road, Los Gatos, CA 95032
<www.woodenhorsetoys.com>

Special event in late April for the National TV Turn Off Week with week-long activities including storytime, arts and crafts, Earth Day celebration, and play day. "Sleepover parties" and play days throughout the year. Check the Web site for special events under the "Community" tab.

Chapter 9
Historical Outings

Historical outings show us what life was like in the old days. This section includes history parks and outings to learn about California history, including Native Americans, Spanish Missions, and the Gold Rush.

LearnCalifornia.org provides information on California's history including California Indians, Missions, the Gold Rush era, and railroad history. The Web site is <**www.learncalifornia.org.**

History Parks & Museums

Ardenwood Historic Farm (All Ages)
(510) 796-0663; 34600 Ardenwood Boulevard, Fremont, CA 94555
<www.ebparks.org/parks/arden.htm>

Description: Ardenwood is the site of many historical and cultural events. See the full entry for Ardenwood Historic Farm Chapter 1: Animal Kingdom—Farms.

- *Johnny Appleseed Day* is in early March.
- *Gathering of the Scottish Clan.* Tartan Day celebration with the Scottish folk. Enjoy highland children's games, bagpipes, dancing, traditional Scottish food, and reenactments with Mary, Queen of Scots, and her Court.
- *Annual Civil War Reenactments* held usually on Memorial Day weekend but was held in mid-August in 2006.
- *Celtic Festival* is in June. Enjoy Celtic dance and Welsh and Irish music along with historic enactments and children's activities.

- *Fire Truck Day* is in mid-June.
- *July 4th: Old Fashioned Independence Day Celebration.*
- *Ardenwood Victorian Christmas* usually during the first weekend in December.

Hours/Cost: See the Web site's event calendar for current event details and costs.

History Park, San Jose (All Ages)

(408) 287-2290; 1650 Senter Road, San Jose, CA 95112
<www.historysanjose.org>

Description: This park has historic buildings and exhibits that showcase an old-fashioned small town, with an operational trolley, antique cars, and trolleys from San Jose's bygone days at the Trolley Barn; a working print shop; an old-fashioned ice cream parlor; an old schoolhouse; and an old firehouse. The old firehouse is open during the guided tour and on special event days. *The Hellenistic Heritage Institute/Museum* and the *Portuguese Museum* are also housed here at the park. Don't miss the bark of the cork tree, which makes the cork we use for wine bottles. There is an old Chinese temple and community center, *Ng Shing Gung,* the last of six San Jose China Towns from the 1880s. For more information on the San Jose China Town: <www.chcp.org> then select "Ng Shing Gung."

Hours: Closed Mondays. *Weekends:* noon–5pm; Vintage Trolley, working print shop, and 2-3 buildings are open on weekends. On the Web site, select the "Visiting" tab, then "History Park at Kelly Park," then "Open Building Schedule" for a list of which buildings and when they'll be open. *Tues–Fri:* noon–5pm, grounds open, most buildings closed during weekdays. Look for special event days such as "Family Day—Athletes United For Justice" in October when most buildings will be open. *Museum Store:* Tues–Sun: noon–5pm. Don't miss the print shop demonstrations on the first and second weekends of each month. Trolleys run every weekend from noon to 4pm.

Cost: $6 parking fee. Free admission.

Bathrooms: Yes.

Facilities: Stroller friendly.

Food: *O'Brien's Ice Cream & Café:* Tues–Sun: noon–5pm.

What to Bring: Cash for parking and tickets, sunscreen, sunglasses, camera, and picnic lunch.

Follow-Up Activities: 1) Happy Hollow Park & Zoo and the Japanese

Friendship Garden are both within Kelly Park. 2) On Cinco de Mayo event weekend, the Portuguese Museum sponsors a Portuguese Heritage Festival with parades, cooking demonstrations, arts and crafts for kids, and music and dancing to celebrate their heritage. 3) Around Memorial Day weekend in late May, History Park sponsors a Multicultural Festival with parades, print shop demonstrations, ethnic foods, music, etc. 4) School programs on historic topics such as the Gold Rush, Victorian school, Ohlone Indians, environmental programs, and the history of Santa Clara Valley and its transformation from an agricultural to a technologically driven society. 5) San Jose Safari Day Camps provide week-long summer camps for kids ages 7–10 at different museums each day.

Hyde Street Pier (Ages 3+)
(415) 561-7100; Visitor Center Info Desk: (415) 447-5000;
Hyde Street at Jefferson Street, San Francisco, CA 94109
<www.maritime.org/calendar.htm>; <www.nps.gov/safr/planyourvisit/events.htm>

Description: 1) Hyde Street Pier hosts a costumed living history event called *A Day in the Life: 1901*. Meet a costumed captain and his wife, cook, and chief engineer. Learn what life was like aboard ship around the turn of the 20th century. This event takes place on a Saturday of select months: 11am–4pm. Check Web site for current schedule. 2) Music of the Sea for kids (ages 6+) is held on the 3rd Saturday of the month: 2–3pm. 3) Chantey Sings are on the 1st Saturday of each month: 8pm–midnight. The kid-appropriate tunes are sung 8pm–10pm. The bawdy tunes are not performed until after the 10pm break. Call (415) 556-6435 for reservations to the Chantey Sings. 4) Every Saturday morning at 9:30am, there's a ship mode building workshop for ages 16+. Call to confirm specific dates. 5) Festival of the Sea in September. See Chapter 6: Transportation Favorites—Boats.
Hours: Open daily: 9:30am–5pm. Extended summer hours Memorial Day to September 30: 9:30am–5:30pm. Closed New Year's, Thanksgiving, and Christmas days.
Cost: $5/adult (18+).
Bathrooms: Yes.
Facilities: Stroller not recommended on ships.
Food: No, restaurants close by.
What to Bring: Sunscreen, sunglasses, camera, jacket, change for parking, and cash for food.

Follow-Up Activities: 1) Field trip programs and overnight camping for Scout & other groups. For reservations & details, call (415) 447-5000. **2)** Visitor Center located directly across the street.

Museum of American Heritage (Ages 4+)
(650) 321-1004; 351 Homer Avenue, Palo Alto, CA 94301
<www.moah.org>

Description: This wonderful little museum is in downtown Palo Alto. There's a model 1920s kitchen, old-fashioned general store, print shop, and radio repair shop. There's a blacksmith workshop out in the back. The museum keeps an archive online of previous exhibits.

Hours: Fri, Sat, & Sun: 11am–4pm. Closed Mon–Thur.

Cost: Free.

Bathrooms: Yes.

Facilities: Stroller friendly.

Food: No, restaurants close by in downtown Palo Alto.

Follow-Up Activities: 1) Kids' Workshops (typically ages 10+) include: "How To Build a Crystal Radio," "Build a Short Wave Radio," "Magnetism & Electromagnetism," "Transistors," "Integrated Circuits," "Printshop," and much more. Check Web site under "Education" tab. **2)** Math & science week-long summer camp in late June covers a wonderful variety of topics. Register by mid-June. **3)** From mid-December to mid-January, there's an annual holiday Lego® creation with running Lego® trains.

National Steinbeck Center (Ages 8+)
(831) 796-3833; One Main Street, Salinas, CA 93901
<www.steinbeck.org>

Description: Situated in Old Town Salinas, the Steinbeck Center serves to educate the public about the life, times, and works of John Steinbeck, author of *East of Eden, Cannery Row, Of Mice and Men, The Grapes of Wrath,* and more. The center not only provides interactive exhibits to bring Steinbeck's experiences to life but also serves as a cultural and artistic venue for lectures, films, art exhibits, and community activities.

Hours: 10am–5pm, 7 days a week. Closed on Thanksgiving, Christmas, New Year's Day, and Easter.

Cost: $10.95/adult; $8.95/senior 62+, student with ID, or military with ID; $7.95/youth 13–17; $5.95/child 6–12; free/child 5 and under.

Bathrooms: Yes.
Facilities: Stroller friendly.
Food: Café open 11am–3pm for lunch.
What to Bring: Sunglasses and cash for food.
Follow-Up Activities: 1) Special events such as Kids Art Festival, Day of the Dead, and the Annual Steinbeck Festival in early August feature tours, films, lectures, and more. Call (831) 796–3833 for additional information or look under *Event Calendar* on the Web site. 2) School and group tours available on a first-come, first-served basis. 1 month advanced reservations required. During the summer, walking tours visit locales frequented by John Steinbeck.

Phoebe Hearst Museum of Anthropology (Ages 5+)

(510) 643-7648; U.C. Berkeley, 102 Kroeber Hall, Berkeley, CA 94720
<hearstmuseum.berkeley.edu>; <www.berkeley.edu/map/maps/DE56.html>

Description: It is located on the edge of the U.C. Berkeley campus on Bancroft Way and College Avenues. The museum's vast collection spans the cultures of the world and time from the past to the present. It is also notable for its comprehensive collection of Native Californian artifacts. The Native California Cultures gallery showcases the diversity of customs, environments, and histories of those who lived here.
Hours: Wed-Sat: 10am–4:30pm, Sun: 12-4pm. Closed Mon-Tues, national holidays & university holidays. Check Web site for specific dates.
Cost: $4/adult; $3/senior 55+, $1/student with ID, free/child 12 & under, museum members, UC faculty, students, and staff. *Free every Thursday.*
Bathrooms: Yes.
Facilities: Stroller friendly.
Food: Restaurants close by.
What to Bring: Cash for food and quarters for meter parking.
Follow-Up Activities: 1) Docent tours for K-12 groups. $2/child & $4/adult. 2) Californian Indian Day in mid-September with docent-led tours of the Native Californian Cultures gallery, craft booths, and Pomo dancers.

Roaring Camp Railroads hosts many living history events. See Chapter 6: Transportation Favorites—Big Trains for the full entry. Here's a list of living history events they've hosted in previous years.

- Memorial Day: Civil War Reenactment.
- August: Summer Gathering of Mountain Men and Great Train Robberies.
- October: 1880s Harvest Fair (wool spinning, weaving, and candle making).

Rosicrucian Egyptian Museum (Ages 5+)

(408) 947-3635; 1342 Naglee Avenue, San Jose, CA 95191
<www.egyptianmuseum.org>

Description: This museum presents Egyptian culture, history, and view of afterlife. There's a collection of Egyptian artifacts with replicas of two tombs. Learn about the mummification process and how they've been able to use modern technology to recreate the face of a 4- to 6-year old Egyptian girl. Learn about hieroglyphics, Egyptian gods, and the kings & queens of Egypt, including Cleopatra, King Tut, etc.

Hours: Mon–Fri: 10am–5pm, Sat–Sun: 11am–6pm. Last admission ½ hour prior to closing. Planetarium shows on Mon–Fri at 2 pm, Sat–Sun: 2 pm & 3:30 pm. Closed on major holidays. In the summer, there're hieroglyphics workshops and scavenger hunts on Saturdays. See calendar on their Web site for special programs.

Cost: $9/adult, $7/senior or student w/ID, $5/child (5–10), free/child under 5. $1 discount available for AAA, KQED, or military members. Planetarium shows are complimentary (ask for tickets at the admissions desk).

Bathrooms: Yes.

Facilities: Not stroller friendly.

Food: No. No picnicking allowed on the property or in the park, but there's a picnic area in the San Jose Rose Garden just down the street on Naglee Ave.

What to Bring: Camera.

Follow-Up Activities: 1) Tours for older students and school group programs. 2) In mid-July, look for the Ancient Egyptian Epagomenal Festival celebrating Egyptian deities with special talks, games, children's activities, and ceremonial reenactments. 3) Summer camps. 4) Visit Web site for a virtual tour, maps of Egypt, and online resources on Egypt.

Wax Museum, Fisherman's Wharf (Ages 5+)
(800) 439-4305; (415) 202-0416
145 Jefferson Street, San Francisco, CA 94133 (between Mason & Taylor Streets)
<www.waxmuseum.com>

Description: This wax museum has a large collection of famous and historically significant people, including King Tut and Cleopatra, U.S. presidents, famous scientists, movie stars, religious and world leaders, and artists and writers. It's a big variety, from the famous to the infamous.
Hours: Weekdays: 10am–9pm, Weekends: 9am–11pm. Special holiday hours. Call to confirm hours. Box office closes 1 hour prior to closing time.
Cost: $12.95/adult, $9.95/junior 12–17 or senior 55+, $6.95/child 6–11, discount for AAA members. Look for discount coupons at <www.fishermanswharf.org> or <www.sanfranciscoonline.com/coupons.html>.
Bathrooms: Yes.
Facilities: Stroller friendly.
Food: Nearby restaurants at Fisherman's Wharf, and Rainforest Café is next door.
What to Bring: Cash for parking, food, etc. Don't forget your jacket and sunglasses.
Follow-Up Activities: Educational programs available. To learn how wax figures are made, visit the Web site for a brief description.

Wilder Ranch State Park (All Ages)
(831) 423-9703; (831) 426-0505; 1401 Old Coast Road, Santa Cruz, CA 95060
(Off of Hwy 1, 2 miles North of Santa Cruz)
<www.santacruzstateparks.org/parks/wilder>; <www.scparkfriends.org>

Description: This park showcases a dairy ranch from the 1900s. It has a small farm with a few animals and restored ranch buildings including a working blacksmith shop and a wood shop with water-powered tools. Don't miss the demonstration of this ingenious wood shop with its water wheel and pulley system that powered a drill, a grinder, and even an electric generator! Tour the Victorian house where the Wilder family lived, and see the exhibits at the visitor center. Guided tours of the ranch and living history demonstrations help us envision what life was like in the old days. The docents dress in period costume. In the spring, around late April/May, both the cliff and barn swallows come back to nest every year. It's a sight to watch them build their nests. A nature preserve is on the property but closed to the public. However, there's an overlook from the Old Cove Landing trail for bird watching.

Hours: 8am–sunset. *Visitor Center:* Thur–Sun, 10am–4pm during most months. Closed Thursdays December-February. Open extra days April-mid-June. *Saturdays:* Ranch tours led by knowledgeable docents. *Some Saturday & Sundays,* there's a Living History Demonstration with costumed docents; call for specific dates. Closed in December during the holiday season. Call to confirm hours prior to visit.

Cost: $6 parking fee.

Bathrooms: Yes, by the parking lot.

Facilities: Stroller friendly. Small bookstore in the visitor center.

Food: No, except for the July 4th celebration.

What to Bring: Cash for parking and binoculars for bird watching. If you visit during the July 4th old-fashioned Independence Day celebration, don't forget to bring your picnic gear, picnic lunch, sunscreen, sunglasses, hat, umbrella for shade, camera, and cash for food/ice cream/drinks.

Follow-Up Activities: 1) Ranger Explorers (6- to 10-year-olds) program in the summer through the Santa Cruz State Parks. Call (831) 335-1743 for additional information. There is also a Jr. Ranger program for younger children. 2) Plenty of school programs. See "Education" tab on the Web site. 3) Very close to both Natural Bridges and to the Seymour Marine Discovery Center site. 3) Special event days:

- July 4th celebration is the biggest event on the ranch. Don't miss this event; the ranch is in full operation with demonstrations, hourly tours, old-fashioned games, music, and food.
- Harvest Festival in October.

Check Web site for events information: <www.santacruzstateparks. org/education/events_list.php> & <www.santacruzca.org>.

Woodside Store (Ages 4+)

(650) 851-7615; 3300 Tripp Road, Woodside, CA 94062; (at Kings Mountain Rd) <www.eparks.net> then select "Parks," then "Woodside."

Description: This is a museum set up as a general store filled with the goods that blacksmiths, wagon makers, lumbermen, or teamsters might have needed in the 1880s. There's a precursor to today's washing machine, a hand-operated laundry machine; racoon, skunk, and other skins to touch; old-fashioned toys, and much more. Don't miss the wonderful antique mechnical banks that take in deposited coins in delightful ways on the store counter. There's also a period dentist's office as well as a recreated blacksmith shop.

Hours: Tues & Thur: 10am–4pm, Sat & Sun: noon–4pm. Closed other days and holidays.

Cost: Free.

Bathrooms: Yes.

Facilities: Stroller friendly.

Food: Snacks only. Food is available from concessions only on Woodside Days. Small souvenirs, books, and snacks available at the store regularly.

What to Bring: Sunscreen, sunglasses, camera, and picnic lunch.

Follow-Up Activities: 1) On Woodside Days (once a year on the first Sunday of May), see demonstrations of horseshoeing, blacksmithing, rope making, butter churning, etc. 2) Arrange field trips through San Mateo County Historical Association. Scheduling opens mid-April for schools in San Mateo County and mid-May for other schools for the subsequent school year.

California History

Almaden Quicksilver Mining Museum (Ages 8+)

(408) 323-1107; 21350 Almaden Road, San Jose, CA 95814

<www.parkhere.org> then "Historical & Cultural," then "Almaden Quicksilver"

Description: Learn about the process and technology as well as history of cinnabar mining, the ore that contains mercury. Mercury, in turn, was used to process silver from silver mines.

Hours: *Fall* (Sept–June): Fri: noon–4pm, Sat & Sun: 10am–4pm. *Summer* (July & August): Fri–Sun: 10am–4pm.

Cost: Free.

Bathrooms: Yes.

Facilities: Stroller friendly.

Food: No. Picnic area.

What to Bring: Sunscreen, sunglasses, camera, picnic lunch.

Follow-Up Activities: Guided walking tours to the town of New Almaden, school tours, etc. Visit Web site, select "For Teachers & Kids" to get the teaching and activity guide.

California Historical Society (Ages 10+)

(415) 357-1848; 678 Mission Street, San Francisco, CA 94105
<www.californiahistoricalsociety.org>

Description: The museum provides information on 300 years of California history. Photography and fine arts collections show the history of California from the pre-Gold Rush era to the early decades of the 1900s.

Hours: Wed–Sat: 11am–4:30pm. Public tours on Saturdays at 2pm, included with admission. Closed Mondays.

Cost: $3/adult, $1/student or senior over 62, free/child under 5. *Free on the first Tuesday of each month.*

Bathrooms: Yes.

Facilities: Stroller friendly.

Food: No. Nearby restaurants.

What to Bring: Cash for admission, food, and parking.

Follow-Up Activities: Virtual exhibit of California's history spanning 300 years: <www.californiahistoricalsociety.org/exhibits/online.html>.

California Museum for History, Women, & the Arts
Out of Area (Ages 10+)

(916) 653-7524
California State Archives Building: 1020 O Street, Sacramento, CA 95814
<www.californiamuseum.org>

Description: This is the first California museum to provide permanent exhibit on influential women in California's history such as Elizabeth Taylor, Amelia Earhart, Sally Ride, Julia Morgan, and many more. There's also a Hall of Fame, which includes notable Californians who have made an impact, including Walt Disney, Ronald Reagan, John Muir, César Chávez, etc.

Hours: Tues–Sat: 10am–5pm, Sun: noon–5pm. Closed major holidays. Last admission half hour prior to closing.

Cost: $7.50/adult, $6/senior 55+, $5/youth 6-13, free/child 5 & under.

Bathrooms: Yes.

Facilities: Stroller friendly.
Food: No. Picnic area.
What to Bring: Cash for parking and food.
Follow-Up Activities: Offers workshops for students in grades 3–12.

Peralta Adobe & Fallon House (Ages 4+)

(408) 993-8300; Tour appointment: (408) 918-1055;
175 West Saint John Street, San José, CA 95110
<www.historysanjose.org/visiting_hsj/peralta_fallon/peralta_fallon.html>

Description: Located in downtown San Jose, these two sites are just across the street from each other. The adobe is the oldest structure in San Jose, with 2 rooms furnished in the style of its day around the turn of the 19th century. The furnishings showcase the lifestyle of early Californians. See a seat made entirely out of whale bone, a bed and window pane made from leather, and a hanging crib with moss used as a natural diaper. Fallon House is a Victorian mansion furnished in the period of the mid-19th century. The best time to visit is during the *San Jose Founders' Day* event in November with costumed docents and hands-on demonstrations such as tortilla making, candle dipping, ceramic bowl making, adobe brick making, and dressing up as a Spanish soldier.
Hours: Only open for tours led by docents. Call to make tour appointments.
Cost: Free.
Bathrooms: Yes.
Facilities: Stroller friendly.
Food: No. Restaurants are nearby.
What to Bring: Sunscreen, sunglasses, and camera.
Follow-Up Activities: Many programs offered to schools through History San Jose. These include "Experience Adobe Days," "Experience Victorian Days," plus many others at the History San Jose site in Kelly Park. See Web site under "Education" tab.

San Juan Bautista State Historic Park (Ages 4+)

(831) 623-4526; Hwy 156: 2nd & Mariposa Streets, San Juan Bautista, CA 95045
Plaza History Association: San Juan Bautista State Historic Park
(831) 623-4881; P.O. Box 787, San Juan Bautista, CA 95045
<www.parks.ca.gov/default.asp?page_id=563>

Description: This historic park, located in downtown San Juan Bautista, includes the Plaza Hotel and stable, blacksmith shop, granary, jail, and several houses. The exhibits display what life was like in the California Mission during the Mexican era and during the precolonial days of the Native American.

Hours: 10am–4:30pm. Living history days are held on the first Saturday of each month with costumed docents who bake bread and do black smithing.

Cost: Free.

Bathrooms: Yes.

Facilities: Stroller friendly.

Food: No. Restaurants are nearby.

What to Bring: Sunscreen, sunglasses, camera, cash for food, and lots of gas in the tank.

Follow-Up Activities: 1) Early Days in San Juan is held annually on Father's Day weekend. The living history event features examples of life in the 1800s with an 1830 Mountain Men encampment, 1860–1870 buildings and clothing, and an 1890 bar room. 2) School trips require reservations with Reserve America at (831) 623-4528. Visit the Web site and look under the "School Groups" section for details.

Sanchez Adobe (Ages 4+)

(650) 359-1462; 1000 Linda Mar Boulevard, Pacifica, CA 94044
<www.sanmateocountyhistory.com>;
<www.eparks.net/smc/department/home/0,,5556687_12313319_12368212,00.html>

Description: Don Francisco Sanchez led Mexican California in battle against the United States. Built in the mid 1800s, the adobe house provides a glimpse into the past with period furnishings, special events, and school tours that give students an opportunity to grind corn, rope a "cow," make adobe bricks, and dip candles.

Hours: Tues–Thur: 10am–4pm, Sat & Sun: 1-5pm.

Cost: Free.

Bathrooms: Yes.

Facilities: Not stroller friendly.

Food: No.

What to Bring: Picnic lunch, sunscreen, and sunglasses.

Follow-Up Activities: 1) Rancho Day in mid-September. 2) Registration for school tours start April 15 for San Mateo County schools and May 15 for all others. Fax reservations to (650) 359-1462.

Native American Indians

Chitactac-Adams Heritage County Park (Age 8+)

(408) 323-0107; 10001 Watsonville Road, Gilroy, CA 95020
<www.parkhere.org>, then "Find a Park"

Description: Chitactac was the name of the village of Mutsun Ohlones who lived in the Gilroy area more than 3,000 years ago. This site is notable for its bedrock mortars where the Ohlones prepared their acorns, nuts, and other foods. The interpretive kiosk has information on Ohlone life and culture as well as information on the bedrock mortars and petroglyphs. There are a few petroglyphs inscribed on the rocks by the Ohlones; however, they are rather hard to see and find. The easiest petroglyph to see is at Station D "Rock Art" on the self-guided interpretive trail. Get the map and guide for the trail just inside the interpretive kiosk. Call for interpretive program schedule. School programs provide an opportunity for students to experience drilling with a pump drill, mashing acorns, and playing Indian games.

Hours: Year round 8am–sunset.

Cost: Free.

Bathrooms: Portables only.

Facilities: Stroller friendly.

Food: No. Picnic area.

What to Bring: Sunscreen, sunglasses, picnic lunch, and camera.

Follow-Up Activities: Interpretive programs for schools or groups offered. Visit Web site: <www.sccgov.org/portal/site/parks> then select "For Teachers & Kids" to get Chitactac's teaching and activity guide as well as to see the selection of school programs.

Coyote Hills Regional Park Visitor Center (Ages 4+)

(510) 795-9385; 8000 Patterson Ranch Road, Fremont, CA 94555
<www.ebparks.org/parks/coyote.htm>

Description: This regional park preserves the Ohlone Indian shellmound site and the rich wetlands surrounding Fremont bay. The visitor center has exhibits on the Ohlone way of life, a tule reed boat made using native American methods by the park staff and volunteers, and the park's wildlife and natural history. There are open houses and tours of the main shell-mound site with a reconstructed tule house, shade shelter, dance circle, and sweat lodge. The shellmound site is only open during open houses and tours, so plan in advance if you'd like to visit. The park also offers wonderful nature, bird watching, and archaeology classes for kids (including preschoolers) for minimal cost.

Hours: *Park:* April–October: 8 am–8pm, October–April: 8 am–6pm. *Interpretive Center:* Tues–Sun: 9:30 am–5pm. Closed on Thanksgiving, Christmas, and New Year's Day. *Butterfly & Hummingbird Garden:* Open on the second Saturday of each month.

Cost: $5 parking. Program fees vary, some free.

Bathrooms: Yes.

Facilities: Stroller friendly.

Food: No. Picnic tables available.

What to Bring: Binoculars, camera, picnic lunch, and cash for parking. Wear comfortable walking shoes.

Follow-Up Activities: Naturalist programs on weekends include wild-flower walks in April, Ohlone Indian crafts such as basket weaving and arrowhead making, and shellmound workdays to learn how to build mats to thatch houses. The first Sunday in October is the Annual Gathering of Ohlone People event with special activities for kids to learn about Ohlone customs and culture. Activities include making a miniature tule boat, making a fire without matches, tasting acorn soup and manzanita cider, and watching demonstrations on basketry, jewlery, and making soaproot brushes. There's dance, song, and storytelling, too.

Miwok Park/Marin Museum of the American Indian (Ages 4+)

(415) 897-4064; Miwok Park: 2200 Novato Boulevard, Novato, CA 94947
<www.ci.novato.ca.us/cd/maint/page79.html>; <www.marinindian.com>

Description: Learn about the history and culture of Native Americans. Best visited as part of a camp or group visit, this museum is a local treasure with basketry, Indian games, and other tools used in everyday life.

Hours: Closed Mondays and Holidays. Tues–Fri: 10am–3pm, Sat & Sun: noon–4pm.

Cost: $5/adult, free/child under 12.

Bathrooms: Yes.

Facilities: Baby carrier.

Food: No.

What to Bring: Picnic lunch.

Follow-Up Activities: 1) Summer camp in July/August for children ages 6–12. 2) Annual Trade Feast Celebration is held in September for American Indians to get together to exchange supplies, foods, tools, songs, stories, and dances. Visit the Web site <www.novato.org/events.cfm> then select "Community Events" for special events for families. 3) *Olompali State Historic Park* is closeby off Hwy. 101 southbound. It has a reconstructed Miwok Village and a mortar rock used by the Miwoks to grind acorns, etc. For more information: <www.parks.ca.gov/default.asp?page_id=465> or (415) 892-3383

Kule Loklo: a Replica Coast Miwok Village (Ages 5+)

Point Reyes National Seashore

(415) 663-1092; Bear Valley Visitor's Center: (415) 464-5100

<www.mapom.com/kuleloklo.htm>; Events: <www.mapom.org>

Description: Kule Loklo is a short walk from the Bear Valley Visitor's Center at the Point Reyes National Seashore. It is a replica of the Coast Miwok Village. Visit the village to learn more about Miwok Indian life.

Hours: Bear Valley Visitor's Center: Mon–Fri: 9am–5pm, Sat/Sun and holidays: 8am–5pm. Closed Christmas Day. Guided tours every Sunday from Memorial Day to Labor Day. Meet at the Bear Valley Visitor Center at Point Reyes National Seashore; call Visitor Center for schedule. Roundhouse tours on select Saturdays at 12:30pm during the spring and fall. These tours meet at the Roundhouse.

Cost: Free.

Bathrooms: Yes.

Facilities: Stroller friendly.

Food: Not usually, but on special event days, yes. Restaurants in Point Reyes Station and Olema.

What to Bring: Sunscreen, sunglasses, cash for food or picnic lunch, and camera.

Follow-Up Activities: 1) Strawberry Festival in late April celebrates the arrival of spring with blessing of the first fruit. There'll be Native American dancers and demonstrators as well as food. 2) Big Time is held in late July on a Saturday, 10am–4pm. Big Time is the traditional California Indian get together for dancing, trading, and socializing. Demonstrations, activities for kids, and Indian foods and crafts are for sale. For additional information, call (415) 464-5100. 3) For an online summary of the Miwok Indians, visit <www.nps.gov/pore/history_miwok.htm>. 4) For additional information, contact the Miwok Archeological Preserve of Marin (MAPOM) at (415) 479-3281, 2255 Las Gallinas Avenue, San Rafael, CA 94903 or through <www.mapom.org>.

Directions: <www.nps.gov/pore/planyourvisit/directions.htm>.

San Mateo County History Museum (Ages 4+)
(650) 299-0104; 2200 Broadway, Redwood City, CA 94063
<www.sanmateocountyhistory.com>

Description: This wonderful museum in downtown Redwood City has exhibits and events showcasing California history from the time of the Ohlone Indians to present day. "Nature's Bounty" exhibit has an Ohlone tule house with an audio recording of Ohlone stories. There are displays on mission life and the evolution from mission life to the Gold rush and whaling. Drawers beneath the mission display contain wool that docents use to demonstrate how the wool can be carded and spun. The "Journey to Work" exhibit shows the changes in transportation from stagecoach to train to automobile and the impact on the economy and development of the peninsula and the suburbs. Included in this exhibit are wonderful examples of the first "party-line" telephones, the telegraph and its accompanying Morse codes, and the community bulletin board on a tree trunk. The temporary exhibit, "Parson's Ships of the World," is a rare gem, featuring Charles Parson's exquisitely detailed handcrafted models of historic ships starting with the first ships to present day naval destroyers.

Hours: Tue–Sun: 10am–4pm.

Cost: $4/adult; $2/senior (65+), youth (6-12) & students; free/child 5 & under.

Bathrooms: Yes.

Facilities: Stroller friendly.

Food: No. Nearby restaurants.

What to Bring: Camera and cash for meter parking.

Follow-Up Activities: 1) Don't miss special events such as "Victorian Days" with docents in period dress and even reenactments. On one visit, a highlight was learning to saw logs and make wood shingles the old-fashioned way. 2) School programs.

Santa Cruz Mission (Ages 5+)

(831) 425-5849; 144 School Street, Santa Cruz, CA 95060
<www.santacruzstateparks.org/parks/mission/>

Description: This mission features exhibits about the Ohlone Indians who lived in the Santa Cruz region for thousands of years prior to the arrival of the Spanish missionaries.

Hours: Thur–Sun: 10am–4pm.

Cost: Free.

Bathrooms: Yes.

Facilities: Stroller friendly.

Food: No. Nearby restaurants.

What to Bring: Picnic lunch, sunscreen, and sunglasses.

Follow-Up Activities: *Tule Harvesting* in late August, *Mission Adobe Day* on the 3rd Saturday of September, *Fiesta* in early October; *Living History Demonstrations* on select days, guided tours on Sundays at 1pm on select months, and many more events throughout the year. Visit the Web site: <www.santacruzstateparks.org/education> for current information on dates and times.

Santa Cruz Museum of Art & History (Ages 3+)

Exhibit on Ohlone Indians who lived in the Santa Cruz area. See the full entry in Chapter 8: Art & Performing Arts—Art Museums.

Missions

To learn more about California's missions, visit <www.ca-missions.org>.

Carmel Mission

(831) 624-1271; 3080 Rio Road, Carmel, CA 93923
<www.carmelmission.org>

Store open 9:30am–4:30pm. Special Web site for fourth graders: <**www. carmelmission.org/4th_grade.htm**>. This is still working as a church as well as a museum. Annual *Fiesta* on the last Sunday of September is free.

Mission Dolores

(415) 621-8203; 3321 16th Street, San Francisco, CA 94114
<www.missiondolores.org>

Open 8am–noon & 1–4pm. This serves as church, school, and museum.

Mission San Jose

(510) 657-1797; 43300 Mission Boulevard, Fremont, CA 94539; (P.O. Box 3314)
<www.ci.fremont.ca.us/Visiting/Attractions/HistoricAttractions.htm#Mission XE "Mission" >

Open 10am–5pm. The museum has a collection of artifacts, vestments, and memorabilia from the days when this served as a mission.

Mission San Juan Bautista

(831) 623-4526; Plaza: 2nd & Mariposa Streets, San Juan Bautista
PO Box 400, San Juan Bautista, CA 95045
<www.parks.ca.gov/default.asp?page_id=563>;

Mission San Rafael Arcangel

(415) 456-3016; 1104 Fifth Avenue, San Rafael, CA 94901
<www.saintraphael.com/museum.html>

Self-guided tours 11am–4pm. Docent led tours available on Sundays. School tours with a docent available with advance reservations. Call for schedule/appointment. Museum is being renovated; call prior to visit.

Mission Santa Clara, Santa Clara University

(408) 554-4023; 500 East Camino Real, Santa Clara, CA 95053
<www.scu.edu/visitors/mission>

Santa Cruz Mission State Historic Park
(831) 425-5849; 144 School Street, Santa Cruz, CA 95060
<www.santacruzstateparks.org/parks/mission/>

See full entry in Chapter 9: Historical Outings—California History: Native American Indians.

Sonoma Mission
(707) 938-9560; 1-866-240-4655 Reserve America for school tours
114 East Spain Street, Sonoma, CA 95476
<www.parks.ca.gov/?page_id=479>
Open 10am–5pm. Docent-led tours: Fri–Sun: 11am, 12pm, 1pm, 2pm. Visit other sites of the Sonoma State Historic Park.

Gold Rush

California's history is intricately linked to the Gold Rush. Use your children's fascination with finding treasure to help them learn about California's Gold Rush history. The following Web sites have Gold Rush history: 1) California State Railroad Museum:<**www.csrmf.org/doc. asp?id=15**>. 2) PBS's program: <**www.isu.edu/~trinmich/home.html**>. 3) Learning California: <**www.learncalifornia.org/doc.asp?id=491**>.

Museum of the City of San Francisco (Ages 8+)
(415) 928-0289; Admin. Office: 945 Taraval Street, San Francisco, CA 94116
<www.sfmuseum.org>

Description: This online museum chronicles the history of San Francisco from its start as a Spanish garrison to the Gold Rush era, the historic 1906 Earthquake, the sinking of the Titanic, the end of World War II, and the more recent 1989 earthquake. The museum offers speakers services and exhibits to organizations.

Oakland Museum of California (Ages 3+)
Virtual Exhibit of *California's Untold Stories: Gold Rush!* at:
<www.museumca.org/goldrush>.

Old Sacramento (All Ages)
Out of Area
(916) 558-3912 Events; (916) 442-7644 Visitor Center,
1004 2nd Street, Old Sacramento, CA
<www.oldsacramento.com>; <www.sacmuseums.org>

Preserving historic Sacramento, Old Sacramento is an historic town within Sacramento with operating businesses and many museums. It is the site of many special events throughout the year. 1) Events include the Old-Fashioned Easter and Parade in April, Steam Train excursions in April, Pony Express Re-ride in June, Gold Rush Days over Labor Day weekend, Fall Harvest Days and Spookomotive Steam Train in October, Santa's Steam Train in November, and Heritage Holidays in December. Look on the Web site under "Calendar." 2) *Sacramento Museum Day* means *free admission* to museums in Sacramento. Event occurs annually in February. Call (916) 264-7777 for more information. Download the brochure on the Web site for maps and building details. Visit **<www.sacmuseums.org>** for details.

Hours: Sun–Fri: 10am–5pm, Sat: 10am–6pm. Closed holidays.
Cost: Free.

Below are the museums and river cruise operators located in Old Sacramento and nearby.

Sutter's Fort
(916) 445-4422; 2710 L Street
<www.parks.ca.gov/?page_id=485>
Description: The original settlement is still available for self-guided tours. Located down the road from Old Sacramento.
Hours: Daily:10am–5pm.

Wells Fargo Museum
(916) 440-4263; 1000 2nd Street, Corner of Second and J Streets
<www.wellsfargohistory.com>
Description: Stagecoaches, gold, mining, business, and commerce are all colorfully interpreted for visitors. Tours are available.
Hours: Daily: 10am–5pm.

Schoolhouse Museum
(916) 483-8818; Front and L Street
<www.oldsacschoolhouse.org>
Description: This replica of an authentic one-room school-

house is available for school group tours.

Hours: Call for hours or to reserve tours.

Crocker Art Museum

(916) 264-5423; 216 O Street, Sacramento, CA 95814
<www.crockerartmuseum.org>

Description: This collection includes early Californian, European, and Asian art; drawings by Old Masters; and contemporary Californian art. Family Sundays special events. Tours and art classes available. Check Web site for schedule.

Hours: Tues–Sun: 10am–5pm. Thur: 10am–9pm.

Cost: $6/adult, $4/senior, $3/student w/ ID, free/child 6 & under. Free admission on Sundays 10am–1pm.

Towe Auto Museum

(916) 442-6802; 2200 Front Street, Sacramento, CA 95818
<www.toweautomuseum.org>

Description: American cars starting with the wagons of the 1800s to today's cars are on exhibit.

Hours: Daily: 10am–6pm.

Cost: $7/adult, $6/senior, $3/high school student, $2/grade school student, free/child 6 & under.

California Military Museum

(916) 442-2883; 1115 Second Street, Sacramento, CA
<www.militarymuseum.org>

Description: An interpretive museum with authentic clothing, equipment, and stories from our nation's rich military past.

Hours: Tues–Thur: 10am–4pm, Fri–Sun: 10am–5pm.

California State Capitol Museum

(916) 324-0333; 10th and L Street, Sacramento, CA
<www.capitolmuseum.ca.gov>;
<www.parks.ca.gov/default.asp?page_id=495>

Description: Learn how the government works and how a bill comes into being, and tour the State Capitol and the surrounding park. Free school tours for grades 4+.

Hours: Open daily 9am to 5pm; guided tours on the hour 9am to 4pm.

California State Indian Museum

(916) 342-0971; 2618 K Street, Sacramento, CA 95816
<www.parks.ca.gov/?page_id=486>

Description: Museum with many examples of basketry, pump drill, mortar and pestle for grinding acorn, dance costumes, musical instruments, and hunting tools of California Indians. **Hours:** Daily 10am– 5pm. Closed Thanksgiving, Christmas, & New Year's.

Leland Stanford Mansion

(916)324-0575; 800 N Street, Sacramento, CA 95814
<www.parks.ca.gov/?page_id=489>; <www.stanfordmansion.org>
Description: Completely renovated museum with original period furnishings and Victorian gardens. Tours available daily 10am–4pm.
Cost: $8/adult, $3/youth 6-17, free/child 5 & under. Visitor Center open 9:30am–5pm. Call to confirm prior to visit for any cancellations.

Riverboat Cruises

(800) 433-0263; (916) 552-2933; 110 L Street, Old Sacramento
<www.spiritofsacramento.com>

River Otter Water Taxi

(916) 446-7704; L Street Landing - On the Waterfront
Operates from April through October; reservations recommended.
<www.riverotter.com>

Discovery Museum (All Ages)
"The Sacramento Museum of History, Science, Space & Technology"
<www.thediscovery.org>

Description: This museum is housed in two separate buildings. The Discovery Museum History Center is located in Old Sacramento and appropriately focuses on historical exhibits. The Discovery Museum Science and Space Center is housed in another location.

Discovery Museum History Center (All Ages)

(916) 264-7057; 101 I Street, Old Sacramento CA 95814

Description: Located in Old Sacramento, next door to the California State Railroad Museum, the History Center has a Gold Rush exhibit, an authentic working print shop in the McClatchy Gallery, and imagination play stations with interactive exhibits to immerse children in history. The Community

Gallery documents Sacramento's evolution from frontier town to a state capitol. The Agricultural Technology Gallery shows a historical survey of the technology used in agriculture.

Hours: Tues–Sun: 10am–5pm. Closed Mondays except for holidays and school tours. Closed Thanksgiving Day, Christmas Day, and New Year's Day. *Summer Hours (July and August):* Daily: 10am-5pm. Call to confirm hours.

Cost: $5/adult, $4/senior 60+, $4/youth 13–17, $3/child 4–12, free/child 3 & under.

Bathrooms: Yes.

Facilities: Stroller friendly.

Food: Snacks only. Restaurants are nearby.

Follow-Up Activities: 1) Many family events on weekends. Visit the Web site "Activities." 2) School group tours available. 3) Gold Rush Days is an Living History event with period costumes. All of Old Sacramento participates. The event takes place over Labor Day weekend. Check the Web site under "Activities" then "Special Events."

Discovery Museum Science & Space Center (All Ages)

(916) 575-3941; 3615 Auburn Boulevard, Sacramento, CA 95821

Description: The Science & Space Center has a planetarium and Nature Discovery room with insects and wildlife. It is also home to the Challenger Learning Center. The nature trail outside the museum provides an opportunity to be among the oaks and redwoods, have a picnic, and bird watch.

Hours: Tues–Fri: noon–5pm, Sat & Sun: 10am–5pm. *Summer Hours (July and August):* Daily: 10am–5pm. Closed Memorial Day and the 4th of July. Every Tues–Fri at 2pm, there's a live animal presentation by the animal educator staff. Planetarium shows on weekends at 1pm & 3pm are free with admission. In the summers, planetarium shows are daily at 3pm.

Cost: $5/adult, $4/senior 60+, $4/youth 13–17, $3/child 4–12, free/child 3 & under.

Bathrooms: Yes.

Facilities: Stroller friendly.

Food: Snacks only. Restaurants are nearby.

Follow-Up Activities: 1) Many family events on weekends. Visit the Web site for "Activities" information. 2) School group tours available. 3) Summer Day Camp.

Challenger Learning Center

Located in the Discovery Museum Science & Space Center.
Description: Simulated Space Missions held on Friday evenings from 6–8:30pm on select days throughout the year. Check Web site for schedule. Visit Web site for the most current information.
Cost: $20/person; $15/member; reservations required: (916) 485-8836.

Seymour Pioneer Museum (Ages 10+)
Society of California Pioneers
(415) 957-1849; 300 Fourth Street, San Francisco, CA 94107
<www.californiapioneers.org>

Description: The museum is home to paintings depicting California landscapes and residents, a collection of costumes and accessories, historical artifacts such as gold pans and other equipment used during the Gold Rush era, and a photo gallery of the evolving California landscape and environment. It also has a photo database online.
Hours: Wed–Fri: 10am–4pm. 1st Saturday of every month: 10am–4pm.
Cost: $3/adult, $1/student or senior.
Bathrooms: Yes.
Facilities: Stroller friendly.
Food: No, restaurants nearby.
What to Bring: Cash for parking.
Follow-Up Activities: Located across from Yerba Buena Gardens, this is close to Zeum, Metreon, ice skating, bowling, and the carousel. Park at the 5th & Mission Street Garage.

Wells Fargo History Museum (Ages 4+)
(415) 396-2619; 420 Montgomery Street, San Francisco, CA 94163
<www.wellsfargohistory.com/museums/sfmuseum.html>

Description: The museum displays artifacts important to the development of the Wells Fargo Corporation, California, and the American West. Exhibits include treasure boxes, the Wells Fargo stagecoach, gold, and original papers from the Wells Fargo office founded 100 years ago.
Hours: Mon–Fri: 9 am–5pm.

Cost: Free.
Bathrooms: Yes.
Facilities: Stroller friendly.
Food: No. Restaurants close by.
What to Bring: Cash for parking and food.
Directions: Portsmouth Square Garage at 733 Kearny, (415) 982-6353.

Out of Area...

The following parks, although out of our immediate area, are included because if you have a child like mine, it's nice to know where to go for gold panning.

Columbia State Historic Park (All Ages)

(209) 588-9128; 11255 Jackson Street, Columbia, CA 95310
<www.parks.ca.gov/default.asp?page_id=552>; <www.columbiacalifornia.com>

Description: This real town's Gold Rush era business district has been preserved from the 1850s with shop owners dressed in period costumes conducting business in the old-style. You can pan for gold by renting a gold pan for $5/person at the Matelot Gulch Mine Supply Store, (209) 532-9693, or take a tour of an active hardrock gold mine at Hidden Treasure Gold Mine. For tours, sign up upon arrival at the Matelot Gulch Mine Supply Store for the Hidden Treasure Mine tour, located within the park at the corner of Washington and Main streets. Don't miss the stagecoach ride in town where you may get "held up" by the highway robber during your tour (209-588-0808). There's a one-room schoolhouse, a general store, a jailhouse, a saloon, a hotel, a wonderful old-fashioned candy store, a firehouse, and a blacksmith making metal puzzles at the blacksmith shop.

Hours: Daily 10am–4pm. Call for winter hours for the gold mine tour and gold panning. Free hour long town tours led by docents on weekends at 11am meet at the museum. Gold Rush Days on the 2nd Saturday of each month 1–4pm. Closed Thanksgiving and Christmas days.

Cost: Free, but tours, rides, etc. cost extra. $5/person to rent the gold pan. Stagecoach ride: $6/adult, $5/child. Gold mine tour: $12/adult, $6/

child.

Bathrooms: Yes, at the parking lot.

Facilities: Stroller friendly.

Food: Restaurants located within the park.

What to Bring: Cash for stagecoach ride, food, and souvenirs.

Follow-Up Activities: 1) On the first weekend in June each year, the town reenacts "Columbia Diggins, Tent Town 1852." Event takes place from 10am–5pm. $5/adult, $3/child 5+. Call for details. 2) Many school programs offered. See Web site for details. 3) Jamestown and the Railtown 1897 Historic Park are just 6 miles away.

Hangtown's Gold Bug Park (Ages 5+)
City of Placerville – Parks & Recreation Department
(530) 642-5207; 2635 Goldbug Lane, Placerville CA 95667
<www.goldbugpark.org>

Description: Gold Bug Mine, museum, and gold panning available. You can also take a tour of the Gold Mine Stamp Mill to learn how it crushes the gold ore to get the gold out of the rock. Watch a virtual tour online.

Hours: April through October: daily 10am–4pm. November to April: Weekends only: noon–4pm. Guided tours are available April through October during the weekdays by appointment only. Cost is $100 minimum for up to 15 people and $7/additional person, with a maximum of 65 people. Call (530) 642-5238 to schedule a tour.

Cost: For self-guided tour (Hattie's Museum): $4/adult, $2/youth 7–16, free/child 6 & under. $2/hour gold pan rental for gold panning.

Bathrooms: Yes.

Facilities: Stroller friendly.

Food: Snacks only.

What to Bring: Picnic lunch.

Marshall Gold Discovery State Historic Park (Ages 5+)
(530) 622-3470; Events: (530) 295-2162; 310 Back Street, Coloma, CA 95613
<www.parks.ca.gov/default.asp?page_id=484>; <www.marshallgold.org/calendar>;
<www.coloma.com/gold>; Events: <www.calparks.org/inside-parks/events>

Description: Try gold panning on the east side of the American River. "Live History Days" every Thursday and Friday in the spring and fall.

For a detailed description of Coloma and the tours available, visit: <www. parks.ca.gov/default.asp?page_id=1142>. Bekeart's Gun Shop also has gold panning.

Hours: *Park Hours:* 8am–5pm. *Museum and Building Hours:* March through June: daily 10am–3pm. Closed Mondays July through February. Closed Thanksgiving, Christmas, and New Year's Day. Guided walking tours on weekends at 12pm from March through October.

Cost: Free. Guided tour: $5/adult, $3/senior or child.

Bathrooms: Yes.

Facilities: Stroller friendly.

Food: Yes.

Follow-Up Activities: 1) Gold Discovery Day in late January 11am–4pm. This living history event features a gold discovery reenactment, tours, and Gold Rush music. 2) Over a weekend in mid-October, there is 49er Family Festival or Coloma Gold Rush Live, a two-day event with gold rush tent encampent reenacting life during the Gold Rush era. Gold panning contests for adults and children alike, and historic trade demonstrations. 3) Sunday in early December, experience an old-fashioned Christmas: Christmas in Coloma. 10am–4pm. 4) Call Reserve America at (866) 240-4655 for self-guided school group tours.

Chapter 10
Seasonal Events

The following events are only available seasonally. Some last only one day, while others last as long as one month. They are listed in chronological order. Many state, county, and city parks stage wonderful celebrations and festivals that bring history alive. For California parks' events, visit: <www.calparks.org/inside-parks/events/index.html>.

Martin Luther King Day (Ages 5+)

Children's Discovery Museum, San Jose (Recommended for Ages 5+)

"Living the Dream" play during Martin Luther King Day. This play provides a very short and concise description of the beginning of the United States and the history of the constitutional amendments giving blacks their freedom and black men the right to vote. Then it describes the everyday realities of segregation during the 1940s–1960s, Martin Luther King Jr.'s experience with prejudice, his rallying cry for civil disobedience, and his dream to make the country a place where all are treated equally. The actors teach the audience *We Shall Overcome,* the rallying song sung by Martin Luther King Jr. The show is wonderfully performed, bringing to life the realities of life in the early half of the 20th century for Black Americans. It covers a lot of ground in 30 short minutes for only $1 per person!

Chinese New Year Parade (All Ages)
Chinese Chamber of Commerce
(415) 982-3071; 730 Sacramento Street, San Francisco, CA 94108
<www.chineseparade.com>

Description: The parade lasts about two hours and features dancing lions and dragons as the main attraction. For information on the Chinese New Year Festival and the Chinese zodiac, visit the Chinese Cultural Center's Web site: <**www.c-c-c.org/culture-resources/holidays**>. See Web site for parade route and schedule.

Schedule: Usually takes place in February, but varies yearly since the Lunar New Year changes with the lunar calendar. Check Web site for specific information on exact dates/times and routes on an annual basis. The parade begins at 5:30pm (plan to arrive no later than 5pm), starting at Market and Second streets. See the Web site for current route, maps, parking, and transportation information.

Cost: Free along the street. You can also purchase bleacher seats for $30/person, plus $4.50/order for shipping and handling by calling (415) 391-9680 or via the Web site. Children under 2 are free. The bleacher seats are located on Kearny Street, between Bush & Sutter streets, and between California & Sacramento streets.

Follow-Up Activities: For the legend of the New Year Chinese Dragon: <**www.moonfestival.org/legends/dragon.htm**>.

Berkeley Youth Arts Festival (Ages 4+)
Berkeley Art Center
(510) 644-6893; 1275 Walnut Street, Berkeley, CA 94709
<www.berkeleyartcenter.org>

Description: Festival provides art exhibition in all media by youths in grades K-8. Over the weekend, there are workshops on screen printing, monotype, building musical instruments, photography, shadow puppets, clay, and papier mache led by professional artists.

Hours: Late February/Early March Wed-Sun 12noon-5pm.

Cost: Free.

Bathrooms: Yes.

Facilities: Stroller friendly.

April/Easter (All Ages)

Many events such as Easter egg hunts are produced through the local community. Check with the Local Parks and Recreation departments for details. Old-fashioned easter parades or egg hunts are held at Old Sacramento, Columbia, Dunsmuir Historic Estate, Ardenwood Historic Farm, Filoli Gardens, Roaring Camp Railroads, and many others. See respective entries.

Cal Day at the University of California, Berkeley (Ages 4+)

(510) 642-2294; U.C. Berkeley: Bancroft & Telegraph, Berkeley, CA 94720
<www.berkeley.edu/calday>; <www.berkeley.edu/map>

Description: A don't-miss event where campus museums are free, and university research museums and university departments, rarely open to the general public, share their collections and new research with the community during this one special day annually. Many children oriented activities. Visit Web site for the schedule of events, map, and parking information. Here's a sample of the huge selection of events:

> Hands-on Archaeology for Kids, Play with Clay, Make Your Own Prehistoric Art, Demonstrating the Magic of Chemistry, Discovering Families of Planets, Robotic Racing Cars, Maps for Kids, Young People's Music Fair, Essig Museum of Entomology open, Museum of Paleontology open with tours, The Physics of Music, Hands on Physics Lab for all ages, and much more.

Hours: Takes place throughout the UC Berkeley campus on a Saturday in mid-April from 9am–4pm.

Cost: Free.

Bathrooms: Yes, throughout the campus.

Facilities: Stroller friendly.

Food: Both on campus and off campus. There are plenty of restaurants and lawns.

What to Bring: Picnic lunch. It's a good idea to wear comfortable walking shoes and to dress in layers. Don't forget to bring your camera.

Community Day at Stanford (All Ages)
Stanford University
(650) 725-1221; Stanford, CA (along Serra Street facing the main quad)
<communityday.stanford.edu>

Description: This event is similar in concept to Cal Day at Berkeley. It features a children's carnival with pony rides, petting zoo, and face painting; demonstrations and lectures from the science departments; music and art tours at the Cantor Arts Center; and more.
Hours: Early April 10am-4pm. This event has become a biannual event occuring in 2007, 2009, etc.
Cost: Free.
Bathrooms: Yes.
Facilities: Stroller friendly.
Food: Yes.
What to Bring: Wear comfortable walking shoes, bring sunscreen, sunglasses, and cash for food.

Cinco de Mayo (All Ages)

Cinco de Mayo Fruitvale Festival and Parade
(510) 536-6084; (510) 434-1678
International Boulevard between 33rd and 40th Avenues, Oakland, CA 94601
<www.oaklandcincodemayo.com>

Description: The parade and festival celebrate freedom for the Mexican people. The festival takes place on International Blvd. between 33rd and 40th avenues.
Schedule: It is held on the first Sunday in May closest to Cinco de Mayo (May 5th). Visit Web site for entertainment schedule.
Cost: Free.
What to Bring: Cash for parking and vendors (food, crafts, etc.).

Cinco de Mayo Festival and Parade, San Jose

(408) 288-9470; Market and Santa Clara streets, San Jose, CA 95113
<www.sjgif.org/cincodemayo.html>

Description: The parade and festival celebrate freedom for the Mexican people. It ends at Almaden Boulevard and Park Avenue, the site of the festival.

Schedule: It is held on the first Sunday in May closest to Cinco de Mayo (May 5th). The parade is from 9am–noon. The festival is from 10am–6pm at Guadalupe River Park.

Cost: $1/person, free/child under 12.

What to Bring: Cash for parking and vendors (food, crafts, etc.).

Follow-Up Activities: For a history of Cinco de Mayo: <**www.carnaval. com/cinco/cinco_history.htm**>.

Cinco de Mayo, San Francisco
Parque De Los Ninos

(415) 206-0577;
Parque de Ninos: 23rd Street (Treat & Folsom streets), San Francisco, CA
<www.cincodemayosf.com>

Schedule: Held usually on the first Friday in May 10am–6pm. Parade starts at Mission Street. Check Web site to confirm details.

Cost: Free.

What to Bring: Cash for parking and vendors (food, crafts, etc.).

Civil War Reenactments (Ages 5+)

Ardenwood Historical Farm has battle reenactments typically on Memorial Day weekend. However, in 2006, the reenactment was in late August. Check annually to confirm. Battle reenactments all three days, with two battles on both Saturday and Sunday at noon and at 3pm. On Memorial Day, there's only one battle at noon. The line at the gate can be time consuming. Plan on at least 30-minute wait at the entry. See entry under Chapter 1: Animal Kingdom—Farms.

Casa de Fruta

(408) 842-7282 Office; (408) 842-9316 Events
10021 Pacheco Pass Highway, Hollister, CA 95023
<www.casadefruta.com>, select "Visit Us," then "News/Events"

Description: Besides being a roadside stand and café, Casa de Fruta has a miniature train and children's playground. Casa de Fruta Country Park is the site of the Civil War reenactment in mid-June and a Renaissance Faire in September and October.

Hours: Sat & Sun 9am–6pm. Train schedule: Sat & Sun 11am–5:30pm. Call (408) 842-9316 to confirm mini-train schedule.

Cost: Train & Carousel: *Fun Pass:* $5.49/person includes 1 ride on the train, 1 carousel ride, and a bag of popcorn. *All Day Pass:* $10.99/person with unlimited rides on the train and carousel. *Annual Pass:* $21.99/person with unlimited rides on the train and carousel. Special Events pricing separate.

Bathrooms: Yes.

Facilities: Stroller friendly.

Food: Casa de Coffee restaurant (open 24 hours), a deli, and a fruit stand for snacks. Casa de Sweets has ice cream, coffee, and pie. Picnic grounds.

What to Bring: Sunscreen, sunglasses, camera, picnic lunch, and cash.

Follow-Up Activities: For a more detailed list of special annual events, visit the Web site: <www.casadefruta.com/events.aspx>. In the past, it has featured the following events. 1) Civil War Reenactment in June, with sutler encampments, medical facilities, cannons, military headquarters, etc. 2) Renaissance Pleasure Faire from mid-September to mid-October. <www.norcalrenfaire.com> 3) Pumpkin patch in October.

Roaring Camp Railroads

See full entry in Chapter 6: Transportation Favorites—Trains.

Dragon Slayers Renaissance Festival (All Ages)
Aptos Village Park

(831) 252-4878; 100 Aptos Creek Road, Aptos, CA 95003
<www.dragonslayersfestival.org>

Description: This renaissance festival is smaller scale, but there are magicians, jugglers, musicians, and dancers as well as a sword demonstration

and a duel show. Historic characters include Queen Elizabeth, Sir Francis Drake, and William Shakespeare.
Schedule: Held on a Saturday in mid-June 10am-6pm.
Cost: $12/adult, $10/child.
Bathrooms: Yes.

Celtic Festival (All Ages)
Ardenwood Historic Farms
(510) 796-0199; 34600 Ardenwood Boulevard, Fremont, CA
<www.ebparks.org/parks/arden.htm>

Description: A festival celebrating traditional Celtic dancing, pipebands, Welsh and Irish music, historic reenactments, and children's activities.
Schedule: Held on a Saturday in early June 10am-4pm.
Cost: $10/adult, $7/senior, $5/child.
Bathrooms: Yes.
Food: Yes.
What to Bring: Sunscreen, sunglasses, camera, and extra cash for food and shopping.

Old Fashioned Independence Day Celebration (All Ages)

Ardenwood Historic Farm
See entry under Chapter 1: Animal Kingdom—Farms.

Dunsmuir Historic Estate
See entry under Chapter 10: Seasonal Events—Holiday Season.

Wilder Ranch State Park
(831) 426-0505; (831) 423-9703; 1401 Coast Road, Santa Cruz, CA 95060
<www.santacruzstateparks.org/parks/wilder>; <thatsmypark.org>

Description: Enjoy an old-fashioned celebration with live music, children's parade, hayrides, games, and crafts. Period costumes and docent-led tours show what a dairy ranch was like 100 years ago.

Hours: 10am–4pm, July 4th

Cost: $6 park entrance fee.

Bathrooms: Yes, at the parking lot.

Facilities: Stroller friendly.

Food: Concessions only during the July 4th celebration. Ice cream, etc.

What to Bring: Cash for parking and concessions, sunscreen, sunglasses, picnic lunch, picnic blanket, and plenty to drink.

Scottish Highland Games (All Ages)
Dunsmuir Historic Estate
(510) 615-5555; 2960 Peralta Oaks Court, Oakland, CA 94605
<www.dunsmuir.org>

Description: A festival celebrating traditional Celtic music, athletic competition, Scottish country and Irish step dancing, clan displays, living history reenactments, children's activities, and craft vendors.

Schedule: Held over a weekend in mid-July 10am–5pm.

Cost: $20/2-day pass, $12/1-day pass, $8/senior, military or student, $5/child 4-13, free/child 3 & under. Tickets available online.

Bathrooms: Yes.

Food: Yes.

What to Bring: Sunscreen, sunglasses, camera, and extra cash for food and shopping.

Scottish Games & Celtic Festival (All Ages)
Toro Park
(831) 647-6311; 501 Monterey-Salinas Highway 68, Salinas, CA 93908
<www.montereyscotgames.com>

Description: A festival celebrating Scottish and Irish traditions and culture. Features include a Celtic concert; clan booths; flights of birds of prey; food; entertainment; and competitions in dancing, bagpipe bands, and traditional athletics, including the caber toss and hammer throws.

Schedule: Held over a weekend in early August 9am–5pm. Kids' games held at 1:30pm.

Cost: $10/child 8-16, $14/adult for 1-day admission, free/child 7 & under. Tickets available online.

Bathrooms: Portables.

Food: Yes.
What to Bring: Sunscreen, sunglasses, camera, and extra cash for food and shopping.

Golden Gate Renaissance Festival (All Ages)
Golden Gate Park
(415) 354-1773;
Speedway Meadow: John F. Kennedy Drive & 25th Avenue, San Francisco CA
Administration: 116 Dorado Terrace San Francisco, CA 94112
<www.sffaire.com>; <www.ggfaire.com>

Description: Two days of live theater and shows along with singing, dancing, storytelling, feasts, fencing, and battles during the times of Elizabeth and Mary. The festival features living history reenactments, craft demonstrations, jesters, falconers, and magicians.
Schedule: Usually held in late August over a weekend; Saturday: 10am–6pm, Sun: 10am–5pm.
Cost: $15/adult; $10/teen 13-17, senior, military; $5/child 6-12, free/child under 6. Tickets also available to purchase online.
Bathrooms: Portables.
Food: Yes.
What to Bring: Sweater, camera, and extra cash for food and shopping.

Highland Gathering & Games (All Ages)
Alameda County Fairgrounds
(800) 713-3160; (925)426-7559; 4501 Pleasanton Avenue, Pleasanton, CA 94566
<www.caledonian.org>; <www.alamedacountyfair.com>

Description: Two days of live history reenactment with Scottish music and Celtic rock along with highland and country dancing, birds of prey, Scottish crafts, children's games and activities.
Schedule: Usually held over Labor Day weekend 8am–6pm.
Cost: $8/parking. $15/1-day admission, $22/2-day admission, $10/child 8-16, $10/senior. Tickets available online.
Bathrooms: Portables.
Food: Yes
What to Bring: Sunscreen, sunglasses, camera, and extra cash for food and shopping.

Moon Festival (All Ages)
(415) 982-6306; 667 Grant Avenue, San Francisco, CA 94108
<www.moonfestival.org>

Description: The Moon Festival is a Chinese celebration of the harvest. Entertainment includes live performances by acrobats, dancers, and singers; martial arts demonstrations; arts and crafts; food; parade with costumed children and artisans holding giant puppets; lion dancers; and marching bands. Visit the Web site for maps and directions, as well as the entertainment schedule.

Schedule: Varies yearly based on the Lunar Calendar of the 15th of the 8th month, which falls usually from late August to September. Check the Web site for specific dates annually. Takes place 11am–6pm over a weekend, usually in September.

Cost: Free.

Follow-Up Activities: For the legend of the Moon Festival, visit this Web site: <www.moonfestival.org/legends/chango.htm>.

Chinese Moon Festival (All Ages)
Overfelt Gardens – Chinese Cultural Gardens
(408) 251-3323; 368 Educational Park Drive, San Jose, CA
<www.chineseculturalgarden.org/moonfestival.htm>

Description: The Moon Festival is a Chinese celebration of the harvest. Entertainment includes live performances by acrobats, dancers, and singers; martial arts demonstrations; arts and crafts; food; lion dancers; etc. Visit the Web site for maps and directions, as well as the entertainment schedule.

Schedule: Takes place 1pm–5pm on the 3rd Sunday in September.

Cost: Free.

Follow-Up Activities: Poetry contest for students in grades K–5.

Ohlone Day (All Ages)
Henry Cowell Redwoods State Park
(831) 335-4598; 101 North Big Trees Park Road, Felton, CA
<www.santacruzstateparks.org/parks/henrycowell>

Description: Learn about Ohlone Indians' culture, music, dance, dress, food, stories, ceremonies, and traditions. Ohlone demonstrators will share songs, stories, tools, musical instruments, language, and history. Kids can throw an atlatl (spear); make a mini-tule boat; play Ohlone games; drill holes with a pump drill; and make fire using a stick, a board, and cotton tail fluff.

Schedule: Takes place in mid-September 10am-4pm.

Cost: $6 parking fee.

What to Bring: Sunscreen, sunglasses, and cash for parking, food, etc.

Follow-Up Activities: Roaring Camp Railroads is just next door (walking distance). Take a walk through the beautiful and mature redwood grove.

Kids Faire California (All Ages)
(866) 444-EXPO

Alameda County Fairground, 4501 Pleasanton Avenue, Pleasanton, CA 94566

<www.thekidsfaire.com>; <www.alamedacountyfair.com>

Description: This fair is dedicated to family entertainment. Funds raised contribute to literacy programs for Head Start and other community programs. There are drop-in arts and crafts, a circus, "Safariland" with camel and pony rides, an area where kids can plant a vegetable garden, "Clown Town" where kids can learn to juggle and watch clown antics and magic shows, NBC-TV where kids can read a news story and be an anchor on TV, and a "Meet the Characters" pavilion where kids can meet famous TV characters (Dora the Explorer, Scooby Doo, Jay Jay the Jet Plane, Sponge Bob Squarepants, etc.). Like all fairs, there are rides, jump houses and slides, and musical entertainment on multiple stages.

Schedule: Mid-September, 10am–5pm on a weekend at the Alameda County Fairgrounds.

Cost: $8/adult, $4/child ages 2–12. $1 off Internet ticket purchase.

Bathrooms: Yes.

Food: Yes.

What to Bring: Sunscreen; sunglasses; and extra cash for parking, food, products, and entertainment.

Renaissance Pleasure Faire (Ages 3+)
Casa de Fruta
(800) 52-FAIRE (523-2473); 10031 Pacheco Pass Highway, Hollister, CA 95023

<www.norcalrenfaire.com>

Description: Do knights, jousts, castles, and armor interest your child?

Visit the Renaissance Pleasure Faire to see what life was like in England during the Renaissance. Costumed actors dressed as well-known historical figures play the roles of their famous characters. Converse with Shakespeare, Queen Elizabeth, Robin Hood, and others. See artisans at work using techniques of the Renaissance. Watch jousts, archery contests, and other games of yesteryear.

Schedule: Annually in the fall from mid-September to mid-October on Sat & Sun: 10am–6pm.

Cost: Free Parking. *Tickets at the Gate*: $22/adult, $10/child 5–11. Weekend (2 days) ticket: $30/ticket. *Advanced Tickets Discount Code*: $5 discount online before start of the faire.

Bathrooms: Yes.

Facilities: Stroller friendly, but dusty trails.

Food: Yes—outside food and drinks are not allowed.

What to Bring: Can be very hot. Bring camera; sunglasses; hats; sunscreen; and extra cash for food, drinks, souvenirs, etc.

Ohlone Day (All Ages)
Deer Hollow Farm
(650) 965-FARM; Rancho San Antonio: Cristo Rey Drive, Cupertino, CA 95014
<www.fodhf.org>

Description: Learn about Ohlone Indians' culture through Ohlone demonstrations: hunting, cooking, acorn grinding, flint knapping, sweathouse, and music. Make a rope, play games, drill shells, and watch fire starting and archery demonstrations.

Schedule: Takes place on a Saturday in mid-October 1–4pm.

Cost: $5/adult, $2/child, free/child 2 & under.

Halloween

Adobe Pumpkin Farm (All Ages)
(707) 763-6416; 2478 E Washington Street, Petaluma, CA 94954
<www.adobepumpkinfarm.com>

Description: This farm has u-pick pumpkins and flowers. It has farm animals, a corn maze, hayrides, horse rides, and a haunted house.

Hours: Open mid-September through October 31. 10am–dusk.

Cost: Free admission, but rides cost extra. 10% discount coupon for pumpkins and flowers for Farm Days on Web site.

Bathrooms: Portables.

Follow-Up Activities: Birthday parties, field trips.

Lemos Farm (All Ages)

(650) 726-2342; 12320 San Mateo Road (Hwy 92), Half Moon Bay, CA 94019
<www.lemosfarm.com>

Description: Petting zoo, pony rides, mini-train, hayride, and jumper. Haunted house (rather scary for little ones), pumpkin patch, and hayrides only in October for Halloween. Best time to visit is probably weekdays in October because the decorations for Halloween are fantastic; the farm is a wonderful backdrop for pictures. The "ghost train" also goes to the "ghost town." Late November through December, Christmas trees go on sale and the farm is decorated for the holiday. Traffic can be challenging during special events such as the Pumpkin Festival Weekend.

Hours: Sat & Sun: 9am–5pm.

Cost: Free admission, but rides cost extra. *Rides:* $5/pony ride or play town, $2.50/train ride, $1/feed cup for petting zoo, $2.50/hay ride (October only). **Day pass:** $15/child for unlimited rides; $5/adult. **October month pass** is a great value if you live nearby: $35/child, $10/adult unlimited visits in October. *Field trips* from August-October: $8.50/child includes pony, train, and hayrides as well as petting zoo, air jumper, and "Scare Zone." These are limited to one ride/visit for each thing. For **mothers' clubs:** $10/child, $2/adult (includes a pumpkin). The rides for the mothers' clubs are unlimited.

Bathrooms: Yes.

Facilities: Stroller friendly.

Food: Yes. Hot dogs, pizza, and snacks. In October, pumpkin ice-cream and pumpkin pie.

Follow-Up Activities: 1) Pony or train birthday parties. 2) **Pastorino's Farm** with similar offerings is just across the street. 3) If you can brave the traffic, consider visiting the Annual Half Moon Bay Art and Pumpkin Festival, which is held on the Saturday and Sunday following Columbus Day 10am–5pm. Events include costume contests, Great Pumpkin Parade, pumpkin carving contest, music and family entertainment on three stages. It is held on Main Street, in Half Moon Bay. Admission is free. For more information: <www.miramarevents.com/pumpkinfest/family_fun.html>. For tips and directions: <www.miramarevents.com/pumpkinfest/tips.html>.

G & M Farm Fall Pumpkin Patch (All Ages)

(925) 447-FARM; 487 East Airway, Livermore, CA 94551
<www.gmfarms.com>

Description: Pumpkin patch, corn and straw bale mazes, farm animals, and pony rides on weekends. School groups call for reservations.
Hours: Open all of October. *Pumpkin patch:* weekends: 9am–6pm, weekdays: 2pm–6pm. *Corn maze* (weather dependent): weekdays: 4pm–9pm, Sat: 10am–10pm, Sun: 10am–8pm.
Cost: $8/person 12+, $7/child 6–11, free/child 5 & under with paying adult.
Bathrooms: Portables only.
Facilities: Stroller friendly.
Food: No.
What to Bring: Sunscreen, sunglasses, camera, and cash.

Pastorino's Farm (All Ages)

(650) 726-6440; 12391 San Mateo Road (Hwy 92), Half Moon Bay, CA 94019
<www.pastorinofarms.com>

Description: Pastorino's is primarily a working nursery and pumpkin farm. In the summer, it has u-pick strawberries. In October, the pumpkin patch has a petting and feeding zoo, pony rides, mini-train, hayride, and giant jumpers and slides. Haunted house (rather scary for little ones) is open on weekends. Also gives docent-led educational tours on how plants and pumpkins grow in October. Late November through December, the gift barn is decorated with Christmas ornaments and gifts, and Christmas trees are for sale. Traffic can be challenging during special events such as the Pumpkin Festival Weekend.
Hours: Mon–Sat: 9am–5pm, Sun: noon–5pm. Pumpkin season: mid-September to end of October: daily 9am–6pm. Rides: 10am–4:30pm.
Cost: Free admission, but rides extra. *Field trips* in October: $8/child includes pony, train, and hayrides as well as petting zoo, air jumper, pumpkin, and a treat. Educational tour: $5/person.
Bathrooms: Yes.

Facilities: Stroller friendly.
Food: Yes. Hot dogs, pizza, and snacks.
What to Bring: Sunscreen and sunglasses, camera, and cash.
Follow-Up Activities: 1) Pony camp <www.friendlyponyparty.com>.
2) Birthday parties 3) Week-long summer farm camp for kids. Call for details. 3) In October, 1-hour educational tours with docents help visitors learn how pumpkins, flowers, and plants are grown. Booking starts a year in advance. 4) In June & August, u-pick strawberries are available. Small, medium, and large plastic bags sell for $5, $10, and $15, respectively. You fill them.

Roaring Camp Railroads has a special event on the *Legend of Sleepy Hollow*. See the full entry in the Transportation: Trains.

Uesugi Farms Pumpkin Patch (All Ages)

(408) 778-7225; (408) 842-1294 Office
14485 Monterey Highway, San Martin, CA 95037
<www.uesugifarms.com>

Description: Learn how pumpkins grow with an exhibit that shows the development of the pumpkin from seed to seedling to plant to baby pumpkin to orange pumpkin. There's an accompanying educational video with pianist George Winston. The grounds are beautifully decorated with scarecrows. There's a miniature train ride through a haunted tunnel and a pumpkin vine covered walk-through tunnel for all to explore. The Storybook Path through the corn maze was new in 2006. On weekend days, there are special entertainmnets and roaming magician, balloon artist, and face painter.
Hours: Open last week of September and all of October. During the first week: 9am–7pm. Extended hours from 9am–9pm as it gets closer to Halloween. Visit Web site for most current times and costs.
Cost: Hayride: $4/person, $3/child 10 & under; Train: $4/person, free/child under 2; Storybook path: $5/family of 4 includes pumpkin; Cow train: $3/person; parking free except on weekends during the second half of October, $2/car.
Bathrooms: Portables only.
Facilities: Stroller friendly.
Food: Hot dogs and snacks available.

What to Bring: Sunscreen, sunglasses, picnic lunch, and cash only.
Follow-Up Activities: Call (408) 778-7225 to schedule school tours.

Founders' Day Fandango (Ages 4+)
Santa Teresa County Park's Historic Bernal Ranch
(408) 846-5632; 372 Manila Drive, San Jose, CA
<www.parkhere.org> then select "Find a Park," then "Santa Teresa"

Description: Held at the Bernal-Gulnac-Joyce Ranch, other wise known as Santa Teresa County Park, this rancho-style fandango celebration commemorates the founders of San Jose with dancing and demonstrations. There are hands-on activities for all ages including lassoing, dressing as a Spanish soldier, and crafts. Don't miss the tour with a docent to the spring and the video in the barn showing Ohlone history and way of life. Interpretive panels around the park explain the chores and daily life at the ranch for kids.
Hours: Usually on a Saturday in mid-November 11am-3pm.
Cost: Free.
Bathrooms: Yes.
Food: No.
What to Bring: Dress warmly, and don't forget to bring your camera.

Holiday Season

Many communities have visits with Santa, breakfast with Santa, children's holiday parades, etc. Check with your local Parks and Recreation Department and its catalog, or your city's civic center, to find details on your community's events.

Allied Arts Guild's Children's Holiday Party (Ages 2–6)
(650) 322-2405; 75 Arbor Road, Menlo Park, CA 94025
<www.alliedartsguild.org>

Description: The Allied Arts Guild has beautiful Spanish architecture and gardens and an annual holiday party that in the past included a wonderful puppet show, arts and crafts, and pictures with Santa. Lunch is included. This is very appropriate for the toddler and preschool crowd.

Hours: Usually on a Saturday: 12:30–3:30pm. Party in early December. Make your reservations early to avoid disappointment.

Cost: Reservations required. $20/person.

Bathrooms: Yes.

Food: Lunch included as part of the event.

What to Bring: Dress warmly. Bring camera and cash.

Dickens' Christmas Fair (Ages 4+)
San Francisco Cow Palace
(800) 510-1558; (415) 469-6065 Cow Palace
2600 Geneva Aveue, Daily City, CA 94014
<www.dickensfair.com>; <www.cowpalace.com>

Description: The Dickens Christmas Fair is a living history event with many forms of entertainment. In the past, it featured Irish and Scottish dance performances, shows such as the *Pirates of Penzance* and *Alice in Wonderland*, a Christmas parade, musicians including a bagpipe performer and a harpist, and carolers, of course. Meet Charles Dickens, Ebeneezer Scrooge, Oliver Twist, chimney sweeps, falcons and other birds of prey, etc. Many attendees come in period costume and it's great to see the beautiful clothes and decorations of a Victorian Christmas. The food is great, albeit pricey. There isn't much offered in the way of arts and crafts activities, and they cost extra. However, the shows, music, and dancing are wonderfully done and well worth the time and cost.

Schedule: Weekends after Thanksgiving to just before Christmas from 11am to 7pm.

Cost: $8 parking at the Cow Palace. *Advance tickets* by phone or online: $16/adult; $6/child (5–11yrs); $13/student, senior, or military personnel. $2 processing charge per order. *At the gate*: $20/adult; $8/child 5-11; $17/student, senior, or military. Coupons available at Longs Drugs.

Bathrooms: Yes, but no baby changing stations. Stroller friendly.

Food: Yes, including fish and chips, hot chocolate, afternoon tea (scones, tea sandwiches, pastries, etc.), roasted chestnuts, English beer, and more.

What to Bring: Dress warmly. Bring your camera and extra cash for parking, food, and shopping.

Dunsmuir Historic Estate Holiday (Ages 3+)

(510) 615-5555; 2960 Peralta Oaks Court, Oakland, CA 94615
<www.dunsmuir.org>

Description: Experience an old-fashioned 19th century Christmas at Dunsmuir Historic Estate. The beautifully decorated mansion is open for tours. When you purchase the tickets, you must select a time to tour the mansion. There are carolers, holiday crafts boutique, teas, carriage rides, children's arts and crafts, and visits with Father Christmas. Holiday Teas are separate and require advanced reservations. Dress in layers and plan on getting a bit messy if your children want to participate in arts and crafts activities. The children's arts and crafts have been hosted by the Museum of Children's Art in Oakland in the past and are included with admission.

Schedule: Late November—mid-December Fri–Sun: 11am–5pm. Gates close at 4pm for entry. Check event schedule on the Web site or call for specific dates.

Cost: *Advance Tickets:* $11/adult, $10/senior (62+), $7/child 6–13, free/child under 6. *At the Gate*, prices increase by $4 per person. Tickets can be ordered in early-mid October. *Holiday Teas*: $23/adult, $16/child advanced reservations required. Reserve early to avoid disappointment. These are very popular! There are also Children's Teas with Father Christmas. Menu for Holiday Teas (served by volunteers in period costumes): holiday blend tea, scones, tea sandwiches, breads, and sweets.

Bathrooms: Yes.

Facilities: Stroller friendly.

Food: Holiday café offers sandwiches, soups, salads, etc. in the Garden Pavilion; no reservation required. Holiday Teas and Children's Teas require reservations in advance.

What to Bring: Camera, warm coats, and cash for snacks and hot cocoa.

Filoli Gardens Children's Luncheon Party (Ages 5+)

(650) 364-8300; 86 Cañada Road, Woodside, CA 94062
<www.filoli.org>

Description: The holiday parties have entertainers such as magicians, ventriloquists, and dancers. There are also visits with Santa and Mrs. Claus.

295

Schedule: Four parties held on a Saturday in early December, at 11am, noon, 1pm, and 2pm.
Cost: $30 per person.
Bathrooms: Yes.
Facilities: Stroller friendly.
Food: Yes.
What to Bring: Camera and warm jacket.

Prince & Princess Tea (Ages 12 & under)
Garden Court, The Palace Hotel
(415) 546-5089; 2 New Montgomery Street, San Francisco, CA 94105
<www.gardencourt-restaurant.com>

Description: The Holiday Tea serves pastries and sandwiches. The belle époque Garden Court provides an opulent backdrop, with crystal chandeliers, mirrored doors, and harp music at teatime. Throughout the year, the Prince & Princess Tea for kids 10 & under is on Saturdays 1–3pm.
Hours: Late November through December Monday through Saturday with seatings at 2pm, 2:30pm, 3pm, and 3:30pm in the Garden Court. Call (415) 546-5089 for reservations. Select teas feature Santa visits and gift for the child, but are priced at $38 per person. Make reservations early to avoid disappointment.
Cost: Holiday Tea: $38/adult, $30/child 12 & under. **Prince & Princess** Tea: $28/child, $34/adult.
Bathrooms: Yes.
Facilities: Stroller friendly.
What to Bring: Camera and warm jacket.

Prince & Princess Tea (Ages 12 & under)
Secret Garden Tea House
(415) 566-8834; 721 Lincoln Way, San Francisco, CA 94122
<www.secretgardenteahouse.com>

Description: Located near Golden Gate Park's 9th Avenue entrance, this tea room serves peanut butter and jelly tea sandwiches; a mini-chocolate brownie; pig in a blanket; petits four; and choice of tea, hot chocolate, or milk for kids.
Hours: Offered year-round Tues–Fri: noon–6pm and Sat & Sun: 11:30pm–5:30pm. Closed Mondays and the first Tuesday of each

month.

Cost: $14.95/child 12 & under, $10.95–$19.95/adult.

Bathrooms: Yes.

Facilities: Stroller friendly.

What to Bring: Camera and warm jacket.

Teddy Bear Tea for Children (Ages 3+)
At The Ritz-Carlton, San Francisco
(415) 773-6198; 600 Stockton Street, San Francisco, CA 94108
<www.ritzcarlton.com/hotels/san_francisco/dining/venues/lobby_lounge>

Description: This event includes holiday storytelling, singing, and dancing with the elf and teddy bear. In the past, the menu included hot chocolate, teddy bear cutout cookies, peanut butter and jelly sandwiches, egg salad, and ham and cheese sandwiches. Traditional afternoon tea served year-round. Visit Web site for menu and details.

Schedule: After Thanksgiving to December 24. There are 2 seatings daily: the first is 10–11:30am and the second is 1–2:30pm. Reservations are required. Call starting August 1, at 9am, to make reservations. Reservations are guaranteed with credit card; cancellations require 3 days prior to the event or a $25 cancellation fee applies.

Cost: *Tea Service*: $58/person. Teddy Bear Tea price includes tax, gratuity, and charity donation.

Bathrooms: Yes.

Facilities: Stroller friendly.

What to Bring: Camera and warm jacket; don't forget cash for parking.

Section II
Classes to Take

Chapter 11
Local Resources

Many community groups offer afterschool classes and summer camps. The major players are the cities' Parks and Recreation Departments, the local YMCAs (Young Men's Christian Associations), and the JCCs (Jewish Community Centers). Although the YMCAs and the JCCs have religious affiliations, they do not require anyone to be any particular religion; access is open to all. The Parks and Recreation Departments of the cities do not require residency in the specific city but may charge a slightly higher fee for nonresidents.

These community centers have a huge assortment of classes, field trips, and community events such as free concerts and shows at the local parks, special holiday events including Christmas Tree lighting, children's holiday parades, breakfasts with Santa, and much more. Look first at these resources because they tend to be cost-effective and are convenient to your locale. Don't forget to check with the neighboring community centers, since each center has a unique offering. A huge range of classes is offered by these centers including art, drama, theater, music, science and nature, computers, sewing, cooking, and sports.

I've included additional resources for classes on science and nature, art, music, drama, swimming, dance, ice skating, and bowling. Remember that these are also wonderful for birthday parties. Most facilities will offer birthday parties. Just ask!

Jewish Community Centers (JCCs)

Addison–Penzak Jewish Community Center
(408) 358-3636; 14855 Oka Road, Los Gatos, CA 95032
<www.svjcc.org>

Albert L. Schultz Jewish Community Center
(650) 493-9400; 4000 Middlefield Road, Building R, Palo Alto, CA 94303
<www.paloaltojcc.org>

Berkeley Richmond & Oakland Piedmont JCC
(510) 848-0237; 1414 Walnut Street, Berkeley, CA 94709;
(510) 530-9222; 4500 Redwood Rd Oakland CA 94619
<www.brjcc.org>

Contra Costa JCC
(925) 938-7800; 2071 Tice Valley Boulevard, Walnut Creek, CA 94595
<www.ccjcc.org>; <www.ccjcc.org/departments.htm>

Jewish Community Center of San Francisco
(415) 292-1200; 3200 California Street, San Francisco, CA 94118
<www.jccsf.org>

Jewish Community Center, Sonoma County
(707) 528-4222; 3859 Montgomery Drive, Santa Rosa, CA 95405
<www.jccsoco.org>

The North Peninsula Jewish Community Center
(650) 212-PJCC; 800 Foster City Blvd, Foster City, CA 94404
<www.pjcc.org>

Osher Marin Jewish Community Center
(415) 444-8000; 200 North San Pedro Road, San Rafael, CA 94903

Local Parks & Recreation Departments

Local city Parks and Recreation Departments are wonderful resources. They offer a myriad of classes and activities, including art, music, theater, gymnastics, dance, ice skating, T-ball, soccer, little league, basketball, volleyball, sailing, fencing, horse riding, martial arts, science, and manners classes. They also offer special field trips and outings, even ski day trips in the winter for older youths, and special holiday events like visits with Santa and gingerbread house decorating. Don't forget to check with your local Parks and Recreation Departments, as they have different offerings. Ask to be put on your favorites' mailing lists so you won't miss the quarterly catalogs, especially the summer ones, which are a wonderful resource for summer camps.

You do not need to be a resident of the offering city to take advantage of these classes. There is usually a slightly higher fee for nonresidents, but the activities are open to everyone. Listed below are online activity guides or catalogs with class descriptions and schedules.

For ski trip information, visit <www.BlueAngelSnow.com> or <www. BayAreaSkiBus.com>.

Alameda Recreation and Parks
(510) 747-7529; 2226 Santa Clara Avenue, Alameda, CA 94501
<www.ci.alameda.ca.us/arpd/index.html>; <www.arpdeplay.com>

Albany
(510) 524-9283; 1249 Marin Avenue, Albany, CA 94706
<www.albanyca.org/dept/rec.html>

Belmont Parks and Recreation Department
(650) 595-7441; 30 Twin Pines Lane, Belmont, CA 94002
<http://activenet4.active.com/belmontparksandrecreation>; <www.belmont.gov>

Belvedere–Tiburon Recreation Department

(415) 435-4355; 1505 Tiburon Boulevard, Tiburon, CA 94920
<www.btrecreation.org>
Summer camps on Angel Island for ages 6–13 from mid-June to August.
Other day camps available for ages 3½–5. Registration starts in early
March.

Berkeley Parks and Recreation

(510) 981-5150; 1947 Center Street, Berkeley, CA 94704
<www.ci.berkeley.ca.us/recreation>

Brisbane Recreation Department

(415) 508-2140; 50 Park Place, Brisbane CA 94005
<www.ci.brisbane.ca.us>

Burlingame Parks and Recreation Department

(650) 558-7300; 850 Burlingame Avenue, Burlingame, CA 94010
<www.burlingame.org>

Campbell Recreation and Community Services

(408) 866-2105; 1 West Campbell Avenue #C-31, Campbell, CA 95008
<www.ci.campbell.ca.us/Recreation>

Concord Parks and Recreation

(925) 671-3404; In Person: 2974 Salvio Street, Concord, CA
By Mail: 1950 Parkside Drive, MS/10, Concord, CA 94519-2578
<www.ci.concord.ca.us/recreation/activityguideinfo.htm>; <www.concordreg.org>

Cupertino Parks and Recreation Department
Quinlan Community Center

(408) 777-3120; 10185 N. Stelling Road, Cupertino, CA 95014
<www.cupertino.org>; <reg4fun.cupertino.org/econnect>

Daly City Parks and Recreation Department

(650) 991-8001 Recreation; 111 Lake Merced Boulevard, Daly City, CA 94015

Danville Community Center

(925) 314-3400; 420 Front Street, Danville, CA 94526

<www.ci.danville.ca.us>

Click on "Residents," then "Recreation Services," then "Activity Guide" for the recreation catalog.

Dublin Parks and Community Services

(925) 556-4500; Registration — In person: 200 Civic Plaza, Dublin, CA 94568; Mail in: 100 Civic Plaza, Dublin, CA 94568

<www.ci.dublin.ca.us>; <www.dublinrecguide.com>

El Cerrito Recreation Department

(510) 559-7000; 7007 Moeser Lane, El Cerrito, CA 94530

<www.el-cerrito.org/recreation>

Emeryville Recreation Department

(510) 596-3782; 4300 San Pablo Avenue, Emeryville, CA 94608

<www.ci.emeryville.ca.us/rec>

Foster City Parks and Recreation

(650) 286-3380; 650 Shell Boulevard, Foster City, CA 94404

<www.fostercity.org/Services/recreation>

Fremont Recreation Services Division

(510) 494-4300; 3300 Capital Avenue, Bldg. B, Fremont, CA 94538

<www.ci.fremont.ca.us/Recreation/ClassRegistrationAndInformation>
<www.regerec.com>

Gilroy Community Services Department

(408) 846-0460; 7351 Rosanna Street, Gilroy, CA 95020

<www.ci.gilroy.ca.us/comserv/recguide.html>

Greater Hayward Area Recreation and Park Foundation (H.A.R.D.)

(510) 881-6700; 1099 E Street, Hayward, CA 94541

<www.haywardrec.org>; <hard.dst.ca.us>

305

Lafayette Parks and Recreation
(925) 284-2232; 500 St. Mary's Road, Lafayette, CA 94549
<www.lafmor-recreation.org>; <www.ci.lafayette.ca.us>

Livermore Park and Recreation District
(925) 373-5700; 4444 East Ave, Livermore, CA 94550
<www.larpd.dst.ca.us>

Los Altos Recreation Department
(650) 947-2790; 97 Hillview Avenue, Los Altos, CA 94022
<www.ci.los-altos.ca.us>

Los Gatos–Saratoga Community Education and Recreation
(408) 354-8700, ext 221, ext 225, or ext 231;
123 East Main Street, Los Gatos, CA 95030
<www.lgsararec.org>

Marinwood Community Center
(415) 479-0775; 775 Miller Creek Road, San Rafael, CA 94903
<www.marinwood.org>

Menlo Park Community Services Department
(650) 330-2200; 701 Laurel Street, Menlo Park, CA 94025
<www.menlopark.org/departments/dep_comservices.html>

Mill Valley Recreation
Mill Valley Community Center
(415) 383-1370; 180 Camino Alto, Mill Valley, CA 94941
<www.millvalleycenter.org>; <www.cityofmillvalley.org>

Millbrae Parks and Recreation
(650) 259-2360; 477 Lincoln Circle, Millbrae, CA 94030

Milpitas Parks and Recreation Services
408) 586-3210; 457 E. Calaveras Boulevard, Milpitas, CA 95035
<www.ci.milpitas.ca.gov>

Monterey Recreation Services
(831) 646-3866; 546 Dutra Street, Monterey, CA 93940
<www.monterey.org/rec>

Moraga Parks and Recreation Department
(925) 284-2232; (925) 376-2520; 2100 Donald Drive, Moraga, CA 94556
<www.lafmor-recreation.org>; <www.ci.moraga.ca.us/park.htm>

Morgan Hill Community and Cultural Center
(408) 782-0008; 17000 Monterey Road, Morgan Hill, CA 95037
<www.mhcommunitycenter.com>

Centennial Recreation Center:
(408) 782-2128; 171 W. Edmundson Avenue, Morgan Hill, CA 95037
<www.mhcrc.com>

Mountain View Recreation Department
(650) 903-6331; 201 South Rengstorff Avenue, Mountain View, CA 94039
<www.mountainview.gov>

Newark Recreation & Community Services
Silliman Activity Center
(510) 742-4400; 6800 Mowry Avenue, Newark, CA 94560

Community Center
(510) 742-4437; 35501 Cedar Boulevard, Newark, CA 94560
<www.newark.org>; <www.ci.newark.ca.us>

Novato Parks, Recreation & Community Services
(415) 899-8200; 75 Rowland Way, #200, Novato, CA 94945
<www.cityofnovato.org/prcs>; <www.novatofun.org>

307

Oakland Parks and Recreation
(510) 238-7557; 250 Frank H. Ogawa Plaza, #3330, Oakland, CA 94612
<www.oaklandnet.com/parks/programs>; <www.oaklandparks.org>

Orinda Community Center
(925) 254-2445; 26 Orinda Way, Orinda, CA 94563
<www.ci.orinda.ca.us/parksandrec>

Pacific Grove Recreation Department
(831) 648-5730; 515 Junipero Avenue, Pacific Grove, CA 93950
<www.pacificgroverecreation.org>

Pacifica Recreation
(650) 738-7381; 1810 Francisco Boulevard, Pacifica, CA
Mail registration to: 170 Santa Maria Avenue, Pacifica, CA 94044
<www.ci.pacifica.ca.us>; <activenet.active.com/pacifica>

Palo Alto Arts & Culture Department
(650) 463-4900; 1305 Middlefield Road, Palo Alto, CA 94301
Palo Alto Arts & Culture Catalog: <www.paenjoy.org>
<www.city.palo-alto.ca.us>, then search "Arts/Culture"

Petaluma Parks & Recreation Department
(707) 778-4380; 320 N. McDowell Boulevard, Petaluma, CA 94954
<cityofpetaluma.net/parksnrec>

Piedmont Recreation Department
(510) 420-3070; 358 Hillside Avenue, Piedmont, CA 94611
<www.ci.piedmont.ca.us>

Pinole Recreation Department
(510) 724-9062; 2131 Pear Street, Pinole, CA 94564
<www.ci.pinole.ca.us/recreation>

Pittsburg Parks and Recreation

(925) 252-4842; 65 Civic Avenue, Pittsburg, CA 94565
<www.ci.pittsburg.ca.us>

Pleasant Hill Recreation and Parks District

Community Center
(925) 676-5200; 320 Civic Drive, Pleasant Hill, CA 94523
Aquatics, Adult/Youth Sports Leagues
(925) 682-0896; 147 Gregory Lane, Pleasant Hill, CA 94523
<www.pleasanthillrec.com>

Pleasanton Parks and Community Services

(925) 931-5340; 200 Old Bernal Avenue, Pleasanton, CA 94566
<www.ci.pleasanton.ca.us/services/recreation>

Portola Valley, Town Center Resources

(650) 851-1701; 765 Portola Road, Portola Valley, CA 94028
<www.portolavalley.net/community>

Redwood City Parks, Recreation & Community Services

(650) 780-7250; 1400 Roosevelt Avenue, Redwood City, CA 94061
<www.redwoodcity.org/safari>

Richmond Recreation & Parks

(510) 620-6793; 3230 MacDonald Avenue, Richmond, CA 94804
<www.ci.richmond.ca.us>

San Anselmo Recreation Department

(415) 258-4640; 1000 Sir Francis Drake, San Anselmo, CA 94960
<www.townofsananselmo.org/recreation>

San Bruno Recreation Services Department

(650) 616-7180; 251 City Park Way, San Bruno, CA 94066
<sanbruno.ca.gov/city_services/recreation>

San Carlos Parks and Recreation
(650) 802-4382; 600 Elm Street, San Carlos, CA 94070
<www.recconnect.net>

San Francisco Recreation & Parks Department
(415) 831-2700; Main Admin: 501 Stanyan Street, San Francisco, CA 94117
<www.parks.sfgov.org>

San Jose Parks & Recreation
(408) 277- 4661; 4 N. Second Street, Ste 600, San Jose, CA 95113
For Recreation Activity Guides : <www.sanjoseca.gov/prns>;
<www.ci.san-jose.ca.us/prns/rcssa.htm>

San Jose Special Events calendar: <www.sanjoseca.gov/prns/prnsevents.asp>

Almaden Community Center
(408) 268-1133; 6445 Camden Avenue, San Jose, CA 95120
Alviso Community Center
(408) 586-7624; 5050 North 1st Street, San Jose, CA 95002
Berryessa Community Center
(408) 251-6392; 3050 Berryessa Avenue, San Jose, CA 95132
Camden Community Center
(408) 559-8553; 3369 Union Avenue, San Jose, CA 95124
Evergreen Community Center
(408) 270-2220; 4860 San Felipe Road, San Jose, CA 95135
Gardner Community Center
(408) 279-1498; 520 W. Virginia Street, San Jose, CA 95125
George Shirakawa Community Center
(408) 277-3317; 2072 Lucretia Avenue, San Jose, CA 95122
Hank Lopez Community Center
(408) 251-2850; 1694 Adrian Way, San Jose, CA 95122
Hoover Community Center
(408) 292-5871; 1677 Park Avenue, San Jose, CA 95126
Houge Park Community Center
(408) 559-7542; 3852 Twillight, San Jose, CA 95124
Kirk Community Center
(408) 723-1571; 1601 Foxworthy Avenue, San Jose, CA 95118
Mayfair Community Center
(408) 729-3475; 2039 Kammerer Avenue, San Jose, CA 95116
Millbrook Community Center
(408) 270-1602; 3200 Millbrook Drive, San Jose, CA 95148

Moreland West Community Center
(408) 871-3820; 1850 Fallbrook Avenue, San Jose, CA 95130
Olinder Community Center
(408) 279-1138; 848 E. William Street, San Jose, CA 95116
Roosevelt Community Center
(408) 998-2223; 901 East Santa Clara Street, San Jose, CA 95116
Sherman Oaks Community Center
(408) 292-2935; 1800A Fruitdale Avenue, San Jose, CA 95116
Solari Community Center
(408) 224-0415; 3590 Cas Drive, San Jose, CA 95111
Southside Community Center
(408) 629-3336; 5585 Cottle Road, San Jose, CA 95123
Starbird Community Center
(408) 984-1954; 1050 Boynton Avenue, San Jose, CA 95117

San Leandro Recreation

(510) 577-3462; Admin: 835 E.14th Street, San Leandro, CA 94577
Marina Community Center: 15301 Wicks Boulevard, San Leandro, CA
<www.ci.san-leandro.ca.us/slrechumansvcs.html>

San Mateo Parks & Recreation

(650) 522-7400; 330 West 20th Avenue, San Mateo, CA 94403
<www.cityofsanmateo.org/dept/parks>; <www.erecreg.com>
Marine Science Institute offers classes via San Mateo Parks & Rec.

San Rafael Community Center

(415) 485-3333; 618 "B" Street, San Rafael, CA 94901
<www.cityofsanrafael.org>; <eplay.livelifelocally.com>

San Ramon Parks and Community Services

(925) 973-3200; 12501 Alcosta Boulevard, San Ramon, CA 94583
<www.ci.san-ramon.ca.us/parks>; <pool12.ci.san-ramon.ca.us/econnect>

Santa Clara Parks & Recreation Department

(408) 615-2260; 1500 Warburton Avenue, Santa Clara, CA 95050
<www.ci.santa-clara.ca.us/park_recreation/pr_dept.html>;
<online.activecommunities.com/santaclara>

Santa Cruz Parks & Recreation Department
(831) 420-5270; 323 Church Street, Santa Cruz, CA 95060
<www.santacruzparksandrec.com>

Santa Rosa Parks & Recreation Department
(707) 543-3282 ; 415 Steele Lane, Santa Rosa, CA 95403
<www.santarosarec.com>

Saratoga Recreation
(408) 868-1248; (408) 868-1249; 19655 Allendale Avenue, Saratoga, CA 95070
<www.saratoga.ca.us/recreation.htm>

Sausalito Parks & Recreation Department
(415) 289-4152; 420 Litho Street, Sausalito, CA 94965
<www.ci.sausalito.ca.us/business/park-rec>; <http://sausalito.recware.com>

South San Francisco Recreation & Community Services
(650) 829-3800; 33 Arroyo Drive, South San Francisco, CA 94080
<www.ssf.net/depts/rcs/default.asp>

Sunnyvale Parks & Recreation
Sunnyvale Community Center
(408) 730-7341; 550 E. Remington Drive, Sunnyvale, CA 94087
<http://ttp://sunnyvale.ca.gov/Departments/Parks+and+Recreation>

Town of Moraga
Parks and Recreation Activities
(925) 284-2232; (925) 376-2520; 2100 Donald Drive, Moraga, CA 94556
<www.ci.moraga.ca.us>; <www.lafmor-recreation.org>

Walnut Creek Recreation Division
Recreation Classes, Heather Farm Community Center
(925) 943-5858; 301 N. San Carlos Drive, Walnut Creek, CA 94598
<www.ci.walnut-creek.ca.us>

Walnut Creek Civic Arts Education Program

(925) 943-5846

<http://arts-ed.org>

Civic Park Campus

N. Broadway and Civic Drive, Walnut Creek, CA 94596

Shadelands Campus

111 N. Wiget Lane & Ygnacio Valley Road, Walnut Creek, CA 94598

Young Men's Christian Associations (YMCAs)

The YMCA (Young Men's Christian Association) has wonderful programs for families. Like the JCCs, no religious afiliation is required, and anyone may join. The Web site for U.S. YMCAs is **<www.ymca.net>**.

The YMCA also has a wonderful *Youth and Government program* (for 10th to 12th graders starting in September) and a *Model United Nations* (for 6th to 9th graders starting in December) for youths to learn about the process of government. These are held on a yearly basis. To join, sign up with your local YMCA. For additional information about these programs, visit: **<www.calymca.org>**. For information about the Model United Nations program: **<www.calymca.org/mun>**.

Berkeley-Albany YMCA

<www.baymca.org>

Albany YMCA

(510) 525-1130; 921 Kains Avenue, Albany, CA 94706

<www.baymca.org/index.php/albany.html>

Downtown Berkeley YMCA

(510) 848-9622; 2001 Allston Way, Berkeley, CA 94704

<www.baymca.org/index.php/downtown.html>

South Berkeley YMCA

(510) 843-4280; 2901 California Street, Berkeley, CA 94709
<www.baymca.org/index.php/south.html>

Mt. Diablo Region YMCA

<www.mdrymca.org>

Concord/Clayton YMCA

(925) 889-1600; 700 Gym Court, Clatyon, CA 94517
<www.mdrymca.org/loc_concord_clayton.php?sid=21>

Delta Family YMCA

(925) 625-9333; 1250 O'Hara Avenue, Oakley, CA 94561
<www.mdrymca.org/loc_delta.php?sid=22>

Irvin Deutscher Family YMCA

(925) 687-8900; 350 Civic Drive, Pleasant Hill, CA 94523
<www.mdrymca.org/loc_irvin.php?sid=23>

San Ramon Valley YMCA

(925) 831-1100; 1029 LaGonda Way, Danville, CA 94526
<www.mdrymca.org/loc_san_ramon.php>

Sonoma County Family YMCA

(707) 545-9622; 1111 College Avenue, Santa Rosa, CA 95404
<www.scfymca.org>

YMCA of the East Bay

<www.ymcaeastbay.org>

Downtown Oakland YMCA

(510) 451-9622; 2350 Broadway, Oakland, CA 94612
<www.ymcaeastbay.org/downtownoakland>

Eden Area YMCA

(510) 259-2928; 24100 Amador Street, Hayward, CA 94542
<www.ymcaeastbay.org/edenarea>

Fremont Newark YMCA

(510) 279-2905; 41811 Blacow Road, Fremont, CA 94538
<www.ymcaeastbay.org/fremont>

Hilltop Family YMCA
(510) 222-9622; 4300 Lakeside Drive, Richmond, CA 94806
<www.ymcaeastbay.org/hilltop>

Tri-Valley YMCA
(925) 475-6100; 4725 First Street, Pleasanton, CA 94566
<www.ymcaeastbay.org/trivalley>

Urban Services YMCA
(510)654-9622; 3265 Market Street, Oakland, CA 94608
<www.ymcaeastbay.org/urbanservices>

West Contra Costa YMCA
(510) 412-5647; 263 South 20th Street, Richmond, CA 94804
<www.ymcaeastbay.org/westcontracosta>

YMCA Camp Arroyo
(925) 371-8401; 5535 Arroyo Road, Livermore, CA 94550
<www.ymcaeastbay.org/camparroyo>

YMCA Camp Loma Mar
(650) 879-0223; 9900 Pescadero Road, Loma Mar, CA 94021
<www.ymcaeastbay.org/camplomamar>

YMCA Camp Ravencliff
(510) 222-9622; 4300 Lakeside Drive, Richmond, CA 94806
<www.ymcaeastbay.org/campravencliff>

YMCA of the Mid-Peninsula
<www.ymcamidpen.org>

El Camino YMCA
(650) 969-9622; 2400 Grant Road, Mountain View, CA 94040
<www.ymcamidpen.org/elcaminoy.php>

East Palo Alto YMCA
(650) 328-9622; 550-B Bell Street, East Palo Alto, CA 94303
<www.ymcamidpen.org/sequoiay.php>

Palo Alto Family YMCA
(650) 856-9622; 3412 Ross Road, Palo Alto, CA 94303
<www.ymcamidpen.org/pafy.php>

Page Mill YMCA
(650) 858-0661; 755 Page Mill Road, Building B, Palo Alto, CA 94304
<www.ymcamidpen.org/pagemilly.php>

Sequoia YMCA
(650) 368-4168; 1445 Hudson Street, Redwood City, CA 94061
<www.ymcamidpen.org/sequoiay.php>

YMCA of San Francisco
<www.ymcasf.org>

Bayview Hunter's Point YMCA
(415) 822-7728; 1601 Lane Street, San Francisco, CA 94124
<www.ymcasf.org/Bayview>

Buchanan YMCA
(415) 931-9622; 1530 Buchanan Street, San Francisco, CA 94115
<www.ymcasf.org/Buchanan>

Central YMCA
(415) 885-0460; 220 Golden Gate Avenue, San Francisco, CA 94102
<www.ymcasf.org/Central>

Chinatown YMCA
(415) 576-9622; 855 Sacramento Street, San Francisco, CA 94108
<www.ymcasf.org/Chinatown>

Embarcadero YMCA
(415) 957-9622; 169 Steuart Street, San Francisco, CA 94105
<www.ymcasf.org/Embarcadero>

Marin YMCA
(415) 492-9622; 1500 Los Gamos Drive, San Rafael, CA 94903
<www.ymcasf.org/Marin>

Mission YMCA
(415) 586-6900; 4080 Mission Street, San Francisco, CA 94112
<www.ymcasf.org/Mission>

North Bay YMCA
(707) 421-8746; 586 E. Wigeon Way, Suisun City, CA 94585
<www.ymcasf.org/NorthBay>

Novato YMCA
(415) 883-9622; 3 Hamilton Landing, Suite#140, Novato, CA 94949
<www.ymcasf.org/Novato>

Presidio Community YMCA
(415) 447-9622; Presidio of San Francisco:
Lincoln Boulevard. & Funston, San Francisco, CA 94129
<www.ymcasf.org/Presidio>

Peninsula Family YMCA
(650) 286-9622; 1877 South Grant Street, San Mateo, CA 94402
<www.ymcasf.org/Peninsula>

Richmond District YMCA
(415) 666-9622; 360 18th Avenue, San Francisco, CA 94121
<www.ymcasf.org/Richmond>

Stonestown YMCA
(415) 242-7101; 333 Eucalyptus Drive, San Francisco, CA 94132
<www.ymcasf.org/Stonestown>

YMCA Camp Jones Gulch
(650) 747-1200; 11000 Pescadero Road, La Honda, CA 94020
<www.campjonesgulch.org>

YMCA Point Bonita
(415) 331-9622; 981 Fort Barry, Sausalito, CA 94965
<www.pointbonitaymca.org>

YMCA of Santa Clara Valley
<www.scvymca.org>

Central YMCA
(408) 298-1717; 1717 The Alameda, San Jose, CA 95126
<www.scvymca.org/central>

East Valley Family YMCA (Milpitas & Berryessa)
(408) 715-6500; 1975 S. White Road, San Jose, CA 95148
<www.scvymca.org/eastvalley>

Mt. Madonna YMCA
(408) 762-6014; 17666 Crest Avenue, Morgan Hill, CA 95037
<www.scvymca.org/mtmadonna>

Northwest YMCA
(408) 257-7160; 20803 Alves Drive, Cupertino, CA 95014
<www.scvymca.org/northwest>

South Valley Family YMCA
(408) 226-9622; 5632 Santa Teresa Boulevard, San Jose, CA 95123
<www.scvymca.org/southvalley>

Southwest YMCA
(408) 370-1877; 13500 Quito Road, Saratoga, CA 95070
<www.scvymca.org/southwest>

YMCA Camp Campbell

(831) 338-2128; 16275 Highway 9, Boulder Creek, CA 95006
<www.scvymca.org/mtmadonna>

Chapter 12
Science & Arts Education

Science & Technology Education

Children are born scientists. They are born with an innate sense of curiosity and wonder. They naturally experiment and try out their theories about how things work, using the process scientists have labeled the "scientific method." Yet children do this process naturally, without being taught. Encourage children's natural curiosity and observation skills by stopping and watching the insects you find anywhere. Learn about the life cycle of butterflies, frogs, and other creatures of interest to your child. Build their natural skills a baby step at a time, and you'll be amazed how quickly they amass knowledge. Don't let the terms "science" and "education" fool you. These classes and programs are lots of fun and probably should be categorized as "edu-tainment." Review the list of possible programs below and you'll see what I mean.

The Lawrence Hall of Science at the University of Berkeley, California has developed a *Consumers' Guide to After-school Science Resources*. Visit Web site for list of book titles: <**www.sedl.org/afterschool/guide/science/index.html**>.

4-H Youth Development Program (Ages 5+)
<www.ca4h.org>; <www.4husa.org>

Description: The 4-H program is a national club that is run by the University of California Cooperative Extension in California, with local branches throughout California. Visit the Web site to find the clubs closest to you. The 4-H Club offers a huge range of topics, depending on the interests of the children participating. The 4-Hs stand for head, heart, health, and hands. The program includes projects working with animals, marine science, sewing, computer programming, whatever interests the children. It is run primarily by parent and other adult volunteers.

California Academy of Sciences Golden Gate Park
Encompasses: Steinhart Aquarium, Natural History Museum, and Morrison Planetarium

(415) 321-8000; 55 Concourse Drive, San Francisco, CA 94118 *(Reopens 2008)*
Temporary Location: 875 Howard Street, San Francisco, CA 94103
<www.calacademy.org>

Description: Look for the Junior Academy when the museum moves back to Golden Gate Park. The Junior Academy offered classes for older children ages 8–14. These classes include topics such as marine mammals, birds, insects, the savanna habitat, manatees, old ways living skills (methods used by early humans to make fire, beads, and string), astronomy, etc. On the Web site, look under "Education Programs." For the calendar of events: <www.calacademy.org/events/calendar>.

Hours: 10am–5pm. Third Thursday of the month: open until 9pm. On Saturday mornings, there's *Children's Story Time* geared for children 3–5 years old. These are held at 10:30 am.

Cost: *First Wednesday of each month is free to the public.* Third Thursday $5 admission from 5pm to 9pm. Normally, $10/adult; $6.50/youth (12–17), student w/ ID, & senior 65+; $2/child (4–11); free/child 3 & under. There are a few days each year where San Francisco residents of certain zip codes may visit for free. (Planetarium closed until 2008.)

Camp Galileo (Ages 5–10)
Galileo Educational Services, LLC

(800) 854-3684; (510) 595-7293; 5237 College Avenue, Oakland, CA 94618
<www.galileoed.com>; <www.campgalileo.com>

Arts, sciences, and the outdoors summer camp. This camp is sponsored by Galileo Educational Services; Klutz, Inc.; and the Tech Museum. Locations served include San Francisco, the peninsula, south bay, and the east bay. Check Web site for dates and locations.

Chabot Space & Science Center (Ages 4+)

(510) 336-7300; (510) 336-7373 Box Office
10000 Skyline Boulevard, Oakland, CA 94619
<www.chabotspace.org>

Description: 1) For children ages 4–7, the Discovery Lab is a wonderful hands-on exploration lab. Call prior to visit for current hours. 2) Summer camps are week-long, half-day, or full day. Past camp topics have included robotics, principles of flight (what does it take to get to outer space?), the moon, Mars, astronaut training camp, etc. These camps are appropriate for children in first through eighth grades. 3) The Challenger Learning Center for grades 5+ allows students to do simulated space missions. For current programs, call (510) 336-7381.

Crab Cove Visitor Center (Ages 3+)

(510) 521-6887; 1252 McKay Avenue, Alameda, CA 94501
<www.ebparks.org/parks/crab.htm>

Description: Besides a small exhibition area, there are wonderful family oriented naturalist programs on the weekends. Center also offers classes during school break and day camps. Visit the Web page for specific programs, dates, and times. Topics include the mud flats habitat, microscopes to view the microbes found nearby, birding hikes, reptiles, and predator vs. prey. Some programs require advanced reservations (510) 521-6887. The center also hosts birthday parties.

Cybercamp (Ages 7–16)

(Nationwide)
1-888-904-CAMP; (206) 442-4500
<www.cybercamps.com>; <www.giantcampus.com/cybercamps>

These weeklong summer camps can be half-day, full day, or residential, depending on the child's age. They provide instruction in Web design, 3-D animation, digital media (graphics, sound, etc), game design, programming, and robotics. In Northern California, these camps have been located at De Anza College (Cupertino), UC Berkeley, and Stanford University. Check the Web site for pricing, locations, and camp courses.

Computer & Lego® Camp (Ages 5–16)
TechKnowHow
(650) 620-9300; 1091 Industrial Road, Suite 270, San Carlos, CA 94070
<www.techknowhowkids.com>

Locations on the peninsula, San Francisco, south bay, and east bay. Camps on Lego®, robotics, game design, and video effects.

Destination Science (Ages 5–11)
(888) 909-2822
<www.destinationscience.org>

Destination Science services Marin, San Francisco, San Mateo, Contra Costa, and Santa Clara counties.

Edventure More (Ages 5–12)
(877) 993-MORE; (415) 731-MORE;
1151 Taraval Street, San Francisco, CA 94116
<www.edventuremore.com>

Edventure More offers camp activities designed by the California Academy of Sciences, the Exploratorium, YMCA of San Francisco, and MOCHA. Summer camps in science and art offered in Marin, San Francisco, and the east bay.

Environmental Volunteers (Ages 7–12)
(650) 961-0545; 3921 E. Bayshore Road, Palo Alto, CA 94303-4326
<http://evols.org/snake_camp.htm>

The Environmental Volunteers who staff the Baylands in Palo Alto with docents offer S.N.A.K.E. Summer Camp. These camps are limited to 32 students in grades 2–6. They are held at the Keys School: 2890 Middlefield Road, Palo Alto, CA 94306, (650) 328-1711. They also offer birthday parties at the Baylands in Palo Alto.

Exploratorium (Ages 3–14)
(415) 563-7337; Palace of Fine Arts: 3601 Lyon Street, San Francisco, CA 94123
<www.exploratorium.edu>
Saturday afternoon science classes are for members only. Past class topics included weather, building bridges, sounds and music, and mirrors.

For the fastest and easiest listing of the classes being offered, go to the Web site, click on the "Visit," then the "Membership" icon, then "Science Classes." Summer science full-day camps for members' kids ages 7–14. For additional information, call (415) 561-0302. The Web site also has many "Web casts" and Web projects that showcase topics such as the biodiversity of life, the science of cooking, and global climate change. It is, in essence, an online classroom.

FIRST (Ages 6-18)
(For Inspiration & Recognition of Science & Technology)
<www.usfirst.org>; <www.firstlegoleague.org> First Lego League (for JFLL also)

Description: Founded by the inventor of the Segway Human Transporter, Dean Kamen, FIRST sponsors four separate robotics programs and tournaments. 1) Junior FIRST LEGO League (JFLL) is for kids ages 6–9, modeled after the First Lego League. 2) FIRST LEGO League (FLL) is for kids ages 9–14. It is run internationally, with teams around the globe. The FIRST LEGO League challenge has two parts. Part one comprises using the LEGO Mindstorms robotics system to build and program a robot to accomplish different specified tasks or "missions." The second part of the challenge is to do a research project that includes selecting a current problem or opportunity, designing a solution or an improvement, and sharing the problem and solution with the community. Each year, the challenge changes missions and topic. For example, in 2006, the challenge theme was nanotechnology. In 2007, the theme is alternative energy resources: meeting the global demand. 3) FIRST Vex Challenge (FVC) is for high schoolers interested in an intermediate robotic program using the Vex Robotics Design system. The competition is based on the FIRST Robotics Competition. 4) FIRST Robotics Competition (FRC) is a varsity program for high schoolers focused on solving an announced challenge within a 6-week time frame. The team builds a robot from a kit of parts and enters the robot into a series of challenges.

Hayward Shoreline Interpretive Center (Ages 1+)
(510) 670-7270; (510) 881-6700 Reservations
4901 Breakwater Avenue, Hayward, CA 94545
<www.haywardrec.org>

Description: Hayward Shoreline Interpretive Center provides an introduction to the San Francisco Estuary's ecology. The Interpretive Center has exhibits as well as weekend programs conducted by naturalists. These programs cover a wide range of topics that have included San Francisco Bay pirate history, the solar system and the universe from the Hubble Space Telescope, how boats float, and builders of the natural world: seashells, snails, and spiders, etc. For the most current list of programs, dates, and times, visit the Web site. Once you're at the home page, click on the "Signature Facilities" on the left column of the window, then click on "Hayward Shoreline Interpretive Center." School programs are available during the weekdays by reservation only. Summer science camps through both the Sulphur Creek Nature Center as well as the Interpretive Center. Check under the "Activities Guide" tab for the Hayward Recreation catalog for additional program information. Sulphur Creek also offers affordable birthday parties.

Hours: Sat & Sun: 10 am–5pm. Administrative office is closed Mondays and Tuesdays.

Cost: Free, some programs require a small fee.

ID Tech Camps (Ages 8–17)
(888) 709-TECH
<www.internaldrive.com>

These camps focus on digital technology, including computer programming, Web design, computer graphics, digital music, and digital videos. These camps are available throughout the U.S. In northern California, they are held at UC Berkeley, Stanford, Santa Clara University, St. Mary's in Moraga, UC Davis, and UC Santa Cruz.

Lawrence Hall of Science (Ages 4–18)
(510) 642-5132; Centennial Dr. near Grizzly Peak Boulevard, Berkeley, CA 94720
<www.lhs.berkeley.edu>

Description: Family workshops for children ages 3 to 7 are on Saturday mornings. During the week, there is a wonderful selection of classes, even for preschoolers, as well as science classes for homeschoolers ages 3 to 14. You may want to consider the affordable workshops/birthday parties. Summer camps (half-day, full-day, or residential) for ages ranging from 4–5 to high school teenagers. Supervised lunch hour and extended day care for summer camps are also available. Check the Web site and calendar for

a full listing of the classes, programs, and summer camps offered.
Hours: Daily: 10am–5pm.

Mad Science of the Bay Area (Ages 3–12)

(877) 390-5437; 5409 Central Avenue, Suite 6, Newark, CA 94560
(650) 342-8342 San Mateo County; (510) 792-2795 Alameda County
(408) 262-5437 Santa Clara County
<www.madscience.org/southbay>

Description: Fun science classes in San Mateo, Santa Clara, and the western portion of Alameda counties. Programs include preschool programs, afterschool classes, workshops, and summer and vacation camps. Check with your local Parks and Recreation Activity Guide to see if it is offered through your Parks and Recreation Department. Birthday parties for kids ages 5+.

Marine Science Institute (Ages 5+)

(650) 364-2760; 500 Discovery Parkway, Redwood City, CA 94063
<www.sfbaymsi.org>

Description: The Marine Science Institute offers classes, marine summer camps, and school programs to educate students on the ecology of the bay. Check the San Mateo Recreation catalog for classes as well <www.erecreg.com>.

Math/Science Nucleus (Ages 5+)

(510) 790-6284; 4074 Eggers Drive, Fremont, CA 94536
<www.msnucleus.org>

Description: Offers afterschool science and math classes during the school year and science summer camps. Offers birthday parties, too.

NASA Robotics Alliance Project (Ages 6+)

<http://robotics.arc.nasa.gov>

Description: The Robotics Alliance Project provides a clearinghouse of robotics competitions. These include: FIRST <www.usfirst.org>, Botball <www.botball.org>, and BattleBots IQ <www.battlebotsiq.org>.

Ohlone for Kids at Ohlone College (Ages 9–17)

(510) 659-6090; 43600 Mission Boulevard, Fremont, CA 94539
<www.ohloneforkids.com>
Description:Summer program for kids at Ohlone College includes Lego Robotics/electronics, science, performing arts, etc. March registration.

Play-Well TEKnologies (Ages 5+)

Marin Engineering Center: (415) 847-9330; 17 Paul Drive, Terra Linda, CA
(415) 457-2841 Napa, Marin, & Sonoma; (415) 377-2384 San Francisco, San
Mateo, & Santa Clara; (510) 459-9620 Alameda & Contra Costa
<www.play-well.org>

Description:This group offers classes, workshops, and summer camps through schools and Parks and Recreation Departments on engineering, building, and problem solving skills, typically with building toys like Lego, K'Nex, etc. The Marin Engineering Center is open during drop-in hours. See Web site for drop-in hours, which vary considerably.

Redwood Grove Nature Preserve (Ages 5+)

Through the Los Altos Parks and Recreation Department:
(650) 941-0950; (650) 917-0342; 482 University Avenue, Los Altos, CA 94022
<www.ci.los-altos.ca.us>

Description: In the spring and fall, a *Nature Fun* program is offered afterschool for ages 5–7. The program includes nature exploration, games, music, and arts and crafts. There are programs for school groups on nature, the Gold Rush, Ohlone Native Americans, archery, and bird watching. Summer programs are extremely popular and are on a first-come, first-served basis. Register as early as possible to ensure placement. Hosts wonderful birthday parties.

Robotics Learning (Ages 9–17)

(408) 910-1176; 586 Pomeroy Avenue, Santa Clara, CA 95051
<www.roboticslearning.com>
Description:Offers workshops in robotics and animation year-round and a week-long summer camp.

Rotary Nature Center (Ages 6–15)

(510) 238-3739; 600 Bellevue Avenue, Oakland, CA 94610
<www.oaklandnet.com/parks/programs/rnc.asp>

Description: Weeklong summer day camps for children 6–15 years old. These science camps focus on different themes each week and include various topics such as bugs, birds, botany, and earth science. They also have extended care during the day.

Sally Ride Science Camps for Girls (Ages 11–14)

1-888-472-4386; Stanford University, Stanford, CA
<www.sallyridecamps.com/ScienceCamp/stanford/index.html>;
<www.sallyrideclub.com>; <www.toychallenge.com>

Description: Astronomer Sally Ride started this camp, which covers topics in astronomy, bioengineering, and structural engineering. These summer camps are held at Stanford University. Sally Ride Science also offers a Toy Challenge for kids in 5th through 8th grades. They work in teams to create and design a new toy or game.

Science Adventures (Ages 5–12)

Science Enrichment Services, Inc.

1-800-4-SCIENCE (1-800-472-4362)
15412 Electronic Lane, Suite 201, Huntington Beach, CA 92649
<www.scienceadventures.com>

Description: Summer camps offered in Alameda, Contra Costa, Santa Clara, Marin, San Francisco, San Mateo, and Sonoma counties. Camps cover a variety of science topics.

Stanford Summer Youth Camps (Ages 7+)

(650) 723-3126; 123 Encina Commons, Stanford, CA 94305
<www.stanford.edu/dept/hds/scs/youth>

Description: Stanford is host to many academic and sports camps during the summer. The academic camps include digital media, junior statesmen summer school (for high shoolers), speech and debate camp, and academic programs from Stanford and Johns Hopkins. See above Web site for details and contact information. See sports camp information in Chapter 13: Physical Activities—Swimming.

The Tech Museum of Innovation (Ages 9–13)
1-800-854-3684; (408) 294-TECH
201 South Market Street, San Jose, CA 95113
<www.thetech.org>

Description: For older children, the Tech runs summer camps in partnership with Galileo. These are weekly half-day camps. The programs vary but generally include robotics, video game design, Web site design, and other science topics.

Youth Science Institute (Ages 3–12)
<www.ysi-ca.org>

Description: The Youth Science Institute has great hands-on science classes for kids from preschool on up. Summer camps and afterschool science classes are popular. These classes range from worms to temperature (such as the science of making ice cream), the planets, animal tracks, gravity, and rockets. Camp registration begins in March. There's an annual Insect Fair in May 10am–4pm at Sanborn Park and a Wildlife Festival in mid-October 11am–4pm at Alum Rock Park, San Jose. This festival is free, but parking is $6/car. Class schedules and family science events are printed in the "Newsletter" on the Web site. You can also request to be placed on the mailing list for the newsletter. There three sites in Santa Clara County.

Vasona Lake County Park
(408) 356-4945; 296 Garden Hill Drive, Los Gatos, CA 95032
Mon–Fri: 9am–4:30pm, Sat–Sun by appointment.

Sanborn Center in Sanborn Park
(408) 867-6940; 16055 Sanborn Road, Saratoga, CA 95070
Tues–Fri: 9:30am–4:30pm, Sat–Sun: 12:30–4:30pm.

Alum Rock Park
(408) 258-4322; 16260 Alum Rock Avenue, San Jose, CA 95127
Tues–Sat: noon–4:30pm.

U.S. Space Camp (Ages 7–18)
Huntsville, Alabama
1-800-533-7281

Description: The NASA-affiliated Space Camp program requires children to be at least 9 years old and be in 4th grade. Space Camp now has three tracks: space, aviation, and robotics. Camps run year-round. This is a residential camp that includes all room and board. There is a *Parent/Child Space Camp* for children ages 7–11; a *Space Academy Camp* for ages 12–14; and an *Advanced Space Academy* for teenagers 15–18. Unfortunately, the Moffett Field Space Camp closed due to financial difficulties. Chabot Space & Science Center offers simulated space missions at its Challenger Learning Center.

Zeum (Ages 2–13)
(415) 820-3565; 221 Fourth Street, San Francisco, CA 94103
<www.zeum.org>

Description: Zeum offers summer camps (ages 8–13) in art, media, and technology, combining creativity and technology. Camps include clay animation, video game creation, TV show production, and animation. Weekend workshops on a variety of creative art and technology topics as well. On Friday afternoons, workshops for preschoolers.

Art Education

Creating art has great benefits. It helps nurture imagination, problem-solving skills, discipline, and patience. Children learn how to problem solve by correcting "mistakes" in the project. They develop their concentration, attention span, and patience since it takes time to complete a project.

When my daughter was three years old, she developed an attitude that things were "too hard" for her. What little concentration she had was tossed out the window when the painting she was working on didn't meet her expectations. She was frustrated and gave up on her self-initiated projects quickly. I had enrolled her in an art class but had some concerns that she wouldn't be able to sit through such a long class. I thought it was going to be very challenging because the class was over an hour long. To my surprise, she loved the class. She developed concentration, and her

329

impatience quickly changed to patience. She brought home wonderful projects that required time and effort to complete. Within a month of starting the art class, she aspired to become an artist when she grew up. The patience and attention span she developed were unintended benefits of these art classes. But in retrospect, it makes a lot of sense that those skills were developed in the course of creating art.

There seem to be two camps in early childhood art education: "Open Art" and "Closed Art." The "Open Art" camp believes that art education for early childhood should be about pure exploration and creativity, that children should explore a variety of materials, textures, two- and three-dimensional projects, etc. Coloring books restrict children's creativity. Projects should not be done with a "cookie cutter" approach where the goal is in the end result looking exactly like the sample. "Open Art is an art process that allows the child to explore an art project on his own, uninhibited by outside expectations. It is a process that tends to lead to multiple interpretations, various end results, and even unpredictable directions. It is a process that thrives in a noncritical environment, in which the child's exploration is allowed to proceed without adult interference or correction. It is a process in which the *process itself* is more important than any adult-judged results."[2]

"The similarity of the work is a result of a ['Closed Art'] process in which the children are shown what they are going to do, shown how to do it, and often assisted in the process." "Closed Art" results in identical pieces of art work because "the *measure* of success is its close resemblance to the sample shown at the beginning of the process." [3]

"Open Art" believes in an open process while "Closed Art" believes in the end results.

As a parent who is neither an artist nor an educated art historian, I have wrestled with these philosophies and approaches. Perhaps my thoughts will help you arrive at your own insights. Here's the conclusion I've come to. I think that the "Open Art" process is very valuable in encouraging creativity and providing a positive and encouraging environment. I also

[2] *Everyday Art for Kids* by Carolyn Holm pp8–9.
[3] *Everyday Art for Kids* by Carolyn Holm pp8–9.

agree with the prescription to withhold judgment, either positive or negative, on the child's work. Instead, factual observations can be made about the child's artwork that help the child see the effects of having mixed certain colors together, or how different use of line created the effects observed in the artwork. However, I saw how frustrated my daughter was in producing or even envisioning the art she wanted to create because she did not have the appropriate techniques and skills. Ideally, "Open Art" provides the techniques, then steps back to allow the child's originality to come through. But in some of the "Open Art" sessions I've seen, there has been very little guidance and basically just the materials are provided.

On the other hand, I was not impressed with the "Closed Art" approach that I saw in many preschools and day care centers, and even some art studios and art books, for the very reasons that Carolyn Holm, author of *Everyday Art for Kids*, cited. "Closed Art" sabotages the creativity that I was trying to nurture in my child.

Because of what I've read about coloring books restricting creativity, I've not asked nor required my daughter during her preschool years to do any coloring within the lines. The result was that my daughter's fine motor control skills were not honed. While coloring books do not encourage creativity, I believe there is a place for them. Learning to color within the lines helps the child learn to develop fine motor control skills. However, I don't recommend coloring books exclusively and I don't believe that coloring is creative. I've found that providing my daughter with blank paper and quality coloring crayons with a clipboard in the car has been tremendously rewarding. She uses the time in the car as art sessions to experiment and be creative. It is open-ended and completely initiated by her. The artistic progress she has made from 4 years old to 5 years old, once I started the crayons and clipboard in the car, has been wonderful to see. I highly recommend it.

There is a compromise approach where the child is guided through a project framework with step-by-step techniques to help gain mastery of skills while providing freedom for individual creativity and variation. The results of this approach are works that look similar because they are the same projects, but with variations in each work.

I've spoken with artists to learn their views on these approaches and how they learned to become artists. They've told me that they were trained by learning the techniques. Creativity is something that comes forth later because they now have the skills to allow their creativity to produce what they envisioned.

One thing that seems to be a general consensus in the arts community is the setup of a workspace for doing art, and an environment where being messy is OK. The accessibility of the art materials helps children incorporate art into their everyday lives. See the recommended books for parents on how to set up the art area in your home.

Here's a guide to what to look for in an art class:
1. Art history introduction at each class, who the artist is, what his technique is, and what to notice about the art.
2. How the teacher talks to the students. Does the teacher encourage the child? There should not be judgmental comments from the teacher. How does the teacher talk about imitation? Imitation of other people's work helps us learn new techniques and can inspire us. The teacher should address the child's feelings of having made a "mistake." There are great children's books that are very appropriate for working with these issues.
3. The techniques being taught in the class. Does the teacher teach about line, colors, composition, perspective, balance, etc?
4. Are there a variety of materials offered? Are they quality materials that are easy and fun to work with? Poor quality materials can be frustrating to use, both for children and adults, and may hinder the creative flow.

Recommended reading for parents:
Everyday Art for Kids by Carolyn Holm
"Projects to Unlock Creativity." "Over 250 fun & easy projects that get kids excited about art. Handy materials reference. Simple guidelines for providing a creative environment."
Doing Art Together by Muriel Silberstein-Storfer with Mablen Jones
"Discovering the joys of appreciating and creating art as taught at The Metropolitan Museum of Art's famous parent-child workshop."

Books about art for the preschooler:

I Am an Artist by Pat Lowery Collins, Robin Brickman (Illustrator).
Regina's Big Mistake by Marissa Moss.

Art Classes

Local community centers, such as the local Parks and Recreation Department, the YMCA, and the JCC, also sponsor art classes. See the listings at the beginning of the Classes section.

Below is a list of the art studios that provide art classes, including classes for young toddlers, in the Bay Area beyond your local community center. They are listed in alphabetical order.

A Painting Studio (Ages 5+)

(415) 333-9515; 300 Chenery Street, San Francisco, CA 94131
<www.ccesf.org>

Almaden School of Music, Art, and Dance (Ages 5+)

(408) 267-3651; 5353 Almaden Expressway #12, San Jose, CA 95118
<www.almadenschool.com>

Art Academia (Ages 5+)

(650) 579-4456; 28 East 3rd Avenue #101, San Mateo, CA 94401
<www.artacademia.com>

Art Beat (Ages 2+)

(408) 370-5002; 68 E. Campbell Avenue, Campbell, CA 95008
<www.theartbeat.net>

Offers classes in clay as well. Look for offerings from local parks and recreation departments as well. Offers open studio to do your own clay and art drop-in project. See Web site.

Art House Kids (Ages 2+)

(408) 975-9987; 1043 Lincoln Avenue, San Jose, CA 95125
<www.arthousekids.com>

Art in Action (Ages 2+)

(650) 566-8339; 3925 Bohannon Drive, Suite 300, Menlo Park, CA 94025
<www.artinaction.org>

Summer art camps throughout the peninsula.

Artful I Studio (Ages 5+)

(408) 517-0377; 5325 Prospect Avenue, San Jose, CA 95129
<http://home.comcast.net/~artfuli>

The Art Room (Ages 4+)

(925) 299-1515; 50 Lafayette Circle, Lafayette, CA 94549
<www.theart-room.com>

California College of Arts and Crafts (Ages 12+)

(800) 447-1ART; (510) 594-3600; (510) 594-3710: Young Artist Studio
5212 Broadway, Oakland, CA 94618
<www.ccac-art.edu>; <www.cca.edu/academics/summer/yasp>;
<www.cca.edu/academics/summer/atelier>

Summer courses for 6th–8th graders in the Young Artist Studio program, the Summer Atelier program for 9th graders, and the precollege program for high schoolers completing sophomore to senior years with three college credits.

Cantor Arts Center at Stanford University (Ages 5+)

(650) 723-4177; Lomita Drive and Museum Way, Stanford, CA 94305-5060
<museum.stanford.edu>

Description: Art classes are offered to families, children, and teens. The class schedule is also available online by selecting "Participate," then "Classes." Registration form online.
Hours: Wed–Sun: 11am–5pm; Thur: 11am–8pm. Closed Mon, Tues, and holidays.

Community School of Music & Arts (2+)

(650) 917-6800; 230 San Antonio Circle, Mountain View, CA 94040
<www.arts4all.org>

Description: Offers art and music classes to preschoolers and up. There are also workshops, camps, performances, and special events throughout the year.

Clay Studio (Ages 5+)

(415) 777-9080; 61 Bluxome Street, San Francisco,CA 94107
<www.theclaystudio.com

Offers clay instruction and hand building for children. After-school and Saturday morning classes are available.

Civic Arts Education (All Ages)

(925) 943-5846; Civic Park Campus: 1313 Civic Drive, Walnut Creek, CA 94596
Shadelands Campus: 111 North Widget Lane, Walnut Creek, CA 94598
<www.arts-ed.org>; <www.walnut-creek.org>

Offers art and music classes for all ages.

Crucible (Ages 12+)

(510) 444-0919; 1260 7th Street, Oakland, CA 94607
<www.thecrucible.org>

Description: Youth classes, camps, and family workshops in blacksmithing, welding, jewelry, neon, woodworking, etc.

De Young Museum (Ages 3+)

(415) 863-3330; (415) 750-3528 Education Department
Golden Gate Park, 50 Hagiwara Tea Garden Drive, San Francisco, CA 94118
<www.thinker.org/deyoung>

Description: 1) On Saturdays (10:30am–noon), there are drop-in art classes for children 3½ to 12 years old. These are free with museum admission. No preregistration required. Members' children have classes 1:30pm–3pm. Classes meet at the Kimball Education Gallery. 2) Free after-school programs for students in grades 4–8. 3) On Friday nights from March to November, there are special art activities and demonstrations for families. Open until 8:45pm on these nights. 4) For high school students, free advanced placement program in art history after school. Check Web site.

Hours: Tues–Sun: 9:30am–5:15pm.

Cost: $10/adult; $7/senior 65+, $6/youth 13–17; free/child under 12.

Doodlebug (Ages 2+)

(415) 456-5989; 641 San Anselmo Avenue, San Anselmo, CA 94960
<www.doodlebugmarin.com>

Offers classes in clay, jewelry, drawing, painting, fashion design, knitting, and sculpture. Drop-in studio for pottery painting available. Birthday parties.

Falkirk Cultural Center (Ages 3+)

(415) 485-3328; 1408 Mission Avenue, San Rafael, CA
<www.falkirkculturalcenter.org>; <http://eplay.livelifelocally.com> for classes.

Classes offered through San Rafael Recreation Department.

Gymboree Play & Music Programs (Ages <5)

<www.playandmusic.com/b2c/customer/programIndex.jsp>

Now has art classes for 16-month-olds to 5-year-olds. Classes include music and creative movement. Available for birthday parties, too.

Habitot Children's Museum (Ages 2+)

(510) 647-1111; 2065 Kittredge Street, Berkeley, CA 94704
<www.habitot.org>

Art area for self-directed art projects. Geared toward toddlers and preschoolers. Wonderful selection of art, music, and drama classes, as well as camps. Available for birthday parties.

Jewish Community Center of San Francisco (Ages 3–14)

(415) 292-1200; 3200 California Street, San Francisco, CA 94118
<www.jccsf.org>

Art and ceramic classes for children. There's an open studio for kids on weekends on a drop-in basis.

Junior Center of Art and Science (Ages 2–17)
Lakeside Park (by Lake Merritt/Oakland's Fairyland)
(510) 839-5777; 558 Bellevue Avenue, Oakland, CA 94610
<www.juniorcenter.org>
<www.oaklandnet.com/parks/facilities/points_junior_center.asp>

Description: Drop-in art activities and pottery studio for all ages, including preschoolers. Afterschool art and science classes 4–6pm for children ages 5+. Registration is required. Summer art camps for children 5–16. During the summer, drop-in activities are also available. Parties available. **Hours:** *September–May:* Tues–Fri: 10am–6pm; Sat: 10am–3pm. *June–August:* Mon–Thur: 8:30am–5:30pm.

Kids N' Clay (Ages 3+)
(510) 845-0982; 1824 5th Street, Berkeley, CA 94710
<www.kidsnclay.com>

Ceramics studio offers classes to children 5 and older (up to teens) after school and on Saturdays. Summer camps available. Ask to be on the mailing list. The mailing goes out in January. Summer camps sign up in February. Look for new sites in San Francisco and Walnut Creek.

Museum of Children's Art (MOCHA) (Ages 18 months+)
(510) 465-8770; 538 Ninth Street, Oakland, CA 94607
<www.mocha.org>

Art studios designed for preschoolers as well as big kids.

Pacific Art League (Ages 4+)
(650) 321-3891; 668 Ramona Street, Palo Alto, CA 94301
<www.pacificartleague.org>

Classes and summer camps.

Palo Alto Art Center (Ages 18 months+)
(650) 329-2366; 1313 Newell Road, Palo Alto, CA 94303
<www.cityofpaloalto.org/community-services/ac-index.html>; <www.paacf.org>

See Palo Alto *Enjoy* catalog for the schedule of classes. Great family workshops on weekends, too.

Purple Crayon (Ages 20 months+)

(415) 831-0693; 301 Cornwall Street, San Francisco, CA 94118
<www.purplecrayon.com>

The Randall Museum (Ages 2+)

(415) 554-9600; 199 Museum Way, San Francisco, CA 94114
<www.randallmuseum.org>

Richards Arts Crafts & Framing (Ages 5+)

(925) 820-4731; 225A Alamo Plaza, Alamo, CA 94507
(925) 447-0471; 4502 Las Positas, Livermore, CA 94550
<www.richardsartsandcrafts.com>

Art project birthday parties, including ceramic painting, tie dye T-shirts, etc. Afterschool and Saturday classes.

Richmond Art Center (Ages 3+)

(510) 620-6772; 2540 Barrett Avenue, Richmond, CA 94804
<www.therichmondartcenter.org>

Sanchez Art Center (Ages 2+)

(650) 355-1894; 1220-B Linda Mar Boulevard, Pacifica, CA 94044
<www.sanchezartcenter.org>

San Francisco Children's Art Center (Ages 2+)

(415) 771-0292; Fort Mason Center, Building C, San Francisco, CA 94123
<www.childrensartcenter.org>

The Santa Cruz Mountains Art Center

(831) 336-3513; 9341 Mill Street, Ben Lomond, CA 95005
<www.mountainartcenter.org>

Children's ceramic, art classes, and camps offered.

Sharon Art Studio (Ages 5+)

Golden Gate Park Arts & Crafts Division at McLaren Lodge
(415) 753-7004; 501 Stanyan Street, San Francisco, CA 94117

Ceramics, glass, jewelry making, drawing, painting, and mixed media classes offered.

Silicon Valley Art Museum (Ages 4–12)

1870 Ralston Avenue, Belmont, CA 94002

<www.svam.org>: Online art lesson plans only.

Studio One Art Center

(510) 597-5027; 365 45th Street, Oakland, CA 94609

<www.oaklandnet.com/parks/facilities/points_studio_one.asp>

The Marvegos Fine Art School

(408) 866-0671; 18776 Cox Avenue, Saratoga, CA (Quito Village)

(408) 770-0671; 40085 Mission Boulevard, Fremont, CA (Mission Valley)

<www.marvegos.com>

Triton Museum of Art (Ages 6+)

(408) 247-3754; 247-9340; 1505 Warburton Avenue, Santa Clara, CA 95050

<www.tritonmuseum.org>

University Art (supply store w/ classes)

(408) 297-4707; 456 Meridian Avenue, San Jose, CA 95126

<www.universityart.com/class.htm>

Young at Art Studio (Ages 4+)

(408) 255-1414; 19701 Stevens Creek Boulevard, Cupertino, CA 95014

<http://yaainc.net>

Art Supplies Stores

Besides taking art classes, it's good to encourage your child to do art at home. *Doing Art Together* author Muriel Silberstein-Storfer suggests setting up a workspace in the home and providing good quality paints, brushes, pastels, paper, etc. Here's a list of Bay Area art supplies stores.

Aaron Brothers
<www.aaronbrothers.com>

Stores: Daly City, San Francisco, Berkeley, Concord, Dublin, Fremont, Pinole, San Ramon, Walnut Creek, Redwood City, San Mateo, Campbell, Cupertino, Sunnyvale, and San Jose.

Blick Art Materials
(510) 486-2600; 811 University Avenue, Berkeley, CA 94710
(510) 658-2787; 5301 Broadway, Oakland, CA 94618
(415) 441-6075; 1414 Van Ness Avenue, San Francisco, CA 94109
<www.dickblick.com>

East Bay Depot for Creative Use
(510) 547-6470; (510) 547-6535; 6713 San Pablo Avenue, Oakland, CA 94608
<www.ciwmb.ca.gov/reuse/Profiles/EastBay.htm>

Lakeshore Learning Store
<www.lakeshorelearning.com>

Walnut Creek, San Jose, and San Leandro. San Leandro store is also a clearance warehouse.

Michaels
<www.michaels.com>

Morrison School Supply
(650) 592-3000; 400 Industrial Road, San Carlos, CA 94070
(408) 749-1114; 560 E El Camino, Sunnyvale, CA 94087
<www.morrisonschoolsupplies.com>

Great source of 11x14 and 8x11 white construction paper. 15% discount coupon on Web site.

RAFT (Resource Area for Teaching)
(408) 451-1420; 1355 Ridder Park Drive, San Jose, CA 95131
<www.raft.net>

For homeschoolers, teachers, and community groups.

Richard's Arts Crafts & Framing
(925) 820-4731; 225A Alamo Plaza, Alamo, CA 94507
(925) 447-0471; 4502 Las Positas, Livermore, CA 94550
<www.richardsartsandcrafts.com>

Scrap—Creative Re-use
(415) 647-1746; 801 Toland Street, San Francisco, CA 94124
<www.scrap-sf.org>

University Art
<www.universityart.com>

Stores in San Francisco, Palo Alto, San Jose, and Sacramento.

Music Education

Learning to play a musical instrument has many benefits. Besides developing music appreciation, the discipline of learning an instrument provides opportunities to learn life lessons. There are times when learning new skills is hard, and the student has great difficulty accomplishing new tasks. Oftentimes, this is when the student wants to quit. It's important to learn that skills and tasks that are hard require practice, but with practice comes mastery. It's important to learn not to give up for trivial reasons, to learn the discipline of having to practice daily, even when it's hard and not so fun.

In the course of dealing with difficulty, the student should also learn to be patient and kind to himself; he must give himself the time to learn. The goal is daily incremental improvement. Sometimes, it's two steps forward and one step backward. It's important not to expect perfection but rather to expect to do one's best. Mistakes are not failures but the means to learn and improve. These are important life lessons that can be learned through the discipline of playing an instrument. Of course, these life lessons can be learned through many different pursuits, including sports and hobbies, as long as there is commitment and dedication.

Playing an instrument demands great physical coordination. It requires the eyes and brain to read the notes and translate them to the hands/ breath, etc. It requires listening to the music and cooperating with other instruments in the orchestra, ensemble, or symphony. These tasks require a great deal from children's brains, resulting in general development of the brain and, therefore, intelligence. In recent years, there has been a product trend of cassettes and videos to increase an infant's intelligence. The most recent study shows that there is an effect while listening to the music, but it is very short-lived. These products try to cash in on the public's misunderstanding that these passive activities increase the baby's or child's intelligence.

From my experience, there are several distinct stages in musical develop-ment in early childhood. The first stage is just music appreciation, which can be developed by the parent or caregiver. Start by singing and allow-ing yourself to be silly to foster creativity. Singing lullabies and children's songs helps develop the child's sense of pitch, rhythm, and—most impor-tantly—love of music. Once the child starts singing along with you, it's time for introductory music classes such as Music Together, Kindermusic, and Gymboree Music. These programs develop music appreciation and basic musicianship in a fun, stimulating, and nonthreatening environ-ment. They all believe that your child is inherently musical and help develop musical skills through play.

Making music at home with your child, and using the skills you've learned in these programs is a great way to encourage daily music play. It's a great idea to start a "music kit" that contains rhythm instruments (maracas, egg shakers, train whistle, drum set, tambourine, sticks, spoons, etc.). Music Together also sells its collections via cassette or CD, with a songbook with lyrics for each collection. This is a great way to bring the Music Together experience home. Gymboree Music and Play Programs also sell CD and rhythm instruments. Look for finger plays, counting and chants for rhythm development, as well as old-time favorite tunes.

Once your child is comfortable with music—singing in pitch and with basic rhythm—it's probably time for a group music class that will prepare your child to take private music lessons. This stage should be in the 4- to 5-year-old range. The goals of the group lessons should be learning the

following concepts and putting these new skills into practice.
1) Rhythm, keeping a steady beat.
2) Keeping count (your child need only be able to count to six, as almost all music measures are 2 beats up to a maximum of 6 beats per measure).
3) Distinguishing whether a musical piece or phrase is fast or slow.
4) Distinguishing whether the note is a high note or low note.
5) Differentiating between right and left hand.
6) Being able to distinguish whether it's a major key (sounds happy) or a minor key (sounds sad).
7) Learning the types of notes (whole notes get 4 beats, half notes get 2 beats, quarter notes get 1 beat, eighth notes get ½ beat, etc.).
8) Learning to read the music: understanding the clefs (treble clef and bass clef), the number of beats per measure, and reading the notes on the musical staff.
9) Being able to identify the piano key to the note on the musical staff. It is possible for young children to learn to read music. In fact, it is easier to learn to read music at the beginning since they are only learning a note or two at a time. Waiting until the repertoire is more advanced to begin reading music just creates more difficulty in having to learn so many notes all at once!

This lays the foundation for private music lessons. However, consider the emotional maturity and the readiness of the child before starting private lessons, as this step requires the discipline and commitment to practice the instrument on a daily basis.

As you begin to look for private lessons, here are some things to consider when evaluating and selecting a music teacher.
1) Proper form and technique must be taught, and bad habits should never be allowed to continue or "let go." It is so easy for the teacher to just mention it but not require the bad habit be corrected. Teachers who care will persist and *continue* to correct bad habits.
2) Teachers who can't do don't understand how to do it for themselves; therefore, they don't and *can't* teach it. That was one of my mistakes in evaluating teachers—I gave the teacher the benefit of the doubt, thinking that if he can't do it, he might still be able to teach it.
3) Teachers should not rush and push the student to play "faster"

without ensuring that the student is properly relaxed. The stress of playing fast can also create tension in the hands, arms, shoulders, etc.; which if left for prolonged periods can lead to serious injury that can be debilitating. Learning to play in a relaxed way while maintaining strength and power is extremely important, and can't be rushed.

4) Teachers should teach not only the correct technique but also the emotional and musical expression of the music. Music should not be played merely as a bunch of notes, with no regard to its emotional component. It is possible even for a young child to learn to do this, if properly taught, and the musical piece is age appropriate.

5) Music theory should be part of the curriculum, along with performance.

6) Performance opportunities in the form of recitals should also be an inherent part of the curriculum.

The Music Teacher Association of California has a directory of the member branches throughout California. Its Web site <**www.mtac.org/branches**> links to the branches' Web sites along with contacts. Once you've located the branches closest to you, visit their Web sites and look for the teacher directory. This is a good place to start looking for a private music teacher. Of course, networking with people in your community is another wonderful way to find a good teacher. Just keep in mind that one person's expectations and standards might be very different from another's.

Music Classes

Local Parks and Recreation Departments also sponsor group music classes for beginners. Don't forget the youth orchestras and symphonies in Chapter 8: Arts & Performing Arts—Youth Symphonies. See Chapter 11: Local Resources—Parks and Recreation Departments.

CradleRock Children's Center (Ages < 6)

(415) 789-KIDS; 642 Tiburon Boulevard, Tiburon, CA 94920
<www.cradlerockmusic.com>

Early music and art classes for young children.

Gymboree Play & Music Programs (Ages < 5)

<www.playandmusic.com/b2c/customer/programIndex.jsp>

Kids in Tune (Ages 18 Months–7 years)

(800) 720-0887; (510) 887-1304; P.O. Box 336, Mt. Eden, CA 94557
The Grange Hall: 743 Diablo Road, Danville, CA 94526; St. John's Episcopal
Church: 1707 Gouldin Road, Oakland, CA 94611; Foothill Congregational
Church: 461 Orange Avenue, Los Altos, CA 94022

Teaching based on the Kodaly method. Offers classes through preschools
and local Parks and Recreation Departments. Call to request brochure for
details. The following cities have Parks and Recreation Departments that
feature Kids in Tune: Alameda, Concord, Fremont, Los Altos, Milpitas,
Newark, Pleasant Hill, Redwood City, San Leandro, and San Mateo.

Kindermusik (Infants & Up)

<www.kindermusik.com>

Provides early childhood instruction in music for newborns to children
age 7. Visit the Web site for curricula information and educator location.

Music Makers (Age 18 months–6)

(415) 461-1066; 240 Tiburon Boulevard, Tiburon, CA 94920
<www.music-makers.org>

Music Together (Age 1–5)

<www.musictogether.com>

Nationwide music and movement program for babies and preschoolers.
Go to the Web site for city locator and program closest to you. The classes
can also be found through various city Parks and Recreation Departments.
Certain locations have International Music Together featuring music and
songs from various countries and languages. You can also purchase the
music collections and rhythm instruments online.

Connect the Tots
(510) 798-4833; 172 Oakes Boulevard, San Leandro, CA 94577
<http://connect-thetots.com>
Serves Fremont, Hayward, Union City, San Leandro, and
Castro Valley.

Delta Music Together
(925) 418-5624;
<www.deltamusictogether.com>
Serves Antioch and Brentwood.

East Bay Music Together
(510) 843-8641; 2316 Webster Street, Berkeley, CA 94705
<http://eastbaymusictogether.com>
Serves Alameda, Albany, Berkeley, Montclair, Moraga, Oakland,
Rockridge, and Walnut Creek.

Fun with Music Together
(510) 521-3676; 2008 Franciscan Way #204, Alameda, CA 94501
<www.funwithmusictogether.com>
Serves Alameda.

Golden Gate Music Together
(415) 884-2710; 3429 Sacramento Street, SF; 2266 California Street, SF
<www.goldengatemusictogether.com>
Serves 3 locations in San Francisco.

Mo Music
(650) 365-5355;
<www.momusic.org>
Serves Foster City, Redwood City, San Carlos, Millbrae, and
Woodside.

Music for Families
(650) 917-2354;
<www.music4families.net>
Serves Sunnyvale, Mountain View, Los Altos, Palo Alto,
Atherton, and Menlo Park.

Music Together in the Tri-Valley
(925) 551-7722;
<www.musictogether.net>
Serves Walnut Creek, Danville, San Ramon, Pleasanton, and
Livermore.

Music Together of Concord

(925) 946-2990; 10 Arlene Lane, Walnut Creek, CA 94595
<www.musictogetherofconcord.com>
Serves Concord, Clayton, and Martinez.

Music Together of Marin

(415) 388-2464; P.O. Box 7043, Berkeley, CA 94707
<www.music4families.com>
Serves Mill Valley, Corte Madera, San Anselmo, Larkspur, San
Rafael, Ross, and Marinwood.

Music Together of San Francisco

(415) 596-0299; P.O. Box 371075, Montara, CA 94037
<www.musictogethersf.com>
Serves San Francisco and Pacifica.

Music Together of the North Bay

(707) 747-9417
<www.musictogethernorthbay.com>
Serves Benicia and Fairfield.

Music Together of the Valley

(408) 227-4803; 3637 Snell Avenue #260, San Jose, CA 95136
<www.musictogether007.com>
Serves San Jose, Morgan Hill, and Fresno.

Music Together with Debbie

(415) 456-3565; 2080 Fifth Avenue, San Rafael, CA 94901
<www.musictogetherwithdebbi.com>
Serves Novato and Sonoma.

Musical Me Inc.

(831) 462-5195;
<www.musicalme.com>
Serves Cupertino, Los Gatos, Saratoga, Campbell, Capitola,
Santa Cruz, Ben Lomond, and Watsonville.

Playing with Music

(831) 229-7440; 813 Larkin Street, Salinas, CA 93907
<www.playingwithmusic.com>
Serves Monterey and Salinas.

Santa Rosa Area Music Together

(707) 544-5747; 3450 Franz Valley Road, Santa Rosa, CA 95404
<www.musiceveryone.com>
Serves Santa Rosa, Healdsburg, and Windsor.

West County Music Together
(707) 823-6893; 7620 Healdsburg Avenue, Sebastopol, CA 95472
<www.westcountymusictogether.com>
Serves Cotati, Petaluma, and Sebastopol.

Alameda School of Music (Ages 3+)
(510) 769-0195; 1307 High Street, Alameda, CA 94501
<http://alamusic.com>

Almaden School of Music, Art, & Dance (Ages 5+)
(408) 267-3651;
Almaden Plaza: 5353 Almaden Expressway, #12, San Jose, CA 95118
<www.almadenschool.com>

Community Music Center (Ages 8+)
(415) 647-6015; 544 Capp Street, San Francisco, CA 94110
(415) 221-4515; 741 30th Avenue, San Francisco, CA 94121
<www.sfcmc.org>

Community School of Music & Arts (Ages 2+)
(650) 917-6800; 230 San Antonio Circle, Mountain View, CA 94040
<www.arts4all.org>

Crowden Center for Music in the Community (All Ages)
(510) 559-6910; 1475 Rose Street, Berkeley, CA 94702
<www.crowden.org>

Offers Music Together, homeschool music (including music theory), and a varied curriculum.

Crystal Children's Choir (Ages 6+)
(408) 725-8328; (510) 656-0388; P.O. Box 66, Cupertino, CA 95015
<www.crystalchoir.org>

Rehearsals at Fremont, Cupertino, San Jose, and Foster City.

Danville Music
(925)743-0788; 3 Railroad Avenue, Danville, CA 94526
<http://danvillemusic.com>

East Bay Center for Performing Arts (Ages 3+)
(510) 234-5624; 339 11th Street, Richmond, CA 94801
<http://eastbaycenter.org>

Harmony Road Music School (All Ages)
Piedmont Piano Company
(510) 652-1222; 4382 Piedmont Avenue, Oakland, CA 94611
<www.piedmontpiano.com/Webpages/musicschool.html>

Marin Children's Chorus (Ages 5+)
(415) 898-3331; P.O. Box 905, Novato, CA 94948
<www.marinchorus.org>

Marin Music Center (Ages 5+)
(415) 897-4131; 1559 South Novato Boulevard, Novato, CA 94947
<www.marinmusic.com>

Music Hatchery (All Ages)
(707) 775-3655; 620 Petaluma Boulevard North, Suite C2, Petaluma, CA 94952
<www.music-hatchery.com>

The Music Place (Ages 1+)
(408) 445-2787 (ARTS); 1617 Willowhurst Avenue, San Jose, CA 95125
<www.musicplace.com>

The Music School (Ages 1+)
(408) 739-9248; 728 W. Fremont Avenue, Sunnyvale, CA 94087
<www.themusicschool.org>

Music Village
(408) 377-2504; 2985 Union Avenue, San Jose, CA
(408) 629-1812; 5885 Santa Teresa Boulevard, San Jose, CA

New Mozart School of Music
(650) 324-2373; Office/lessons: 305 N. California Avenue, Palo Alto, CA 94301
Private lessons: 220 University Avenue, Palo Alto, CA 94301
<www.newmozartschool.com>

Pacific Boychoir Academy (Ages 6+)
(510) 652-4PBA; 410 Alcatraz Avenue, Oakland, CA 94609
<www.pacificboychoir.org>

Peninsula Girls Chorus (Ages 9+)
(650) 347-6351; 1443 Howard Avenue, Burlingame, CA 94010
<www.peninsulagirlschorus.org>

Peninsula Piano School (Ages 3+)
(650) 854-7006; (888) 742-6680;
Office: 405 El Camino Real #232, Menlo Park, CA 94025; Classes at Cubberley
Community Center: 4000 Middlefield Road Room M7, Palo Alto, CA 94303
<www.penpiano.com>

Piedmont Choir (Ages 6+)
(510) 547-4441; 401-A Highland Avenue, Piedmont, CA 94611
<www.piedmontchoirs.org>

Polonsky Piano School (Ages 4+)
(408) 828-7641; 4055 Evergreen Square Village, Room 230, San Jose, CA 95135
<www.polonskypianoschool.com>
Offers piano and violin classes. Summer arts camp.

Ragazzi Boys Chorus (Ages 7+)
(650) 342-8785; 20 N. San Mateo Drive, Suite 9, San Mateo, CA 94401
<www.ragazzi.org>

San Francisco Boys Choir (Ages 4+)
(415) 861-SING(7464); 333 Hayes Street, Suite 116, San Francisco, CA 94102
<http://sfbc.org>

San Francisco Conservatory of Music (Ages 4+)
Preparatory Division
(415) 864-7326; 50 Oak Street, San Francisco, CA 94102
<www.sfcm.edu>

Provides early childhood music education for children ages 4–9. Private lessons are also available.

San Francisco Girls Chorus (Ages 4+)
(415) 863-1752; 44 Page Street, Suite 200, San Francisco, CA 94102
<www.sfgirlschorus.org>

Singers Marin (Ages 6+)
(415) 383-3712; 1038 Redwood Hwy. Bldg. A, Mill Valley, CA 94941
<www.singersmarin.org>

Sonoma Music Arts School
(707) 996-7661; 901 Broadway Street, Sonoma, CA 95476
<www.sonomamusicarts.com>

Yamaha Music Education (Ages 4+)
(510) 523-4797; Starland Music Center: 1631 Park Street, Alameda, CA
(925) 691-5220; F.A.M.E. Music Center:
1630 Contra Costa Boulevard #210, Pleasant Hill, CA
<www.yamaha.com> then select "Music Education" at bottom of page.

Drama & Speech Education

Children love to pretend and dress up. It's a wonderful way to develop their imagination and creativity. In addition, they're developing their public speaking skills and self-confidence. Using "baby steps," it's possible to lead even a shy youngster to speak with confidence. Start with pretend play, then show and tell and puppet shows at home, then musical theater, and drama, to eventually lead to confidence in public speaking and presentation skills. There's a relatively new company on the scene that focuses on speech and debate, starting at the prepublic-speaking level. I'm excited to see this offered to kids in the elementary and middle school levels in addition to the high school level. Many of the companies listed below provide drama classes, as well as performances, for children, so don't overlook these as a source for performances to attend.

Alameda Children's Musical Theatre (Ages 6–16)
(510) 521-6965; PO Box 2378, Alameda, CA 94501
<www.acmtkids.org>

Arts Express (For schools: grades 4–12)
(408) 277-2859; email: arts.express@sanjoseca.gov
<www.sanjoseculture.org/artsexpress>

Free arts experiences for San Jose and Santa Clara County schools.

California Theater Center Conservatory (Ages 6+)
Summer Theater Conservatory
(408) 245-2979; P.O. Box 2007, Sunnyvale, CA 94087
<www.ctcinc.org>

Children's Fairyland Children's Theater (Ages 5+)
(510) 452-2259; 699 Bellevue Avenue, Oakland, CA 94610
<www.fairyland.org/schedule.html#daily>

City Lights Theater Company of San Jose (Ages 6+)
(408) 295-4200; 529 South Second Street, San Jose, CA 95112
<www.cltc.org>

Coastal Repertory Conservatory (Ages 4+)
(650) 726-0627; 1167 Main Street, Half Moon Bay, CA 94019
<www.coastalrep.com>

Conservatory of Performing Arts (Ages 4+)
Children's Musical Theater, San Jose
(408) 288-5437 x22; 1401 Parkmoor Avenue, Suite 100, San Jose, CA 95126

Offers classes for children starting at age four. Tiny Tots Song & Dance (ages 4–5), Junior Talents Revue (ages 6–8), Rising Stars Revue (ages 9–12), and Master Acting Class (ages 12–20). Summer camps are available.

Communication Academy (Ages 5+)

(408) 777-8876; 7337 Bollinger Road, Suite #E, Cupertino, CA 95014
<www.communicationacademy.com>
Offers classes from prepublic-speaking through speech and debate. Also offers classes through local Parks and Recreation Departments.

Glitter & Razz Productions (Ages 4+)

(510) 845-8542 x351; 2640 College Avenue, Berkeley, CA 94704
<www.glitterandrazz.com>

Hillbarn Theatre & Conservatory (Ages 4+)

(650) 349-6411; 1285 East Hillsdale Boulevard, Foster City, CA 94404
<www.hillbarntheatre.org>

Imagine Performing Arts (Ages 4+)

(925) 551-0200; 6620 Dublin Boulevard, Dublin, CA 94568
<www.imagineperformingarts.org>

Classes offered through the Imagine Performing Arts Academy. Offers classes and camps in acting, singing, improv, and dance. Birthday parties offered. A few courses are through the Parks and Recreation Departments of Livermore, Pleasanton, and San Ramon. These courses include "City Theatre Arts," "Creative Dramatics," and "Acting Is for Me." See the Parks and Recreation section under these cities for the Web sites.

Kids on Broadway (Ages 6+)

(831) 425-3455; P.O. Box 3461, Santa Cruz, CA 95063
<www.kidsonbroadway.org>

Afterschool classes, workshops, and summer camps in theater arts for kids 6 and older. Classes include acting, voice, dance, improvisation, lighting, set construction, and costume design.

Marin Theatre Company Conservatory (Ages 7+)
(415) 388-5200; 397 Miller Avenue, Mill Valley, CA 94941
<www.marintheatre.org/conservatory.htm>

Palo Alto Children's Theater (Ages 5+)
(650) 463-4930; (650) 463-4970: Tickets
1305 Middlefield Road, Palo Alto, CA 94301
<www.city.palo-alto.ca.us/community-services/theater-index.html>;
<www.paenjoy.org> for class information

Wonderful summertime theater for kids, including preschoolers, in an outdoor environment. You can bring a picnic and blanket. You can purchase cookies and hot dogs, too. Camps and classes throughout the year.

Peninsula Youth Theatre (Ages 3½+)
(650) 988-8798 x302; 2500 Old Middlefield Way, Mountain View, CA 94043
<www.pytnet.org>

Offers classes and camps.

Pinole School of Performing Arts (Ages 3+)
(510) 724-9844; Community Playhouse: 601 Tennent Avenue, Pinole, CA 94564
<www.ci.pinole.ca.us/recreation/performarts.html>

Register classes through Pinole Parks and Recreation Department.

Roberta Jones Junior Theatre (Ages 4+)
Santa Clara Community Recreation Center
(408) 615-3161; 969 Kiely Boulevard, Santa Clara, CA 95051
<www.ci.santa-clara.ca.us/park_recreation/pr_dept.html>;
<online.activecommunities.com/santaclara>

Register through the Santa Clara Parks and Recreation Department. For more information, see the Santa Clara Parks and Recreation Department in Chapter 11: Local Resources—Local Parks and Recreation.

San Jose Repertory Theater (Ages 7+)
(408) 367-7291; 101 Paseo de San Antonio, San Jose, CA 95113
<www.sjrep.com>

Creative Dramatics Summer Workshop: write and perform original play.

Stage Door Conservatory (Ages 8+)

(510) 521-6250; 909 Marina Village Parkway, Box 501, Alameda, CA 94501
<www.stagedoorconservatory.org>
Spring and summer camps in the theater arts held at 3 different venues.

Starstruck (Ages 4+)

(925) 944-1565; Rehearsal at Diablo Light Opera Company Firehouse:
1948 Oak Park Boulevard, Pleasant Hill, CA 94523
<www.dloc.org/youththeatre>

Sunnyvale Community Players (Ages 8+)

(408) 733-6611; P.O. Box 60399, Sunnyvale, CA 94088
<www.sunnyvaleplayers.org>;
<http://sunnyvale.ca.gov/Departments/Parks+and+Recreation>

Tabard Theatre Company

(408) 979-0231; Office: 5663 Chambertin Drive, San Jose, CA 95118
<www.tabardtheatre.org>

Television & Video Production (Ages 8–14)
KMTV15 Community Television

(650) 968-1540; 1400 Terra Bella Avenue, Suite M, Mountain View, CA 94043
<www.kmvt15.org/workshops/youth.html>

Offers after-school workshops and summer camps on television and
video production. In partnership with the Peninsula Youth Theater, offers television acting workshops to middle schoolers.

Willows Theatre Conservatory (Ages 8+)

(925) 798-1300; 1975 Diamond Boulevard, Concord, CA 94520
<www.willowstheatre.org>

Young Performers Theatre (Ages 3–15)
Fort Mason Center

(415) 346-5550; Building C, Room 300, San Francisco, CA 94123
<www.ypt.org>

Besides wonderful children's theater at very affordable prices, there are
classes for even the youngest pretenders. Available for birthday parties.

Chapter 13
Physical Activities

Physical activity is not only fun, it is absolutely necessary for children's well being. Motor skill development is as important as academic development. A great time to visit toddler playgrounds is in the first two years, after babies learn to walk and are fairly confident on their feet. Many gymnastics programs have classes for infants to 4-year-olds. Some swimming classes accommodate children as young as six months. Dance classes usually require the child to be at least 2 years old, generally 3 years old. Ice skating usually accommodates children three and older. Bowling seems to work well for kids more than 3 years old.

Parks

The California Department of Fish and Game has created a *Fishing in the City* program, with free 45-minute clinics showing kids ages 5–15 how to fish. Equipment and tackle are provided to participants. These clinics rotate to different parks throughout the Bay Area. Visit <**www. dfg.ca.gov/oceo/fishcity**> or call (415) 892-0460 for events close to you. Don't forget to bring your driver's license to get a rod, and two kids per adult are allowed.

National & State Parks

National Parks
1-888-GO-PARKS
<**www.nps.gov**>
<**www.nationalparks.org**>

California State Parks
(916) 653-6995
<http://parks.ca.gov>

County Parks

East Bay Regional Park District
<www.ebparks.org>

Includes Alameda and Contra Costa counties.

Marin County Parks
<www.marinopenspace.org>; <www.marincountyparks.org>

Monterey County Parks
<www.co.monterey.ca.us/parks>

San Francisco Parks
<www.parks.sfgov.org/site/recpark_index.asp>

San Mateo County Parks
<www.co.sanmateo.ca.us/smc/department/esa/home/0,2242,5556687_
10575168,00.html>

Santa Clara County Parks
<www.parkhere.org>; <http://claraweb.co.santa-clara.ca.us/parks/index.html>

Santa Cruz County Parks
<www.scparks.com>

Sonoma County Parks
<www.parks.sonoma.net>

Neighborhood Parks

Here are Web site for each city's neighborhood parks. Don't forget to check Chapter 11: Local Resources—Local Parks & Recreation for recreation activities, too. Some parks have water play areas. For those, it's a good idea to bring flip-flops, bathing suits, sunscreen, towels, a picnic lunch, and drinks. Don't forget your sunscreen, sunglasses, and some change for metered parking, too.

Alameda: <www.ci.alameda.ca.us/arpd/parkfacil.html>
Belmont: <www.belmont.gov>
Berkeley: <www.ci.berkeley.ca.us/parks/parks.html>
Brentwood: <www.ci.brentwood.ca.us/department/pr/cob_par/parks/>
Burlingame: <www.burlingame.org>
Campbell: <www.ci.campbell.ca.us/Recreation/parks>
Concord: <www.cityofconcord.org/recreation/parks/playgrnd.htm>
Cupertino: <www.cupertino.org/just_visiting/what_to_do/index.asp>
Danville: <www.ci.danville.ca.us>
Dublin: <www.ci.dublin.ca.us/DepartmentSub.cfm?PL=Rec&SL=prkfac>
El Cerrito: <www.el-cerrito.org/recreation/parks.html>
Emeryville: <www.ci.emeryville.ca.us/rec/parks.html>
Foster City: <www.fostercity.org/Services/recreation/ParkGrid.cfm>
Fremont: <www.fremont.gov/Recreation/Playgrounds/default.htm>
Gilroy: <www.ci.gilroy.ca.us/comserv/parks.html>
Hayward: <www.hard.dst.ca.us>; <www.ebparks.org>
Livermore: <www.larpd.dst.ca.us/facilities_fs.html>
Los Altos: <www.losaltoschamber.org/parks_recreation.html>
Los Altos Hills: <www.losaltoshills.ca.gov/recreation/open-space.html>
Los Gatos: <www.los-gatos.org/main/parks.html>
Menlo Park: <www.menlopark.org/departments/com/parks.html>
Mill Valley: <www.cityofmillvalley.org>
Millbrae:< www.ci.millbrae.ca.us/parksandrec/parklocations.html>
Milpitas: <www.ci.milpitas.ca.gov/citydept/planning/recreation/parkfacili-
tyreservation.htm>
Monterey Area: <www.monterey.com/mc3/mc3a2.html>
Moraga: <www.ci.moraga.ca.us/moraga_parks_recreation.php>
Morgan Hill: <www.morganhill.org/maps/cityparks.htm>

Mountain View: <www.ci.mtnview.ca.us/city_hall/comm_services/parks_and_trails/city_parks.asp>

Napa: <www.cityofnapa.org/Menu/MnuCommunityResources.htm>

Newark: <www.newark.org/play/parks.html>

Novato: <www.ci.novato.ca.us/parks>

Oakland: <www.oaklandnet.com/parks/facilities/parks.asp>

Orinda: <www.ci.orinda.ca.us/parksandrec/parksandtrails/parksandtrails.html>

Pacific Grove: <www.pacificgroverecreation.org>

Palo Alto: <www.paloaltoonline.com/things_do/open_space.php>

Petaluma: <http://cityofpetaluma.net/parksnrec/cityparks.html>

Piedmont: <www.ci.piedmont.ca.us/html/visitor/parks.htm>

Pleasant Hill: <www.pleasanthillrec.com/Rentals.htm#Parks>

Pleasanton: <www.ci.pleasanton.ca.us/pdf/sumag03pgs6465.pdf>

Portola Valley: <www.portolavalley.net/community/cr_parks_recreation.shtml>

Redwood City: <www.redwoodcity.org/parks/parksandpools>

Richmond: <www.ci.richmond.ca.us/index.asp?nid=424>

San Anselmo: <www.townofsananselmo.org/parks>

San Carlos: <www.cityofsancarlos.org/gov/depts/parks_rec/park_information>

San Francisco: <www.sfgov.org/site/recpark_index.asp?id=1503>

San Jose: <www.sjparks.org/listofparks2.asp>
   For the list of parks within San Jose with water play:
   <www.sjparks.org/Features/waterfeatures.asp>

San Leandro: <www.ci.san-leandro.ca.us/slparks.html>

San Mateo: <www.cityofsanmateo.org/dept/parks/directory.html>

San Rafael: <www.cityofsanrafael.org/Residents/Parks.htm>

San Ramon: <www.ci.san-ramon.ca.us/parks/parks.htm>

Santa Clara: <http://cho.ci.santa-clara.ca.us/park_recreation/pr_parks.html>

Santa Cruz: <www.santacruzparksandrec.com/parks/neighborhoodparks.html>

Santa Rosa: <www.santarosa.fl.gov/parks/locatepark.html>

Saratoga: <www.saratoga.ca.us/recreation/park_reservation.htm>

Sausalito: <www.ci.sausalito.ca.us/business/park-rec/parks.htm>

Sonoma: <www.parks.sonoma.net>; <www.sonomacity.org/Uploads/4338.pdf>

Sunnyvale: <http://sunnyvale.ca.gov/Departments/Parks+and+Recreation/Parks/>

Union City: <www.ci.union-city.ca.us/leisure/Map.htm>

Walnut Creek: <www.ci.walnut-creek.ca.us/header.asp?genericId=1&catId=5&subCatId=13>

Swimming

The American College of Pediatrics recommends waiting until a child is 4 years old to introduce swimming lessons. For its policy statement regarding swimming programs for infants and toddlers, refer to the Web site: <www.aap.org/policy/re9940.html>. It concludes that children under 4 years of age do not have sufficient motor skills and that swim classes can lead parents to the false belief that their child is water safe.

I believe another reason infants should not take swim classes is because their little bodies lose body temperature too quickly, even in a 30-minute class and in an enclosed, heated pool. I've been in classes with 6-month-old infants who were so cold they were shivering in the middle of summer.

I started my child around her 2nd birthday. I found that to be the optimal age because she had not developed a major fear and aversion to the water yet. Children starting at an older age may have a tougher introduction to the water. Additionally, parent/child introductory swimming classes, offered to children under three years old, are wonderful transition classes prior to the child-only classes at the age of 3. The parent/child classes use songs and games to promote a secure and fun environment. It's absolutely critical that we, as parents, do not delude ourselves into believing that our children are water safe just because they have had swim classes. Parents should always supervise their children, especially when their children are in the pool, even if they have had swim classes.

You must decide for yourself when to introduce your children to swim classes, if ever. You should also consider your children's temperament to gauge when they are ready.

I think it's sufficient to take swim classes only during the warm weather, from late spring to early fall. During the winter, it gets very cold, even in an indoor heated pool. There can be quite a change in temperature from being in the pool to getting out of the pool, into the dressing area, and getting dressed. Also, during the cold weather season, so many kids have colds or the flu and yet continue to go to swim classes that I think it's better to avoid this environment entirely. After I stopped my daughter's winter swimming lessons, I noticed that she got sick less often. Lastly, I have not seen any significant regression when I've taken my daughter out of swim classes during the winter. I believe that classes during warm weather provide sufficient progress.

Many people find that the frequency of swimming classes plays an important role in how fast the child's swimming progresses. During the summer, it's ideal to provide multiple swimming sessions each week to help reinforce skills learned. Some swim schools provide summer intensive sessions that run daily for two weeks. Others provide 2 or three classes per week during the summer. I find that a class once a week is sufficient if you have access to a pool during the summer to allow your child the chance to practice what she has learned and just to play.

Be aware that pool facilities vary from site to site. Some facilities are indoor; some outdoor with a dome; while others are outdoor, exposed to the sun and weather. Some pools are very shallow teaching pools, while some are much deeper. Some pools are heated to 90°F, appropriate for young children who lose body temperature very quickly in the water, while other pools are cooler, appropriate for older kids and adults. It is important that the facility you choose be a good fit with your needs. If you have very young children, choose a pool that is well heated (to 90°F), indoor, or domed, to prevent sun damage to tender baby skin. Shallow pools are wonderful for the very first classes because they help children feel more comfortable and secure. However, shallow pools can also become crutches that impede progress because children depend on their ability to stand up and fail to gain confidence in their ability to swim in deeper water.

When my daughter was three, she learned to do the dog paddle at a deeper pool. A beautiful new indoor teaching pool opened and I switched her to this school, since it was winter and I wanted her to stay warmer. Unfortunately, my daughter's skills and confidence regressed because this pool was shallow and it became a crutch. During the two sessions that she took classes at this pool, she became afraid to go into deeper pools and was afraid to swim on her own. When I switched her back to the previous swim school, her confidence returned very quickly and she was again swimming on her own.

Teaching methods also vary from school to school. Some methods are very gentle and are suitable for sensitive children. However, the gentler methods may take more time to produce results. Other methods are more no-nonsense, with faster progress, but not appropriate for all personalities. As a parent, you know your child and what style works best. So, in your search for swimming classes, consider both the facility and the school's teaching methods. To get a better feel for the teaching methods and approaches, it's a great idea to visit the schools, see the facilities firsthand, and talk to other parents there.

Even within a school, different teachers have different styles. You may not be able to choose teachers at a particular school. Each swimming school has its pros and cons. You must judge what works best for your child.

Local Parks and Recreation Departments, JCCs, and YMCAs offer swimming classes at least in the summer. Your local high school or community colleges may also have swimming instruction, especially during the summer. Don't forget to check out the swim clubs/swim teams section because some of those also have swim schools.

Stanford's summer sports camps cover a huge variety of sports for kids ages 7–18 include swimming, gymnastics, basketball, soccer, rowing, sailing, golf, football, rugby, and many many more. Visit the Web site for details: <www.gostanford.com/camps>.

Swim Schools

Adventure Sports Unlimited
(831) 458-3648; 303 Potrero Street #15, Santa Cruz, CA 95060
<www.asudoit.com>

Aitken's Peninsula Swim School
(650) 366-9211; 1602 Stafford Street, Redwood City, CA 94063
<www.peninsulaswim.com>
Indoor/outdoor pool heated to 90°F.

Almaden Valley Athletic Club (AVAC)

(408) 267-4032; 5400 Camden Avenue, San Jose, CA 95124

<www.avac.us/swim.htm>

Indoor pool heated to 90°F, shallow teaching pool (2 feet deep).

Ann Curtis School Of Swimming

(415) 479-9131; 25 Golden Hinde Boulevard, San Rafael, CA 94903

<www.anncurtis.com>

Bay–O–Vista Swim School

(510) 357-8366; 1881 Astor Drive, San Leandro, CA, 94577

<www.bovswim.com>

Bear Swim School (Ages 4+)

(510) 527-5639; 1563 Solano Avenue #373, Berkeley, CA 94707

<www.bearswimming.com>

Betty Wright Swim Center

(650) 494-1480; 3864 Middlefield Road, Palo Alto, CA 94306

<www.c-a-r.org/swim.html>

Specializes in swimming lessons for kids with developmental or physical disabilities.

Cabrillo Threshers (Ages 4+)

(831) 688-3613; 6500 Soquel Drive, Aptos, CA 95003

<www.cab-threshers.org>

Lessons during the summer only.

California Sports Center

(408) 732-2257; 1283 Sunnyvale-Saratoga Road, Sunnyvale, CA 94087

<www.calsportscenter.com/swimless.htm>

Lessons at the Fremont High School pool.

Centennial Recreation Center

(408) 782-2128; 171 W. Edmundson Avenue, Morgan Hill, CA 95037

Club Sport of San Ramon (Ages 6–18)

(925) 735-8500; 350 Bollinger Canyon Lane, San Ramon, CA 94583
<www.clubsportsr.com>

Club Sport (Ages 5–12)

(510) 226-8500; 46650 Landing Parkway, Fremont, CA 94538
(925) 463-2822; 7090 Johnson Drive, Pleasanton, CA 94588
(925) 938-8700; 2805 Jones Road, Walnut Creek, CA 94597
<www.clubsports.com>

Contra Costa Jewish Community Center

(925) 938-7800 x234; 2071 Tice Valley Boulevard, Walnut Creek, CA 94595
<www.ccjcc.org>
Outdoor 74°F pool. Open May–September.

DACA Swim School (All Ages)

(408) 446-5600; 1080 S. De Anza Boulevard, San Jose, CA 95129
<www.daca.org>
Indoor pool heated to 90°F.

Doug Senz Swim Lessons

(925) 356-2226; Pleasant Hill, CA
Starts in February.

Fremont Hills Country Club Swim School

650) 948-8261, ext 207; (650) 948-8261
12889 Viscaino Place, Los Altos Hills, CA 94022
<www.fremonthills.com>
Summer program.

Fremont Swim School/American Swim Academy

Fremont: (510) 657-7946; 42400 Blacow Road, Fremont, CA 94539
Livermore: (925) 373-7946; 2821 Old First Street, Livermore, CA 94550
Newark: (510) 794-7946; 37400 Cedar Boulevard, Newark, CA 94560
Dublin: (925)479-7946; 6948 Sierra Court, Dublin, CA 94568
<www.fremontswimschool.com>; <www.americanswimacademy.com>

Golden Gateway Tennis & Swim Club

(415) 616-8802; 370 Drumm Street, San Francisco, CA 94111
<www.ggtsc.com>

Happy Fish Swim School

(510) 226-SWIM; 4831 Davenport Place, Fremont, CA 94538
<www.swimhappyfish.com>

Harriet Plummer Aquatic School

(925) 943-7331; 1150 Nogales Street, Lafayette, CA 94549
<www.harrietplummer.com>

Harvey West Swimming Pool

(831) 420-6140; 275 Harvey West Boulevard, Santa Cruz, CA 95060
<www.santacruzparksandrec.com/>
Classes offered through the Santa Cruz Parks and Recreation
Department.

Highlands Swim School
Dolphins Swim Team

(650) 341-4251; 1851 Lexington Avenue, San Mateo, CA 94402
<www.highlandsrec.com>

Jim Booth Swim School

(831) 722-3500; 25 Penny Lane, Watsonville, CA 95076
<www.jimboothswimschool.com>

Jim Gorman's Swimming & Diving Instruction
Ladera Oaks

(650) 854-3101; 3249 Alpine Road, Portola Valley, CA 94028
<www.laderaoaks.com>
Pool heated to mid-80°F.

Joinville Swim Center

(650) 522-7460; 2111 Kehoe Avenue, San Mateo, CA 94403
<www.cityofsanmateo.org/dept/parks>

Junipero Serra High School: Swim School

(650) 345-7331; (650) 345-8207; 451 W 20th Avenue, San Mateo, CA 94403
<www.serrahs.com>

Summer program.

Kona Kai Swim & Racquet Club

(408)984-8880; 680 Hubbard Avenue, Santa Clara, CA 95051
<www.konakaiclub.com/swimming.html>

Le Petit Baleen

(650) 588-7665; 434 San Mateo Avenue, San Bruno, CA 94066
(650) 726-3676; 775 Main Street, Half Moon Bay, CA 94019
<www.swimlpb.com>

Livermore Valley Tennis Club (6 months+)

(925) 443-7700; 2000 Arroyo Road, Livermore, CA 94550
www.lvtc.com

Swim classes for children more than 6-months old. Tennis classes for children from 3 to 18 years old.

Los Gatos Swim & Racquet Club

(408) 356-2136; 14700 Oka Road, Los Gatos, CA 95032
<www.lgsrc.com>

Outdoor pool heated to 82°F.

Menlo Swim and Sport

(650) 328-7945; 501 Laurel Street, Menlo Park, CA 94025
<www.menloswim.com>

Mission San Jose Aquatics

(510) 226-6752; P.O. Box 3079, Fremont, CA 94539
<www.swimmsja.org>

Summer program only. Uses the Ohlone College Pool at 43600 Mission Blvd. in Fremont and the American High School Pool at 36300 Fremont Blvd. in Fremont.

Newark City Silliman Family Aquatic Center

(510) 739-2620; 6800 Mowry Avenue, Newark, CA 94560

<www.newark.org>

Through Newark Parks and Recreation Department.

Rafael Racquet & Swim Club

(415) 456-5522; 95 Racquet Club Drive, San Rafael, CA 94901

<www.rafaelracquetclub.com/swimlessons>

Summer program.

San Ramon Olympic Pool and Aquatic Park

(925) 973-3240; 9900 Broadmoor Drive, San Ramon, CA 94583

<www.sanramonrecguide.com> or <www.ci.san-ramon.ca.us/parks/index.htm>

Once on the Web site, choose the Parks and Recreation Activities Guide and select the appropriate brochure for the season. Outdoor pool heated to 80°F, open spring–fall. Birthday parties, too.

Santa Clara Swim Club

Santa Clara International Swim Center

(408) 246-5003; 2625 Patricia Drive, Santa Clara, CA 95051

<www.santaclaraswimclub.org>

Santa Cruz Swim School

(831) 426-7946; P.O. Box 455, Santa Cruz, CA

<www.santacruzswimschool.com>

Summer program held at the Elks Lodge.

Sherman Swim School

(925) 283-2100; 1075 Carol Lane, Lafayette, CA 94549

<www.shermanswim.com>

Summer session begins in mid-June, Mon–Fri 3–7pm.

Strawberry Canyon Recreation Area Aquatics

UC Berkeley (summer program)

(510) 643-2267; (510) 643-4397

Strawberry Canyon Center: 1 Centennial Drive, Berkeley, CA 94720

Sue's Swim School
(925) 837-2428; 2701 Stone Valley Road, Alamo, CA 94507
<www.sueswimschool.com>

Strawberry Recreation Center
(415) 383-1610; 118 E. Strawberry Drive, Mill Valley, CA 94941
<http://strawberry.marin.org/aquatics.html>

Taft Swim School
(650) 349-7946; 57 E 40th Avenue, San Mateo, CA 94403

Terra Linda Recreation Center
City of San Rafael Parks and Recreation Department
(415) 485-3344; 670 Del Ganado Road, San Rafael, CA
<http://eplay.livelifelocally.com>

Water Babies Swim School
(408) 377-4626; 973 Apricot Avenue, Campbell, CA 95008
<www.waterbabiesswim.com>
Outdoor pool: March–September season.

San Francisco Parks and Recreation Swimming
<www.parks.sfgov.org/site/recpark_page.asp?id=1867>
Call the senior swimming instructor of each pool for specific dates and
times. See Web site for schedule and hours.
Cost: $5/adult (18 and older)/swim, $34/10-swim scrip ticket. $2 /child
(17 and younger). Swim Lessons: $1 plus regular admission fee.

Balboa Park & Pool
(415) 337-4701; San Jose Ave and Havelock, San Francisco, CA 94112
Indoor pool at 80°F.

Coffman Pool (reopens fall 2007)
(415) 337-4702; Visitacion and Hahn Streets, San Francisco, CA
Indoor pool at 80°–85°F.

Garfield Pool
(415) 695-5001; 26th and Harrison Streets, San Francisco, CA
Indoor pool at 80°–85°F.

Hamilton Pool
(415) 292-2001; Geary Boulevard and Steiner Street, San Francisco, CA
Indoor pool at 81°F.

Martin Luther King Jr. Pool
(415) 822-2807; 3rd Avenue and Carroll Street, San Francisco, CA
Two indoor pools at 80°F.

Mission Pool
(415) 695-5002; 19th Street and Linda, San Francisco, CA
Ooutdoor pool, open in the summer only.

North Beach Pool
(415) 391-0407; Lombard and Mason Street, San Francisco, CA
Indoor pool at 80°F.

Rossi Pool
(415) 666-7014; Arguello and Anza Streets, San Francisco, CA
Indoor pool at 80°F.

Sava Pool
(415) 753-7000; 19th Avenue and Wawona Street, San Francisco, CA
Indoor pool at 80°F.

Swim Clubs & Teams

While some swim clubs and swim teams focus on competitions, many have noncompetitive programs as well. Many swim clubs/teams also provide swimming lessons for young infants and preschoolers. Don't overlook these for your young child just because they sound competitive. Each club or team has its own philosophy, so check out the Web sites, call, and visit to get a feel for the team and to see if it's a good fit for your needs.

The United States Swimming Teams are associated with the U.S. National Swim Team. To find more swim teams, visit the U.S. National Swim Team Web site: <www.usswim.org>.

Alameda Island Aquatics (Ages 5+)
(510) 865-5484; 215 Beach Road, Alameda, CA 94502

Burlingame Aquatic Club (Ages 6+)

(650) 558-1298; Burlingame Aquatic Center: PO Box 281, Burlingame, CA
<www.burlingameaquatics.com>
Uses the Burlingame High School pool. Burlingame Aquatic Center:
851 Oak Grove Avenue, Burlingame, CA 94010.

Cabrillo Threshers Swim Team

(831) 688-3613; P.O. Box 1686, Soquel, CA 95073
<www.cab-threshers.org>
Uses the Cabrillo College pool at 6500 Soquel Drive, Aptos, CA

Courtside Swim Team (Ages 5+)

(408) 395-7111; 14675 Winchester Boulevard, Los Gatos, CA 95032
<www.courtsideclub.com/web/site/benefits/kids/aquatics.jsp#team>

DACA (De Anza Cupertino Aquatics)

(408) 253-SWIM (7946); P.O. Box 436 , Cupertino, CA 95015
<www.daca.org>
Uses the De Anza College and Saratoga High School pools.

Daly City Dolphins Aquatics Club

Giammona Pool: 131 Westmoor Avenue, Daly City, CA 94015
<www.dalycitydolphins.org>

East Bay Silver Dolphins Swim Team

(510) 799-8229; 2001 Refugio Valley Road, Hercules, CA 94547
<www.ci.hercules.ca.us>

Foothill Tennis and Swim Club

(650) 493-0920; 3351 Miranda Avenue, Palo Alto, CA 94304
<www.foothills-club.org>

Fremont Area Swim Team (F.A.S.T.) (Ages 6+)

(510) 226-SWIM; 4831 Davenport Place, Fremont, CA 94538
<www.swimhappyfish.com/swim_team.htm>
Summer program. Uses the outdoor Washington High School pool.

Gilroy Gators Swim Team

(408) 847-2424 #2261; 777 First Street, PMB 183, Gilroy, CA 95020
<www.gilroygators.org>
Swims at the Gilroy High School Pool at 750 W. 10th Street, Gilroy, CA 95020

Golden Bear Swim Club (Ages 4+)

(510) 527-5639; 1563 Solano Avenue #373, Berkeley, CA 94707
<www.bearswimming.com>

Livermore Blue Dolphins

(925)-447-SWIM; 6546 Village Drive, Livermore, CA 94551
<www.dolphinswimming.org>

Los Altos Mountain View Aquatics Club

(650) 599-2213; P.O. Box 1269, Los Altos, CA 94023
<www.lamvac.org>
Uses the Foothill College Pool: 12345 El Monte Road, Los Altos Hills; Eagle Pool: off Church St. and S. Shoreline Blvd; and Rengstorff Pool at Rengstorff Park: Crisanto Ave and S. Rengstorff Avenue.

Los Gatos Swim Club

(408) 356-2136; 14700 Oka Road, Los Gatos, CA 95032
<www.lgsrc.com>

Lynbrook Aquatics

(408) 377-3020; 3130 Jennifer Way, San Jose, CA 95124
<www.lynbrookaquatics.com>
Lynbrook High School pool: 1280 Johnson Ave, San Jose, CA 95129
Kona Kai Swim and Racquet Club: 680 Hubbard Ave, Santa Clara, CA

Marin Pirates Swim Team

(415) 892-2269: Indian Valley Campus, Novato; (415) 756-0678: College of Marin, Kentfield; (415) 455-5952: Cañon Club, Fairfax

Mavericks Swimming
(877) 410-1608; P.O. Box 521, Half Moon Bay, CA 94019
<www.mavericks-swim.org>

Mid Peninsula Mariners
(650)235-5072;
Joinville Swim Center: 2111 Kehoe Avenue, San Mateo, CA 94403
<www.eteamz.com/mpm>

Mission San Jose Aquatics
(510) 657-MSJA; P.O. Box 3079, Fremont, CA 94539
<www.swimmsja.org>

Montclair Swim Club
(510) 339-8013; 1901 Woodhaven Way, Oakland, CA 94611

Morgan Hill Swim Club
(408) 782-0088; 16200 Condit Road, Morgan Hill, CA 95037
<www.morganhillmakos.com>

Napa Valley Swim Team
(707) 257-SWIM; College: 2277 Napa-Vallejo Highway, Napa, CA 94558
<www.napavalleyswim.com>

Oakland Barracuda Aquatics
(510) 451-2832; Mail: 4200 Park Boulevard, #121, Oakland, CA 94602
Live Oak Pool: 1055 MacArthur Boulevard, Oakland, CA 94610
<www.oaklandbarracudas.org>

Orinda Aquatics
(408) 268-9752; Campolindo High/Soda Aquatics Center:
300 Moraga Road, Moraga, CA 94556
<www.teamunify.com/Home.jsp?team=oapb>

Osprey Aquatics (6+)
(408) 268-9752; 757 Harry Road, San Jose, CA 95120

Pacific Coast Marlins Swim Club

(415) 456-1153; Rafael Racquet Club: 95 Racquet Club Drive, San Rafael, CA
<www.pacificcoastmarlins.com>

Palo Alto Stanford Aquatics

(650) 328-6536; 526 Waverley Street, Palo Alto, CA 94301
<www.paloaltoswimclub.org>

Peninsula Covenant Aquatics Swim Team

(650) 364-6272; 3623 Jefferson Avenue, Redwood City, CA 94062
<www.pcaswimteam.com>

Piedmont Swim Team

(510) 812-4449; (510) 655-5163; 777 Magnolia Avenue, Piedmont, CA 94611
<www.piedmontswimteam.org>

Pleasanton Seahawks Swim Team

(925) 847-7946; P.O. Box 1675, Pleasanton, CA 94566
<www.pleasantonseahawks.org>

Santa Clara Swim Club

(408) 246-5050; 2625 Patricia Drive, Santa Clara, CA 95051
<www.santaclaraswimclub.org>

Santa Cruz County Aquatics

(831) 246-2059; SCCA, P.O. Box 1616, Soquel, CA 95073
<www.santacruzcountyaquatics.com>

Santa Rosa Neptune Swim Club

(707) 579-9502 (Santa Rosa); (707) 433-1109 (Healdsburg);
P.O. Box 317, Santa Rosa, CA 95402

Silicon Valley Aquatics Association (SVAA) Club

(408) 227-5884; Silver Creek Office: (408) 239-0504;
P.O. Box 36205, San Jose, CA 95159
<www.siliconvalleyaquaticassociation.org/introprogram.htm>
Uses Gunderson High School pool: 622 Gaundabert Lane, San Jose, CA

Sunnyvale Swim Club

(408) 235-9874; P.O. Box 2580, Sunnyvale, CA 94087
<www.sunn.org>
Uses the Fremont High School & Sunnyvale Middle School pools.

Terrapin Swim Team (Ages 5+)

(925) 680-8372; 4180 Treat Boulevard, Suite. K, Concord, CA 94518
<www.terrapinswim.com>

Walnut Creek Aquabears

(925) 939-5990; P.O. Box 3462, Walnut Creek, CA 94598
<http://aquabears.org>
Uses Clarke Memorial Swim Center at Heather Farm Park.

West Coast Aquatics

(408) 259-4522; P.O. Box 32188, San Jose, CA 95152
<www.westcoastaquatics.org>
Uses the Independence High School and the Silver Creek High School
pools.

Dancing

Dance is a great way to help young children develop motor coordination. It also helps them develop an understanding of rhythm and exposes
them to the idea that musical rhythm and motion can go together. Since
performance is part of a dance curriculum, don't overlook these dance
companies as a wonderful source of dance performances. For performance
schedule and additional information, visit the Web sites or call.

Dance Schools

For more dance studios: <www.dancemastersofcalifornia.org/studios. htm>.

Axis Dance Company (Ages 5+)
(510) 625-0110; 1428 Alice Street, Suite 200, Oakland, CA 94612
<www.axisdance.org>

Beaudoins School Of Dance (Ages 3+)
(650) 326-2184; 464 Colorado Avenue, Palo Alto, CA 94306
<www.beaudoins-studio.com>
Tap, ballet.

Branham Dance Center (Ages 3+)
(408) 269-1363; 1088Branham Lane, San Jose, CA 95136
<www.thebranhamdancecenter.com>
Tap, jazz, ballet, hip-hop, modern, and lyrical.

California Academy of Performing Arts (Ages 2+)
(925) 376-2454; P.O. Box 6147, Moraga, CA 94570
Studio: 370 Park Street, Suite E & F, Moraga, CA 94556
<www.capadance.net>
Ballet, jazz, tap, and hip-hop.

Center Stage Dance Co.
(408) 723-2623; 1095 Malone Road, San Jose, CA

Dance 10 Dancers (Ages 3+)
(510) 339-3345; Studio: (510) 522-5678;
900 Santa Clara Avenue, Alameda, CA 94501
<www.dance10.org>
Ballet, jazz, hip-hop, tap, lyrical, yoga, and musical theater.

Dance Academy USA (Ages 2+)

(408) 257-3211; 21269 Stevens Creek Boulevard #600, Cupertino, CA 95014
<www.danceacademyusa.com>
Ballet, jazz, hip-hop, tap, lyrical, hula, musical theater, and martial arts.

Dance Affair (Ages 3+)

(408) 243-4834; 850 North Winchester Avenue, San Jose, CA 95128
<www.thedanceaffair.com>
Hip-hop, jazz, tap, and musical theater.

Dance Attack! (Ages 2+)

(408) 356-6456; 14110 Blossom Hill Road, Los Gatos, CA 95032
<www.danceattackstudios.com>
Ballet, jazz, hip-hop, tap, break dancing, modern, voice, and acting lessons offered.

Dance Attack! LLC (Ages 2+)

(408) 245-5432; 120 Carroll Street, Sunnyvale, CA 94086
<www.danceattack.com>
Ballet, tap, jazz, lyrical, and hip-hop. Has some of the same teachers as Dance Attack! Los Gatos but different owners.

Dance Arts Project (Ages 4+)

(510) 5212270; 1201 Chestnut Street, Alameda, CA 94501
<www.danceartsproject.com>

Dance Connection (Ages 3+)

(650) 322-7032; 4000 Middlefield Road, Palo Alto CA 94303
<www.danceconnectionpaloalto.com>
Jazz, ballet, hip-hop, tap instruction. *Nutcracker* performance in early December. There's a tea party prior to the performance to help the little ones understand the story.

Dance Effects (Ages 3+)

(408) 374-6123; 58 E. Campbell Avenue, Campbell, CA 95008

Dance with Miss Tilly (Ages 3+)

(415) 923-9965; 5499 California Street, San Francisco, CA 94118
Enroll early; long wait lists.

Dance with Sherry Studio (Ages 4+)

(415) 499-1986; 4140 Redwood Highway, Suite 8, San Rafael, CA 94903
<www.dancewithsherrystudio.com>
Tap, jazz, hip-hop, break dance, and musical theater. Birthday parties.

Dance Mission Theatre (Ages 2½+)

(415) 273-4633 x 4; 3316 24th Street, San Francisco, CA 94110
<www.dancemission.com>

Danspace (Ages 3½+)

(510) 420-0920; 473 Hudson Street, Oakland, CA 94618
<www.danspace.com>

East Bay Dance Center (Ages 3+)

(510)336-3262; 1318 Glenfield Avenue, Oakland, CA 94602
<www.eastbaydancecenter.org>
Ballet, tap, jazz, and hip-hop.

Happy Feet

(415) 381-0811; 15 Montford Avenue, Mill Valley, CA 94941
Ballet, tap, jazz.

Imagine Performing Arts

(925) 551-0200; 6620 Dublin Boulevard, Dublin, CA 94568
<www.imagineperformingarts.org>

Offers classes and camps in acting, singing, improv, and dance. Birthday parties offered.

Jazz N Taps (Ages 3+)

(925) 484-0678; 1270-A Quarry Lane, Pleasanton, CA 94566
<www.jazzntaps.com>
Ballet, tap, jazz, and hip-hop

Jensen Performing Arts (Ages 2+)

(408) 262-0770; 1491 N. Milpitas Boulevard, Milpitas, CA 95305

<www.jpadance.com>

Ballet, tap, jazz, lyrical, tumbling, voice/song/dance, TnT Dancers.

Kids 'N Dance (Ages 14 mos+)

(925) 284-7388; 3369 Mt. Diablo Boulevard, Lafayette, CA 94549

(510) 531-4400; 3841 MacArthur Boulevard, Oakland, CA 94610

<www.kidsndance.com>

Ballet, tap, jazz, hip-hop, gymnastics, and musical theater.

Luna Kids Dance (Ages 3+)

(510) 644-3629;

Julia Morgan Center for the Arts: 2640 College Avenue, (Studio C),Berkeley, CA

Mills College: 5000 MacAurthur Boulevard, Oakland, CA

Knights of Columbus Hall: 167 Turnstead Avenue, San Anselmo, CA

<www.lunakidsdance.com>

Martis Dance School (Ages 3+)

(650) 947-8699; 1140 Riverside Drive, Los Altos, CA 94024;

1334 S. Mary Avenue, Sunnyvale, CA

<www.martidance.com>

Menlo Park Academy of Dance (Ages 2+)

(650) 323-5292; 1163 El Camino Real, Menlo Park, CA 94025

<www.mpaod.com>

Ballet, tap, jazz, tumbling hip-hop, and voice.

Mission Dance & Performing Arts (Ages 3+)

(510) 651-2783; 42068 Osgood Road, Fremont, CA 94539

<www.missiondancefremont.com>

Ballet, break dance, hip-hop, jazz, tap, lyrical, and more.

Presidio Dance Theatre Academy (Ages 3+)

(415) 561-3958; 1158 Gorgas Road, San Francisco, CA 94129

San Juan School of Dance (Ages 3+)

(650) 948-6287; 140 3rd Street, Los Altos, CA 94022
(408) 267-5525; 1557 Meridian Avenue, San Jose, CA 95125
<www.sanjuandance.com>
Ballet, pointe, tap, jazz, lyrical, song and dance.

Saratoga School of Dance (Ages 1½+)

(408) 866-4691; 18778 Cox Avenue, Saratoga, CA 95070
<www.saratogaschoolofdance.com>
Ballet, tap, and jazz.

Shawl–Anderson Dance Center (Ages 1+)

(510) 654-5921; 2704 Alcatraz Avenue, Berkeley CA 94705
<www.shawl-anderson.org>
Ballet, jazz, and modern dance classes.

Stapleton School of Performing Arts (Ages 1+)

(415) 454-5759; P.O. Box 331, San Anselmo, CA 94979
Main Studio: 118 Greenfield Avenue, San Anselmo, CA 94960
Satellite Studio: 2240B Fourth Street, San Rafael, CA
<www.stapletonschool.org>
Ballet, hip-hop, boys' and teen classes offered.

Valley Dance Theatre (Ages 2+)

(925) 243-0925; 243-0927 Box Office
2247 Suite B, Second Street, Livermore, CA 94550
<www.valleydancetheatre.com>
Ballet and modern dance classes.

Yoko's Dance & Performing Arts Company (Ages 3+)

(510) 651-STAR (7827); 42400 Blacow Road, Fremont, CA 94539
<www.yokosdance.com>
Tap, jazz, lyrical, hip-hop, and ballet.

Ballet Schools

Academy of American Ballet (Ages 3+)
(650) 366-1222; 275A Linden Street, Redwood City, CA 94061
<www.americanballet.com>

Academy of Classical Ballet (Ages 5+)
(510) 452-5140; 452 Santa Clara Avenue, Oakland, CA 94610
<www.acb-oakland.com>

Alonzo King's LINES Ballet
(415) 863-3040 ext. 248; 26 Seventh Street, 5th Floor, San Francisco, CA 94103
<www.linesballet.org>

Ballet San Jose Silicon Valley School (Ages 4+)
(408) 288-2820, ext. 223; 40 North First Street, San Jose, CA 95113
<www.balletsanjose.org>

The Open Division for children ages 4 to 14 has classes once a week and Saturday classes. The Adult/Teen Division is on a drop-in basis. The Professional Division is for students 8–18 years old who are interested in professional ballet.

Berkeley Ballet Theater (Ages 2+)
(510) 843-4687; (510) 843-4689; 2640 College Avenue, Berkeley, CA 94704
<www.berkeleyballet.org>

Berkeley City Ballet (Ages 4+)
(510) 841-8913; 1800 Dwight Way, Berkeley, CA 94703
<www.berkeleycityballet.org>

City Ballet School (Ages 4+)
(415) 626-8878; 32 Otis Street, San Francisco, CA 94103

Conservatory of Classical Ballet (Ages 3½+)
(510) 568-7728; 1035 MacArthur Boulevard, San Leandro, CA 94577
<www.conservatoryofballet.com>

Contra Costa Ballet Centre (Ages 3½+)
(925) 935-7984; 2040 North Broadway, Walnut Creek CA 94596
<www.contracostaballet.org>

Los Gatos Ballet (Ages 3+)
(408) 399-7577; 16 Lyndon Avenue, Los Gatos, CA 95030
<www.lgballetpilates.com/ballet>

Marin Ballet Center for Dance (Ages 3+)
(415) 453-5894; 100 Elm Street, San Rafael, CA 94901
<www.marinballet.org>

Marin Dance Theatre (Ages 3+)
St. Vincent's School Campus
(415) 499-8891; One St. Vincent Drive, San Rafael, CA 94903
<www.mdt.org>

Mountain View Ballet Company & School/Western Ballet School (Ages 4+)
(650) 968-4455; 914 N. Rengstorff Avenue, Mountain View, CA 94043
<www.westernballet.org>

Pacific Ballet Academy (Ages 3½–15)
(650) 969-4614; Mailing: P.O. Box 765, Los Altos, CA 94023
Campus: 295B Polaris Avenue, Mountain View, CA
<www.pacificballet.org>

Professional Ballet School (Ages 3+)
(650) 598-0796; 425 Harbor Blvd. #3, Belmont, CA 94002

San Francisco Ballet School (Ages 6+)
(415) 553-4642; 455 Franklin Street, San Francisco, CA 94102
<www.sfballet.org/school>

Santa Clara Ballet School (Ages 3+)
(408) 247-9178; 3086 El Camino Real, Santa Clara, CA 95051
<www.santaclaraballet.org>

Gymnastics

For toddlers and young preschoolers, playgrounds at the local parks are probably sufficient. During winter, when it's cold and rainy, you might want to consider the Gymboree Play, Junior Gym, Little Gym, or My Gym Programs.

Gymboree Play Programs (Ages <5)
1-877-4-GYMWEB (1-877-449-6932)
<www.playandmusic.com/b2c/customer/programIndex.jsp >

(925) 685-7773; Willows: 1975 Diamond Boulevard #C-130, Concord, CA 94520
(510) 528-3002; 700 El Cerrito Plaza, El Cerrito, CA 94530
(510) 739-6150; 39138 Fremont Hub #221, Fremont, CA 94538
(925) 283-4896; 3482 Mt. Diablo Boulevard, Lafayette, CA 94549
(650) 949-5798; 664 Los Altos Rancho, Los Altos, CA 94024
(415) 383-9771; 329 Strawberry Village Shopping Center, Mill Valley, CA 94941
(510) 834-0982; 3433 Lakeshore Avenue, Oakland, CA 94610
(925) 249-0006; Oakhills: 5460-9 Sunol Boulevard, Pleasanton, CA 94566
(650) 364-3420; 2531 El Camino Real, Redwood City, CA 94061
(415) 242-5637; Lakeshore: 1525 Sloat Boulevard, San Francisco, CA 94132
(408) 629-5813; Oakridge: 925 Blossom Hill Road #1169, San Jose, CA 95123
(408) 378-5318; 1600 Saratoga Avenue, #517, San Jose, CA 95129
(650) 358-9943; Laurelwood: 3180 Campus Drive, San Mateo, CA 94403
(925) 866-8315; 3191-A Crow Canyon Place, San Ramon, CA 94583

Junior Gym (Ages 6 months+)
(650) 548-9901; 101 South B Street, San Mateo, CA

Parent/toddler classes for babies 6 months–3 years old, gymnastics classes for kids 3–10 years old, sports skills class for kids 4+, cheerleading skills for girls 5+, yoga for kids 6+, and self-defense for kids 5+.

The Little Gym (Ages 4 months–12 years)
<www.thelittlegym.com>
(650) 596-0550; 390 El Camino Real, Unit F, Belmont, CA 94002
<www.tlgbelmontca.com>
(925) 736-3141; 3490 Blackhawk Plaza Circle, Danville, CA 94506
<www.tlgdanvilleca.com>
(408) 262-3333; 305 S. Abbott Avenue, Milpitas, CA 95035
<www.tlgmilpitasca.com>
(408) 776-8125; 15750 Vineyard Boulevard, Suite 190, Morgan Hill, CA 95037
<www.tlgmorganhillca.com>
(650) 961-8100; 1910-F West El Camino Real, Mt View, CA 94040
<www.tlglosaltosmtviewca.com>
(510) 794-6660; 5700 Newpark Mall Road, Newark, CA 94560
<www.tlgnewarkfremontca.com>
(925) 798-1800; 115 Crescent Drive, Pleasant Hill, CA 94523
<tlgpleasanthillca.com>
(408) 723-7222; 1375 Blossom Hill Road, Suite 45, San Jose, CA 95118
<www.tlgssanjoseca.com>
(408) 366-2222; 5357 Prospect Road, San Jose, CA 95129
<www.tlgsanjoseca.com>
(415) 289-0600; 170 Donahue Street, Sausalito, CA 94965
<www.tlgsouthmarinca.com>

MiniGym Explorations (Ages 8 months–8 years)
(408) 559-4616; 559-3631; 4115 Jacksol Drive, San Jose, CA 95124
<www.minigymexplorations.com>

Parent/me classes for babies 8 months–3 years old; "Exploragym Preschool" for children 3–4 years old; and summer camps for children 3½ –8 years old. Birthday parties available for kids up to 7 years old.

My Gym Children's Fitness Center (Ages 3 months–9 years)
<www.my-gym.com>
<www.my-gym.com/franchisee.asp?gymid=328> Marin County
(650) 330-1760; 2655 Middlefield Road, Palo Alto, CA 94306
(707) 769-0900; Petaluma, CA

(415) 643-5500; 901 Minnesota Street, San Francisco, CA 94107
(408) 279-9700; 1262 S. Bascom Avenue, San Jose, CA 95128
(925) 244-1171; 180 Market Place, San Ramon, CA 94583
(707) 575-4975; 3267 Airway Drive, Santa Rosa, CA 95403
(925) 952-9791; 2256 Oak Grove Road, Walnut Creek, CA 94598

Gymnastics and exercise incorporating dance, music, and games. Birthday parties are offered also.

Traditionally the following schools catered to the older child. However, these schools have now expanded coverage to the toddler and preschool crowd. These school are part of the USA Gymnastics association: <www.usa-gymnastics.org>.

AcroSports (Ages 1½+)
(415) 665-2276; 639 Frederick Street, San Francisco, CA 94117
<www.acrosports.org>
Offers circus arts, too.

Airborne Gymnastics (Ages 1+)
(408) 986-8226; 2250 Martin Avenue, Santa Clara, CA 95050
<www.airborne-gymnastics.com>

Almaden Valley Gymnastics Club (Ages 1+)
(408) 268-1272; 19600 Almaden Road, San Jose, CA 95120
<www.almadengymnastics.com>

American Gymnastics Club (Ages 1+)
(415) 731-1400; 2520 Judah Street, San Francisco, CA 94122
<www.americangymnasticsclub.com>

Bay Aerials Gymnastics (Ages 1+)
(510) 651-5870; 4883 Davenport Place, Fremont, CA 94538
<www.bayaerials.com>

California Gymnastics Academy (Ages 2+)
(925) 245-0331; 180 Wright Brothers Avenue, Livermore, CA 94551

California Sports Center (Ages 1½+)

(408) 360-9400; 100 Great Oaks Boulevard, Suite 150, San Jose, CA 95119
(408) 269-5437 (KIDS); 832 Malone Road, San Jose, CA 95125
(408) 280-5437; 336 Race Street, San Jose, CA 95126
(408) 264-5439; 3001 Ross Avenue, San Jose, CA 95124

<www.calsportscenter.com>

Also offers classes through Sunnyvale and the Santa Clara Parks and Recreation Departments.

Champions Academy (Ages 3+)

(408) 776-1858; 18855 Adams Court, Morgan Hill, CA 95037
<www.causa.us>

Demaray's Gymnastics Academy (Ages 1½+)

(510) 661-0576; 40511 Albrae Street, Fremont, CA 94538
<www.demarays.com>

Diablo Gymnastics School (Ages 1+)

(925) 820-6885; 2411-J Old Crow Canyon Road, San Ramon, CA 94583
<www.diablogym.com>

Encore Gymnastics (Ages 1+)

(925) 932-1033 ; Mail: P.O. Box 30113, Walnut Creek, CA 94598
999 Bancroft Road, Concord, CA 94518
(925) 240-1133; 2490 Sand Creek Road, Brentwood, CA
<www.encoregym.com>

Rock climbing also.

Gold Star Gymnastics Academy (Ages 1+)

(650) 694-7827; 240 South Whisman Road, Mountain View, CA 94041
<www.goldstargym.com>

Golden Bear Gymnastics (Ages 1½+)

(510) 642-9821; UC Berkeley: 25 Sports Lane #4428, Berkeley, CA 94720
<www.oski.org>

Available for birthday parties.

Golden Gate Gymnastics (Ages 1½+)

(925) 674-9683; 1441 C Franquette Avenue, Concord, CA 94520
<http://goldengategymnastics.com>

Gymfinity Gymnastics (Ages 1+)

(925) 960-9440; 1001 Shannon Court, Suite A, Livermore, CA 94550
<www.gymfinitygym.com>

Gymtowne Gymnastics (Ages 1+)

(650) 589-3733; 300 Piedmont Avenue, Ste 604, San Bruno, CA 94066
(650) 563-9426; 850 Airport Street, Unit 7, Moss Beach, CA 94038
<www.gymtowne.com>

GymWorld Academy (Ages 1½+)

(415) 482-8580; 555 E. Francisco Boulevard #19, San Rafael, CA 94901
<www.gymworldmarin.com>

Head Over Heels (Ages 1½+)

(510) 655-1265; 4701 Doyle Street, Building F, Emeryville, CA 94608
<www.hohgymnastics.com>

Also has dance program and a circus program for kids.

Liberty Gymnastics Training Center (Ages 1½+)

(925) 687-8009; 2330 A Bates Avenue, Concord, CA 94520
<www.libertygymtrainingcenter.com>

Livermore Gymnastics Center (Ages 1+)

(925) 371-1688; 4039 First Street, Livermore, CA 94550
<www.livgym.com>

Marin Elite Gymnastics Academy (Ages 2+) (MEGA)

(415) 257-MEGA; 72 Woodland Avenue, San Rafael, CA 94901

Menlo Park Gymnastics (Ages 1+)

(650) 330-2224; 501 Laurel Street, Menlo Park, CA 94025
<www.menlopark.org/departments/com/gymnastics.html>

San Francisco Gymnastics (Ages 1+)

(415) 561-6260; P.O. Box 29427, San Francisco, CA 94129
920 Mason Street, The Presidio, San Francisco, CA 94129
<www.sanfranciscogymnastics.com>

San Rafael Gymnastics Club (Ages 1½+)

(415) 491-1290; 129 Carlos Drive, San Rafael, CA 94903
<www.srgym.com>
Available for birthday parties. Cheerleading program.

Santa Cruz Gymnastics Center (Ages 1½+)

(831) 462-0655; 2750-B Soquel Avenue, Santa Cruz, CA 95062
<www.scgym.com>

Santa Rosa Gymnastics Center (Ages 1+)

(707) 525-1720; 2210 Bluebell Drive, Santa Rosa, CA 95403
<www.srgymnastics.com>

Top Flight Gymnastics (Ages 1½+)

(510) 796-3547; 5127 Mowry Avenue, Fremont, CA 94538
<www.topflightfremont.com>

Twisters Gym

(650) 967-5581; 2639 Terminal Boulevard, Mountain View, CA 94043
<www.twistersgym.com>

West Coast Olympic Gymnastics Academy (Ages 1½+)

(925) 846-1010; 1056-B Serpentine Lane, Pleasanton, CA 94566

West Valley Gymnastics School (Ages 1 +)
(408) 374-8692; 1190 Dell Avenue #1, Campbell, CA 95008
<www.wvgs.com>

Ice Skating

Ice skating has become an extremely popular sport in recent years. It is a wonderful summertime activity to escape from the heat. It is also a great birthday party destination. Be advised that public skating sessions vary from facility to facility, so plan ahead; get information on public sessions to avoid disappointment prior to your outing. For skating classes, don't forget to check your local Parks and Recreation Departments, as their programs may provide better times or values than participating directly with the facility. Ice skating classes are typically for kids 3 years and older.

Belmont Iceland
(650) 592-0533; 815 Old County Road, Belmont, CA 94002
<www.belmonticeland.com>
Admission includes skate rental: $7/adult, $6/youth 17 & under, $4/child 4 & under, $3/skate rental only.

Berkeley Iceland
(510) 647-1620; 2727 Milvia Street, Berkeley, CA 94703
<www.berkeleyiceland.com/eastbay/berkeley>
Admission includes skate rental: $7/adult, $6/youth 17 & under, $4/child 4 & under, $3/skate rental only.

Dublin Iceland
(925) 829-4445; 7212 San Ramon Road, Dublin, CA 94568
<www.dubliniceland.com/eastbay/dublin>
Admission includes skate rental: $7/adult, $6/youth 17 & under, $4/child 4 & under, $3/skate rental only.

Ice Center, Cupertino
(408) 446-2906; 10123 N. Wolfe Road, Cupertino, CA 95014
<www.icecenter.net/cupertino>

$10/admission includes skate rental, $7/admission only, $5/senior admission and rental, $4/skate rental only.

Ice Center, San Mateo
(650) 574-1616; 2202 Bridgepointe Parkway, San Mateo, CA 94404
<www.icecenter.net/sanmateo>

$10/admission includes skate rental, $7/admission only, $5/senior admission and rental, $4/skate rental only.

Ice Oasis
(650) 364-8090; 3140 Bay Road, Redwood City, CA 94063
<www.iceoasis.com>

$8/person 13 & older; $7/child 12 and under, $7/senior; $3/skate rental.

Kristi Yamaguchi Embarcadero Center Ice Rink (Outdoor)
Embarcadero Center in Justin Herman Plaza
(415) 956-2688; 1 Market Street, San Francisco, CA 94111
<www.embarcaderocenter.com/ec/attractions/rink_details.html>

Open only November–January each year. Sun–Thur: 10am–10pm; Fri–Sat: 10am–11:30pm. 90-minute public skate sessions begin on every even hour starting at 10am. Parking is validated up to four hours after 5pm on weekdays and after 10am on weekends.

Cost: Monday until Friday 6pm:$7/adult, $3.50/child 10 and under, $3.5/skate rental only. Add $.50 to cost after Friday at 6pm.

Logitech San Jose Ice Center
(408) 279-6000; 1500 S. 10th Street, San Jose, CA 95112
<www.logitechice.com>

$7.50/person 13+, $6.50/child 12 & under, $3.50/skate rental only.

Oakland Ice Center
(510) 268-9000; 519 18th Street, Oakland, CA 94612
<www.oaklandice.com>

$7.50/adult, $6.50/child 12 & under, $6.50/senior, $2.50/skate rental.

Redwood Empire Ice Arena
(707) 546-7147; 1667 W. Steele Lane, Santa Rosa, CA 95403
<www.snoopyshomeice.com>
$7/ person 12 & older, $5.50/child under 12, $2/skate rental only.
Weekend and holidays: rates are higher. Special parent and child rate.

San Jose Downtown Ice (Outdoor)
(408) 279-1775; in front of 110 South Market Street, San Jose, CA 95113
<www.sjdowntown.com>
Open only November–January each year. $7.50/person 13+, $6.50/child
12 & under, $4.50/senior, $3.50/skate rental only.

Sharks Ice at Fremont
(510) 623-7200; 44388 Warm Springs Boulevard, Fremont, CA 94538
<www.sharksiceatfremont.com>

$7.50/person 13+, $6.50/child 12 & under, $4.50/senior, $3.50/skate
rental.

Walnut Creek On Ice (Outdoor)
(925) 935-SNOW; Civic Park: 1375 Civic Drive, Walnut Creek, CA 94596
<www.iceskatewalnutcreek.com>
Open only mid-November to mid-January each year. $10/person, $5/
skate rental.

Winter Lodge (Outdoor)
(650) 493-4566; 3009 Middlefield Road, Palo Alto, CA 94306
<www.winterlodge.com>

Open late September to April each year. $7/admission, $3/skate rental.

Yerba Buena Ice Skating & Bowling Center

(415) 820-3532; 750 Folsom Street, San Francisco, CA 94107
<www.skatebowl.com>

$8/adult, $6.25/child 12 & younger, $5/senior; $3/skate rental only.

Bowling

300 San Jose

(408) 578-8500; 5420 Thornwood Drive, San Jose, CA 95123
<www.300sanjose.com>

AMF Bowling Centers

<www.amfcenters.com>

Boulevard Lanes: (707) 762-4581;
1100 Petaluma Boulevard, South Petaluma, CA 94952
<www.amf.com/boulevardlanesca>

Mel's South Shore Bowl: (510) 523-6767; 300 Park Street, Alameda, CA 94501
<www.amf.com/southshorelanes>

Mission Lanes: (408) 262-6950; 1287 South Park Victoria, Milpitas, CA 95035
<www.amf.com/missionlanes>

Moonlite Lanes: (408) 296-7200; 2780 El Camino Real, Santa Clara, CA 95051
<www.amf.com/moonlitelanes>

Mowry Lanes: (510) 794-7777; 585 Mowry Avenue, Fremont, CA 94536
<www.amf.com/mowrylanes>

Pinole Lanes: (510) 724-9130; 1580 Pinole Valley Road, Pinole, CA 94564
<www.amf.com/pinolevalleylanes>

Redwood Lanes: (650) 369-5584;
2580 El Camino Real, Redwood City, CA 94061
<www.amf.com/redwoodlanes>

Bel Mateo Bowl

(650) 341-2616; 4330 Olympic Avenue, San Mateo, CA 94403

Boardwalk Bowl
(831) 426-3324; 115 Cliff Street, Santa Cruz, CA 95060
<www.boardwalkbowl.com>

Brentwood Bowl
(650) 583-1056; 237 El Camino Real, South San Francisco, CA 94080
<www.newbrentwoodbowl.com>

Brunswick Delta Bowl
(925) 757-5424; 3300 Delta Fair Boulevard, Antioch, CA 94509
<www.deltabowl.net>

Cambrian Bowl
(408) 377-2354; 14900 Camden Avenue, San Jose, CA 95124
<www.cambrianbowl.com>

Castro Village Bowl
(510) 538-8100; 3501 Village Drive, Castro Valley, CA 94546
<castrovillagebowl.net>

Classic Bowling Center
(650) 878-0300; 900 King Drive, Daly City, CA 94015
<www.classicbowling.com>

Clayton Valley Bowl
(925) 689-4631; 5300 Clayton Road, Concord, CA 94521
<http://claytonvalleybowl.com>

Cloverleaf Family Bowl
(510) 656-4411; 40645 Fremont Boulevard, Fremont, CA 94538
<www.cloverleafbowl.com>

Danville Bowl
(925) 837-7272; 200 Boone Court, Danville, CA 94526

Diablo Lanes
(925) 671-0913; 1500 Monument Boulevard, Concord, CA 94520
<www.diablolanes.com>

Double Decker Lanes
(707)585-0226; 300 Golf Course Drive, Rohnert Park, CA 94928
<www.doubledeckerlanes.com>

Earl Anthony's Dublin Bowl
(925)828-7550; 6750 Regional Street, Dublin, CA 94568
<www.earlanthonysdublinbowl.com>

Fourth Street Bowl
(408) 453-5555; 1441 N. Fourth Street, San Jose, CA 95112
<www.4thstreetbowl.com>

Gilroy Bowl
(408) 842-5100; 7554 Monterey Street, Gilroy, CA 95020

Granada Bowl
(925) 447-5600; 1620 Railroad Avenue, Livermore, CA 94550
<www.granadabowl.com>

Harvest Park Bowl
(925) 516-1221; 5000 Valfour Road, Brentwood, CA 94513
<www.harvestparkbowl.com>

Homestead Lanes
(408) 255-5700; 20990 Homestead Road, Cupertino, CA 95014
<www.homesteadlanes.com>

Manor Bowl
(510) 351-2101; 887 Manor Boulevard, San Leandro, CA 94579

Napa Bowl
(707) 224-8331; 494 Soscol Avenue, Napa, CA 94559

Paddock Bowl
(925) 685-7812; 5915 Pacheco Boulevard, Pacheco, CA 94553
<paddockbowl.com>

Palo Alto Bowl
(650) 948-1031; 4329 El Camino Real, Palo Alto, CA 94306
<www.paloaltobowl.com>

Presidio Bowling Center
(415) 561-2695; 93 Moraga, San Francisco, CA 94129
<www.presidiobowl.com>

Serra Bowl
(650) 992-3444; 3301 Junipero Serra Boulevard, Daly City, CA 94014
<www.serrabowl.com>

Sea Bowl
(650) 738-8190; 4625 Coast Highway, Pacifica, CA 94044
<www.seabowl.com>

Yerba Buena Ice Skating & Bowling Center
Rooftop at Yerba Buena Gardens
(415) 820-3532; 750 Folsom Street, San Francisco, CA 94107

Appendices

Appendix A
Regional Index

This regional index is provided to help you find organizations in a particular area. The index is broken down into very big regional categories: north bay, peninsula, east bay, Silicon Valley, and Santa Cruz.

East Bay

Academy of Classical Ballet
Alameda and Oakland Ferry Service
Alameda Children's Musical Theatre
Alameda County Public Libraries
Alameda Island Aquatics
Alameda Recreation and Parks
Alameda School of Music
Albany YMCA
AMF Mel's South Shore Bowl
AMF Mowry Lanes
AMF Pinole Lanes:
Ardenwood Historic Farm
Art-Gecko Creative Studio
Aurora Creative Studios
Axis Dance Company
Bacchini's Fruit Tree
BART (Bay Area Rapid Transit)
Bay Aerials Gymnastics
Bay Area Storytelling Festival
Bay-O-Vista Swim School
Bear Swim School
Berkeley Art Museum & Pacific Film
  Archive
Berkeley Ballet Theater
Berkeley City Ballet
Berkeley Iceland
Berkeley Public Library

Berkeley Richmond JCC
Berkeley Youth Arts Festival
Blackhawk Museum
Blick Art Materials
Brentwood Farms
Brunswick Delta Bowl
Brush Strokes Studio
Cal Day at the University of California
Cal Performances
California Academy of Performing Arts
California Ballet
California College of Arts and Crafts
California Gymnastics Academy
California Shakespeare Festival
California Shakespeare Theatre
  Midsummer Stage
Canciamilla Ranch
Castro Village Bowl
Celtic Festival
Chabot Space & Science Center
Children's Fairyland
Cinco de Mayo Fruitvale Festival and
  Parade
Civic Arts Education
Civic Park Campus
Clayton Valley Bowl
Cloverleaf Family Bowl
Club Sport
Color Me Mine
Community Concerts

Appendix A: Regional Index

Silicon Valley

Out of Area....

Appendix B
Calendar Index

This calendar is provided to help you plan your outings. I have pulled out the follow-up activities' special events from the entries to help you search for outings based on the time of year. For more detailed information, use the alphabetical index to locate the entries.

For a general San Francisco Bay Area events Web site: <www.sfgate. com/eguide/events>

Third Saturday of each month:
- Young Eagles program (free flight): Hiller Aviation Museum, San Carlos Airport

January
- Gold Discovery Day: Marshall Gold Discovery State Historic Park, Coloma
- Great blue heron & great egret nesting season (arriving late January– early March): Elkhorn Slough Reserve
- Monarch butterflies: Natural Bridges State Beach, Pacific Grove Monarch Preserve, Ardenwood Historic Farm
- Northern Elephant Seals: Natural Bridges State Beach, Point Reyes National Seashore

February
- Chinese New Year Parade, San Francisco
- Expanding Your Horizons Conference (for girls interested in math & science careers): Lawrence Livermore National Labs' Discovery Center, Livermore
- Lunar New Year Celebration: Oakland Museum of California, Oakland

- Old Sacramento: Free Museum Day
- Monarch butterflies: Natural Bridges State Beach, Pacific Grove Monarch Preserve, Ardenwood Historic Farm
- Northern Elephant Seals: Natural Bridges State Beach, Point Reyes National Seashore
- Registration for summer camps begins: note early discounts

March

- Departure of Northern Elephant Seals: Natural Bridges State Beach, Point Reyes National Seashore
- Monarch butterflies leave on migration routes: Natural Bridges State Beach, Pacific Grove Monarch Preserve, Ardenwood Historic Farm

Early March

- Berkeley Youth Arts Festival: Berkeley Art Center, Berkeley
- Farm Days events: Slide Ranch, Muir Beach
- Great American Train Show: Cow Palace, Daly City (see South Bay Historical Railroad Society entry)
- Johnny Appleseed Day: Ardenwood Farm

April

- Cal Day: U.C. Berkeley (Chapter 10: Seasonal Events)
- Children's Concerts series for K-grade 3: San Francisco Symphony, San Francisco
- Community Day at Stanford University (Chapter 10: Seasonal Events)
- Earth Day Celebration: Junior Center of Art & Science, Oakland
- Model Railroad Show: South Bay Historical Railroad Society, Santa Clara
- Strictly Sail Pacific boat show: Jack London Square, Oakland
- Young Pianists' Beethoven Competition: San Jose State University, San Jose

Easter

- Baby chicks and ducklings on farm tours April–June: Deer Hollow Farm, Cupertino
- Easter Egg Hunt: Casa de Fruta, Holister and Filoli Gardens, Woodside

- Easter Egg Hunt: Filoli Gardens, Woodside
- Gardens
- Old Fashioned Easter and Parade: Old Sacramento
- Wildflower walks: See Nature Preserves section

Late April

- Berkeley Bay Festival: Shorebird Nature Center, Berkeley Marina
- Earth Day Celebration: Junior Center of Art & Science, Oakland
- Pacific Coast Dream Machines: Half Moon Bay
- Steam train excursion: Old Sacramento
- Strawberry Festival (Native American celebration): Kule Loklo, Point Reyes National Seashore

May

- Bay Area Storytelling Festival: Kennedy Grove Regional Recreation Area, El Sobrante
- Bug Day: Randall Museum, San Francisco
- Bug Day: Henry Cowell Redwoods State Park, Felton
- Celebration Weekend: Sunset Magazine Gardens, Menlo Park
- Cinco de Mayo: Oakland, San Jose, and San Francisco
- Cinco de Mayo weekend: Portuguese Heritage Festival: History Park, San Jose
- Garden Tour: Heather Farms, Walnut Creek
- Hillsborough Classic Car Show & Carnival, First Sunday in May
- History Cruise on the San Francisco Bay. May–October on Thursdays & Saturdays: Presidential Yacht Potomac, Oakland
- May Day celebration of spring with Maypole dancing: Hayward Shoreline Interpretive Center
- May Fireworks: Angel Island/Tiburon Ferry
- Migratory Bird Day: Don Edwards San Francisco Bay National Wildlife Refuge, Newark
- Port of Oakland Tour: Jack London Square, Oaklad (May – October)
- Strawberry picking: Chapter 2: Plant Kingdom—Coastal Berry Picking Farms section
- Wings of History Air Museum sponsors an air show; Young

Eagles get to ride for free: South County Airport
- Woodside Days, first Sunday in May: Woodside Store
- Yerba Buena Gardens Festival: Yerba Buena Gardens Esplanade, San Francisco (May-October)
- Young Eagles Flight Rally: Watsonville Airport, Watsonville (May – November)
- Youth Concerts series for grades 4-9: San Francisco Symphony, San Francisco

Late May
- Cherry picking season begins
- Civil War Reenactment: Casa de Fruta, Roaring Camp & Railroad, & Ardenwood Farm (Moved to mid-August in 2006)
- Insect Fair: Youth Science Institute Sanborn Nature Center, Saratoga
- Multicultural Festival: History Park, San Jose
- Watsonville Fly-In & Air Show: Watsonville Airport

June
- Dragon Slayers Renaissance Festival: Aptos Village Park, Aptos
- International Russian Music Piano Competition: Le Petit Trianon, San Jose
- Irving M. Klein International String Competition: California Music Center, San Francisco
- Port of Oakland Tour: Jack London Square, Oaklad (May – October)
- Stern Grove Festival: Stern Grove, San Francisco (Mid-June to mid-August)

Early June
- Celtic Festival: Ardenwood Farm, Fremont
- Columbia Diggins, Tent Town 1852: Columbia State Historic Park, Columbia (Out of Area)
- History Cruise on the San Francisco Bay. May–October on Thursdays & Saturdays: Presidential Yacht Potomac, Oakland
- "Sheep to Shawl" Day: Elkus Youth Ranch, Half Moon Bay
- San Francisco Youth Arts Festival: De Young Museum, San Francisco
- Wildlife Fair: Sulphur Creek Nature Center, Hayward

Mid-June

- Early Days in San Juan Living History Event: San Juan Bautista State Park, San Juan Bautista
- Father's Day tide pooling trip: Seymour Marine Discovery Cente, Santa Cruz
- Fire Truck Day & Antique Engine Show: Ardenwood Farm, Fremont
- Fruit picking–boysenberries, olallieberries, & strawberries: coastal farms; nectarines, plums, and apricots: Brentwood farms
- Heritage Day: Old Borges Ranch, Walnut Creek
- Vertical Challenge Helicopter Air Show: Hiller Aviation Museum, San Carlos Airport

Late June

- Palo Alto Concours D'Elegance, Classic Car Show: Stanford University

July

- Ancient Egyptian Epagomenal Festival: Rosicrucian Egyptian Museum, San Jose
- Berry & fruit picking—boysenberries, raspberries, nectarines, peaches, plums, and apricots
- Big Time (Native American celebration): Kule Loklo, Point Reyes National Seashore
- Cable Car Bell Ringing Competition: Union Square, San Francisco
- History Cruise on the San Francisco Bay. May–October on Thursdays & Saturdays: Presidential Yacht Potomac, Oakland
- Independence Day Celebration: U.S.S. Hornet Museum
- July 4th celebration with fireworks: Jack London Square, Oakland
- Old Fashioned Independence Day Celebration: Ardenwood, Fremont & Wilder Ranch State Park, Santa Cruz
- Port of Oakland Tour: Jack London Square, Oaklad (May – October)
- Ringling Brothers & Barnum & Bailey Circus, July – August
- Scottish Highland Games: Dunsmuir Estate, Oakland
- Shakespeare Festival Theatre Ensemble: Oak Meadow Park, Los Gatos
- Shakespeare in the Park (Free): Bay Area wide, various venues

- Shakespeare Santa Cruz: UCSC Theater Arts Center & Festival Grove, Santa Cruz
- Summer program to watch the stars open to the public (July–September): Lick Observatory, San Jose

August

- Early August: Annual Steinbeck Festival: National Steinbeck Center, Salinas
- Golden Gate Renaissance Festival: Golden Gate Park, San Francisco
- Civil War Reenactment: Ardenwood Farm, Fremont
- History Cruise around San Francisco Bay. May–October on Thursdays & Saturdays: Presidential Yacht Potomac, Oakland
- Open House: Blackhawk Museum, Danville
- Port of Oakland Tour: Jack London Square, Oakland (May – October)
- Scottish Games & Celtic Festival: Toro Park, Salinas
- Shakespeare Festival Theatre Ensemble: Oak Meadow Park, Los Gatos
- Shakespeare in the Park (Free): Bay Area wide, various venues
- Shakespeare Santa Cruz: UCSC Theater Arts Center & Festival Grove, Santa Cruz
- Shakespeare: Shady Shakespeare Company, Sanborn Park, Saratoga
- Summer Gathering of Mountain Men: Roaring Camp & Railroads
- Wings Over Wine Country Air Show: Pacific Coast Air Museum, Santa Rosa

Late August/September

- Fruit picking—asian pears
- Kenneth C. Patrick Visitor Center: Labor Day Sunday Sand Sculpture Contest: Point Reyes National Seashore
- Tule harvesting, storytelling: Santa Cruz Mission
- Moon Festival: San Francisco

September

- Californian Indian Day: Phoebe Hearst Museum of Anthropology, Berkeley

- Boat Show: Jack London Square, Oakland
- Festival of the Sea: Hyde Street Pier, San Francisco
- Fiesta: Carmel Mission, Carmel
- Gold Rush Days over Labor Day weekend: California State Railroad Museum
- Great Train Robberies reenactment: Roaring Camp Railroads, Felton
- Hawk Talk: Hawk Hill, Marine Headlands
- Highland Gathering & Games: Labor Day Weekend: Alameda County Fairgrounds, Pleasanton
- Historic Rail Fair: Labor Day weekend: Ardenwood Historic Farms, Fremont
- History Cruise on the San Francisco Bay: May–October on Thursdays & Saturdays: Presidential Yacht Potomac, Oakland
- Kids Faire California: Alameda County Fairgrounds, Pleasanton
- Mission Adobe Day: Santa Cruz Mission, Santa Cruz
- Ohlone Day: Henry Cowell Redwoods State Park, Felton
- Port of Oakland Tour: Jack London Square, Oaklad (May – October)
- Rancho Day: Sanchez Adobe, Pacifica
- Shakespeare in the Park (Free): Bay Area wide, various venues
- Shakespeare: Shady Shakespeare Company, Sanborn Park, Saratoga
- Tapestry Arts Festival: Labor Day weekend: Downtown San Jose
- Walk in the Gardens: Bonfante Gardens, Gilroy
- Watsonville Airport Open House in the Fall

Mid-September:
- Fruit Picking—apples
- Harvest Festival: Wilder Ranch State Park, Santa Cruz
- Moon Festival: Chinese Cultural Gardens at Overfelt Gardens, San Jose
- Renaissance Pleasure Faire: Casa de Fruta
- Trade Feast Celebration: Miwok Park/Marin Museum of the American Indian, Novato

October
- Airport Open House: Watsonville Airport, Watsonville

- Boo at the Zoo, Oakland Zoo, Oakland
- Community Day: Lawrence Livermore National Labs' Discovery Center, Livermore
- Fall Harvest Days: Old Sacramento
- Fall Pumpkin Harvest: Smith Family Farm, Brentwood
- Fleet Week & Parade of Ships: Marina Green, Fisherman's Wharf, & Ferry Building, San Francisco
- Ghost Train & Reenactment of the Legend of Sleepy Hollow: Roaring Camp Railroads, Felton
- Goblin Jamboree: Bay Area Discovery Museum, Sausalito
- Hawk Talk: Hawk Hill, Marine Headlands
- History Cruise on the San Francisco Bay: May–October on Thursdays & Saturdays: Presidential Yacht Potomac, Oakland
- Jack O'Lantern Jamboree: Children's Fairyland, Oakland
- Open House: Don Edwards San Francisco Bay National Wildlife Refuge, Newark
- Pumpkin Patches: Adobe Pumpkin Farm, Casa de Fruta, G & M Farm, Lemos Farm, Nicasio Valley Farm, Pastorino's, Smith Family Farm, Uesugi Farms, and Western Railway Museum
- San Leandro Monarch Tours: Oct-Jan, San Leandro
- Star Party: Junior Center of Art & Science, Oakland

Early October

- Community Day: Gamble Garden, Palo Alto
- Fiesta: Santa Cruz Mission
- Fleet Week Cruise: Angel Island/Tiburon Ferry, *SS Jeremiah O'Brien*
- Gathering of Ohlone People: first Sunday in October: Coyote Hills Regional
- Harvest Festival: Emma Prusch Farm, San Jose
- Harvest Festival at the Farm: UC Santa Cruz Farm & Garden, Saturday in early-October
- Port of Oakland Tour: Jack London Square, Oakland (May – October)
- Shakespeare in the Park (Free): Bay Area wide, various venues
- Wildlife Education Day: McClellan Ranch Park, Cupertino

Mid-October

- 49er Family Festival or Coloma Gold Rush Live: Marshall Gold Discovery State Historic Park, Coloma

- Apple Butter Festival w/ apple butter making, canning, pumpkin patch, etc.: Gizdich Ranch
- Autumn Festival: Railtown 1897 State Historic Park, Jamestown (Out of Area)
- California International Air Show: Salinas Municipal Airport
- Harvest Celebration: Slide Ranch, Muir Beach
- Haunted Train: Ardenwood Farm, Fremont
- Pumpkin Patch Trains: Western Railway Museum, Suisun
- Wildlife Education Day: Santa Clara Valley Audubon Society
- Wildlife Festival: Youth Science Institute, Alum Rock Park, San Jose

Weekend after Columbus Day
- Annual Half Moon Bay Art & Pumpkin Festival: Lemos Farm

Late October
- Halloween Swamp Tour: Jelly Belly Factory, Fairfield
- Haunted Forest and the Phantom Express Train: Oak Meadow Park, Los Gatos
- Monarch butterflies return to Natural Bridges, Pacific Grove, Ardenwood Farms, and Point Lobos State Reserve, etc.
- Ohlone Day: Deer Hollow Farm, Cupertino
- Spookomotive Halloween Train: California State Railroad Museum, Old Sacramento

November
- Bird watching season for migratory birds: see Chapter 1: Animal Kingdom—Nature Preserves section
- Chestnuts: U-pick: Chapter 2: Plant Kingdom—Fruit Farms & Orchards
- Dickens Christmas Fair, Cow Palace, San Francisco: See Seasonal Events section
- Founders' Day Fandango: Santa Teresa County Park, San Jose
- Great American Train Shows: Alameda County Fairgrounds, Pleasanton (see South Bay Historical Railroad Society entry)
- Old Fashioned 19th Century Christmas: (mid-November–mid-December): Dunsmuir Historic Estate, Oakland
- Model Railroad Show: South Bay Historical Railroad Society, Santa Clara
- Victorian Christmas: Ardenwood Farm, Fremont

December

- Brunch with Santa: Jelly Belly Factory: Fairfield
- Christmas in Coloma (old-fashioned Christmas): Marshall Gold Discovery State Historic Park, Coloma
- *Deck the Halls, Peter & the Wolf*: San Francisco Symphony
- Dickens Christmas Fair: Cow Palace, San Francisco
- *Fantasy of Lights* drive through: Vasona Lake Park, Los Gatos
- Heritage Holidays: Old Sacramento
- Historic Trolley Service: Light-rail San Jose
- Holiday Teas: Dunsmuir Historic Estate, Oakland
- Holiday Train: Billy Jones Wildcat Railroad, Oak Meadow Park Los Gatos
- Holiday Train of Lights: Niles Canyon Railway & Museum, Sunol Depot
- Kwanzaa Celebration: Bay Area Discovery Museum, Sausalito
- Lamplight Tours: Old Sacramento
- Northern elephant seals breeding season (December—March): Año Nuevo State Reserve, Point Reyes National Seashore
- *Nutcracker* Ballet: See Chapter 8: Art & Performing Arts—Ballet Performance section
- Santa Trains: Western Railway Museum, Suisun
- Santa's Yuletide Express: California State Railroad Museum
- Winter Family Day: Elkus Youth Ranch, Half Moon Bay

Early December

- Children's Parties: Filoli Gardens, Woodside
- Children's Puppet Show & Holiday Teas: Gamble Garden, Palo Alto
- Holiday Craft Day: Randall Museum, San Francisco
- Holiday Hoe Down: Old Borges Ranch, Walnut Creek
- Holiday Open House: Luther Burbank Home & Gardens, Santa Rosa
- Victorian Christmas: Ardenwood Historic Farm, Fremont

Mid-December

- Holiday Lego with Lego trains: Museum of American Heritage, Palo Alto (mid-December to mid-January)
- Victorian Christmas: Roaring Camp Railroads, Felton
- Winter Family Day: Elkus Youth Ranch, Half Moon Bay

Appendix C
Free Activities Index

Many activities are free, such as performing arts, parks, and special free days at museums and zoos. However, remember that the free days at the museums and zoos may also mean crowds. So, expect to be in a crowded space and prepare accordingly. It's also probably a good idea to visit early in the morning before the crowds get too big. Please refer to the Alphabetical Index to help you locate the entries.

First Tuesday of Every Month:
- Asian Art Museum
- California Historical Society
- Cartoon Art Museum "Pay What You Wish" Day
- Conservatory of Flowers
- De Young Museum
- Legion of Honor
- San Francisco Museum of Modern Art
- Seymour Marine Discovery Center

First Wednesday of Every Month:
- Asian Art Museum, Civic Center
- California Academy of Sciences (comprised of Steinhart Aquarium, Natural History Museum, and Morrison Planetarium)
- Coyote Pointe Museum
- Exploratorium
- San Francisco Zoo

First Thursday of Every Month:
- Berkeley Art Museum (Free admission on Cal Day in April)
- U.C. Berkeley Botanical Garden

First Friday of Every Month:

- Santa Cruz Museum of Art and History (MAH)

Second Saturday of Every Month:

- Bay Area Discovery Museum

Second Sunday of Every Month:

- Oakland Museum of California

Every Thursday

- Phoebe Hearst Museum of Anthropology
- San Francisco Museum of Modern Art has ½ price every Thursday night, 6pm–9pm.

Free Everyday (When open)

- Agate Beach County Park, Bolinas: tide pooling: (415) 499-6387; <www.co.marin.ca.us/depts/pk/main/pos/pdagatebch.cfm>
- Almaden Quicksilver Mining Museum, San Jose: (408) 323-1107; <www.parkhere.org>
- Arastradero Preserve, Palo Alto: (650) 329-2423; <www.arastradero.org>
- Art galleries
- Asilomar State Beach: Tide pooling
- Bay Model Visitor Center, Sausalito: (415) 332-3871; <www.spn.usace.army.mil/bmvc/>
- Baylands Nature Preserve, Palo Alto: (650) 329-2506; <www.paloaltoonline.com/things_do/baylands.shtml>
- Berkeley Marina Shorebird Nature Center, Berkeley: (510) 981-6720; <www.ci.berkeley.ca.us/marina/marinaexp/naturecenter.html>
- Berkeley Youth Arts Festival: (510) 644-6893; <www.berkeleyartcenter.org>
- Bolinas Lagoon Preserve, Stinson Beach: (415) 868-9244; <www.egret.org>
- Cal Day at U.C. Berkeley (April): (510) 642-5215; <www.berkeley.edu/calday>
- Cantor Art Center, Stanford University, Stanford: (650) 723-4177; <museum.stanford.edu>
- Chitactac-Adams Heritage County Park, Gilroy: (408) 323-0107;

<www.parkhere.org>
- Children's Events (at libraries and stores)
- Chinese Moon Festival, San Jose: (408) 251-3323; <www.chineseculturalgarden.org/moonfestival.htm>
- Cinco de Mayo, San Francisco: (415) 206-0577; <www.cincodemayosf.com>
- Cinco de Mayo Fruitvale Festival and Parade, Oakland: (510) 536-6084; (510) 434-1678; <www.oaklandcincodemayo.com>
- Chinese New Year Parade, San Francisco: (415) 982-3071; <www.chineseparade.com>
- Community Concerts, East Bay: <www.CommunityConcerts.com>
- Community Day at Stanford University, Stanford: (650) 724-2933; <communityday.stanford.edu>
- Community School of Music & Arts: Free concert series, Mountain View: (650) 961-0342; <www.arts4all.org>
- Computer History Museum History Center, Mountain View: (650) 810-1010; <www.computerhistory.org>
- Crissy Field, San Francisco: (415) 561-7690; <www.crissyfield.org>
- Deer Hollow Farm: Rancho San Antonio Preserve, Los Altos: (650) 903-6430; <www.fodhf.org>
- Don Edwards San Francisco Bay National Wildlife Refuge, Fremont and Alviso: (510) 792-0222 & (408) 262-5513, respectively; <http://desfbay.fws.gov>
- Emma Prusch Farm, San Jose: (408) 926-5555; <www.pruschfarmpark.org>
- Federal Reserve Bank Tour, San Francisco: (415) 974-3252; <www.frbsf.org/federalreserve/tours.html>
- Fitzgerald Marine Reserve, Moss Beach: (650) 728-3584; <www.fitzgeraldreserve.org>
- Foothill Observatory, Foothill College, Los Altos Hills: (650) 949-7334; <www.foothill.edu/ast/fhobs.htm>
- Founders' Day Fandango, San Jose: (408) 846-5632; <www.parkhere.org>
- Gamble Garden, Palo Alto: (650) 329-1356; <www.gamblegarden.org>
- Gardens at Heather Farms, Walnut Creek: (925) 947-6712; <www.gardenshf.org>
- Gold Rush Trail, San Francisco: (415) 981-4849;

<www.goldrushtrail.org>

- Golden Gate Fortune Cookie Company, San Francisco: (415) 781-3956; <www.chinese-fortune-cookie.com>
- Golden Gate Live Steamers Club, Tilden Park, Berkeley: free train rides on Sundays noon–3pm. <www.ggls.org>
- Golden Gate Model Railroad Club, San Francisco: (415) 346-3303; <www.ggmrc.org>
- Half Moon Bay: Annual Half Moon Bay Art & Pumpkin Festival on weekend following Columbus Day (See Lemos Farms entry)
- Hawk Hill, Marin Headlands: (415) 331-0730; <www.ggro.org>
- Hayward Shoreline Interpretive Center: (510) 670-7270; <http://hard.dst.ca.usl>
- Intel Museum, Santa Clara: (408) 765-0503; <www.intel.com/museum>
- Japanese Friendship Garden, San Jose: (408) 277-5254
- Japanese Tea Garden, San Mateo: (650) 522-7440
- Jelly Bean Factory Tour, Fairfield: (800) 953-5592; <www.jellybelly.com>
- Junior Center of Art and Science, Oakland: (510) 839-5777; <www.juniorcenter.org>
- Kule Loklo, replica Coast Miwok Village: (415) 464-5100; <www.mapom.com/kuleloklo.htm>
- Lawrence Livermore National Lab's Discovery Center, Livermore: (925) 423-3272; <www.llnl.gov>
- Levi-Strauss Visitor Center, San Francisco: (415) 501-6000; <www.levistrauss.com/Heritage/OurArchives.aspx>
- Linden Tree: Wednesdays in the Courtyard Music Series, Los Altos: (650) 949-3390; 1-800-949-3313
- Luther Burbank Home & Gardens, Santa Rosa: (707) 524-5445; <www.lutherburbank.org>
- Marin French Cheese Company Tour, Petaluma: (800) 292-6001; <www.marinfrenchcheese.com>
- Marin Wild Care: (415) 453-1000; <www.wildcaremarin.org>
- Marine Mammal Center, Marin Headlands: (415) 289-7325; <www.tmmc.org>
- Maritime Museum, San Francisco Maritime National Historic Park (Reopens 2009): (415) 561-7100; <www.maritime.org>

- Marshall Gold Discovery State Historic Park, Coloma: (530) 622-3470; Events: (530) 295-2162; <www.parks.ca.gov/default.asp?page_id=484>
- McClellan Ranch Park, Cupertino: (408) 777-3149
- Mee Mee Bakery, San Francisco: (415) 362-3204; <www.meemeebakery.com>
- Memorial Park Amphitheater: Summer Concerts, Cupertino: (408) 777-3120; <www.cupertino.org/event_calendar>
- Mid-Peninsula Open Space Preserve: (650) 691-1200; <www.openspace.org>
- Moon Festival, San Francisco: (415) 982-6306; <www.moonfestival.org>
- Monarch Grove Sanctuary, Pacific Grove: (831) 375-0982
- Monterey Bay Chocolates, Seaside: (800) 648-9938; <montereybaychocolates.com>
- Museum of American Heritage, Palo Alto: (650) 321-1004; <www.moah.org>
- Museum of Children's Art (MOCHA), Oakland: (510) 465-8770; <www.mocha.org>
- Music at Noon series at University of Santa Clara: (408) 554-4429; 554-4015; <www.scu.edu/cpa/events/musicatnoon.cfm>
- NASA Exploration Center, Mountain View: (650) 604-6274; <www.nasa.gov/centers/ames/home/exploration.html>
- Nicasio Valley Farm (October only): (415) 662-9100
- Noon Concert Series, U.C. Berkeley's Hertz Hall: (510) 642-4864; <music.berkeley.edu>
- NUMMI Factory Tour, Fremont: (510) 498-5649; <www.nummi.com>
- Oakdale Cheese Factory Tour, Oakdale: (209) 848-3139; <www.oakdalecheese.com>
- Oakland Discovery Center, Oakland: (510) 535-5657, (510) 832-3314
- Old Borges Ranch, Walnut Creek: (925) 934-5860
- Organic Gardens
- Overfelt Gardens/Chinese Cultural Gardens, San Jose: (408) 251-3323; <www.chineseculturalgarden.org>
- Pacific Grove Museum of Natural History: (831) 648-5716; <www.pgmuseum.org>

- Palo Alto Junior Museum & Zoo, Palo Alto: (650) 329-2111; <www.cityofpaloalto.org/community-services/museum-index.html>
- Peralta Adobe & Fallon House, San Jose: (408) 993-8300; Tour appointment: (408) 918-1055; <www.historysanjose.org/visiting_hsj/ peralta_fallon/peralta_fallon.html>
- Point Reyes National Seashore: <www.nps.gov/pore/home.htm>
- Port of Oakland Tour: (510) 627-1188; <www.portofoakland.com/communit/serv_tour.asp>
- Randall Museum, San Francisco: (415) 554-9600; <www.randallmuseum.org>
- Richardson Bay Audubon Center, Tiburon: (415) 388-2524; <www.tiburonaudubon.org>
- San Francisco Cable Car Museum, San Francisco: (415) 474-1887; <www.cablecarmuseum.com>
- San Francisco Conservatory of Music: free concert series, San Francisco: (415) 864-7326 (SFCM); <www.sfcm.edu>
- San Francisco Fire Department Museum, San Francisco: (415) 563-4630; <www.sffiremuseum.org>
- San Francisco Youth Arts Festival: (415) 750-8630; <www.sfyouthartsfestival.org>
- San Leandro Monarch Butterfly Tours; (510) 577-6085
- San Juan Bautista State Historic Park: (831) 623-4526; <www.parks.ca.gov/default.asp?page_id=563>
- Sanchez Adobe (650) 359-1462; <www.sanmateocountyhistory.com>
- Santa Cruz Mission: (831) 425-5849; <www.santacruzstateparks.org/ parks/mission/>
- Scharffen Berger Chocolate Maker Factory Tour, Berkeley: (510) 981-4050; <www.scharffenberger.com>
- Shakespeare in the Park <www.sfshakes.org/park/index.html>
- Shoreline Lake, Mountain View: (650) 965-7474 Boathouse; (650) 965-1745 Café; <www.shorelinelake.com>
- Sigmund Stern Grove Festival, San Francisco: (415) 252-6252; <www.sterngrove.org>
- South Bay Historical Railroad Society, Santa Clara: (408) 243-3969; <www.sbhrs.org>
- Stanford Linear Accelerator Tour, Menlo Park: (650) 926-2204; <www2.slac.stanford.edu/tours>
- Strybing Arboretum & Botanical Gardens, San Francisco:

(415) 661-1316; <www.strybing.org>

- Sulphur Creek Nature Center, Hayward: (510) 881-6747; <www.hard.dst.ca.us>
- Sunset Magazine's Demonstration Gardens, Menlo Park: (650) 321-3600; <www.sunset.com>
- Tapestry Arts Festival, San Jose (September): (408) 494-3590; <www.tapestryarts.org>
- Tiburon Railroad–Ferry Depot Museum, Tiburon: (415) 435-1853; <www.landmarks-society.org/landmarks.html>
- Tilden Regional Park: <www.ebparks.org/parks/tilden.htm>
- Tilden Botanic Garden Berkeley: (510) 841-8732; <www.nativeplants.org>
- Triton Museum of Art, Santa Clara: (408) 247-3754; <www.tritonmuseum.org>
- U.C. Berkeley's Noon Concert Series: (510) 642-4864; music.berkeley.edu/noon.html
- U.C. Santa Cruz Arboretum, Santa Cruz: (831) 427-2998; <www2.ucsc.edu/arboretum>
- U.C. Santa Cruz Farm & Garden: (831) 459-3240; <http://zzyx.ucsc.edu/casfs/community/tours.html>
- U.S. Geological Survey, Menlo Park: (650) 329-4390 Recording, (650) 329-5392 Tour requests
- Wells Fargo History Museum: (415) 396-2619; <www.wellsfargohistory.com/museums/sfmuseum.html>
- Whole Foods Groceries Store Tours: See Chapter 7: How Things Work—Site Tours section.
- Woodside Store: (650) 851-7615; <www.eparks.net> then select "Parks," then "Woodside."
- Yerba Buena Gardens Festival, San Francisco: (415) 543-1718; <www.ybae.org>

Appendix D
Alphabetical Index

Appendix D: Alphabetical Index

Appendix D: Alphabetical Index

Z

Appendix E
Rainy Day Ideas

Here are more ideas if you don't find anything after first looking through the Free Activities Index. Use the Alphabetical Index to find an entry.

- Aquariums: Steinhart Aquarium at the California Academy of Sciences, Seymour Marine Discovery Center, etc.
- Art outings: ceramic painting, drop-in art at children's museums and art museums, art museums.
- Children's museums: Children's Discovery Museum, Coyote Point Museum, Habitot, Palo Alto Junior Nature Museum & Zoo, Randall Museum.
- Libraries & store events (book stores, Lakeshore, toy stores).
- Museums: California Academy of Sciences, Chabot Space and Science Center, Exploratorium, Intel Museum, Lawrence Hall of Science, NASA Exploration Center, The Tech Museum, Zeum, etc.
- Nature and visitor centers at parks or wildlife museums like Lindsay Wildlife Museum, Marin Mammal Center, Sulphur Creek Nature Center, Don Edwards San Francisco Bay National Wildlife Refuge.
- Natural History Museums: Santa Cruz Natural History Museum, Pacific Grove Natural History Museum, etc.
- History Museums: Rosicrucian Egyptian Museum, Oakland Museum of California, Phoebe Hearst Anthropology Museum, San Mateo County History Museum, Santa Cruz Museum of Art & History.
- Physical outings: bowling or ice skating.
- See a show: children's theater, dance, or music performance.
- Transportation Museums: Blackhawk Museum, Hiller Aviation Museum.
- Take a tour: Jelly Belly Factory, Mrs. Grossman's Sticker Factory, NUMMI, Scharffen Berger Chocolate Maker, Stanford Linear Accelerator, Whole Foods, etc.

Checklist — Before You Go

1) Call to confirm dates, times, costs, and directions.

2) Print out maps/directions from the destination's Web site.

3) Bring some cash, in various denominations from quarters and dollar bills to larger bills for parking and food.

4) Extra changes of clothing and shoes in the car (at least for the kids, but it's a good idea for the adults, too) for unexpected messes.

5) Bring lots of bottled water or drinks because fun can be a thirsty business. It's always a great idea to bring a cooler with some fruit, yogurt, cheese sticks, or other snacks handy for the trip home.

6) Sunscreen.

7) Sunglasses.

8) Jackets.

9) Binoculars.

10) Camera.

11) Umbrella.

About the Author

Elina Wong is a former product line manager in the health care industry and a former market researcher with Apple Computers, Inc. She has a bachelor's degree in biochemistry from U.C. Berkeley and a master's degree in health finance and management from the Johns Hopkins Bloomberg School of Public Health.

She lives in Los Gatos, California, with her husband and two young daughters. She has been an active full-time mom for the past six years, with many adventure miles logged on her car.

Both of her parents were music teachers. Her hobbies include piano and photography. She is passionate about her children's education.

Feedback Please!

Thanks for your feedback!
Please send to: **Kids Edventures**
P.O. Box 1090, Los Gatos, CA 95031-1090
or e-mail to: info@kidsedventures.com

Have you had a wonderful outing or class? Have you had a lousy experience? I'd love to hear from you, especially if you have any ideas that will make this book even better. Please send me an e-mail at info@kidsedventures.com or write me a note, and tell me what you think.

Please circle:
Are you a parent, educator, homeschooler, scout troup leader, or friend?

How old are the kids?

Where do you live?
City, State: Postal Code:
Country

Would you like to receive a free copy of my e-mail newsletter with updates and events? If yes, please provide your e-mail address: